Baptists and Public Life in Canada

McMaster Divinity College Press

McMaster General Series 2

Volume 1 in the Canadian Baptist Historical Society Series

Baptists and Public Life in Canada

edited by
GORDON L. HEATH
and
PAUL R. WILSON

PICKWICK *Publications* • Eugene, Oregon

BAPTISTS AND PUBLIC LIFE IN CANADA

McMaster Divinity College General Series 2

McMaster Divinity College Press
1280 Main Street West
Hamilton, Ontario, Canada
L8S 4K1

Pickwick Publications
An Imprint of Wipf and Stock Publishers
199 W. 8th Av.e, Suite 3
Eugene, OR 97401

www.wipfandstock.com

ISBN 13: 978-1-60899-681-0

Cataloging-in-Publication data:

Baptists and public life in Canada / edited by Gordon L. Heath and Paul R. Wilson.

x + 400 p. ; 23 cm. Includes bibliographical references and indexes.

McMaster Divinity College Press General Series 2

ISBN 13: 978-1-60899-681-0

1. Baptists — History in Canada. I. Heath, Gordon L. II. Wilson, Paul R. III. Title. IV. Series.

BX6251. B25 2012

Manufactured in the U.S.A.

Contents

BAPTIST INITIATIVES AND PUBLIC LIFE

Contributors

EDITORS AND CONTRIBUTORS

GORDON L. HEATH is Associate Professor of Christian History at McMaster Divinity College, and also serves as Director of the Canadian Baptist Archives. He received his PhD from St. Michael's College at the University of Toronto. His publications include *A War with a Silver Lining: Canadian Protestant Churches and the South African War, 1899–1902* (Montreal and Kingston: McGill-Queen's University Press, 2009) and *Doing Church History: A User-friendly Introduction to Researching the History of Christianity* (Toronto: Clements, 2008). He is co-author with Stanley E. Porter of the *The Lost Gospel of Judas: Separating Fact from Fiction* (Grand Rapids: Eerdmans, 2007). Gord is an ordained minister with the Convention of Atlantic Baptist Churches.

PAUL R. WILSON was for thirteen years the Director/Professor of General Education Studies at Heritage College and Seminary. He is presently an independent scholar. In 1996, he completed his doctorate in history at the University of Western Ontario. He has published a number of articles on Baptist history, and is currently co-editing *T. T. Shields: Reflections on the Legacy of a Baptist Fundamentalist*. Paul was ordained by the North American Baptist Conference, and served in that denomination as a pastor. He and his wife Yvonne live in Cambridge, Ontario.

OTHER CONTRIBUTORS

DOUG ADAMS is currently pursuing a PhD in history at the University of Western Ontario. His father was a loyal supporter of Shields and in time became the principal of Toronto Baptist Seminary. Doug studied at the seminary and graduated in 1977 with a Master of Divinity degree. He went on to serve as an associate pastor in Briscoe Street Baptist Church

and later as Pastor of East Williams Baptist Church, a position he occupied for twenty years. During that time, Doug also pursued further
education at the University of Western Ontario and by the mid-1990s
achieved his Master of Arts degree. Doug also served as the Professor
of Church History at Toronto Baptist Seminary for nearly twenty years.
Involvement in both Shields' school and his church gives Doug unique
opportunities to study the life of Dr. Shields. Jarvis Street Baptist Church
has graciously granted him access to their extensive archives, which contain most of the Shields papers. Doug is currently writing his dissertation
on Shields as something of a revisionist biographical account of Shields's
life and ministry.

SANDRA BEARDSALL is Professor of Church History and Ecumenics at St.
Andrew's College in Saskatoon, Saskatchewan, where she has served since
1997. Raised in Brampton, Ontario, she served as an ordained minister
with congregations of the United Church of Canada in Newfoundland,
Labrador, and eastern Ontario, and holds a ThD from Emmanuel College,
Toronto. She teaches history of Christianity, ecumenism, and pastoral
theology in the Saskatoon Theological Union, and participates in research and writing related to Protestant spirituality, history of the United
Church of Canada, the social gospel movement, theological education,
and the theology and practice of local ecumenical ministries.

SHARON M. BOWLER enjoys teaching elementary school children at the
Hamilton-Wentworth District School Board. She has a background in
Child and Youth Studies and has completed post-professional studies in
Child Life from the Health Sciences Department at McMaster University.
She received her MEd from Brock University in 2002 in Organizational
and Administrative Studies with her work on understanding the role of
the Protestant Conscience in Ontario's Education system. She continued
her graduate studies at the Ontario Institute for Studies in Education in the
Theory and Policy Studies Department, graduating in 2006 with an EdD.
Her thesis was entitled "Biography as Thesis: Dr. Jonathan Woolverton
and Protestant Conscience in Nineteenth-Century Ontario." She has had
opportunity to lecture at both Centennial College and Tyndale University
in the area of Child Studies. She is currently working on a biography of
Dr. Woolverton with the University of Toronto Press, and has previously
published an article on his life in the *Historical Papers of the Canadian*

Society of Church History (2006). She has recently accepted a position overseeing the promotion of the Canadian Baptist Women of Ontario and Quebec's *The Link and Visitor* magazine across all churches in her Baptist association.

DONALD A. GOERTZ is Associate Professor of Church History at Tyndale University College and Seminary, Toronto. He has published numerous book chapters, articles, and encyclopedia entries on Baptist history, as well as the book-length urban case study, *A Century for the City: Walmer Road Baptist Church 1889–1989*. His other areas of research interest are focused on issues around the engagement of gospel and culture throughout history, with a particular focus on the Canadian context. He is an ordained pastor with the Canadian Baptists of Ontario and Quebec.

DANIEL C. GOODWIN is Professor of History at Crandall University, Moncton, NB. He has published in the areas of nineteenth- and twentieth-century Canadian religion and the history of philosophy and culture. His most recent book is *Into Deep Waters: Evangelical Spirituality and Maritime Calvinistic Baptist Ministers 1790–1855* (Montreal and Kingston: McGill-Queen's University Press, 2010). He is currently working on a study of evangelical religion and modernity in New Brunswick, 1830 to 1930.

JAMES TYLER ROBERTSON is currently a doctoral student at McMaster Divinity College studying the response of Canadian churches (Catholic and Protestant) to times of war and/or national crisis in the first half of the nineteenth century. His interest is primarily focused on how the church teaches its members during times of national conflict, but he is also interested in the growth of fundamentalism in the early twentieth century as well as incidents of violent insurrection that have occurred on Canadian soil. James has published articles and chapters in a variety of academic journals and books. He is the pastor of Mountsberg and Westover Baptist Churches in Flamborough, Ontario.

ROBERT R. SMALE has been teaching history, philosophy, comparative religion, and other social science courses for the Toronto District School Board for the past twenty-two years. He also lectures in history at the University of Toronto's School of Continuing Studies and is an Adjunct Professor (Teacher Mentor) for the Faculty of Education at York

University. He holds an MDiv (Northwest Baptist Theological Seminary), an MA in historical theology (Briercrest Theological Seminary), and an MEd in history and philosophy of education and the EdD (2001) from the Ontario Institute for Studies in Education at the University of Toronto. His publications include a number of papers related to Baptist history and Canadian immigration policy. Robert resides in Alliston, Ontario.

C. MARK STEINACHER is a Baptist pastor who has served in Alberta and Ontario. A graduate of the University of Toronto (BA, MDiv, ThM, ThD), he is currently a member of the faculty at Tyndale Seminary, where he created and launched the Seminary's online program. He has taught at McMaster Divinity College, where he also was Acting Director of the Canadian Baptist Archives. His main research interests are nineteenth-century Ontario church history, chaos/complexity theory, eschatology, the doctrine of the church, the history of religious freedom, and Christian pacifism. A former President of the Canadian Baptist Historical Society, he is currently Vice President. He is the author of numerous book chapters, encyclopedia articles, and dictionary entries, and his first monograph, a history of the Congregational Christian Churches in Canada, is forthcoming.

Introduction

THE RECENT DISCUSSION AND debate about Marci McDonald's *The Armageddon Factor: The Rise of Christian Nationalism in Canada* demonstrates that the role of religion in Canadian public life is still able to command considerable attention and engender a wide range of responses.[1] Although public discourse and debate about the relationship between religion and public life in Canada can be heated at times, the historical study of the many expressions of this relationship has recently become the focus of thoughtful historical inquiry. The efforts of Marguerite Van Die in *Religion and Public Life in Canada: Historical and Comparative Perspectives*, David Lyon and Marguerite Van Die in *Rethinking Church, State, and Modernity: Canada between Europe and America*, and Gary Miedema in *For Canada's Sake: Public Religion, Centennial Celebrations, and the Remaking of Canada in the 1960s* have significantly improved our understanding of the role that Christian religious beliefs, traditions, and practices have played in Canadian public life. These studies have also helped to shift the attention of historians away from the debate over secularization and on to new ground that examines the role of Canada's largest Christian denominations within the public domain. The experience of Canada's smaller Protestant Christian groups, however, has remained largely unexplored. This is particularly true in the case of Canada's Baptists.

This volume of historical essays, the first produced by the Canadian Baptist Historical Society, seeks to fill a number of sizeable gaps in knowledge about the connections between the Baptist faith and Baptist

1. McDonald, *Armageddon Factor*. Essentially, McDonald argues that Prime Minister Harper is enabling evangelicals to advance an American-style socio-political agenda in Canada. For reviews of McDonald's book, see Molly Worthen, "Onward, Christian Nationalists," *Globe and Mail*, 14 May 2010, F10; Douglas Todd, "New Book Digs Deep into Christian Political Activism in Canada," *Vancouver Sun*, 18 May 2010, B2; Gary Nicholls, "Marci MacDonald's Biggest Blunder," *National Post*, 20 May 2010, A14.

activity in the public domain. The collection of essays in this volume expands the focus of the existing scholarship to include a wide range of Canadian Baptist beliefs, attitudes, perspectives, and actions related to the relationship between Baptist faith and practice and public life.

For anyone acquainted with Baptist distinctives, a volume about Baptists and public life may seem somewhat ironic. After all, Baptists have had a long tradition of belief in the separation of church and state. As William Brackney noted in his study entitled *Baptists in North America*, "Government, leading Baptists contended, was to refrain from interference in matters of the spiritual realm."[2] This separation did not mean, however, that Baptists became political or social isolationists. As Brackney suggests, "Baptists did not cease from interposing their opinions upon the civic order."[3] Indeed, when it came to assessing the quality of those involved in their country's political life, Canadian Baptists were often both critical and complimentary. As an 1871 editorial in the *Canadian Baptist* wryly noted, "Accident may have brought to the surface of politics a good many who float by reason of the cork-like lightness of their brains; but on the whole, our public men are as able as those of other countries."[4] Such views were common fare in the public discourse of Canadian Baptists.

It is also important to note that within the Canadian context, Baptists followed the example of their British and American brothers and sisters and became ardent proponents and practitioners of voluntarism and separationism.[5] From this standpoint, in the eighteenth and nineteenth centuries Baptists called for an end to all forms of religious favoritism and the adoption of Anglo-Saxon Protestant values in public policy. Consequently, the issues that garnered attention from Canadian Baptists covered a broad range. They advocated for the abolition of slavery, an end to clergy reserves, the elimination of religious tests for office, and the creation of a public education system. In the twentieth century, Baptists who held widely divergent views of their religious identity, such as fundamentalists and social gospellers, became outspoken advocates of moral reform and social justice. Often Canadian Baptists sided with

2. Brackney, *Baptists*, 41.

3. Ibid., 42.

4. "Canadian Progress," *Canadian Baptist*, 28 September 1871, 1.

5. See, for example, Brackney, *Baptists*, 39–42, 50–54, and Pitman, *Baptists and Public Affairs*, 1–13.

other Protestants in their nation-building efforts and their construction of a broad evangelical moral socio-cultural consensus. At times, however, Baptists, particularly at the individual or regional levels, chose to pursue a more counter-cultural course that stood in contrast to more mainstream Protestant beliefs and values.

Previous historians have explored some of the Baptist contributions to Canada's public life, and their endeavors have provided both a foundation and a stimulus for this book. Unfortunately, some of this earlier material is now dated, limited in its scope or still in the form of unpublished papers and dissertations. Education has received the most attention. On this theme G. A. Rawlyk's *Canadian Baptists and Christian Higher Education* is perhaps the best example of a study that provides a careful analysis of how Baptist identity and belief shaped the denomination's educational activities. Among the many notable contributions related to Atlantic Canada are the articles by David Britton on the life of the New Brunswick preacher and politician Joseph Crandall, and Margaret Conrad on the efforts in Nova Scotia and New Brunswick of Baptist educator Theodore Harding Rand.[6] Works that discuss central Canadian Baptists and public life have tended to stress the role of key individuals such as Theo Gibson's biography of Robert Alexander Fyfe, Charles Johnston's analysis of William McMaster in the first volume of his McMaster University history, and Dale Thomson's biography of Alexander Mackenzie.[7] Institutions such as McMaster University and Walmer Road Baptist Church in Toronto have also received some attention, although the study of many key institutions is still in its infancy as are examinations of many central Canadian Baptist initiatives.[8] In the western context, Canadian historians have written a number of biographies about notable Baptist political figures, such as William Aberhart, Tommy Douglas, and John Diefenbaker, but often the linkages between their Baptist faith and public life are ignored altogether or treated superficially or tangentially. Still, not all historians are guilty of these faults. David Elliott's studies of William Aberhart show clearly the many connections between Aberhart's evolving and ever-changing religious views

6. Britton, "Joseph Crandall"; Conrad, "An Abiding Conviction of the Paramount Importance of Christian Education."

7. Gibson, *Robert Alexander Fyfe*; Johnston, *McMaster University* 1:18–44; Thomson, *Alexander Mackenzie*.

8. See Johnston, *McMaster University*; Goertz, *A Century for the City*.

(including Baptist) and the development of his social credit political ideology.[9] Similarly, the work of Walter E. Ellis and Robert Burkinshaw has drawn our attention to western Baptist participation in politics and a variety of educational initiatives.[10] The efforts of these historians have given us a partial picture of Baptists in public life.

While previous historical studies have provided some analysis of the Baptist experience in Canada's public life, there are many individuals, institutions, initiatives, and responses that remain shrouded in obscurity. The present volume begins with four articles that examine the endeavors of individual Baptists. The first two articles analyze aspects of the contributions made by two iconic Baptist figures: T. C. "Tommy" Douglas and T. T. Shields. Sandra Beardsall traces Douglas's family, educational, and occupational experiences and connects each with his prairie Baptist outlook and his intellectual and theological development. Beardsall also tackles the thorny question of whether Douglas retained his Baptist identity after his acceptance of the social gospel, ecumenism, and democratic socialism. According to Beardsall, Douglas's adherence to the strict morality of his Baptist upbringing and his evangelistic fervor provide sufficient evidence that he remained within the Baptist fold. Douglas Adams examines the political and social activism of the fundamentalist pastor T. T. Shields in the 1930s and 1940s through his interactions with Ontario's Roman Catholic Premier Mitchell Hepburn, and Prime Minister Mackenzie King. Adams argues that Shields overestimated his political acumen, demonstrated a considerable amount of political naïveté, but still proved to be a formidable critic and opponent of both Hepburn and King.

Two lesser known but no less important Baptists are examined in the articles by Sharon Bowler and Daniel Goodwin. Bowler examines the linkages between Dr. Jonathan Woolverton's Baptist faith and his involvement in the implementation at the local level of the public education system in Ontario. The picture that emerges is of a Baptist professional who was not only deeply religious and upwardly mobile, but also deeply committed to an emerging theological and socio-cultural evangelical Protestant consensus that motivated many talented, ambitious, and altruistic evangelicals in the mid-nineteenth century to es-

9. See Elliot and Miller, *Bible Bill*; Elliot, "Antithetical Elements."

10. See, for example, Ellis, "What the Times Demand"; Ellis, "Baptists and Radical Politics"; Burkinshaw, *Pilgrims in Lotus Land*, 55–99.

tablish the foundational social and political institutions of the province. Bowler argues that Woolverton's contribution was indicative of a rising professional class that was anxious to find its place in the public domain. Daniel Goodwin introduces us to the life and career of the Maritime Baptist intellectual Wilfred Currier Keirstead. Goodwin chronicles in detail the progression of Keirstead's thought and his attempts to combine his Baptist beliefs with the philosophies of Christian Personalism and Modernity. As Goodwin astutely observes, Kierstead's decision to leave a plum pastoral charge in Illinois, turn down an offer to teach at the University of Chicago, and return to New Brunswick, where he served as both pastor and intellectual, set him apart from many of his Maritime Baptist peers, many of whom chose to live and work in much more prominent positions in the United States. Goodwin's chapter and the other three biographical articles in this volume fill some important gaps in our current knowledge about the efforts of individual Baptists to practice their Baptist faith in a variety of public contexts.

The next two articles examine Baptist perspectives and responses related to events that threatened to disrupt the peace and derail the process of nation-building. Gordon Heath examines the response of the Baptist press to the Riel Rebellion of 1885. Heath argues that Baptist newspapers in every region of the country were committed to nation-building, and all shared the belief that the country's Protestant churches must play a central role in the creation of a Christian nation. Furthermore, Riel represented an obstacle and threat to westward expansion, law and order, patriotism, white dominance, and the assimilation of aboriginal peoples. The Baptist press was unanimous in its denunciation of the Rebellion, although Heath's findings challenge pre-existing views and assumptions about the nature and level of such denunciations. Particularly insightful is Heath's observation that the Maritime Baptist press was far more jingoistic in its response than the *Canadian Baptist* in central Canada. In a related vein, James Robertson examines the Ontario Baptist response to the Fenian invasion of 1866. As one would expect, he finds that Baptists in Canada West (Ontario) consistently condemned the Fenian invasion of 1866 and steadfastly opposed the Fenian cause. In addition, Baptists rejected any notion of a passive response and called for armed resistance to the incursions of the Fenian invaders if such resistance was necessary to preserve order and provide justice. The work of Heath and Robertson clearly demonstrates that Canadian Baptists often held views of key national events that were in lock-step with those of other Canadian Protestants.

The final section of this book contains four chapters that examine a variety of Canadian Baptist initiatives and responses within particular public domains. Paul Wilson examines the philanthropic and moral reform efforts of Toronto's Baptists, from the city's incorporation to the end of the First World War. Wilson argues that these efforts served a dual purpose: the living out of religious altruism and the achievement of middle class status and social respectability. He also observes two patterns of behavior that lay at the center of the endeavors by upwardly mobile Baptists to achieve their socio-cultural goals: relocation to middle class neighborhoods and the creation of physical and moral separation between themselves and those they served. Mark Steinacher employs chaos-complexity theory in his examination of the admission of non-Baptist students at McMaster University. Essentially, Steinacher argues that, as an institution committed to religious voluntarism, McMaster served as a faith-based alternative to the more scientifically-oriented and secular University of Toronto. Eventually, however, McMaster succumbed to the pressures of secularization and joined the mainstream of Ontario's public higher education system. In doing so, McMaster lost its identity as a distinctively Baptist and Christian University. Another Baptist initiative is covered in Donald Goertz's article about the Forward Movement. Here was a Baptist attempt to unify all Baptists behind the goals of increased outreach and social service. As Goertz notes, this was a significant attempt by Baptists to work towards shared spiritual and social objectives as one cohesive group. Although well-intentioned, the Forward Movement failed to make the dreams of unified action and a higher level of public involvement a reality. Finally, Robert Smale analyzes Canadian Baptist responses to immigration between 1880 and 1939. He finds that nativist, assimilationist, and ethnocentric attitudes prevailed until Watson Kirkonnell challenged Baptists to rethink their position in the 1930s by proposing a more pluralistic multi-cultural view of Canadian society. Smale also demonstrates that for Canadian Baptists, evangelization and Canadianization were synonymous for much of the period that he examines. Again, these studies of Canadian Baptist initiatives open new windows on the Canadian Baptist experience within the public domain.

The material contained in this volume is intended to stimulate further discussion and research even as it fills a number of gaps in our understanding of the complex and ever-changing relationship between religion and public life in Canada. The Baptist story, we believe, is one that deserves to be told and studied. *Baptists and Public Life in Canada* makes no claim to be the definitive study of its subject. But it is a beginning, and we are grateful to the authors for their contributions.

Gordon L. Heath
Paul R. Wilson
July 2011

BIBLIOGRAPHY OF THE INTRODUCTION

Brackney, William H. *Baptists in North America*. Oxford: Blackwell, 2006.

Britton, David. "Joseph Crandall: Preacher and Politician." In *An Abiding Conviction: Maritime Baptists and Their World*, edited by Robert S. Wilson, 109–33. Hantsport, Nova Scotia: Lancelot, 1988.

Burkinshaw, Robert K. *Pilgrims in Lotus Land: Conservative Protestantism in British Columbia 1917-1981*. Montreal & Kingston: McGill-Queen's University Press, 1995.

Conrad, Margaret. "'An Abiding Conviction of the Paramount Importance of Christian Education': Theodore Harding Rand as Educator, 1860-1900." In *An Abiding Conviction: Maritime Baptists and Their World*, edited by Robert S. Wilson, 155–95. Hantsport, Nova Scotia: Lancelot, 1988.

Elliot, David R. "Antithetical Elements in William Aberhart's Theology and Political Ideology." *Canadian Historical Review* 59 (1978) 38–58.

Elliot, David R., and Miller, Iris. *Bible Bill: A Biography of William Aberhart*. Edmonton: Riedmore, 1987.

Ellis, Walter E. "Baptists and Radical Politics in Western Canada." In *Baptists in Canada: Search for Identity amidst Diversity*, edited by Jarold K. Zeman, 161–82. Burlington, ON: Welch, 1980.

———. "What the Times Demand: Brandon College and Higher Education in Western Canada." In *Canadian Baptists and Christian Higher Education*, edited by George A. Rawlyk, 63–87. Montreal and Kingston: McGill-Queen's University Press, 1988.

Gibson, Theo T. *Robert Alexander Fyfe: His Contemporaries and His Influence*. Burlington, ON: Welch, 1988.

Goertz, Donald. *A Century for the City: Walmer Road Baptist Church, 1889-1989*. Toronto: Walmer Road Baptist Church, 1989.

Johnston, Charles Murray. *McMaster University. I. The Toronto Years*. Toronto: University of Toronto Press, 1976.

Lyon, David, and Van Die, Marguerite. *Rethinking Church, State, and Modernity: Canada between Europe and America*. Toronto: University of Toronto Press, 2000.

McDonald, Marci. *The Armageddon Factor: The Rise of Christian Nationalism in Canada*. Toronto: Random House, 2010.

Miedema, Gary. *For Canada's Sake: Public Religion, Centennial Celebrations, and the Remaking of Canada in the 1960s*. Montreal and Kingston: McGill-Queen's University Press, 2005.

Pitman, Walter G. *The Baptists and Public Affairs in the Province of Canada, 1840-1867*. New York: Arno, 1980.

Rawlyk, George, ed. *Canadian Baptists and Christian Higher Education*. Kingston and Montreal: McGill-Queen's University Press, 1988.

Thomson, Dale C. *Alexander Mackenzie: Clear Grit*. Toronto: Macmillian, 1960.

Van Die, Marguerite, ed. *Religion and Public Life in Canada: Historical and Comparative Perspectives*. Toronto: University of Toronto Press, 2001.

1

Jonathan Woolverton

Education Advocate, 1811–1883

SHARON M. BOWLER

THE FIRST SCHOOL OPENED in Upper Canada in 1785, with the first Education Act passed in March 1807, and the first Common School legislation enacted in 1816.[1] Annual parliamentary grants of varying amounts were in place to support Upper Canada's Common Schools as early as the 1816 School Act. Advocates for educational improvement, like John Wilson of Saltfleet[2] and Robert Baldwin of Hastings,[3] suffered considerable opposition to their education bills. It was a difficult task to provide a system of education that was free and open to all children and welcomed by the people of the province.

Historians of education have documented the fact that early Protestant advocacy was instrumental in ensuring that the first common school education acts guaranteed Protestants of both Upper and Lower Canada a form of schooling that would meet their faith needs.[4]

1. Until 1816, elementary education was not formally recognized by the government. For a history of the Upper Canada school system, see Hodgins, "Historical Sketch of Education in Upper and Lower Canada."

2. "The Hon. John Wilson of Saltfleet," 94. This source provides a biographical sketch of an early education advocate, beginning with his legislative career in 1808.

3. "Sketch of the System of Public Elementary Instruction in Upper Canada." This source provides additional information on Robert Baldwin.

4. For a most informative contextual understanding of Ontario's educational system beginnings, see Axelrod, *Promise of Schooling*.

In drafting the First Common School Act of 1841, the First Parliament of the United Canadas faced the dilemma of meeting the needs of both Catholics, primarily in Lower Canada, and a varied number of Protestant groups, primarily in Upper Canada, including congregations from Anglican, Methodist, Presbyterian, and Baptist religious faiths. Public objection to different aspects of education law, teacher education, teacher conduct, student conduct, and faith-based needs can be found throughout the Education Department correspondence and newspapers of the nineteenth century.[5]

The First Parliament of the Canadas resolved differences in educational faith-based needs by implementing a public system of separate schooling for those of Catholic faith and a public non-denominational method of schooling for those of a Protestant faith. The reading of the Bible, clergy visitations, and daily prayers within the public Protestant classrooms was initially guaranteed through Education Act legislation.

After confederation, as a greater number of people immigrated into the province, Ontario began to change from a predominantly bicultural community to a multicultural community.[6] Although challenges to the Protestant influence in Ontario's educational practice were expressed during this period of multicultural growth, Ontario classrooms remained little changed, and the reading of the Bible, clergy visits, and daily prayer continued throughout much of the province. Not until the 1980s and the Canadian Charter of Rights and Freedoms did Ontario classrooms experience dramatic reform. The secularization of classrooms eliminated all indoctrination and the use of Protestant-only prayer, religious instruction, and Scripture readings.

Although the Catholic public system of education was given guarantees based on Education Act legislation that was in place at the time of Confederation, no similar guarantee was provided for the public Protestant half that was in place at the time of Confederation. The Protestant voice that was equally represented in the initial Education Act legislation was clearly not considered equally significant to the Catholic voice, because the Catholics were more unified and able to speak with a singular voice. This being said, this chapter seeks to document one pre-

5. Archives of Ontario, "Incoming Correspondence," provides a number of examples of public outcry.

6. For discussions concerning the multi-cultural change within Ontario's educational system, see Gidney, *Hope to Harris*.

Confederation Protestant voice, that of the Baptist education advocate Jonathan Woolverton, in order to not lose sight of his efforts and to better understand his role in the development of Ontario's public education system.

This work is important in two ways. First, it examines yet another example of "religio-scientific synthesis" or the "blurring of worlds" that many historians, including Craig James Hazen, Kenneth Dewar, Nathan Hatch, Catherine Albanese, Lynne Marks, and William Westfall, have argued was the experience of many in nineteenth-century Ontario.[7] Hazen has argued that many nineteenth-century individuals "blurred" their beliefs in science and religion. Many refused to compartmentalize their faith into private areas and openly opted to have it encompass all aspects of their lives. The subject of this chapter, Jonathan Woolverton, is representative of a number of early education advocates that formed complex and interrelated faith-based schemas that served as guides in their daily, professional, and spiritual lives. He lived by what Peter Jensen has identified as a Protestant Conscience, a state of mind that motivated the one who possessed it to live consistently with this blurring of worlds.[8]

Second, the purpose of this chapter is to begin to fill the void in our knowledge of early local-level education advocates and administrators. Many histories have focused on the work of major figures, such as the Methodist Reverend Egerton Ryerson and the Anglican Bishop John Strachan, who held prominent upper-tier positions within their denominations and contributed significantly to education in the province. Historians have often ignored or minimized the role of local-level middle-tier administrators.

In attempting to meet these two objectives, I have chosen to use a micro-historical analysis. John Webster Grant provided the inspiration for this research when he wrote, "much of the religious history of Ontario has perished with those who made it." Many "Ontarians did not put their inmost thoughts on paper" and therefore, "we attach undue weight to the writings that have come down to us, which represent in the main the opinions of clerics and heretics, or we draw such inferences as we can from the public activities of Ontarians." Grant hoped

7. Hazen, *Village*; Dewar, *Charles Clarke*; Hatch, *Democratization*; Albanese, *Nature Religion*; Marks, *Revivals*; Westfall, *Two Worlds*.

8. Jensen, "Protestant Conscience."

that "perhaps someday a massive exploration of private diaries will make possible a more thorough exposé of the religious mind—or minds—of the province."[9] This chapter, therefore, provides a micro-historical rather than a macro-historical analysis using a considerably shortened biographical account of a Baptist who had a significant role and influence in the initial implementation of the public education system in his community.

I have selected Dr. Jonathan Woolverton (1811–1883) as the illustration of a life filled with a Protestant Baptist faith that permeated his professional, political, and private life. The primary source for this biographical sketch is all the material available in the journals, diary, and letters from his hand.[10] Much of this material consists of Woolverton's reflections about aspects of reform politics, community benevolence, education, and the Baptist religion. For thirty years (1832–1862) he kept a reflective diary that recorded his personal and professional stresses and joys. His Education Speech Journal and his letters to the Department of Education for the years 1850 through 1865 document his public expressions that show how he combined his Baptist faith with the more secular public good. The secondary nineteenth-century sources examined include newspaper articles, books, government reports, letters, and legislation. Taken together, these records offer rich insights into the inner life of a public man who was profoundly influenced by his Baptist faith.

Woolverton was the son of an MP, a husband, father, traveler, surgeon, physician, Temperance Society president, first Local School Superintendent for Lincoln County, medical school professor, grammar school board chair, Justice of the Peace, and member of the Clinton Baptist Church. We may be surprised to see such a vast array of interests, opportunities, and responsibilities reflected in only one life. Woolverton, however, was not unique, but representative of a number of nineteenth-century professionals who shared broad interests and skills. These people were remarkably linked to one another through travel, educational experience within the university setting, and the written word.[11]

9. Grant, *Profusion of Spires*, ix.

10. These documents are cited throughout this chapter with a note of gratitude to the archivists at the Grimsby Museum, the Grimsby Historical Society, the Archives of Ontario, and a special thanks to Woolverton family members, specifically Dr. Ralph Woolverton, who contributed family papers and provided access to family artefacts.

11. For an informative discussion on this topic see, Gidney and Millar, *Professional Gentlemen.*

The study of Woolverton's life has resulted in a fascinating exploration of the interconnectedness of working, living, and communication in a relative wilderness at a time of great instability and rapid educational and political reform. For the purpose of this short chapter, only a focus on the impact of Woolverton's faith in relation to his work in the Upper Canada educational system is explored.

In order to explore Woolverton's work in the Upper Canada educational system, it is necessary to develop two areas of understanding. First, a clear understanding of his Baptist faith is necessary, and second, a clear understanding of his role as a Local School Superintendent must be developed. Both the exploration of the complexity of the nineteenth-century non-clerical Baptist Protestant conscience and the role of a nineteenth-century Local School Superintendent warrant more analysis, and for that reason, this chapter includes two discussions that are intended to provide the contexts in which one can analyze Woolverton's educational work. These discussions provide some valuable new insights into the belief systems of non-clerical Baptists and the importance of the work of middle-tiered nineteenth-century educational administrators.

WOOLVERTON'S PROTESTANT BAPTIST CONSCIENCE

Woolverton was schooled in his faith and religious practice by his grandfather, who was the only Baptist family member during Jonathan's youth. The senior Woolverton's request to join the Baptists in 1810 may have come as a result of a missionary effort by the Rev. Daniel Hascall of Vermont, a Baptist missionary with the Shaftesbury Association.[12]

Woolverton's grandfather, also named Jonathan, provided a verbal statement before the church agreeing to the articles of faith and the church covenant.[13] These affirmations in front of the Clinton Baptist Church were important, because the evangelical teachings of the elder Woolverton had a profound impact on the spiritual development of his grandson. During the young Woolverton's early years, it is likely that his grandfather shared with him the following basic tenets of his faith, which resulted in Jonathan's similar desire to join with the Baptists in his twenty-second year. Woolverton's grandfather affirmed in front of the Clinton Baptist Church that there was one God in the form of the Trinity.

12. Gibson, *Fyfe*, 37.
13. Clinton Baptist Church papers.

He stated that God was the Creator of all things, and it was through the Bible that God's words provided the unerring rules of faith and practice. Jonathan's grandfather believed that although humanity was created to be just, the fall in the Garden of Eden resulted in an eternal punishment that could only be eliminated through God's grace and Christ's atonement at the cross. He noted that he believed in predestination. His grandfather believed that there would be a time when Jesus would once again come to judge the world, at which time there would be a resurrection of all the dead, with the wicked suffering punishment and the good celebrating in eternal happiness. The senior Jonathan agreed to honor the doctrines of believer's baptism by immersion and the congregational participation in closed communion. He also promised to attend church every Sunday and devote himself to the duties of the church.

Proper living was outlined in the church covenant that Jonathan's grandfather willingly accepted. Temperance in all things was emphasized, along with following the Bible. He promised to support the other church members and devote himself fully on the Lord's Day to the service of God and church. The senior Jonathan accepted that prayer and worship needed daily attention. He also dedicated himself to the prosperity of the church and God's kingdom on earth, and he promised that wherever he might be in the world he would seek to become a member of a church of the same faith and doctrine.

Young Woolverton's family subculture varied in many ways from that of his Grimsby neighborhood. Parental division on both religious and political lines placed Jonathan in a awkward and unusual situation. His mother considered herself a United Empire Loyalist with strong ties to the Anglican Church. Her family shared loyalties to the Crown and the Family Compact Conservatives. Jonathan's "American" father was not of the United Empire Loyalist or Anglican majority of Grimsby. In politics, Jonathan's father was a Member of Parliament who demonstrated allegiance to the Reform cause. Within this divided family, Jonathan Woolverton was exposed to a variety of ideas regarding politics and religion.

John Webster Grant has shown that religion and party allegiance were intertwined. Grant makes some interesting observations, noting that "Baptists could be counted on to vote the Reform ticket" and "defenders of Anglican privileges were almost uniformly Tory." Grant clearly acknowledges that the relationship between religion and party affiliation was a complex one that was reflected in fluctuating institutional, individual, and party goals that sometimes divided allegiances and resulted in congregational and electoral tensions. Grant concludes, however, that although "issues and alignments would change," the basic "religious underpinnings would remain significant" throughout the nineteenth century.[14]

Ruby Janet Powell, a local Grimsby historian, has argued that, according to the Woolverton family history, the marriage of Jonathan's parents, Dennis and Catharine, was "not a perfect union." Dennis the "American" had Baptist religious beliefs and Reformer politics that were in opposition to "Loyalist" Catherine's Anglican views and strong Tory politics.[15] Jonathan's father Dennis seems to have held no Baptist membership until the 1840s, while Jonathan's mother never abandoned her Anglican faith.

Woolverton was baptized by the Rev. Alexander Stewart into the Baptist faith in April 1832, while he was away at a York grammar school.[16] Theo Gibson has described Reverend Stewart's practice of interviewing candidates requesting membership in the church. Once the candidates were accepted, a baptismal service would take place, and the new member would then be entitled to participate in communion services.[17] In some ways, the York March Street Baptist Church where he was baptized, and Jonathan's grandfather's church, the Clinton Baptist Church, shared similar professions of faith and church covenant. However, the

14. Grant, *Profusion of Spires*, 98–99.

15. Powell, *Annals of the Forty No. 9*. Dennis's Baptist convictions that Powell refers to do not become established until years later as recorded in 1843 by Dr. Woolverton: "The most extensive revivals of religion that have ever been known in Canada or America, have taken place this year. There have been added to the church in Beamsville during the past few months nearly 100 members among which number I am very thankful that I can enumerate a Father and Sister." Woolverton, "Diary," 56.

16. York was the former name of the city of Toronto.

17. Gibson, *Fyfe*, 108–9. Reverend Stewart was a Baptist minister who came from Edinburgh in 1816 and worked as a schoolmaster in York. He worked in several schools, experiencing some difficulties receiving payment allegedly due to the fact that he was not with the Church of England. In 1829, he opened the March Street Baptist Church, later called the Jarvis Street Baptist Church, with a Mr. Caldicott, a Baptist teacher, taking over the school responsibilities. Stewart's church was only the second Baptist church in York; the first was a church organized just previously by a group of escaped slaves from the United States.

York church had a documented history with another denomination, the Church of Christ.

Reuben Butchart, a Canadian historian for the Church of Christ, was able to show that Alexander Stewart was one of his denomination's Canadian founders.[18] The fact that Jonathan joined this particular church is of significance for understanding Jonathan's open denominational philosophies in later years. The early teachings to which Stewart exposed Jonathan were likely influential in making him open to other ideas. In fact, exposure to differing beliefs within his family may have given him an opportunity to develop an openness to consider the teachings of other denominations and a respect for the differing beliefs of revival missionaries.

Stewart had numerous arguments with York's Anglican rector and President of the General Board of Education, John Strachan, who was a firm advocate for Anglican control over the common school system. Stewart likely shared his experiences and his Reform philosophies with Woolverton. Stewart had become involved with the Reformers during a 10 December 1830 rally in York.[19] The rally eventually resulted in a petition from ten thousand members who called themselves, "The Friends of Religious Liberty." Their leader, Robert Baldwin, along with Reverend Stewart and George Ryerson, urged that the petition be sent to England, where it apparently was well-received but ineffective in promoting change. Stewart likely introduced Jonathan to many of the prominent individuals from the Reform movement during the early 1830s, providing Jonathan with an opportunity to gain greater insight into Upper Canada politics.

Woolverton moved several times to further his medical education. His moves included York, Montreal, and Philadelphia, and he recorded his Baptist church attendance at each location. He attended a relatively new Baptist church in Montreal in 1832–33, and reported that he attended John Gilmore's services "with interest and delight." However, while in Montreal he experienced personal conflicts within his chosen denomination.

Gilmore had helped found St. Helen Street Baptist Church in 1831.[20] Gilmore believed in open communion and interdenominational coop-

18. Gibson, *Fyfe*, 169.

19. Ibid., 98.

20. Ibid., 25.

eration. In addition, the St. Helen Street Baptist Church practiced "open membership, twelve of its twenty-five charter members being unimmersed persons."[21] Jonathan found himself in the middle of a Baptist debate. Gibson has identified the Baptist open-communion question as "beyond doubt the most divisive question plaguing Canadian Baptists for many decades."[22]

Some time during his Montreal stay, Woolverton decided that he wished to join the St. Helen Street Baptist Church, and as was the practice of the Baptist church, he was required to request a letter of transfer from his home congregation in York.[23] He was surprised and disappointed to find, however, that his home pastor, Alexander Stewart from York, raised strong objections. These objections were based on the open and closed communion question and likely open membership, although Woolverton never refers to this second point. Jonathan decided that open communion was not offensive to him, but as he would likely remain in Montreal only a short time, he decided against joining the Montreal church. He likely felt that his relationship with Stewart would carry on longer than his relationship with Gilmore. However, as noted below, Gilmore would later figure prominently in Woolverton's life.

Woolverton believed in one God who provided him with his Word in the Bible, and it was by the use of Scripture that he refined, maintained, and integrated his faith throughout his life's work. He clearly indicated that good works did not make a good person, believing that an active, accomplished, and intellectual person may, in fact, have "neglected to educate aright his moral and religious powers," resulting in a person of good works being capable of taking "advantage" of a fellow human being.[24]

In Woolverton's opinion, those with a pure conscience would be able to rejoice in *mens sana in corpore sano*, or a sound mind in a healthy body. Woolverton believed that if the "mind is at all times free and unclouded," the individual will be "prepared for every emergency," anticipating "the coming storm" and remaining sheltered from such because such a one "forseeth the evil," by hiding from it.[25] Honoring the manner

21. Ibid., 172.
22. Ibid., 171.
23. Clinton Baptist Church papers.
24. Woolverton, "Speech Journal," 79–81. From an educational speech dated 1850.
25. Ibid., 30. This material is taken from a temperance speech dated January 1848.

in which the apostle James in the New Testament developed the analogy of a human being to a ship, Woolverton instructed his community at public meetings to "not permit [their] judgements be dethroned nor wander with its 'helm of reason lost,'" in order that they be "enabled to pursue 'the even tenor of [their] way' unruffled by the storms and commotions of life."[26]

Woolverton believed that in order to reduce the opportunity for evil that existed in society, an educational system had to be established "to guide and guard us safely through this state of our probation to bring us to our end in peace and give us a blessed hope of immortality beyond this transitory scene of our existence." Based on his studies in the sciences, he believed that within either the "dance in the transient sunbeam" or "the depths of the great abyss," a person should become, "equally surprised, delighted and astonished at the Wisdom, the Goodness, the adaptation, and the perfection displayed in the manifold works of God."[27]

Woolverton's reflections with regard to science and religion indicate that he found no conflict between these two fields of study, and both provided him with the foundations for his life's work. Woolverton's writings provide the historian with a window into the ways in which secular and religious themes were negotiated and reconciled within one individual's life.

In his diary, Woolverton often mentioned that he sought hope through his faith. He believed that his life-path would be guided by his God. In a time of difficulty and decision he noted that "all things were under the direction and guidance of a just, wise, and merciful God, my murmuring ceased and I could say, it is the Lord let Him do what seemeth Him good."[28] He also vowed that no matter the outcome, he would continue to serve God and trust in God's plan. Woolverton could trust in his God because he was "fully convinced that the words of the apostle are true that all things shall work together for good to those that love God." He resigned himself "into His hands, to be directed by His providence, and to bear with cheerfulness those dispensations, which in His great

26. Here Woolverton quotes from James 3:4.

27. Woolverton, "Speech Journal," 151. All the quotations in this paragraph are taken from an educational speech dated 1850.

28. Woolverton, "Diary," 10–11. This entry was written some time during the fall of 1832.

Wisdom and goodness, He may be pleased to call me to pass through."[29]
This kind of unwavering faith permeated his thirty-year-long diary.

THE ROLE OF A LOCAL SCHOOL SUPERINTENDENT

In 1843, the second Common School Act was passed, which included
the first provision for the Office of Chief Superintendent of Schools. In
1844, this office was filled by Egerton Ryerson a Methodist minister and
educator. Knowing that he had to gain public support and confidence by
applying his knowledge to the public discourse, he insisted that the education department be non-political. He also demanded that he be given
a year-long leave to examine the educational systems in both Europe and
America.[30] Ryerson's international experience gave him the grounding
necessary to discuss, design, and implement a system of education for
Upper Canada.

Ryerson emphasized that school law and a school fund did not
guarantee a successful system of education in a community. Education
depended, in Ryerson's view, on the ability of the Local School
Superintendent to inspire the people into action that would implement
the intentions of the law. Local School Superintendents were required to
accept Ryerson's demand that the Local School Superintendent inspire
the people through public lectures. The political climate with respect to
common schools was generated and controlled in part through these
public school lectures, which were the responsibility of Local School
Superintendents after 1850.

Throughout his career, Ryerson used the educational methods
and reform experiences of other countries to his advantage. Most importantly, he remained vigilant in his monitoring of new educational
methods after their introduction. He was also careful not to create too
many laws too hastily or in a way that was not conducive to generating
public support. Comments that Ryerson made regarding the implementation of the 1850 Common School Act are indicative of the political
philosophy that he held throughout his career. He was also insistent that
all those who worked to promote education in the province should hold
such views. Ryerson worked on a principle of maintaining the public's

29. Ibid.
30. "Sketch of the System of Public Elementary Instruction in Upper Canada."

support, and he demanded the same from men such as his Local School Superintendents.

Ryerson believed that the School Act of 1850 was only a beginning.[31] The Act was meant to be improved and was, in effect, representative of only a small part of his vision for the province, which he had published earlier in 1846. Ryerson felt that in 1850, the Upper Canada population was not yet ready to accept his vision for the province's educational system, and rather than risk defeat, he would implement his vision in steps with the help of Local School Superintendents.

In his Educational Reports, his correspondence, and frequently in the *Journal of Education*, Ryerson made many references to the state of education in other countries. He urged his readers to heed the advice of and take warning from the errors made in other jurisdictions.[32] Writing about the history of the school system of Upper Canada in the year 1852, Ryerson discussed the tension created by the law enforcing the concept of a free school, and he reinforced his personal philosophy of delaying implementation until public support was established.[33] Ryerson felt that a law too hastily implemented would prove difficult to maintain as years went by. It did not mean that the public accepted the law if it was only forced upon them.

Ryerson was much attuned to the need to satisfy the public with a process of efficient school management. In fact, the method of education governance was itself a contentious topic in the early years. For example, the role of Local Superintendent underwent major change from its first introduction in the School Act of 1843, its repeal in 1846, and its modified form reintroduced in 1850. In his "Report on Education" in 1846, Ryerson quoted a District Superintendent as representative of the public's objections to the concept of a Township Superintendent.[34]

31. For an account of Ryerson's work on the Act of 1850 see, Hodgins, *Documentary History*.

32. For example, on an 1852 letter received by Ryerson from Woolverton, Ryerson's office penned a response concerning Free Schools and Funding, noting that a recommendation should be made to read the article, "The Efficiency of a School System Not Dependent on a Large School Fund," *Journal of Education for Upper Canada* 3 (April 1850), 130–32. An essay by the Superintendent of Schools for the State of Connecticut advocated for the spirit of education in applying school law.

33. Ryerson, "Spirit," 303.

34. "Report on Education," Appendix "P," *Journals of the Legislative Assembly of the Province of Canada* 5, 20 March to 9 June 1846.

The measure clearly was not popular. Many were convinced that there were not enough capable people to fill the positions. In 1846, because of the public outcry and internal criticism, the new Common School Act of 1846 abolished the role of Township Superintendent. Even Ryerson voiced his objections to the role of Township Superintendent in a letter to the Secretary of the Province in March 1846, citing public objections as his determining factor.[35]

Although the role of Township Superintendent was eliminated in 1846, it would be reintroduced. From September through December 1847, Ryerson toured Upper Canada in order to gather information about the public's perception regarding the system of education in the province. In an 1848 letter from Ryerson to the Education Secretary of the Province, Ryerson commented that his own public meetings had sparked an interest and excitement in the province that he believed should be maintained through "annual visitation."[36] Ryerson surely realized the scope and power of this "annual visitation" and the need to have a number of highly influential local individuals to assist in the performance of this duty.[37] The Common School Act of 1850 was modified to include a clause to guarantee the delivery of these "annual lectures" and, in effect, resulted in the legislating of a method of education advocacy throughout the province.

In Ryerson's August 1850 Circular to County Councils and Local Superintendents, he stated, "A most important duty, which the new School-Act devolves upon the County Council, is the annual appointment of Local Superintendents of Schools."[38] The amended sections outlined the duties of the Local Superintendents to include that they become knowledgeable about public "interests," confer on these "interests" at the district level, and provide public lectures of public "interest."[39] This formed the political foundation for a system of education advocacy.

35. This information is taken from a letter dated 3 March 1846, from Ryerson to the Secretary of the Province (Appendix "N," *Journals of the Legislative Assembly of the Province* 9, 14 May to 10 August 1850).

36. Appendix "ZZZ," *Journals of the Legislative Assembly of the Province of Canada* 8, 1849.

37. For an example of Ryerson's familiarization with the role of Local Superintendents in other jurisdictions, see his discussion of an 1844 article on the Common School System of the State of New York (Ryerson, "Chief Superintendent's Circular," 11).

38. Ibid., 9.

39. Appendix "N," *Journals of the Legislative Assembly of the Province* 9, 14 May to 10 August 1850.

Ryerson declared that "the greatest increase in the duties and efficiency of the department [of education] was made by the Act of 1850,"
and he particularly stressed that there was "an increase in the number of
superintendents of from twenty to two hundred and fifty."[40] With these
legislated Local Superintendents, each of whom had directives to implement annual lectures in a manner to meet public interest while confer-
ring at the district level, Ryerson was able, in theory, to maintain direct
communication with the public, readers and non-readers alike.

Ryerson knew that the role of Local Superintendent would be of
critical importance to him in maintaining public support of education.
He set about to educate those in authority to select appropriate persons
for the position and then direct those new superintendents in the process of interacting with the public through annual lectures that were
both stimulating and focused on school improvement and system maintenance.[41] This was not an easy task, as the public was not yet ready to
embrace the concept of free education. Ryerson needed superintendents
that could generate both public trust and confidence. Only with competent people could Ryerson hope to tackle problems such as public objection to free schools or public apathy with regard to school improvement.

Ryerson did not want his system of education to fail. The role of
Local Superintendent, therefore, became a critical focus of his attention
after the 1850 Education Act established the position. Ryerson realized
that the selection of the right persons for the task was most important.
The 1856 *Journal of Education for Upper Canada* summarized Ryerson's
vision for the position of Local School Superintendent.[42] County
Councils were asked to appoint people who could fulfill the various
miscellaneous duties, examine teachers, schoolhouses, and pupils, and
successfully perform the lecture component of the job. He wanted persons of sound judgment and knowledge, who could "command public
attention as lecturers." Ryerson believed that the Council needed to seek
out those who understood school organization and improvement. He
urged councils to select solely on the grounds of "personal qualification

40 Appendix "B," *Journals of the Legislative Assembly of the Province of Canada* 13,
5 September 1854 to 30 May 1855.

41. Keele, *Magistrate's Manual.* The role of Superintendent with regard to public
lectures is outlined as follows: "To deliver in each school section a public lecture on
practical education once a year, and to stimulate parents and guardians to improve the
schools and secure sound education."

42. Ryerson, "Chief Superintendent's Circular," 9.

and character, and irrespective of party considerations." He also insisted that the Local Superintendents needed to stay clear of partisan bias.

The philosophy that education advocacy should stay clear of partisan bias was explained in Ryerson's 1850 Circular to County Councils and Local Superintendents.[43] Ryerson had witnessed in many school sections how party politics had impeded the successful implementation of School Law. He predicted that a zeal for one party over the other would "degenerate into mere party strife, and petty, personal bickerings," and "ensure disaster and defeat to the best and noblest cause."

Placing the focus on a party bias would detract from the primary arguments educators wished to address. Focusing arguments on the educational subject at hand and away from political interests helped to ensure that the primary message was heard. The messages that needed communication had to be identified by Ryerson in order that his superintendents could consistently and successfully promote the envisioned system of education. Ryerson did not fail in providing Local Superintendents with a purpose and focus for their public lectures. He made sure that the *Journal of Education* and "Reports on Education" were readily available to members of the Upper Canada reading public, and supplied them to each school section and Local School Superintendent. These superintendents regularly consulted the *Journal of Education*, *Annual Reports on Education* and school circulars, and used these documents to supplement school lectures, make decisions, and petition Ryerson for change.

Ryerson felt that education was of such importance to the country that he needed to ensure that every community became firm supporters of the new public education system. He needed his superintendents to "excite and maintain, as widely and in as high a degree as possible, among all classes of the community, a correct appreciation of the nature and importance of popular education, and a spirit of intelligence, philanthropy and patriotism and the adoption of the diversified means necessary for the attainment of that end." Ryerson made it the job of the superintendent to introduce and maintain "a moral influence, an energy, a vitality" for education by providing the community with the information they needed to support their schools.

Maintaining an interest in the educational cause and educating the public on the system of education would ensure the public sup-

43. Ryerson, "Spirit," 303.

port Ryerson needed. Politically it was wise of him to ensure that Local School Superintendents had a clear understanding of the purpose of the law and the required implementation strategies necessary to maintain stakeholder support. He cautioned superintendents to balance education advocacy and implementation of school law with political strategies.

Ryerson instructed Local Superintendents with a number of political strategies. Superintendents were warned that the rapidly advancing state of education would demand great caution. He demanded that a sense of mutual cooperation be promoted between the community and the Department of Education. Superintendents were urged to practice with "conciliation and forbearance." Lectures were to discuss the principles of education intelligently, with practical examples, and stress the importance of education to the good of the country. Ryerson urged superintendents to listen to objections in order to respect the differing opinions of others. He cautioned that, "There is a latent pride and spirit of resistance in the bosom of almost every man, which, if imprudently, or incautiously, aroused, will result in a settled opposition to the favourite theories of others."[44]

Ryerson realized that the acceptance of any school law could be secured by making people fear the repercussions of breaking the law, but it was best that the Law be implemented with community support. Ryerson was clearly very politically astute. His directives to Local Superintendents clearly advocated the implementation of the law in combination with education advocacy. The necessity to provide factual information prudently and cautiously, in a manner that was non-partisan, persuasive, and sympathetic to differing points of view would politically help to ensure the acceptance and successful implementation of the school law.

Ryerson's 1850 circular outlined the requirements necessary in fulfilling the public lecture duties of superintendants.[45] Only those committed to the delivery of public lectures should remain in office. He also demanded that superintendents who failed to generate their community's support of education must accept the full responsibility and disgrace they deserved.

44. Ibid.

45. Ryerson, "Chief Superintendent's Circular," 9–10.

LOCAL SCHOOL SUPERINTENDENT AND GRAMMAR SCHOOL BOARD CHAIR JONATHAN WOOLVERTON

In 1834, Dennis Woolverton, Jonathan's father, was elected as a member of the Lower House of Parliament and joined his son in York.[46] In addition to his York medical experiences with the sick and dying, and his opportunities to discuss spiritual matters with his pastor Alexander Stewart, Jonathan Woolverton also filled his days observing political activities in the province. He regularly visited his father in Parliament, noting that he "was much gratified and interested with the debates on several measures." But, as he also recorded, all was not well in Parliament. He recognized that the "two houses were much opposed to each other," accurately predicting that "the Legislative Council by their obstinacy and illiberality are fast hastening their own downfall. Before many years they must show a little more disposition to comply with the majority of the lower house, or the supplies will be stopped."[47]

In fact, when Dennis Woolverton did leave the Lower House in 1836, his last efforts were to have the supplies stopped. In 1835 Parliament faced a crisis. Jonathan Woolverton had the opportunity to witness events first hand as he sat and watched the house debates. Even when resolutions and bills were brought forward in the Lower House, he saw how many of them were defeated in the Legislative Council. The majority, who were Reformers, could not make a difference when the Legislative Council blocked most of their bills.

Dennis Woolverton supported a motion on 15 April 1835 to draft a letter to the King seeking his intervention.[48] The lengthy letter made the King aware of the Legislative Council's rejection of bills concerning the protection of agricultural interests, distribution of property of persons dying intestate, impartial juries, militia laws, improvement of schools, the King's College charter, selling of Clergy Reserves, voting by ballot, and the support of the Grantham and Bath Academies. A demand for responsible government and local responsibility was put forth with a

---

46. R. J. Powell, *Annals of the Forty* rough note papers, Grimsby Museum. Powell states: "Dennis became a member of the Legislative Assembly of Upper Canada from 1834–1836. He was urged to be a candidate in the election of 1836 but refused probably because at this time Rebellion was rearing its ugly head."

47. Woolverton, "Diary," 35–36.

48. *The Journal of the House of Assembly of Upper Canada*, 1835. CIHM: 9 00941 11.

threat to withhold the annual grant to support the government if a reso-lution was not found.

Jonathan Woolverton had the opportunity to become familiar with many of the Reform issues and to develop associations with many of the reformers pushing the government for change. Dennis was either a member or a chair for many of the subcommittees considering the issues raised by the rejected bills. The rejected Act to Promote Education within the province included twenty-two points including: the estab-lishment of local school superintendents, financial support for scholars needing education out of their district, examination of schoolmasters, establishment of local education funds, and the establishment of an an-nual process for Local Board of Education communication with the gov-ernment.[49] Jonathan had opportunity to discuss educational issues with his father, and when the position of Local Superintendent was finally established in 1850, and he was invited to take the position. He likely felt well prepared to take on the role.

In 1838, Jonathan Woolverton's path crossed once again with John Gilmore. Gilmore and Dr. Benjamin Davies, a professor sent by the Baptists in England, spent the day with Jonathan to consider the pos-sibility of a Baptist institution in the province. The Baptist Society in England had sent funds to the Baptist Canadian Missionary Society for the establishment of a Baptist College in the colony.[50] The initial request for funds had come from Montreal, so Davies was sent to Montreal from England to become a professor in the new institution. In the meantime, a second request arrived from Upper Canada, sparking a debate in England and Canada as to the location of the new Baptist College. Davies found himself in the middle of this debate and visited with the four Upper Canada congregations who wished that the college be located in their area. One of the four churches was Clinton Baptist Church, Woolverton's home church when he lived in Grimsby. Woolverton ended up acting as church representative during the Gilmore and Davies visit. The visit by the Reverends Gilmore and Davies illustrates the emerging nineteenth-century direction of the Baptist Church and the interconnections with the educational system in the province.

In 1838, Davies also found himself in the middle of a political de-bate that allied him with Egerton Ryerson, the future Superintendent of

49. See "An Act to Promote Education, Bill 24."

50. Gibson, *Fyfe*, chap. 5.

Education in the Province. Gibson has documented that there were protests from 1836 through 1838 regarding the implementation of fifty-seven rectories (government land allocations for a church, clergy residence, and often a school that would be staffed by Anglican clergy) that were established with the help of Anglican Archdeacon Strachan.[51] Egerton Ryerson through the *Guardian*, and the Baptists through the *Register*, urged their members to take action. Action was taken in September 1838 when a Montreal rally passed seven resolutions, which may have led Lord Durham to consider that the questions regarding ecclesiastical conflicts might best be solved through responsible government. Rally attendees resolved to reject the establishment of a state church, pursue independence from England if a state church was implemented, appeal to the public for support, demand the proceeds of the sale of the Clergy Reserves[52] to be used for the universal good, suggesting that these funds be used for education, and resolve to resist through legal means the establishment of rectories.[53]

It may have been during Woolverton's earlier meeting with Davies and Gilmore that he decided to focus a greater amount of his time on the concerns of education in the province. Woolverton had previously been exposed to his father Dennis's failed attempts in 1835 to change the delivery of education in the province, and he was likely able to share a number of these ideas with his Baptist guests. Woolverton became directly involved in this movement when he accepted the role of Local School Superintendent and later Chairman of the Grimsby Grammar School Board. His meeting with Davies and Gilmore presented an opportunity for him to merge the questions of Baptist education, evangelism, revival, and the political state of schooling in the province.

Jeffery McNairn provides some insight into the political climate of the time, which illustrates how important Dr. Woolverton's community involvement was to him. McNairn points out that post-Rebellion Upper Canadians were living at a time of critical change and rapid prog-

51. Ibid., 101–2.

52. Clergy Reserves were the lands set aside in the Constitutional Act of 1791 for the maintenance of "Protestant Clergy." They constituted one-seventh of all Crown lands. The constitution was initially interpreted to mean that these lands were for the support of the Anglican Church (which collected rents on these lands), although the Church of Scotland was later included. Baptists believed that such government support of only one or two denominations should come to an end.

53. Ibid., 102.

ress. The Rebellion, and the resulting implementation of Responsible Government, demanded a voice from the people to provide and implement Canadian ideas. Professionals like Woolverton, who had an ability to express their ideas clearly and represent others, were needed to speak for the people as well as the government. As McNairn notes, "words mattered" in Upper Canada. The community and government were searching "for ways to govern and understand themselves that best reflected the lessons of the science of politics, their diverse experiences, and their hopes and fears for Upper Canada and the broader North Atlantic world." McNairn concludes that the people of Upper Canada "cared passionately about politics" and that the times were filled with serious debate, with those of ability taking on central roles in helping the country settle "the principles of legitimate authority; and the best mechanisms for reflecting them."[54]

When Woolverton decided to accept responsibility for his community's system of education, he was prepared. He was certainly a bright and capable individual, but he also carried with him experience that many individuals in his community lacked. His knowledge of the role, direction, history, and goals of Responsible Government grew from his earliest years. And as he sat at his journal in 1850, recording pertinent school law, his mind must have been on the responsibility and the power that he was assuming in his new role of Local School Superintendent.

Woolverton served as Local School Superintendent from 1850 into the 1860s. He addressed his lectures to a wide audience and used many communication techniques to maintain audience focus. He covered a wide range of topics including educational law, methods and curriculum, evangelism, childcare and health, parenting, science, libraries, school architecture, corporal punishment, temperance, and citizenship. Throughout his time as Local School Superintendent, Woolverton fulfilled Ryerson's directives by advocating for the acceptance and improvement of the school system.

Woolverton had been a student in Grimsby and was well aware of the issues that his grandfather and father had to contend with in ensuring that the common school was available for his family. Woolverton was also aware of the objections and disparities suffered within the Grimsby community. Despite public objections, legislators who believed

---

54. McNairn, *Capacity*, 211.

in a Common School system held firm to their belief in the good of an improved legislated system of education.

Woolverton's many hours spent observing Parliamentary debate and his Temperance Society public lectures had given him the confidence to accept Ryerson's directives with full faith that he would be successful in the role, yet Woolverton knew changes were necessary at both the local and Department of Education levels of government.

An article in the 1853 *Niagara Chronicle* gives some insight into the public culture in which Woolverton likely went about performing his Local School Superintendent tasks.[55] Many in Niagara were not sending their children to school or paying much attention to the system of education in the province. Inhabitants were apathetic and indifferent when it came to education. It was reported that even the prominent men and women failed to visit the local school to provide even just a little encouragement for the learning that was taking place there. The newspaper urged all citizens to become active and aware of the education that was taking place in the community.

The role of Local Superintendent required a person of power and knowledge of the system of education to inspire interest in the schools. The process of finding the best person for the difficult role of Local Superintendent was not an easy task, as illustrated by a Hastings Local Superintendent's Annual Report for 1851.[56] The report claimed that a number of men were appointed to the role of Local Superintendent who had no previous knowledge or interest in education and were incapable of doing the job. According to this Superintendent, the process of appointment was flawed, because the appointment was usually made by the Township Reeve who was not always honest. It is likely that Woolverton received his own appointment because of his father's role in the township government.

The Superintendent from Hastings also complained that those qualified for the position of Local Superintendent were often unwilling to accept the appointment. Professionals were unable to devote enough time to fulfill the required duties adequately. As a physician, Woolverton most certainly would have interrupted his duties as Local School Superintendent to provide assistance to the sick and dying. It

55. "The Schools," *Niagara Chronicle*, 26 August 1853.

56 Appendix "JJ," *Journals of the Legislative Assembly of the Province of Canada* 11, 19 August 1852 to 14 June 1853.

is impossible from his words to determine how he balanced his roles as father, Local School Superintendent, physician, and later Justice of the Peace. It is known that he ventured away from his community for extended periods of time and that at these times his brother may have covered his medical practice; yet it is unclear how his many community commitments were handled.

The Superintendent from Hastings also advocated that people take the position only if they could demonstrate a sound understanding of the practical and theoretical aspects of education and the ability to devote their "whole" time to educational advocacy. This superintendent felt that the ones who accepted the position of Local School Superintendent should be men of "talent and learning, and above all, men of untarnished character, whose advice and opinions will have some influence in reconciling such differences as frequently arise in school sections." He concluded by predicting that the system of education would fail unless appropriate superintendents were found to fill the role.

Woolverton accepted an enormous and difficult responsibility when he took over the task of Local School Superintendent. Woolverton's Speech Journal, letters to Egerton Ryerson, and articles in the *Journal of Education for Upper Canada*, provide the only documentation of his work as Superintendent.[57] He recorded his annual school lectures, examination questions, short essays on curriculum topics, and parts of the School Law in his Speech Journal. These records provide an insight into Woolverton's role as spokesman for the Department of Education.

Like his boss, the Methodist evangelical Ryerson, the Baptist evangelical Woolverton used "revivalist" techniques to aid his attempts to reform the province's education system further. To ensure that the entire community was reached, Ryerson, who was most familiar with the techniques of revival in his role as a minister in the Methodist Church,

---

57. Education Speeches were transcribed from Dr. Woolverton's "Speech Journal." This source is used with the permission of the Grimsby Museum and with a special thank you to Margaret Gibson, a local historian, who was able to locate this journal and help me identify Woolverton as the writer. Dr. Woolverton's correspondence with Egerton Ryerson has been transcribed from the original documents in the Archives of Ontario: Incoming correspondence has been transcribed from the original paper documents in RG 2-12 Boxes 9 through 103. Outgoing correspondence has been transcribed form the original draft documents in RG 2-9 and from the microfilmed letter books in MS 925. Information has been collected from the Annual Education Report files and the Local School History files for Grimsby in RG 2-87, and the Teaching Experiences files in RG 2-97.

put revival practices such as circuit-riding into place for Local School Superintendents like Woolverton.

Woolverton correctly interpreted Ryerson's directives to mean that indoctrination in a particular faith would not be tolerated, but a general "evangelistic" call to a common set of Christian principles was expected by the Department of Education. Woolverton became such an evangelist. Quoting from Scripture, he communicated to those in attendance at his Lectures on Education the basic Protestant principle of salvation, that "God so loved the world that he gave his only begotten son to die that whosoever believeth on him might not perish but have everlasting life."[58] Furthermore, Woolverton felt that the words of God should "be assiduously impressed upon the mind and especially upon the minds of the young." The teaching of students within the Common School system, while clearly focused on Protestant principles, was also evaluated by Woolverton as needing to be free from "any sectarian bias" or "any peculiar dogmas."[59]

Woolverton had opportunity to observe discipline in the classroom. In one of his speeches about school discipline, he stated that sometimes "moral suasion" had to be backed up with corporal punishment via the rod when the offender lacked appropriate feeling and duty. Woolverton stressed that "the great majority of children may be influenced, restrained and directed by proper and opportune moral management," and he noted that "much harm is likely to ensue by the too frequent and severe infliction of Corporal punishment." He also acknowledged that there were "many instances and those not a few, in which the rod discreetly used is actually necessary to bring the offender back to feeling and to duty."[60] Woolverton advocated corporal punishment because he believed that it was biblically sound and necessary.

In his instruction to teachers on when to use corporal punishment, he advocated for the child, suggesting that "if a child can but be brought to feel that he has done wrong, to feel sorrow for his fault, and promise amendment for the time to come, the great object of discipline is already accomplished," and corporal punishment is not needed. Before administering corporal punishment, Woolverton urged teachers to "appeal to his [the student's] intellect, to his knowledge of right and wrong, to the

58. Woolverton, "Speech Journal," 79–81. Quoting from John 3:16.

59. Ibid.

60. Woolverton, "Speech Journal," 134, from an Education Speech of 1850.

impropriety, and the injurious tendency of his conduct," highlighting the aspect of respect for self and others, and the need to strive toward wisdom and usefulness while steering away from impropriety, "shame and disgrace."[61]

Woolverton believed that it was feelings and affection to duty and the knowledge required to do good that ought to be instilled in the pupil. Although the rod was seen as valuable in accomplishing this goal, Woolverton also recognized the possibility of the rod's misuse. He urged teachers to use the rod with "judgement and discretion," never striking the child in "excitement, or passion." He also cautioned the teacher not to "strike the child about the head or face, as should any ill consequences follow he would be liable to damages."[62] Although he believed that the rod was a biblically justified form of child discipline, Woolverton emphasized to his teachers that they must practice such discipline within the confines of the law. In his speeches he clearly demonstrated an advocacy for the proper treatment of students.

Woolverton's education speeches also demonstrate how he resolved his study of science with his Baptist faith. In reference to the study of astronomy and geology, Woolverton described to his audience his feelings regarding the "grandeur and sublimity of the works of Nature; the beauty and harmony of her designs, and the accuracy and truthfulness of her laws." He eloquently described God's creation from the smallest molecule to the largest body in the heavens and declared that he was "equally surprised, delighted and astonished at the Wisdom, the Goodness, the adaptation, and the perfection displayed in the manifold works of God." He offered a challenge to those who could not resolve the study of science with the works of God, announcing that, "An undevout Astronomer is Mad."[63] He justified this remark by concluding that astronomy provides "enlarged views of the greatness, goodness and power of our creator; or correct views of our own weakness, nothingness, and dependence." Woolverton saw God in science and challenged those so inclined to engage in scientific studies to do the same. Whether scientists looked at the smallest of molecules or the vast expanse of the heavens, Woolverton challenged them to reflect on God's power, goodness, and creative design.

61. Ibid., 135.
62. Ibid., 133–36.
63. Ibid., 151 and 49 (out of order).

Woolverton noted that many schoolhouses were not properly built. Schoolhouses that were overcrowded, poorly ventilated, confining, and hot, created, in Woolverton's view, "dull, languid and stupid" children with irritated lungs, oppressed breathing, poorly circulating blood, headaches, and disease.[64] Another amenity for which Woolverton advocated was adequate and comfortable furnishings for the schoolroom, noting that inappropriate desks could harm the body.[65]

Woolverton called the elementary school pupil a "man in miniature" and noted that it was often overlooked that children had similar needs to adults both in "our physical organization, as well as to our mental faculties."[66] He hoped that his audience would recognize that pupils needed more than intellectual stimulation, and he considered regular exercise to be a necessary school activity. He challenged those in his audience who thought that a child could be hurt through too much physical activity. Woolverton assured listeners that a child would stop if tired or sleep if necessary, and the opportunity to exercise would strengthen and help develop a child's organs. Parents were urged to stop their over-anxiety and over-protectiveness. Some children in Grimsby were restricted to sunless rooms at home. Woolverton wanted healthy children, so he directed parents to allow their children to play outdoors, under the sun, in the fresh air, and with the ability to explore and enjoy the environment.

Woolverton emphasized the importance of education in the development of the whole person: physical, social, emotional, intellectual, and spiritual. He declared that "education includes everything that tends to make men wise, useful, and virtuous, everything that tends to promote health of body and strength of mind, finally everything that is calculated to make them happy in this life and in that which is to come."[67]

Modern nineteenth-century teaching techniques were seen by Woolverton as responsible for improving the capacity of a child to learn. He believed that as a result of the new techniques children were learning skills at an earlier age, and the earlier children learned the longer their learning would be retained. Woolverton highlighted the need to provide a sound moral and biblically-based education by including Scripture

64. Woolverton, "Speech Journal," 123.

65. Ibid., 129.

66. Ibid., 58–60.

67. Ibid., 52–53.

references in his speeches.[68] He also urged the community to be vigilant in their use of biblical principles as the basis for the delivery and content of the curriculum. When he advocated improvements in education, Woolverton often used biblical language and symbolism. For example, in one speech he compared the student to a vine and the teacher and parent to the gardener, emphasizing that "the training of their vines is among their most important duties. We all know that how swift and how luxuriant ever a vine may grow, yet if it is not properly trained it will not bear fruit to any amount nor bring it to proper maturity."[69]

Woolverton often provided his audience with a brief history of education and a view of how children as learners were wrongly perceived. He noted that past generations had felt that some subjects of study were inappropriate for children. These included arithmetic, grammar, geography, and philosophy. In contrast, Woolverton advocated for inclusion of all of these subjects in the school curriculum.[70] In a classic application of Lockean philosophy, he argued that a child started life with a blank mind, consequently he spent considerable time eloquently illustrating the benefits of knowledge.[71]

Woolverton urged the Trustees and the Board of Public Instruction to select their teachers wisely. He believed education was not only critical to the development of the individual but also critical to the development of a nation that needed contributing citizens. Most importantly, he felt that education provided a source of protection and was a gift of opportunity to the citizenry. He advised students "to attend to your studies well whilst at school that thus you may not be found lacking when you come to be men."[72]

Since it was often argued in the mid-nineteenth century that children learned from imitation, the good morality and temperance of the teacher were seen as essential for inculcating the best characteristics into the country's growing citizens. Woolverton, therefore, urged that those responsible for hiring teachers be vigilant in their choice in order that they might select persons of the "proper stamp."[73] Yet, he was also

68. Ibid., 54–55.
69. Ibid., 57.
70. Ibid., 56.
71. Ibid., 61–63.
72. Ibid., 140–41.
73. Ibid., 115.

clear that adults were not entirely responsible for the success or failure of their children's education. Children were warned that they also had duties to perform. For example, Woolverton maintained that children had the duty to be diligent and purposeful. He urged them to "improve all your time, whilst at school to the best advantage, that there you may not only attain the appellation of dutiful and studious children; but also the approbation of your Parents and Teacher and grow up wise, useful and responsible members of Society."[74]

Woolverton also encouraged the spiritual growth of children, and he used his annual lectures to "evangelize" his audience. Woolverton pointed out to his listeners that good intellectual powers and good opportunities did not make a good individual. Teachers and parents were instructed to "be especially careful that they neglect not at the same time to impress [children's] minds with those higher and more important principles: A love to God and love to man; to follow out the Golden rule. 'To do unto others as it would they should do unto us.'"[75] As a God-fearing evangelical Baptist, Woolverton stressed to his audience that the Bible needed to be used and taught in order to provide the child with an opportunity to secure a place in heaven. The teaching that he offered was Protestant, non-sectarian, and non-denominational. Parents were to maintain similar teachings at home. However, if parents did not wish their child to participate in the spiritual activities of the school, they were permitted to withdraw their child during times of spiritual instruction.[76]

Woolverton did not view the spiritual component of school as confined to specific scheduled times in the day or to part of a particular curriculum. He merged sciences with spirituality, and described the subjects of mathematics, astronomy, and science as being subject areas where a student could witness the power of God.[77]

His use of the role of Local School Superintendent for evangelization provides an illustration of Westfall's claims regarding the spiritual within secular spaces in Victorian society.[78] Woolverton also merged his Temperance activism with his annual school lectures. He instructed his audience on the ills of intemperance and advocated the temperate

74. Ibid., 115–17.

75. Ibid., 78–81.

76. Ibid., 114.

77. Ibid., 148–61.

78. Westfall, *Two Worlds*, 206–7.

lifestyle, supported by his Baptist and Protestant values.[79] Woolverton intended that all spiritual instruction be taken beyond the walls of the schoolhouse, and in his many speeches, he openly expressed his wish that pupils would take their Bible studies to heart by applying these teachings to their lives and accepting Jesus as their personal Savior in order to ensure their place in heaven. It was education, Woolverton believed, that held the key to merging scientific inquiry with spiritual growth. He believed that it was through education that people would learn how to think and reason and come to their own conclusions concerning God's creation. He once noted that "without the magic influence of education applied to these developing powers assisted by reflection and attention, the mind will present (not withstanding its capabilities) but a barren and dreary waste."[80]

McNairn has noted that there was an important relationship between public discourse and Parliamentary power.[81] Not everyone in his district shared Woolverton's evangelical zeal, opinions, or desire for change. Nineteenth-century individuals such as Woolverton, however, did not always value the breadth of "public opinion." McNairn argues that some of these individuals strived to use the power of "public opinion" to justify their own personal views. In Woolverton's case, he tried to promote his Baptist beliefs and values to the community through his speeches and lectures. In this public discourse he melded his faith and his professional responsibilities as physician, Local School Superintendent, and Temperance Society president.

Jeffery McNairn and Carol Wilton's analysis of governmental control over the direction of public institutions, such as schools, is critical for understanding Woolverton and his world.[82] The Department of Education, led by Egerton Ryerson, deemed it necessary to create and place in authority people such as Woolverton to implement the ideals of the state. The importance of School Law, therefore, cannot be underestimated. Both Wilton and McNairn emphasize the fact that in analyzing local discourse it is imperative that the historian recognize that even with the implementation of Responsible Government in the 1840s, there remained a significant degree of governmental power over the direc-

79. Woolverton, "Speech Journal," 124–26 and 144–47.
80. Ibid., 153–54.
81. McNairn, *Capacity*, 433.
82. Ibid.

tion of institutions such as schools.[83] Woolverton had a duty to represent and implement current government policy and law; therefore, his public discourse about education combined his version of Ryerson's views with certain elements of his evangelical Baptist faith. As a local representative of the Department of Education, Woolverton took seriously his responsibility to implement the laws and decisions of those over him. Woolverton's public speeches and correspondence tell us much about his ability to merge his faith with his professional activity and his role as a local representative and spokesman for the Department of Education.

Of course, Woolverton's role of Local School Superintendent was not confined to public lectures. He met with other Local School Superintendents, visited with personnel in the Department of Education, and was often in correspondence with Egerton Ryerson. His letters and Annual Reports to Ryerson show a high level of advocacy. He wished to see many changes to the system of education in Upper Canada, and he petitioned the Department of Education on a broad range of issues including teacher accreditation, teacher pensions, school funds, and educational statistics.

As a Local School Superintendent, Woolverton also had the responsibility of reporting statistics annually to the Department of Education. The annual report forms that he had to fill out, however, never satisfied him. The system of communication through reports between the local school teachers, trustees, and the Local School Superintendent and then on to the Department of Education was viewed by Woolverton as flawed. Throughout his time as Local School Superintendent, Woolverton frequently petitioned Ryerson to change the forms and the process. His many suggestions were sometimes implemented and often ignored. Despite this reception, Woolverton continued to believe that he knew of ways to improve communication and accountability in the province's education system.[84]

Woolverton also implored Ryerson to reconsider the ways in which government grants were distributed. The student attendance statistics that Woolverton reported did not, in his opinion, reflect the needs of

83. Wilton, *Popular Politics*, 233.

84. The letters have been transcribed from the Archives of Ontario RG 2-12, Boxes 9 through 103, and RG 2-9 and the microfilmed letter books in MS 925, and are referenced by date. The letters dealing with forms are: 30 August 1852; 27 January 1855; 29 March 1855; 3 February 1859; 7 February 1860; 8 February 1865.

Grimsby, and he wanted either the reporting system or the grant distribution criteria to be changed. Woolverton saw some results. In July 1854, Ryerson changed the criteria for the distribution of the grants and allowed each Local Superintendent to apportion the monies as they saw fit. Woolverton also urged Ryerson to examine the way that different districts used these monies. Some employed the lowest class of teacher, because they did not see any need for their children to attain a higher level of education. Woolverton argued that all children deserved an education that might lead to higher education, and he pushed Ryerson to consider making changes in School Law so that local boards would spend more money on hiring more qualified teachers.[85]

Woolverton also suggested to Ryerson that all teachers be certified by the province. In this way, municipalities would be relieved of a burden for which they were ill-equipped and the province would achieve its goals of putting more qualified and suitable teachers in the classroom. Woolverton did not believe that local examinations in any way were able to predict the ability of a teacher to teach. In part, Woolverton based his claims on personal experience. In April 1853, Woolverton and Reverend Lundy, a local school trustee, attended the Board of Public Instruction for the purpose of admitting several teachers and lifting a suspension on a schoolmaster. After the meeting, while Woolverton and Reverend Lundy were at supper, they were shocked to see the teacher, whose suspension they had lifted, drunk in the streets.[86] Woolverton realized that a better system of certifying teachers needed to be put in place. From observation he knew that a number of sections employed unqualified individuals as teachers.[87]

Woolverton believed that it was most important that all teachers participate in some form of Normal School training. It did not matter to him where the teacher candidates obtained their training or how long they participated. He advocated for an examination board so that each teacher would be certified under the same standards. This impulse arose

85. Incoming and outgoing correspondence, 10 March 1852; 30 August 1852; 1 September 1852; 4 July 1854; 23 July 1854; 28 February 1856; 17 July 1856.

86. F. J. Lundy, 1853 "Diary." Archives of Ontario, MS 3. Entry dated 11 April 1853.

87. Archives of Ontario, "Incoming Correspondence," 27 February 1853. Dr. Woolverton continued his petitioning for improvements in teacher training and certification into the 1860s. See letter of 11 March 1862.

from the conviction that teachers were professionals and deserved a training that was available to other professionals, such as physicians.[88]

Gidney and Millar have explored the three founding professions in Upper Canada: lawyer, physician, and clergy.[89] They explore aspects of the complex role of professional judgment and judgments of professionals, which set a context for Woolverton's petitions. Woolverton lived at a time when his work as a medical doctor was struggling to secure professional status. He was familiar with the difficulties in promoting a new profession. For the profession of physician, Gidney and Millar are able to identify a number of nineteenth-century issues including educational requirements, the therapeutics employed, licensing board regulations, parliamentary law, quackery, competition, and community and peer judgment. Physicians found themselves practicing under a fair amount of stress. Woolverton had a personal understanding of the struggles within his own profession and, therefore, he empathized with those in the teaching profession.

Woolverton's role as Local School Superintendent continued into the 1860s. His interest in education from the point of view of a father complemented his professional interest as Local Superintendent. On 21 June 1856, Dr. Woolverton began to correspond with Egerton Ryerson concerning the possibility of opening a Grammar School in Grimsby.[90]

Already in 1852, Woolverton had noted that there were relatively few Grammar Schools in existence and they were only of benefit to students residing close by or having the ability to secure room and board. As a result, Woolverton advocated for a Grammar School to be available in every village containing enough citizens to support its operation. In Woolverton's opinion, the Common Schools were unable to prepare a pupil sufficiently for the University, as the prerequisite subjects required for the University needed the advanced attention of a Grammar School. Woolverton argued that the community and the country would benefit by an increased level of education within the population.[91]

88. Archives of Ontario, "Incoming Correspondence," 28 December 1852; 13 February 1853; 23 July 1854.

89. For an excellent history of the professions in the nineteenth century, see Gidney and Millar, *Professional Gentlemen*.

90. For additional information on schooling in the Lincoln area, see Love, *Education in the Niagara Peninsula*; Houston and Prentice, *Schooling and Scholars*; and Gidney and Millar, *Inventing Secondary Education*.

91. Archives of Ontario "Incoming Correspondence," 1 September 1852; 13 February 1853.

Woolverton prefaced his requests for a Grammar School by assuring Ryerson that Grammar Schools would be of benefit to the Education Department. Woolverton believed that a higher number of successful teacher candidates would enter the province's Normal School if these students had access to Grammar Schools. He suspected that many candidates entered the Normal Schools directly from the "plough and the mechanic shops." He felt that local Grammar Schools would provide an increased supply of better qualified Normal School entrants.[92]

In 1853, Grammar School Laws were designed to replace the District Schools with schools that would link the Common Schools with the University system.[93] Grammar Schools were to offer instruction in Latin, Greek, French, English, Mathematics, Geography, History, Physical Science, Writing, Drawing, and Vocal Music, with consideration of Gymnastics for males and Callisthenics for females. Students would select their areas of study based on the entrance requirements stipulated by the University.[94]

Woolverton had some reservations about children moving away from home. He advocated for children to remain under the roof of the parents while gaining their education. He believed that a Grammar School in the village would allow for the "welfare of the child and the happiness of the parents," because children could remain in the home.[95] Undoubtedly, Woolverton was disappointed with Ryerson's response to his requests to establish a Grammar School in Grimsby. Ryerson replied that with three other Grammar Schools in Lincoln County he suspected that the County Council would not find the Grammar School Fund sufficient to provide a fourth Grammar School.[96] Without the support of Ryerson or the County Council, Woolverton decided to take matters into his own hands, and in 1857 his community activism was rewarded with the establishment of Grimsby's first Grammar School.

1857 was an important year for the Grammar School movement. In York, the Educational Museum and Model Grammar School were established. The Model Grammar School was designed to "exhibit the

92. Ibid., 27 February 1855.

93. Hind, *Eighty Years' Progress*, 432. Also, Hind, *Grammar Schools*, 1–8.

94. For information on Educational Law, see, *Laws Relating to Grammar and Common Schools*, and Hodgins, *School House*, 121.

95. Archives of Ontario, "Incoming Correspondence," 21 June 1856.

96. Ibid., 6 July 1856.

best system of grammar school organization, discipline, and teaching."[97]
It also served as a training facility for grammar school masters and as-
sistants. Woolverton likely visited the facility to acquaint himself with
the newest teaching innovations.

The Grimsby Grammar School Trustees initially met in February
1857, and Woolverton was elected chairman.[98] Woolverton maintained
his role as Local Superintendent while also functioning as Chairman of
the Board of Grimsby Grammar School. He was not able to gain access
to Grammar School Funds until May 1857. Unable to find funds for an
appropriate building to house the new Grammar School, Woolverton
suggested the use of his home, an offer that was accepted by the trustees.
Woolverton's home was used until 1859, when a new facility could finally be financed. Throughout the early history of the Grammar School,
the Nelles, Woolverton, Pettit, and Nixon families supported the school
through voluntary subscriptions.

Grimsby Grammar School was not a free school. Fees were charged
and only students who had been examined and had their fees paid
were admitted. Woolverton as Chairman, the Board secretary, Trustee
Reverend Lundy and the headmaster, Mr. Campbell, were responsible
for examining students for entrance and selecting textbooks.[99] The daily
routines were based on the Common School Act and included daily
Scripture readings and prayers.

The first class consisted of twelve male students among whom
Woolverton was pleased to see his sons Edgar and Algernon. Considering
the number of young men and women in Grimsby, this was a relatively
small portion of the population. Females were admitted the following
year in 1858, alleviating the need for families to send their girls to the
Ladies Academies.[100] The admission of females to Grammar schools was
not common in the rest of Upper Canada. In fact, a resolution at the
annual meeting of the Baptist Missionary Convention in October 1859
resulted in a petition to the Education Department stating that it was

97. Hind, *Eighty Years' Progress*, 456.

98. The information regarding the history of the Grimsby Grammar School is provided from a letter dated 28 June 1894, in Archives of Ontario, "Local School Histories,"
on Grimsby.

99. For a discussion on textbook selection, see Curtis, "Schoolbooks"; Baldus and
Kassam, "Make Me Truthful."

100. For a discussion on women's experiences in Upper Canada classrooms, see
Heap and Prentice, *Gender and Education*.

a grand omission in our provision for higher education in Canada, that nothing has been done by the Council of Education to provide facilities for the superior education of females; that whilst many thousands of pounds are annually expended for the education of boys & young men in branches not provided for in Common Schools, nothing has been given for their sisters & future companions.[101]

Woolverton was likely responsible for pushing for female entry, as he had already pushed for female voting at the Annual School meetings, which caused some friction in the community and some complaints to the Education Department.[102]

With the example provided by the Model Grammar School and the directives found within the Grammar School Law, Woolverton must have known that his Grammar School was lacking.[103] As a man of science, being knowledgeable about the apparatus needed in a school to promote the teaching in the higher classes, Woolverton must have been most concerned about his school's lack of funds. He likely struggled with the fact that the other Grammar Schools in the district were better provided for than the Grimsby school.

An interesting solution to his predicament was articulated in Woolverton's next request to Ryerson. He proposed the creation of a district library. Woolverton did not promote this scheme solely on the basis of his Grammar School's need; instead, he saw his recommendation as a way of promoting the consistent use of educational apparatus within the province. Woolverton often used a similar technique when making such a request. He presented the request as a benefit to the Department of Education and not simply as a benefit for his own hometown. He suggested that Local Superintendents should promote the use of educational apparatus in their Annual Lectures in order to ensure that every schoolhouse was well supplied, and Superintendents had the necessary equipment for their demonstrations. No doubt, Woolverton would have loved to provide demonstrations for the Grammar School rooms housed in his

---

101. Archives of Ontario, "Incoming Correspondence," 4 November 1859.

102. Ibid., 26 January 1852.

103. Dr. Woolverton read the *Journal of Education* and likely had a copy of the laws. He made reference to the articles of the School Law in his letters. The directives from the Education Department were clear even down to the supply of architectural suggestions. See *Laws Relating to Grammar and Common Schools.*

own home.[104] Ryerson's response was disappointing. The Department of Education was willing to provide catalogues of apparatus, and although Ryerson appreciated the concept, he felt that it was not feasible for his Local Superintendents to travel around with demonstration apparatus.[105]

Keeping the Grammar School within the village also proved to be a problem. As early as April 1857, Woolverton was plagued by complaints from the neighboring village of Smithville. The people of Smithville wanted to have the County Council relocate the Grimsby Grammar School to their village. Woolverton appealed to Ryerson to save the Grimsby school. His concerns were based on the fact that the School Law could be interpreted to allow the movement of schools without the Board of Trustee's approval.[106] From a letter sent to Ryerson from Smithville, it appeared that the people of Smithville felt that they had been given prior approval for a Grammar School and were only trying to protect their interests.[107] Ryerson left the decision to the County Council, and the final decision favored Grimsby. Thus, Woolverton was successful in retaining the Grimsby Grammar School. Consequently, Smithville was unable to secure their Grammar School until 1864.[108]

The location of the Grammar School sparked a controversy over Common School locations and taxation in Smithville and sections bordering Woolverton's district. Woolverton found himself in a battle with section trustees. Many letters began to be sent to the Education Office complaining about Woolverton's decisions in the Smithville sections.[109]

Financial concerns began to be a problem in 1858, for the Township of Grimsby was experiencing a financial crisis that had a negative impact on school funding. Woolverton was disappointed that the Clergy Reserve funds were going to be directed to the town rather than to the school system. He complained to Ryerson that suggestions rather than laws regarding the distribution of Clergy Reserve funds were insuffi-

104. Archives of Ontario, "Incoming Correspondence," 3 March 1857.

105. Ibid., 7 March 1857.

106. Ibid., 30 April 1857.

107. Ibid., 4 May 1857.

108. Ibid., 4 January 1864; 21 January 1864; 26 December 1864; 29 December 1864; 13 January 1865.

109. Ibid., 15 May 1857; 27 May 1857; 19 June 1857; 23 January 1860; 2 February 1861; 9 February 1863; April 1863; 20 May 1863.

cient. Woolverton wanted School Laws that required the distribution of Clergy Reserve funds to schools.[110]

Woolverton also wanted other changes. He became concerned with the number of teachers leaving the profession because of poor wages. He wished that Ryerson would change School Law in order to put in place certification requirements tied to pay scales for all Common and Grammar school teachers in order to insure that teachers stayed in the profession. Woolverton complained that the "country is flooded with inefficient persons holding certificates to teach; competition is rife; wages are put down to a mere living point; the really competent teacher is too often crowded out, or finds it pays better to turn his energies in some other channel." Although the Normal Schools were producing a number of competent teachers, Woolverton identified the fact that only "a small fractional part" was actually able to find employment in the Common Schools within the province, because a cheaper teacher could be had. Woolverton advocated for Common School teachers, stating "that the business of school teaching should be elevated to the rank of a 'Profession,' and at least the same care should be taken in granting them certificates."[111]

Woolverton found yet another cause for concern. He became an advocate for retired teachers and their families.[112] Despite Woolverton's concern for ill and infirm teachers who were left in poverty by their adverse circumstances, nothing was done to address the situation.

Edgar-Andre Montigny's research on poverty advocacy in the nineteenth century has shown that, despite calls like those voiced by Woolverton, a social crisis did not exist in Upper Canada. Montigny found that most of the aged population was not ill, infirm, destitute, dependent, or abandoned by their families. Montigny documented a request for social assistance made by John Moore, a teacher and relative of Dr. Woolverton's. Montigny concluded that "principles of communal reciprocity and interdependence among neighbours" formed the basis of many appeals for government assistance.[113] In other words, many

110. Ibid., 6 February 1858.

111. Ibid., 11 March 1862. Teacher advocacy is also noted in Woolverton's correspondence of 4 February 1863.

112. Ibid., 3 February 1859.

113. Montigny, *Foisted*, 70.

requests for government assistance flowed from a sense of entitlement rather than legitimate need.

Pay rates and pensions were on Woolverton's personal agenda, and for an apparently valid reason, as indicated in his letters to the Department of Education. He perceived an injustice in the teaching community. Yet, Montigny's study points out the fact that the teachers Woolverton worried about may not have been representative. Montigny suggests that advocates such as Woolverton may have brought specific cases to the attention of the government in the hope of changing government social policy. Montigny suggests that advocates may have looked for examples to help their reform cause. This may or may not have been the case for Woolverton.

By 1860, Woolverton was proud of the Grimsby Grammar School and the healthy condition of education in the County of Lincoln.[114] The Grammar School had thirty students and the new facility was able to offer several rooms of study. Woolverton had opportunity to observe the role that the Grammar School played in relation to the operation of the Common Schools. As Chairman of the Grammar School Board and Local School Superintendent, he was able to exert control over the teaching staff and student enrolments. Woolverton had made some critical changes in schooling in Grimsby, and he reported these changes to Ryerson hoping that other villages throughout the province would follow his lead.

With the introduction of the Grammar School, neighboring Common School sections were able to send their oldest and most advanced students to the Grammar School. The Common Schools were then free to offer services to only the younger and less advanced students. This change permitted the Common Schools to hire more female teachers who were paid less and had fewer credentials, but were more than capable of fulfilling their duties. The cost of running the Common School system was thereby reduced substantially.

Woolverton recognized that if this method of school delivery was implemented throughout the province, substantial savings would be made, and a better quality of educational delivery could be maintained. In Woolverton's mind, local responsibility for the school system would guarantee a healthier system, because the best sites for Grammar

114. Archives of Ontario, "Incoming Correspondence," 2 February 1860; 11 April 1860.

Schools would be selected, thereby generating even more local support. A provincially controlled system would, in Woolverton's opinion, create schools that were unwanted, unused, and inappropriate. Consequently, Woolverton urged Ryerson to maintain local responsibility, accountability, and partial local financial support.[115] In 1860, with the Grimsby Grammar School safely in position, Woolverton's role as Grammar School Chairman of the Board ended.[116]

Woolverton turned his concern to other school issues. In 1862, he surveyed his school sections and noted that a number of children were not attending school.[117] He was proud of the school system in Lincoln, and could not understand why so many children were not in attendance at school. In his words, he felt that "in nine cases out of ten, it arises from sheer indifference, and neglect on the part of the parents, or Guardians of such children." Woolverton wanted Ryerson to legislate school attendance by placing a fine on parents not sending their children to school.

The role of Local Superintendent was not an easy one, especially for a superintendent who also had competing roles as Justice of the Peace and physician.[118] The interpretation of the School Law was not always clear, and Local School Superintendents sometimes found themselves interpreting School Law differently than the Department of Education, School Trustees, or the parents. In his role as Local Superintendent, Woolverton was forced in the 1860s to proceed legally against some Common School Trustees for questionable use of funds.[119] Other legal concerns also plagued Woolverton. The elections of trustees caused some questions that Woolverton had to direct to Ryerson.[120] A threat of a lawsuit initiated by a parent placed Woolverton into another conflicted position. Parents in one of Woolverton's schools wanted a child suspended for having the "itch." Woolverton would not make a diagnosis or step in to suspend the child, likely because he was in a conflict of

115. Ibid., 16 April 1861. In 1861, amendments to the Grammar School Act were being considered and Dr. Woolverton petition Ryerson to reconsider.

116. Ibid., 2 February 1860.

117. Ibid., 12 February 1862.

118. Dr. Woolverton accepted the role of Justice of the Peace in 1857.

119. Archives of Ontario, "Incoming Correspondence," 25 February 1860; 2 March 1860; 16 April 1866.

120. Ibid., 12 January 1862; 14 September 1863.

interest between his role as physician and superintendent. The trustees appealed to Ryerson for a decision.[121]

Woolverton had other issues that he needed to contend with, including issues between teachers and trustees. In 1862, one of the Trustees and a teacher in Grimsby came into conflict over a matter of discipline with the result that the Trustee made physical threats against the teacher.[122] Conflicts between teachers and the local examining boards also caused problems. When teachers were turned down for first class certificates, or their rehiring was not confirmed, Dr. Woolverton found himself in stressful situations.[123]

The final comment that Woolverton wished to make in his diary was that in all the personal "chastisement" that he had experienced in life he maintained a trust and a confidence in the guidance received from his God. He assured himself that he believed that "all things work together for good to all that are exercised thereby; to all that love God." He penned his last words with the following poem: "In each event of life, how plain, Thy ruling hand I see; Each blessing of my life more dear; Because conferred by Thee."[124]

CONCLUSION

The use of the biographical genre has provided the unique opportunity to explore the ways in which Dr. Jonathan Woolverton's Baptist faith worked at the level of everyday experience to affect the ways in which he understood his own life and his relation to the world. Woolverton was a complex man of intertwining background, ability, faith, compassion, and opportunity. He was a man who documented his commitment to his community, profession, country, and God. He lived at a time of instability in his country and profession. Woolverton is an example of an ordinary nineteenth-century individual who modeled through his life as Local Superintendent and Grammar School Chair a desire to serve others, not only in their physical needs, but intellectually, emotionally, socially, culturally, and spiritually.

121. Ibid., 19 June 1862. The outcome was not documented.
122. Ibid., 14 July 1862.
123. Ibid., 30 October 1862; 4 November 1863; 5 October 1863; 4 November 1864.
124. Woolverton, "Diary," 66. This entry was written 22 February 1862.

This biographical study is important, because it helps to shed some light on faith outside of the nineteenth-century "church," and the interconnection between the secular and spiritual. Woolverton was an Upper Canada education mid-tier administrator who saw education as a vehicle for the acquiring of scientific, political, and spiritual knowledge. This belief inspired him to pursue his educational advocacy within the community. Through ongoing reflection on his personal faith and his conscience through his written prayers and explanations regarding his faith in God, he was able to find hope, support, and a life focus, and to leave behind a witness and an example of an ordinary Baptist nineteenth-century man.

The use of the biographical genre has provided the opportunity to explore the complexity and interconnectedness of a Protestant faith to varying aspects of nineteenth-century politics and education. Jensen argues that the word Protestant "in our context of the word is almost dead on its feet."[125] Today, the development and fruits of the kind of Protestant Conscience that Woolverton and Ryerson had is not easy to understand, because it remains relatively undocumented and private, and is a process that evangelist John MacArthur has noted is "vanishing."[126] No doubt, many analyzing Jonathan Woolverton's writings would conclude that if he were alive today, his Protestant Conscience would be possessed by only a dwindling minority. Woolverton provides an example of an individual who attempted to guard his conscience from the secularization of society.

Applying the kind of nineteenth-century conscience that Woolverton had in the present day in Canada, however, poses difficulties. Although the development, maintenance, and manifestations of a Protestant Conscience may have, for some, been possible and useful within the system of education throughout the nineteenth and much of the twentieth century, Jonathan Woolverton's Protestant-minded advocacy for school reform would no longer be acceptable in today's Ontario under current Education and Canadian law. Today the primary facilitation of the development and maintenance of Protestant Conscience is not in the public arena, but within the private domain as protected by the Charter of Rights and Freedoms. While the development, maintenance, and manifestation of a Protestant Conscience is just as possible and

125. Jensen, "Protestant Conscience."
126. MacArthur, *Vanishing Conscience*.

necessary today, it is private and will only become public if challenged under Section 2a of the Charter of Rights and Freedoms, which may happen as Protestants face increasing challenges to their faith within the Ontario public system of education.

Biography, using the historical analysis of one man's writings as exemplified in this study, may provide the most appropriate way of exploring this private conscience. The ability to analyze an ordinary Upper Canada citizen's Protestant Conscience will assist those who have an interest, for any number of reasons, in Protestant Conscience. Research such as this will provide insight into an individual's perceptions and how they developed, maintained, and acted on their conscience.

This study has shown that John Webster Grant's challenge to explore private diaries in order to "make possible a more thorough exposé of the religious mind" is not only appropriate but feasible.[127] Continued historical research into the complexity of conscience in ordinary individuals using this form of biographical genre will likely yield a rich body of historical data that will prove invaluable for anyone interested in studying any number of different conscience types in action and thought. This biography of Woolverton has also provided an example of a biographical methodology and process, which could prove most informative to other researchers interested in linking the complex study of faith within the vast and interconnected micro-historical contexts of their subjects' lives. The vast number of diaries and letters currently available in private and public collections will provide a rich body of primary source documents from which historians will be able to explore the complexity of individual minds in relation to their public, private, and professional duties.

127. Grant, *Profusion of Spires*, ix.

BIBLIOGRAPHY

"An Act to Promote Education, Bill 24." Appendix to the *Journal of the House of Assembly of Upper Canada* (1835). CIHM: 9 000942 11.[128]

Albanese, Catherine L. *Nature Religion in America: From the Algonkian Indians to the New Age.* Chicago: University of Chicago Press, 1990.

Archives of Ontario. "Department of Education Incoming General Correspondence," RG 2-12 boxes 9 through 103.

———. "Department of Education Drafts and Outgoing Correspondence," RG 2-9.

———. MS 925. In "Department of Education Drafts and Outgoing Correspondence," RG 2-9.

———. "Department of Education Local School Histories and Teaching Experiences," RG 2-87.

Axelrod, Paul. *The Promise of Schooling: Education in Canada, 1800–1914.* Toronto: University of Toronto Press, 1997.

Baldus, Bernd, and Kassam, Meenaz. "'Make Me Truthful, Good and Mild': Values in Nineteenth Century Ontario Schoolbooks." *Canadian Journal of Sociology* 21, no. 3, (1996) 327–58.

Curtis, Bruce. "Schoolbooks and the Myth of Curricular Republicanism: The State and the Curriculum in Canada West, 1820–1850." *Histoire Sociale/Social History* 16, 32 (November, 1983) 305–29.

Dewar, Kenneth C. *Charles Clarke: Pen and Ink Warrior.* Montreal: McGill-Queen's University Press, 2002.

Gibson, Theo T. *Robert Alexander Fyfe: His Contemporaries and His Influence.* Burlington, ON: Welch, 1988.

Gidney, R. D. *From Hope to Harris: The Reshaping of Ontario's Schools.* Toronto: University of Toronto Press, 1999.

Gidney, R. D., and Millar, W. P. J. *Inventing Secondary Education: The Rise of the High School in Nineteenth-Century Ontario.* Montreal: McGill-Queen's University Press, 1990.

———. *Professional Gentlemen: The Professions in Nineteenth-Century Ontario.* Toronto: University of Toronto Press, 1994.

Grant, John Webster. *A Profusion of Spires: Religion in Nineteenth-Century Ontario.* Toronto: University of Toronto Press, 1988.

Hatch, Nathan O. *The Democratization of American Christianity.* New Haven: Yale University Press, 1989.

Hazen, Craig James. *The Village Enlightenment in America: Popular Religion and Science in the Nineteenth Century.* Urbana: University of Illinois Press, 2000.

Heap, Ruby, and Prentice, Alison. *Gender and Education in Ontario.* Toronto: Canadian Scholars, 1991.

Hind, Henry Youle. *An Act to Amend the Law Relating to Grammar Schools in Upper Canada.* Quebec: J. Lovell, 1853. CIHM: 9 05686.

———. *Eighty Years' Progress of British North America.* Toronto: L. Stebbins, 1863. CIHM: 64288.

Hodgins, J. George. *Documentary History of Education in Upper Canada 1851–52.* Vol. 10. Toronto: Cameron, 1903.

128. CIHM is the Canadian Institute for Historic Microreproduction. The numbers are references to the items as stored in CIHM.

————. "Historical Sketch of Education in Upper and Lower Canada." In *Eighty Years' Progress of British North America*, by Henry Youle Hind, 50.

————. *The School House: Its Architecture.* Toronto: Lovell & Gibson, 1857. CIHM: 59365.

"The Hon. John Wilson of Saltfleet." *Journal of Education for Upper Canada* 12, no. 6 (June 1860) 94.

Houston, Susan E., and Prentice, Alison. *Schooling and Scholars in Nineteenth Century Ontario.* Toronto: University of Toronto Press, 1988.

Jensen, Peter. "The Protestant Conscience." Address given at St. Andrews House, Sydney, Australia, 5 April 2005. Online: http://www.sydneyanglicans.net/images/uploads/sydneystories/The_Protestant_Conscience.pdf.

Journal of the House of Assembly of Upper Canada, 1835. CIHM: 9 00941 11.

Journals of the Legislative Assembly of the Province of Canada. Available at Early Canadiana Online. CIHM: 9 00952.

Keele, William Conway. *Magistrate's Manual.* Toronto: H. Rowsell, 1858. CIHM: 9 01695.

The Laws Relating to Grammar and Common Schools, in Cities, Towns, and Villages in Upper Canada. Toronto: Department of Public Instruction for Upper Canada, Lovell & Gibson, 1855. CIHM: 63684.

Love, James. *Education in the Niagara Peninsula.* St. Catharines: Vanwell, 1988.

MacArthur, John. *The Vanishing Conscience: Drawing the Line in a No-Fault, Guilt-Free World.* Nashville: Thompson Nelson, 1994.

Marks, Lynne. *Revivals and Roller Rinks: Religion, Leisure, and Identity in Late-Nineteenth-Century Small-Town Ontario.* Toronto: University of Toronto Press, 1996.

McNairn, Jeffrey L. *The Capacity to Judge: Public Opinion and Deliberative Democracy in Upper Canada, 1791–1854.* Toronto: University of Toronto Press, 2000.

Montigny, Edgar-Andre. *Foisted upon the Government? State Responsibilities, Family Obligations, and the Care of the Dependent Aged in Late Nineteenth Century Ontario.* Montreal: McGill-Queen's University Press, 1997.

Powell, R. Janet. *Annals of the Forty No. 9: 1753–1833 R to S.* Grimsby, ON: Grimsby Historical Society, 1939.

Ryerson, Egerton. "Chief Superintendent's Circular to County Councils and Local Superintendents, August 1850." *Journal of Education for Upper Canada* 9 (January 1856), 9–10.

————. "The Spirit in Which the Present Educational Movement Should Be Directed." In *The Documentary History of Education in Upper Canada, 1851–1852*, edited by J. George Hodgins. Vol. 10. Toronto: Cameron, 1903, 303.

"Sketch of the System of Public Elementary Instruction in Upper Canada." *Journals of the Legislative Assembly of the Province of Canada* 13, no. 5 (5 September 1854).

Westfall, William. *Two Worlds: The Protestant Culture of Nineteenth Century Ontario.* Montreal: McGill-Queen's University Press, 1989.

Wilton, Carol. *Popular Politics and Political Culture in Upper Canada, 1800–1850.* Montreal: McGill-Queen's University Press, 2000.

Woolverton, J. "Dairy." In the Grimsby Museum, Grimsby Ontario. Labelled as "Book B and Prescription Journal."

————. "Speech Journal." In the Grimsby Museum, Grimsby, Ontario.

T. T. Shields
Pastor of Jarvis Street Baptist Church
(Karsh Photograph—Original in the Jarvis Street Baptist Church
Archives). Used by permission of Jarvis Street Baptist Church.

2

Fighting Fire with Fire

T. T. Shields and His Confrontations
with Premier Mitchell Hepburn
and Prime Minister Mackenzie King, 1934–1948

DOUG ADAMS

TWENTY-FIRST-CENTURY ONTARIO BAPTISTS ARE not particularly renowned for their militancy. Such, however, was not always the case. In the early years of the twentieth century there were many battling Baptists who were notable for their militant opposition to the rising tide of moral decay in both church and state. Nevertheless, in the public mind only one man truly personified the title of "militant Baptist." In 1949, Gerald Angelin published an article in *Maclean's* entitled, "The Battling Baptist." Since he was renowned by that time for his highly publicized skirmishes with Ontario Premier Mitch Hepburn and the Canadian Prime Minister Mackenzie King, few Canadians would have missed the reference to Toronto's Dr. Thomas Todhunter Shields. "Reverend T. T. Shields is again on the warpath" was a common byline in the contemporary press.[1] Jean Graham, a reporter for *Saturday Night*, in 1931 remarked on Shields's popularity. She spoke of the reporter who said, "I hope that Dr. Shields will never die." Asked why, the reporter responded, "Because he makes such beautiful copy." Graham also noted

1. Angelin, "Battling Baptist," 15. Note Shields's reaction to such headlines in Shields, *Hepburn Government's Betrayal*, 3. Cf. "Dr. Shields on the Rampage," *Mail*, 30 March 1936, in the *Toronto Telegram* Clippings File (hereafter TTCF), no.132. The TTCF can be accessed on microfiche in the D. B. Weldon Library, University of Western Ontario.

that in an earlier time, Shields would have been popular with the famous Dr. Johnson. Johnson claimed he loved a "good hater." Graham concluded, "Dr. Shields could easily have qualified for a Johnsonian favorite."[2]

Renown as the "hatingest" man in all of Ontario was perhaps not the most flattering reputation to be tagged with for a leading Baptist clergyman. Dr. Shields's notoriety, however, arose out his undeviating pursuit of that "righteousness that exalts a nation" and his public and vigorous denunciation of every evil that threatened to bring ruin upon the social fabric.[3] Shields's controversial bent was first evidenced in his own denomination as early as 1918. Having come fresh from a visit to Europe and scenes of jubilation in Paris, Brussels, and London celebrating the victorious conclusion of the war, Shields arrived home filled with the determination to uphold the gains he imagined had been won for the cause of righteousness.[4] After discovering an article in the *Canadian Baptist* that challenged one of the fundamental elements of evangelical orthodoxy, Shields went to war. Over the next dozen years he was the most prominent figure in both Canada and the United States in the Fundamentalist battle against the inroads of rationalism. The fight led him all over the continent, and in January 1926, he was able to boast of having travelled over 30,000 miles in only ten months.[5] During those years he acted as the President of the Baptist Bible Union, a militant Fundamentalist organization that fought "modernism" aggressively on the convention floors of the Northern Baptist Convention in the United States and the Baptist Convention of Ontario and Quebec. He led the Fundamentalist cause in the purchase of Des Moines University, where he became its president. He was influential among the Bible Institutes, which were seen by some as the Fundamentalists' last line of defense against the modernist attack.[6] When modernism threatened the Bible

2. Jean Graham, "Among Those Present," *Toronto Telegram*, 11 July 1931, in *TTCF*, no. 107.

3. Shields, "The Real Heart of the Matter," *The Gospel Witness* (hereafter *GW*), 16 May 1935.

4. Shields witnessed the celebration of the Armistice in London, then the following Sunday the celebration in Paris, and thereafter traveled to Brussels with Canadian officers to witness the return of King Albert of Belgium. Cf. Shields, *Plot*, 79.

5. Letter from Shields to Rev. Stewart Robertson, 9 January 1926, Jarvis Street Baptist Church Archives (hereafter JBCA), Toronto.

6. *Breaking the Bible School Defense Line*, 1. In box 3 of "Shields' Correspondence," JBCA.

Institute of Los Angeles, Dr. Shields was at once brought across the continent to help in the Institute's restructuring. At home he confronted modernism as it raised its specter among the professors of McMaster University, the official educational institution of Ontario Baptists. With many convention officials and McMaster supporters among the membership of his own church, Jarvis Street Baptist, it soon became the primary battle ground. Years later, Shields published his account of this struggle in *The Plot That Failed*. He concluded:

> Modernism, as touching the inspiration and integrity of the Bible; Modernism in the matter of amusements; Modernism in vaudeville performances in Sunday School entertainments; Modernism in opposition to the Regular Baptist position in the matter of the ordinances; Modernism in church choirs; Modernism hydra-headed, and in its many-coloured forms, raised its head in Jarvis Street Baptist church—and Modernism was vanquished![7]

The decade-long fight precipitated a significant division among Canadian Baptists, and the Fundamentalists withdrew from the Baptist Convention of Ontario and Quebec in 1927 to form the Union of Regular Baptist Churches. Shields assumed leadership of this new venture and served as president for most of its existence. With the loss of McMaster University to the forces of modernism in 1927, Shields founded his own theological training institution patterned after C. H. Spurgeon's College of Pastors. From his position as the pastor of Jarvis Street Baptist Church Shields served as the president of this church-run school, Toronto Baptist Seminary, until his death in 1955. Needing a vehicle to carry his message of war against evil to the world, Shields created the *Gospel Witness* in 1922. For the next thirty-three years Shields exercised total control over this weekly publication and was often its primary contributor. The publication was his principal weapon, both within his own denomination and in the world at large. At the height of its influence it was sent into over sixty countries and to over thirty thousand subscribers.[8] At one point, over three thousand pastors subscribed to the paper, leading Shields's biographer to comment, "It could probably be stated without exaggeration that this weekly magazine edited by a busy pastor was one of the most powerful organs of the fundamentalist movement of the

---

7. Shields, *Plot*, 356.
8. Angelin, "Battling Baptist," 15.

1920s and 1930s."[9] In 1930, he added another weapon to his arsenal as he began a radio broadcast. Initially, he had envisioned a "super-station that would carry the message over the entire continent." He took out a license in 1925 in the name of the church for the operation of a radio station to be known as CJBC, the last three letters standing, of course, for Jarvis Street Baptist Church.[10] The dual challenges of rising broadcasting costs and the depression forced him to surrender the permit, but in May 1930, Jarvis Street began broadcasting over Canada's most powerful station, CKGW. For $150.00 a week the evening service of Jarvis Street was broadcast. Two hours were booked to allow Dr. Shields sufficient time to preach his sermon.[11] Correspondence still extant in the archives of Jarvis Street Baptist Church bears testimony to the wide influence Shields enjoyed through this endeavor.

Contemporary opinions of Shields were mixed. "T. T. Shields," commented historian George Rawlyk, "was either loved or hated, respected or detested," considered as a true "disciple of Christ" or as a "minion of Antichrist."[12] Shields's supporters saw him as the Spurgeon of Canada.[13] Some went so far as to liken him to such men as Jeremiah, the Apostle Paul, and Martin Luther.[14] His opponents were just as prone to exaggeration. He was denounced vociferously as "'a self-appointed bishop' and 'the Pope of Jarvis Street.'" The media treated him to such designations as "'dictator,' 'hypocrite,' 'vain,' 'egotistical,' 'destructive' and . . . 'a man without a Christian heart.'"[15] In Ontario he became a household name and a favorite target of the press. Quebecers were infuriated by him, and their "plea was that the Minister of Justice should imprison 'Pasteur' Shields." Some even called for "his public hanging."[16] Lord Bennett, in a personal visit, praised his anti-catholic efforts and affirmed Shields in his predictions of a coming civil war.[17] Premier Hepburn kept a "dirt file" on him.

9. Tarr, *Shields of Canada*, 110.

10. CJBC became a CBC station.

11. Tarr, *Shields of Canada*, 121.

12. Rawlyk, *Champions of the Truth*, 76.

13. Tarr, *Shields of Canada*, 3. According to the fly-leaf, one of the first to call him this was Sir W. R. Nicol, editor of *The British Weekly*. It is a comparison often made in both Canadian and British newspapers (cf. *Toronto Telegram*, 9 May 1921).

14. Slade "Forward," 3.

15. Anglin, "Battling Baptist," 50.

16. Tarr, *Shields of Canada*, 132.

17. Shields, "Scandalous Manipulation of Canada's National Revenue Service," *GW*, 27 September 1951, 2.

Prime Minister King once declared from the floor of parliament that he had "nothing but contempt" for Dr. Shields.[18]

Historical interest in Dr. Shields began early and has proved to be as ambivalent as public opinion. Only one biography has been published, although Shields himself published autobiographical material relative to his first decade in Jarvis Street entitled *The Plot That Failed*. The sole biography was commissioned by the pastor and deacons of Jarvis Street Baptist Church in 1967 as a memorial of Shields to commemorate Canada's centennial year. They felt it appropriate to celebrate the memory of one who was given "the extraordinary ability and genius to defend the political, spiritual and moral interests of the people of Canada in such full measure."[19] Its author, Leslie K. Tarr, was personally acquainted with Dr. Shields and worked for many years with him. The biography was hagiographic in nature and contained little in the way of critical assessment. Though Tarr acknowledged that Shields was the "Soldier of Christ," fighting particularly as a defender of "civil liberty," he argued that Shields would better be characterized as a "shepherd of souls," a pastoral figure who was loved by his church. The aloof, contentious, and bitter personality that many identified in Shields, Tarr alleged, was a creation of the public press that continually demonized him.[20] Tarr's contention throughout was that the simple appellation, "the man of God," best characterized Shields. "He was indeed God's man," claimed Tarr, "unmoved by either taunts or flattery, the servant of the Lord, conscious of his great mission."[21]

Much of the published material on Shields, outside of the public media, came in the context of the study of Fundamentalism.[22] These evaluations were often influenced heavily by presuppositions concerning the fundamentalist/modernist debate itself and tended to be highly

18. King, quoted in "Reply to Premier King and Other Parliamentary Critics," *GW*, 25 February 1943, 2. The full quote of King is: "Speaking here as a member of the Protestant Church, I wish to say that I have the utmost contempt for Dr. Shields and all the utterances he can make."

19. Tarr, *Shields of Canada*, flyleaf.

20. Ibid., 165.

21. Ibid., 184.

22. Fundamentalism is a term coined in 1920. Cf. Curtis Lee Laws, "Convention Side Lights," *Watchman-Examiner*, 1 July 1920, 834. He wrote, "We suggest that those who still cling to the great fundamentals and who mean to do battle royal for the fundamentals shall be called 'Fundamentalists.'"

critical of men like Shields.[23] While Shields was only incidental to these early works, he became the focal point of several scholarly works that particularly evaluated the role played by Shields in the development of Fundamentalism. Most of these adopted a critical or overtly hostile stance toward Shields and focused primarily upon evaluations of the controversy surrounding McMaster University in which Shields was the leading figure.[24] Some balance was brought to this discussion by the works of Clark Pinnock and Paul Wilson. Dr. Shields was somewhat co-incidental to their works but both of these helped identify factors in the controversy that were not attributable to Shields and to which Shields justly reacted.[25]

In 1993, John G. Stackhouse published an important survey of Canadian Evangelicalism.[26] Noting the prominence of Dr. Shields in the controversies in the first part of the twentieth century, Stackhouse began his account with a discussion of Shields's particular place in the Canadian evangelical scene. Stackhouse acknowledged that Shields occupied the central place in Canadian fundamentalism. "Church historians may debate definitions of fundamentalism," he noted, "but standing squarely in the middle of anyone's definition is Canada's best-known and most influential fundamentalist, Thomas Todhunter Shields." Stackhouse also provided a useful biographical account of Shields, although it was heavily dependent on Tarr's *Shields of Canada*. Stackhouse, however, tried to find a balance between the "hagiographically uncritical" approach of Tarr and the "patronizingly critical" approach most commonly evident from those "studies that originated in the academy."[27] He certified

23. Older historiographies characterize the decade of the 1920s as the decade of the Fundamentalist-Modernist conflict. Cf. Cole, *History of Fundamentalism*, and Furniss, *Fundamentalist Controversy*.

24. Carder, "Controversy," 374. Also see Dozois, "Shields in the Stream of Fundamentalism"; Ellis, "Social and Religious Factors"; Elliot, "Three Faces"; Rawlyk, "T. T. Shields' Impact," in *Champions of the Truth*, 76–102; Parent, "Christology of T. T. Shields."

25. Pinnock countered the assumption of some like Carder that modernism had little real presence in Canadian churches (Pinnock, "Modernist Impulse"). Wilson, like Ellis, looked at sociological factors in the fundamentalist/modernist schism. Wilson found significant roots of the struggle in the gradual secularization of the church by business interests within its membership (Wilson, "Baptists and Business").

26. Stackhouse, *Canadian Evangelicalism*; Cf. also Stackhouse, "Thomas Todhunter Shields," and "Proclaiming the Word."

27. Stackhouse, "Thomas Todhunter Shields," 400.

Shields's concern for orthodoxy and noted the renown Shields achieved for the eloquence of his preaching. However, in chorus with most other historians before him, Stackhouse pointed to Shields's contentiousness that in the end led to notoriety rather than fame. By the end of his life his militancy was viewed by most as "dogmatism, if not sheer arrogance." Stackhouse concluded: "Most Christians . . . sooner or later decided to separate from the most prominent ecclesiastical separatist in Canada, T. T. Shields."[28] So far as his influence was concerned, Shields marked "out the fundamentalist limit of Canadian evangelicalism" but sat well outside the mainstream of Canadian evangelical life.[29]

Historians have long debated the merits of Shields's fundamentalist crusade. However, little has been done to evaluate the paradox implicit in Stackhouse's observations. Dr. Shields, in his lifetime, was one of the most central figures in Canadian Evangelicalism, and by the end of it, one of the most marginalized. It is the contention of this chapter that at least some of the answer to the puzzle of why this was so can be found in Shields's exploits in the public realm. While the stories of Shields's ecclesiastical skirmishes are told and retold, little has been done to evaluate his role in public life. The historians' interest in Shields largely ends at the high point of fundamentalist influence and the demise of the most prominent of the fundamentalist agencies with which he was affiliated. However, Shields saw himself as always engaged in the same fundamentalist struggle to the end of his life. His focus and methodology shifted in the years after the death of the Baptist Bible Union, and a defense of Western ideological forms, Protestant liberties, and evangelical hegemony became the stuff of his fundamentalist tirades. This paper focuses primarily upon his social and political activism and the methodology associated with it. It is the story of a shift in emphasis from the spiritual weaponry that so characterized his early career to the carnal weapons of political activism and demagoguery that so dominated his efforts in later life. Ironically, the evangelical hegemony that he championed was the most conspicuous casualty of his misplaced zeal.

Pastor T. T. Shields first came to the attention of the Toronto media in 1912. Within two years of taking up his tenure at Jarvis Street Baptist Church he was already throwing in his lot with the city's social reformers. When the St. Clair affair erupted in September 1912, Shields was

28. Ibid.

29. Stackhouse, *Canadian Evangelicalism*, 34.

front and center in the battle with city officials that ensued. When Rev. R. B. St. Clair, the secretary of the Toronto Vigilance Association, published and distributed a pamphlet exposing the indecent performance "The Darling of Paris" that had been presented in Toronto's Star Theatre, he was arrested and convicted for "circulating obscene literature."[30] The irony of the fact that a prominent clergyman could be arrested for circulating obscenity, while the police morality squad refused to lay charges against the theatre itself, was too much for many of the outraged citizens of Toronto. Three prominent clergymen denounced the whole proceeding, but Shields particularly dominated the headlines with his suggestion that "An open cesspool in front of the City Hall would be less injurious to the public health than that place of so-called entertainment is to the moral health of those that frequent it."[31] Shields deliberately courted the newspapers. According to the *Globe* reporter, Shields announced his title, "How the Devil's Work is Covered Over in Toronto," and held up his "manuscript and said he took full responsibility for all he said, and hoped the newspapers would enlarge his audience." As for Staff Inspector Kennedy, Shields noted "that he was utterly disqualified to be a judge of moral questions, as disqualified for his special work as one would be for Medical Health Officer who would recommend an open sewer down Yonge Street." Noting the hypocrisy of city officials, he pointed out that he had read of some that "were denounced for straining at a gnat and swallowing a camel, but here are some that strain at a pamphlet and swallow a theatre."[32] In a manner that would also characterize his later dealings with public officials, Shields defied and taunted the governing authorities:

> After what I have said you must not be surprised to hear that I have been arrested by the edict of the sultan of the Morality Department and duly photographed and measured. And disinclined and unaccustomed as I am to the work of scavenger, I am disposed to feel that such an experience would not be altogether unwelcome, because of the opportunity it would afford me to assist the Morality Department to clean house. I would not

30. "Judges Comment on St. Clair Bulletin," *The Globe*, 27 November 1912, 9. The Toronto papers gave prominent coverage to this issue. For further reading on this issue, see Wilson, "Caring for Their Community." Cf. also Campbell, "A Slub in the Cloth."

31. "Theatre Worse Than Open Cesspool," 8. Cf. "Clergymen Condemn Way Police Censors Do Work," *Toronto Star*, 30 September 1912, 3.

32. "Theatre Worse Than Open Cesspool," 8. cf. Matt 23:24.

promise under such circumstances to use a dustless and noiseless vacuum cleaner.[33]

In this first public skirmish Shields had much cause to be encouraged. In part, Shields's agitation for the reform of the police board led to the creation of a citizens' committee of "One Hundred" that was established to direct future protests. A formal call was issued to the citizens of Toronto for a mass meeting. This call was signed by "fifty-two prominent men," among whose signatures were those of T. T. Shields and one of his prominent deacons, James Ryrie.[34] When the meeting was convened at Massey Hall on 1 November, Ryrie was the chairman while Shields was one of the featured speakers. Also, Shields was prominent as one who presented resolutions pertinent to the reconstitution of the Police Commission. Four thousand citizens were in attendance. The meeting also saw the formation of a committee of forty "for the purpose and with authority to convene public meetings of citizens, when in its opinion such meetings are desirable in the interests of public morals."[35] Again, Shields was included in the committee, and it is clear that he took his role seriously. When he visited London, England three years later he took the opportunity as a member of the committee to make inspection of a local theatre. Mistaken for a member of the Lord Chamberlain's office, Shields delighted in making the manager squirm. "The thing was remarkable for its silliness," remarked Shields, "it would be very tame in the *Star* in Toronto. I learned something for the Committee of Forty, & incidentally gave the manager an uncomfortable quarter of an hour."[36] In the St. Clair affair, the public pressure was too much, charges were laid against the manager of the Star Theatre, and despite the Toronto mayor's protests, changes were made to the criminal code, and the police board was enlarged.[37]

Nearly thirty years later, Dr. Shields was still fighting in the public forum. By his own admission, his militancy over the years had escalated, and by 1943 he boasted, "I have sounded no different note in my preaching or my writing the last few years than that which I have sounded from

33. Ibid.

34. "Fifty-Two Names Signed to Call," *The Globe*, 26 October 1912, 9.

35. "Clean House, Demand of 4,000 Citizens," *The Globe*, 2 November 1912, 9.

36. Shields circular letter to family members, 23 July 1915, in JBCA.

37. "Indictment Follows Charges of St. Clair," *The Globe*, 11 December 1912, 9. cf. "Radical Amendment to Criminal Code," *The Globe*, 5 December 1912, 9.

this pulpit now for more than thirty years. The only difference in the present situation is that the menace is more imminent, the gangsters are nearer to their prey; hence their description and identity meets with a more raucous response."[38] The "gangsters" Shields had in mind were the political leaders with whom he was wrestling. His two most notable political foes of this era were Premier Mitch Hepburn and Prime Minister Mackenzie King.

PREMIER MITCHELL HEPBURN

Dr. Shields's controversy with Ontario Premier Mitchell F. Hepburn was a particularly colorful affair. As Kenneth Johnstone of the *Standard* put it, "for once Mitch had met his match in the gentle art of invective. First [Shields] announced that Hepburn was a vulgarian demagogue. Then he noticed that Hepburn strongly resembled Hitler. He asked the pertinent question: Did Rome assist Hepburn? Finally he lit upon the golden phrase of "Hepburn's Alliance with Rum and Rome."[39] Hepburn in turn responded by labeling Shields "an offensive temperance crank."[40]

The Beer Parlor Question

Shields was a firmly entrenched opponent of the alcohol industry, and he was an outspoken prohibitionist. Some of his first public pronouncements on the issue surfaced in his public addresses concerning the First World War. Shields had traveled coast to coast sharing his personal observations of the war at the behest of the Borden government and the British Ministry of Information.[41] His observations concerning the liquor trade were delivered with typical Shields pugnacity:

> Personally, I am a Prohibitionist. I would prohibit the Liquor Traffic everywhere, just as I would prohibit a man-eating tiger from wandering at large. I am not a chemist, but it seems to me that there is enough of the devil in whisky to afford material for high explosives of some sort; and I should like to turn the chem-

38. Shields, "Challenging Answer," 4.

39. Kenneth Johnstone, "Toronto's Dr. Shields," *The Standard*, [Month and day unknown] 1946, 11.

40. "Dr. Shields Should Not Be Surprised."

41. Shields, "Letter to the Deacons." Cf. Tarr, *Shields of Canada*, 58. Some of these addresses included "England in Wartime," "Imperial London at War," "The Fall of Lucifer," and "The Sword of Victory" (JBCA).

ists of the Empire loose upon what supplies we have in stock, with instructions to convert them into stuff to blow up Prussianism with. I say this to make my own attitude unmistakable plain. The damning and damnable record of this traffic everywhere merits the unsparing, unmitigated, curse of earth and heaven.[42]

Over the years, Shields would continue to make headlines on the issue. He attacked the record of the Ontario Government of Howard Ferguson in the 1929 election, because Ferguson in 1927 had replaced the *Ontario Temperance Act* with the *Act to Regulate and Control the Sale of Liquor in Ontario* creating the Liquor Board of Ontario. "Sweeping aside all camouflage and subterfuge," charged Shields, "the plain unmistakable matter of fact is that Premier Ferguson in this day has become the agent of the brewers and distillers and a reactionary measure has been forced upon this province that undoes the progress of 30 years or more."[43] It is not at all surprising then that Hepburn's move of the Liberal party away from a "Dry" platform had Shields up in arms.[44]

Shields's first attack on Hepburn over his alcohol policy came in 1934 after Hepburn's Liberal victory in the July election. Shields's editorial in the *Gospel Witness* was entitled "Modernism and Beer." Challenging the decline in liquor controls under the law, Shields decried the "freer beer privileges" allowed through the opening of "beverage-rooms" all over the city. His concern was pastoral as he noted that "in the vicinity of Jarvis Street Church during the last few weeks we have witnessed such drunken orgies as were never seen in Toronto in the days of the open bar."[45] Shields's opening salvo in his campaign protesting Premier Hepburn's legislation amending the Liquor Control Act was fired from the pulpit of his church under the heading "Will Ontario Tolerate the Present Deluge of Liquor?"[46] With the media broadly pub-

42. Shields, "England in Wartime," 6. This was an address first presented in Toronto on 29 September 1917. However, the last page includes a listing of 25 other locations in which it was presented. These are mostly in and around Ontario, but the list also includes Montreal; Jamestown, NY, and Saginaw, MI. Congregation sizes are also included and range from 150 to 1500.

43. "Shields Lifts Voice against Ferguson Govt," *Evening Telegram*, 28 October 1929, 15.

44. For a discussion of Hepburn's move away from the "dry" platform, see Saywell, *Just Call Me Mitch*, chap. 3.

45. Shields, "Modernism and Beer," *GW*, 9 August 1934, 5.

46. Shields, "Will Ontario Tolerate the Present Deluge of Liquor?" *GW*, 13 August 1934, 3.

licizing Shields's demands, and Jarvis Street Church's own advertising and circulation of "protest slips," Shields delivered a second salvo the following Sunday evening entitled "Ontario's Shame."[47] The church was packed, and it was estimated that over 3,000 people crowded into the auditorium, adjacent halls and grounds surrounding the church. By means of amplifiers, the audience outside the auditorium was able to listen in. In addition to this audience, Shields estimated that further "hundreds of thousands" tuned in to the broadcast over CFRB, the church's regular Sunday evening broadcast.[48] Within weeks Shields had collected over 40,000 protest slips challenging Hepburn's liquor legislation.[49]

Shields acknowledged that the legislation had been drafted by the previous Henry government, but he held the present administration responsible for its enactment. Premier George Henry had made the amendments conditional upon his return to office. However, the Henry government was defeated. Shields interpreted this defeat as a rejection of Henry's government rather than as a vote for Hepburn. Shields maintained that he himself voted Liberal, not as a vote for Hepburn but as a vote against Henry. "I felt," declared Shields, "the Henry government had grossly betrayed its trust and had outstayed its welcome."[50] However, Shields's welcome for the new government of Mitchell F. Hepburn was brief, and Hepburn's adoption of the Henry government's liquor policies soon had him up in arms. "True," said Shields, "the beer parlor legislation is the Henry Government's baby that was left on Premier Hepburn's doorstep. Notwithstanding, it is now apparent that from the moment he opened his official door and found the baby on his door step, Mr. Hepburn fell violently in love with it, as though it were his own child, and has, in fact adopted it as his own, and handed it over to Nurse Odette to bring it up for him."[51] A few weeks later Shields openly questioned the "paternity of this supposed 'child' of the Henry Government." "In fact," argued Shields, "the more the child grows the more it resembles its

47. "Dr. Shields Demands Closing of Jarvis St. Beverage Rooms." Cf. "Shields Leads Drive to Cancel Licenses," *Toronto Star*, 20 August 1934, 3; "Jarvis St. Baptists Protest Beer Parlors by Church," *Evening Telegram*, 20 August 1934, 11.

48. Shields, "More about Ontario's Shame," *GW*, 30 August 1934, 1.

49. "I'd Like to Be M.P.P.," 1.

50. "Attacking Administration Not Beer Law, Says Shields," *Toronto Star*, 5 o'clock ed., 30 August 1934, 8.

51. "Would Kill New Beer Act Declares Doctor Shields," *Toronto Telegram*, 24 August 1934. In *TTCF*, 111.

foster-parents." Clearly, the affection of the present government for the bill led to the determination "that the ugly child shall have full freedom to disturb the well being of the whole province."[52]

For Shields, the disturbance of the province's well-being was clearly illustrated on Jarvis Street. He identified a violation in the present governmental practice of the fundamental principle laid down in earlier legislation forbidding the sale of liquor within established limits around schools and churches. Pointing to the case of Jarvis Street, Shields was able to identify five educational institutions within two blocks of his church and nine licensed beverage rooms within three blocks. He charged that "licenses were scattered like confetti."[53] Even in the midst of a two-month trip to England combining a honeymoon and a preaching tour arranged by the "Spurgeon Centenary Mission," the Ontario liquor question filled his thoughts. He wrote home:

> I have been nearly seven weeks in London; I was in Liverpool, in Glasgow and Edinburgh. I was in Cork and Dublin in the Free State, and in Belfast in Northern Ireland. In all that time I did not see as much evidence of drunkenness as I could see on Jarvis St. in two hours from the steps of Jarvis St. Baptist church. I am more convinced than ever that conditions in Ontario are such as to make every decent Canadian blush for shame.[54]

What is perhaps most surprising about the Shields/Hepburn controversy was the degree of personal invective hurled back and forth between the two protagonists. Both men were renowned for their provocative and controversial methods. Hepburn had earned quite a reputation for his "barbed-wire eloquence."[55] However, it was Pastor Shields who kept the media entertained with the taunts and personal insults he directed at the Premier. Hepburn's initial reaction to Shields's attacks was to dismiss him "as an offensive temperance crank." Shields fired back that Hepburn's way of dealing with his opposition had been simply to fire all those who did not agree with him. Those he could not fire he called names "in the manner of an angry schoolboy."[56] However,

52. "Alcoholic Foundling Looks Like Hepburn."

53. Shields, "Ontario's Shame," *GW*, 30 August 1934, 2.

54. "Shields Sees More Drunks on Jarvis St. Than on Trip," *Toronto Star*, 5 o'clock ed., 13 November 1934, 23.

55. McKenty, "Hepburn and the Ontario Election," 303.

56. "Dr. Shields Should Not Be Surprised."

rather than take the moral high ground, Shields was determined to meet fire with fire. He deliberately took a swipe at Hepburn's barnstorming campaign in the recent election by suggesting he would match his efforts in the liquor fight. In 1934, he claimed that when he came back from his England honeymoon he would go from one end of the province to the other and "show Mr. Hepburn that I can speak as well as he can. I am not a reformer. Primarily I am a preacher, but I will take my hand at reform. You may nominate me for the Legislature if you like, but I promise you that they shall hear from me."[57] He concluded, "So far as this 'temperance crank' is concerned, I am resolved to become even more offensive."[58]

When Shields returned home, the liquor fight was renewed with a vengeance. Hepburn's curt dismissal of every delegation requesting a hearing on moral issues brought charges of insolence and arrogance from Shields.[59] Though his original intent had been to seek an audience with Hepburn armed with over 40,000 protest slips, Shields quickly abandoned that plan: "I have not yet presented them to Premier Hepburn, because I do not propose to expose myself to that gentleman's insolence." Shields went on to add, "If it were possible to reduce this remarkable person to a chemical analysis to show what he is composed of, I think we would find 5 percent ability and 95 percent conceit."[60]

Two major concerns occupied Shields's mind: the morality of the province and the rule of law versus the arbitrary rule of Hepburn. Shields particularly feared the moral consequences of the beverage room provision and denounced the "debauchery, the whoring, and the demoralization of the young that had overtaken the province."[61] Capitalizing on the sensational headlines of the previous week documenting the kidnapping and release of beer tycoon John S. Labatt, Shields with an ironic twist declared that the liquor business was a "kidnapper a thousand times more dangerous than any of the kidnapping gangsters of the United States or Canada." "It tears the husband from the side of his wife," Shields argued, "the son from his mother and alas, in many instances the mother from her children. It reduces the victim's family to such a condition that none

---

57. "Rev. Dr. Shields Promises Cleanup on Beer Parlors," *Evening Telegram*, 27 August 1934, 21.

58 "Alcoholic Foundling Looks Like Hepburn."

59. Shields, "Hepburn's Alliance with Rum and Rome," 3.

60. "I'd Like to Be M.P.P.," 1.

61. Saywell, *Just Call Me Mitch*, 175.

of them can by any means redeem his brother nor give any sort of ransom for him."[62]

Shields, along with many others, including Prime Minister King, was aghast at the seeming sellout to liquor interests. Hepburn's first announcement to the press after his first cabinet meeting was that Henry's liquor act had been passed and that "beer would flow on 24 July."[63] Since Hepburn had appointed his friend, the heavy-drinking Eddie Odette, to the position of Liquor Commissioner, 24 July witnessed the issuance of "authorities for ninety-nine standard hotels, three clubs, and two steamship companies with a thousand licenses to come." From the outset the consequences were obvious. Beer sales were up 120 per cent by the end of August, and over one million dollars had been paid or was immediately pending to the Provincial Treasury from the "issuance of authorities."[64] Conversion of any old shack into a hotel, some without any sleeping facilities, was rampant. The case of the Breadalbane became celebrated when its circumstances were publicized in the Toronto papers.[65]

For Shields the situation was intolerable and made a mockery of Hepburn's pretensions at a fiscally responsible government. Shields contended that despite Hepburn's promises to cut government expenses by 50 percent, the auctioning of government vehicles, the closure of the lieutenant-governor's residence and the slashing of unneeded public service employees, the social cost of alcohol consumption would be much more. Speaking of Hepburn's refusal of an invitation to a state dinner at Government House,[66] Shields accused him of hypocrisy:

> Personally, we have always had the strongest natural antipathy for that kind of Pharisaical hypocrisy, whether religious or political, which, "strains at a gnat, and swallows a camel"; and we have

62. "Dr. Shields Demands Closing of Jarvis St. Beverage Rooms." For a discussion of the Labatt kidnapping, see Goldenberg, *Snatched! The Peculiar Kidnapping of Beer Tycoon John Labatt*.

63. Saywell, *Just Call Me Mitch*, 170.

64. "Profits Made on Authorities and at Stores," *The Globe*, 30 August 1934, 1.

65. Saywell, *Just Call Me Mitch*, 175. Cf. "Breadalbane Hotel Case Examined by Commissioner," *The Globe*, 30 August 1934, 1.

66. Since the 1934 campaign, Hepburn had promised to close Chorley Park, the official residence of the Lieutenant Governor, which Hepburn called "a haven for broken-down English aristocrats who should be paying for their rooms at the hotels." Given his stance on Government House, Hepburn refused ever to take a meal there. Cf. McKenty, *Mitch Hepburn*, 139.

still less respect for that economic Pharisaism which strains at a dinner menu, and swallows an ocean of beer. If Mr. Hepburn were really bent upon economy, if he were really a friend of the common people, if he really had the moral and material welfare of the Province at heart; and if such benevolent attitude toward his fellows were accompanied by an enlightened judgment, can anyone suppose he would be willing to accept responsibility for the measure which takes an additional twenty-five millions of dollars out of the pockets of the people of Ontario—mostly of young people—by his beer and wine parlours?[67]

A second ground for complaint was soon added to Shields's hit list. When Hepburn governed for eight months by "order-in-council" and the legislature did not meet, Shields noted that "for eight months the electors of the Province of Ontario . . . have been disfranchised." With Hepburn's refusal to attend the state dinner hosted by the Lieutenant-Governor, Shields denounced Hepburn's "offence against good manners," and he had further evidence of Hepburn's disregard for legal authority.[68] In September of 1935, Shields accused Hepburn of defying a Supreme Court decision: "His government is continuing the sale of liquor in three counties where a judgment of the Supreme Court of Canada has said it cannot legally be sold. Mr. Hepburn openly defies the Supreme Court."[69]

As early as September of 1934, Shields had compared Hepburn to Hitler. Commenting on Hepburn's "'wholesale dismissals' from the government services" Shields remarked, "The Premier of Ontario now speaks as though he is already dictator of Canada. I wonder who his political ideal is? I think it must be Adolph Hitler, and a little bit of Mussolini."[70] The charge was repeated in March of 1935. Speaking of his refusal to seek a hearing with Hepburn, because of Hepburn's previous refusal to give a fair hearing to various delegations seeking redress to the issues, Shields remarked: "But I shall not submit these names to the Premier, for what are forty thousand, six hundred and seventy-nine voters to this miniature, intellectually diminutive imitation of Hitler!"[71] This kind of rhetoric would continue and escalate as Shields increasingly

67. Shields, "The Malady of Hepburnism," *GW*, 7 February 1935, 3.

68. Ibid.

69. Shields, "A Canadian Menace," *GW*, 5 September 1935, 5.

70. "Organ Plays to Drown Shouts of Combatants; Man and Woman Ejected," *Mail*, 3 September 1934. In *TTCF*, 112.

71. Shields, "Hepburn's Alliance with Rum and Rome," 3.

found grounds in Hepburn's actions to identify his leadership style as dictatorial and fascist. In the East Hastings by-election, George Drew would echo these sentiments, and with Hepburn's denunciation of an Ontario Court of appeal decision as a "hollow verdict . . . a hog's head of law and a thimbleful of justice," Drew demanded his resignation for contempt of court. He asked: "Who is this Mussolini . . . ? This is Fascism. Mussolini has suspended the courts recently in his totalitarian State. Now this man says he will suspend Ontario's courts. He should haul down the Union Jack and hoist the Jolly Roger. He is a pirate."[72]

Throughout the liquor controversy, Hepburn's response was largely to discount the influence of Shields as too narrow-minded to have much influence. On the occasion that Hepburn was informed of some of Shields's more caustic remarks and the suggestion that Shields would like a seat in the Legislature to better confront him, Hepburn replied, "I don't think that any constituency would elect any man so narrow-minded as Dr. Shields."[73] Two years later his assumptions were indirectly put to the test in the East Hastings by-election and Hepburn would have cause to reflect on the consequences of underestimating Dr. Shields and his following.

The Separate School Question

From early in the Hepburn regime, questions began to arise about reopening the Separate School question.[74] By March of 1935, Shields began to express his concerns about a renewed attack upon the Public School system.[75] Shields's fears proved prophetic, and in April an act to amend the Assessment Act was passed into legislation. Shields immediately reacted. On 14 April 1935, he delivered an address in Jarvis Street Baptist Church entitled, "The Hepburn Government's Betrayal of Its Public Trust by Diverting Public School Revenue to Support of Roman Catholic Separate Schools." Two weeks later he addressed a larger crowd at Massey Hall under the heading, *The Roman Catholic Horseleach*. In both of these addresses, Shields professed that he was not attacking Catholicism as a religion but as a political system that was

72. Saywell, *Just Call Me Mitch*, 272.

73. "I'd Like to Be M.P.P., 1.

74. McKenty, *Mitch Hepburn*, 76.

75. Shields, "Hepburn's Alliance with Rum and Rome," 2.

threatening to make Canada a Catholic nation. Shields argued that one of the primary strategies of Catholicism was to gain control over the educational systems of the country and use the tool of education for the propagation of the Roman Catholic faith. Shields drew a parallel with the Irish situation. A guest of the Irish Ministry of Information in 1918, Shields was given an extensive tour of Ireland during which he was able to meet representatives of all walks of Irish life. Concerning his experiences he boasted at the time, "The Ministry of Information tells us that to no others have so many Irish leaders spoken, & so freely, as to us."[76] At the conclusion of the trip he was invited to dinner with Lord Carson.[77] When Carson pressed him for his understanding of the Irish problem, Shields professed to him that the matter was an educational one. He argued that the children in Irish schools were taught "to nurse the grievances of two hundred and fifty years ago." Shields's solution was "a system of purely secular education, making all religions equal under the law, and allowing all churches to teach with absolute freedom their own tenets—at their own expense." Carson's response was "you propose an impossibility. The Roman Catholic Church will never surrender its control of . . . education . . . , for the reason that her very life depends upon it."[78] It was Shields's conviction that it was the Roman Catholic hierarchy's goal to destroy all secular education in Canada and to replace the secular system with a Catholic educational program. In the present bill, concluded Shields, "The Roman Catholic hierarchy makes a raid upon the national revenue for the propagation of Roman Catholicism."[79]

In the Assessment Act amendment Shields saw a blatant attempt by the Hepburn government "to secure a larger proportion of public funds for the support of Separate Schools." The problem for Shields was that this funding was not to come from the "taxation of some virgin field," but involved "diverting such funds from the treasury of the Public Schools."[80] As Shields understood the act, and he confessed that it was so confusing that even the men that framed it could not really understand

76. Shields, "Letter to the Deacons."

77. Lord Carson was a leader of the Ulster Unionist Party and held many positions in the Cabinet of the United Kingdom. The standard biography is Hyde, *Carson*. For more recent treatment, see Hostettler, *Sir Edward Carson*.

78. Shields, *Hepburn Government's Betrayal*, 12.

79. Ibid., 23.

80. Ibid., 20.

it, this amendment provided for the taxation of corporations for educational purposes. The proportion of funds divided among Public and Separate schools would be according to "the shares held respectively by Protestants and Roman Catholics." While this in itself might be fair, the problem lay in the fact that most corporations were so large and their shares were "so widely scattered through subsidiary companies that it would become impossible to ascertain the religion of each individual shareholder."[81] The rule that was to apply in such circumstances was that the division of funds to Public and Separate boards would be based not on the faith of the share-holders but rather upon the faith of the inhabitants of the district in which the corporation primarily functioned. The ratio of Catholics to Protestants in any given district would be the determining factor for the allotment of tax funding to the respective systems. "Thus," concluded Shields, "there is more than a probability that in the aggregate, millions of dollars of property held by Protestants will be taxed for the propagation of the dogmas of Rome."[82]

Shields's attack on Hepburn centered on his appraisal of Hepburn's motives in introducing the bill. Shields noted that since the bill favored the Roman Catholic constituents who were in a minority in Ontario there must be some particular reason that Hepburn's government had introduced it. He could not find the answer in the constituency of the party, because there Catholics were not in the majority. Nor was there any particular evidence of any kind of religious zeal among Hepburn's colleagues. He hinted broadly that the "House was dragooned into the passage of this Bill . . . for the sake of O'Connor's friendship." It is not entirely clear whether Shields was the first to make this connection, but hereafter, George Drew would make large use of the O'Connor friendship in his own attempts to embarrass Hepburn. [83] Hepburn, for his part, declared that Frank O'Connor was a friend and that "he did not intend to give up that friendship no matter what George Drew, Earl Rowe, and Toronto's Catholic-baiting Baptist minister, the Reverend T. T. Shields, had to say about it."[84] However, whether the legislation was the result of O'Connor's influence or not Shields asserted dogmatically,

81. Ibid., 21.

82. Ibid., 23.

83. Ibid., 24. Senator Frank O'Connor was a "candy millionaire" and close friend of Hepburn. Throughout the subsequent controversy, George Drew would label Hepburn "O'Connor's puppet." Cf. McKenty, *Mitch Hepburn*, 82.

84. McKenty, *Mitch Hepburn*, 83.

Surely one can only conclude that Mr. Hepburn and his party were under some sort of compact to the Roman Catholic church to deliver the goods—and this, remember, is only the first installment. The circumstantial evidence in support of that assumption is overwhelmingly convincing. I think we must conclude that the present Government is under Roman Catholic direction and control.[85]

With this assertion Shields clearly hit a sore point in Ontario politics. Anti-Catholic sentiment ran deep, and a perceived attack upon the province's educational system by the Catholic hierarchy was enough to stir up tremendous opposition. Shields played to this fear and declared, "If Rome challenges us to battle in the political arena, let us respond to her challenge with a declaration of war."[86] With his declaration Shields also delivered a plan of attack:

To this end, *the public must be informed*. False statements must be corrected, and false impressions removed. Let us this evening highly resolve that we will enlist in this war. I suggest that meetings ought to be held all over this city, large meetings and small, wherever people can be assembled—in churches, in halls, and everywhere. Let us evoke such an expression of sentiment that Maple Leaf Gardens will not be large enough to contain the militant Protestants bold enough to declare themselves openly. And when we have done that, let us carry our message to every city, town, village, and hamlet—to every riding in Ontario, from one end of the Province to the other.[87]

Unwittingly, Mitchell Hepburn soon provided the perfect opportunity for Shields to put his plans into action. When J. F. Hill, the Tory member for East Hastings, died on 15 October 1936, Hepburn ignored the advice of friends and associates and called a snap by-election for 9 December, 1936. In his speech at the nominating convention on 6 November, Hepburn largely conceded that the real battle would surround the contentious issue of his separate school legislation. Arguing that the new tax would bring a measure of relief from cities and corporations to rural schools and that it would also bring a "measure of justice to the Catholic minority," Hepburn declared, "If defeat is the penalty

85. Shields, *Hepburn Government's Betrayal*, 26.

86. Shields, *Roman Catholic Horseleach*, 18.

87. Ibid., 20.

for doing what is right and just, then send us down to defeat."[88] His opponents, with the Reverend T. T. Shields prominent in the mix, were determined to do just that.

The Liberal party entered the campaign with all they could muster. Even the federal minister from the Northumberland riding, William "Billy" Fraser," moved his campaign machinery into East Hastings.[89] Hepburn personally led the fight, and by the end of the campaign was largely living in the riding. In the dead of winter he traveled from one end of the riding to the other, from one speaking appointment to another, with an urgency born of desperation. He fought for his record and argued that the Assessment Act amendment was an economic issue and not a religious one.[90] However, he could not overcome the religious prejudices that were endlessly exploited by the opposition. Earl Rowe, the leader of the opposition, suggested that the Liberals were "tools of Rome."[91] George Drew, the future Conservative Party leader and future premier of Ontario, argued that if the Catholics were going to "bring faith into politics" then the war was on. A "whisper campaign" suggested that Hepburn's wife was Catholic, that "crowns on the King's Highways would be replaced by romish crosses," and that a "papal residence was being prepared at Casa Loma." Some suggested that the candidates themselves were "drowned out by the strident oratory emanating from squads of outsiders pouring into every corner of the riding."[92] While not the only one, certainly the voice of T. T. Shields was prominent in the hullabaloo.

Shields gave at least three addresses in the East Hastings riding in the days leading up to the December by-election. *Globe* reporter Ralph Hyman spoke of meetings in Deseronto and Canniston where Shields's speeches were described as "vigorous" and "aggressive."[93] In Deseronto, Shields's claim that "no true, devout Catholic who follows the teachings of his church can be a loyal citizen of any non-Catholic government," brought pandemonium as Catholics in his audience erupted in anger.

88. Saywell, *Just Call Me Mitch*, 272.

89. McKenty, *Mitch Hepburn*, 82. Fraser was known as the "chief political 'fixer' for Central Ontario."

90. Ibid., 83.

91. Ibid., 81.

92. Ibid., 82.

93. Hyman, "Anti-Hepburn Vote Asked by Shields," 3.

News reports of the Deseronto address told of repeated heckling and an argument between Shields and the member of the legislature for Windsor, Mr. J. H. Clarke.[94] In Truro, which had the only separate school in the East Hastings riding, Shields's speech was much more subdued and resembled "an academic address."[95] However, the Chairman, Cecil Armstrong, identified later by Hepburn as "a Toronto civic employee,"[96] was greeted by "twenty minutes of terrific heckling."[97] Shields described the opposition as consisting of "about twenty-five small boys and girls" who were "from the one Separate School in the riding." These were re-inforced by "about seventy-five of the roughest men I ever saw." When Armstrong tried to make his preliminary remarks, Shields noted that "these little children . . . began to make a noise, booing, hissing, and shouting; and the seventy-five men at the back joined them." The Truro meeting boasted a large contingent of police officers, who separated the seventy-five men from the rest of the audience. According to the report made to Shields, a plot against him had been discovered and so the Provincial inspector came "twenty-six miles to take charge."[98] At the conclusion of the meeting, fearing mob action after the dispersal of Shields's supporters, the police escorted Shields from the scene. Shields commented:

> I went out, and was escorted to my car by two or three police-men. Police were on either side of the car. Opening the door on the driver's side, one policeman put down the window and then put himself inside the car while standing on the running-board. Policemen got on both running-boards, and then the officer-in charge said, "Drive on"—and we went off under police escort.[99]

In response to this meeting, Hepburn complained that "every ef-fort" was being made "to inflame the Protestants against the Catholics, who for years have lived here as neighbors and friends." He condemned Armstrong's involvement as chairman in Shields's campaigns:

94. "'You're Crazy' Yells Heckler as Shields Attacks Catholics," *The Globe and Mail*, 2 December 1936, 2.

95. Hyman, "Anti-Hepburn Vote Asked by Shields," 3.

96. Oliver, "Tories Inflaming Religious Strife," 3.

97. Hyman, "Anti-Hepburn Vote Asked by Shields," 3.

98. Shields, "Menace of Present-Day Roman Catholicism," 4. Cf. J. H. Fisher, "Police Guard Dr. Shields from Threatening Crowd," *Evening Telegram*, 4 December 1936, 15.

99. Shields, "Menace of Present-Day Roman Catholicism," 4.

Mr. Armstrong, I understand . . . is drawing his salary while attending those meetings down here. I wonder if he has stopped to realize that while he is here attacking the Catholics so viciously his salary is being paid in part by the Catholic rate payers of Toronto.[100]

Despite Hepburn's protests, Dr. Harold Boyce, Hepburn's candidate for the East Hastings riding, went down to a "crushing defeat." The previous Tory majority of 418 strengthened considerably to 1,136. Hepburn complained that the by-election had been "fought purely on religious bigotry."[101] For the most part, Hepburn laughed off Shields's allegations "as the ranting of a lunatic fringe of sanctimonious, psalm singing preachers."[102] However, when looking for someone to blame for his East Hastings defeat, and the subsequent withdrawal of the Assessment Act, Shields was a handy target. On 24 March 1937, when Hepburn conceded the fight and accepted George Henry's motion to repeal the separate school bill, he accused the opposition of having "intimidated the small Catholic minority so much that they were afraid to vote." While Rowe and Drew were the primary targets of his hour long speech, Shields also was named. Hepburn deprecated Shields's insults of Catholic citizens and condemned Shields's questioning "of the loyalty of devout Catholics." He argued that the opposition had "opened up religious and racial sores which will not heal in the lifetime of this country." He concluded: "It is my responsibility to forestall the possibility of a religious war in this Province."[103] Shields, always the one to have the last word, responded:

When Mr. Hepburn accepted the proposal of the Opposition, that the Amendment be repealed, in his speech in the Legislature he did me the honour of blaming me, among others, for stirring up religious strife. I said, he did me the honour of blaming me—and it was an honour, for to be blamed by Mr. Hepburn for anything is tantamount to a certificate of character.[104]

For some time Shields had publicly expressed his complete confidence that at the first opportunity Hepburn would be defeated at the

100. Oliver, "Tories Inflaming Religious Strife," 3.

101. McKenty, *Mitch Hepburn*, 84.

102. Saywell, *Just Call Me Mitch*, 407.

103. "It Is My Duty to Forestall Religious War," *The Globe and Mail*, 25 March, 1937, 1.

104. Shields, "What Ought Ontario to Do with Hepburn?" 9.

polls. As early as March 1935 Shields predicted Hepburn's electoral demise:

> I find some compensation, however, in the reflection that with every passing day your crudities are serving to enlighten the understanding of intelligent voters all over the Province; for I have, myself, had contact with many hundreds of people who cast their votes in your support at the last election, who are eagerly awaiting an opportunity, as I am, to atone for their folly. . . . I attempt no argument: I can see nothing but for the Province, with what fortitude it can command, to resign itself to suffering the indignity of your premiership, until by the lapse of time the citizens of this Province, in the exercise of their constitutional right, will be able to cast you into the political oblivion which your personal insolence so richly merits.[105]

In his Massey Hall address about the Assessment Act, Shields expressed an increasing confidence that Hepburn's days were numbered: "I cannot believe that the Province of Ontario would ever again entrust the government of its affairs to a man responsible for the beverage rooms and their administration, and now for this iniquitous school law in the form of an amendment to the Assessment Act."[106] Late in 1936, Shields forcefully articulated his view that Hepburn would not survive another election: "And let me tell you friends, when the next election comes around Premier Hepburn will find that there are hundreds of thousands of dictators who will say in no uncertain terms: 'Get out!'"[107] A month later Shields's optimism seemed to be confirmed by the results of the East Hastings by-election, and when Hepburn a year later announced a provincial election, Shields enthusiastically predicted Hepburn's defeat. Noting the "40,679 signed protests" of the beer parlor legislation and the broad response to the broadcast of his addresses to "tens of thousands of people throughout the Province," Shields felt confident in his outlook. Despite being silenced for several months by a heart attack, Shields felt obligated to respond to the appeal of "the inquiring and expectant attitude of the tens of thousands" who now looked for his opinion on the subject of Hepburn's premiership.[108] He observed that there had to be

105. Shields, "Hepburn's Alliance with Rum and Rome," 4.

106. Shields, *Hepburn Government's Betrayal*, 31.

107. "'Failed as Dictator' Shields Answers Charge," *Evening Telegram*, 2 November 1936, 12.

108. Shields, "What Ought Ontario to Do with Hepburn?" 6.

some way by "which an outraged electorate could inflict punishment upon a Government that has betrayed its trust."[109] His conclusion was simple: "There is but one answer to the question, What should Ontario do to Hepburn? *WITH BOTH HANDS AND A STRONG RIGHT FOOT, THROW HIM OUT!*"[110]

Shields's prognostications proved to be as empty as his demagoguery was ineffective. For all his bravado about being tempted to run for office himself as another Cromwell "to drive out the Hepburn gang of outlaws,"[111] Shields was more demagogue than politician. Shields's reading of the political pulse in Ontario proved to be completely incorrect. Despite his best efforts to remind the electorate of the moral ills brought down upon Ontario during Hepburn's tenure, Hepburn, the savvy politician, had already in 1937 picked the opportune time to take his record to the voters of Ontario. Having just defeated the attempts of the CIO to infiltrate the Ontario labor scene, Hepburn sidestepped the opposition's defense of labor rights by boasting of his defeat of communist agitators.[112] In his handling of the Oshawa strike, even Shields was a reluctant admirer.[113] Hepburn's economic record was excellent. He had cut taxes, and at the same time brought about the first budget surplus in many years.[114] He was viewed as having defeated the power barons, and he alone was responsible for lower hydro rates. Hepburn was riding a wave of popular support. The election results were almost as strong as his first showing in 1934. He was down three seats from his previous total in 1934, but had managed to increase his share of the popular vote.[115] Shields's paper the *Gospel Witness* was silent on the matter. Except for the comment, "there never was a time when organized religion was held in greater contempt than it is to-day," and an appeal for divine intervention, Shields offered no commentary on the election.[116]

109. Ibid., 10.

110. Ibid., 13.

111. "Catholics Planning Move Dr. Shields Warns Voters," *Evening Telegram*, 27 March 1937, 33.

112. McKenty, *Mitch Hepburn*, 137.

113. "Fight of Premier Hepburn on Union Stained by Blood Lauded by Dr. T. T. Shields," *Evening Telegram*, 14 April 1937, 16.

114. McKenty, *Mitch Hepburn*, 137.

115. Ibid., 136.

116. Shields, "Let God Arise," *GW*, 21 October 1936, 1.

Another five years lapsed before Hepburn was driven from the political playing field, and even then it was another enemy that was the biggest cause of his political demise. Shields continued to snipe at Hepburn throughout those years, but by the first years of the Second World War, Shields's attention was diverted by a new and greater threat. Somewhat ironically, by the early 1940s, Shields and Hepburn found themselves fighting the same adversary—Prime Minister William Lyon Mackenzie King.

PRIME MINISTER MACKENZIE KING

It is a matter of some historical irony that at a time when Liberal party fortunes were at such a high point in Ontario and with both the provincial and federal branches of the party in power, provincial-federal relations were at an all time low. The cause of this political dysfunction was in large part the result of a personal animus directed towards Prime Minister King by Ontario's premier. McKenty has argued that nearly all of Mitch Hepburn's policies in the late 1930s were directed by his personal hatred of Prime Minister King.[117] With the outbreak of the Second World War, it seemed momentarily that the hatchet might be buried and that the two men would work together in pursuit of the war effort. Having returned from an Australian trip at the beginning of 1939, Hepburn arrived at home with the realization that international relationships were rapidly deteriorating and that it was time for Canada to arm itself. In the Ontario legislature, Hepburn presented a resolution "petitioning the federal government 'that in the event of a war emergency, the wealth and manpower of Canada shall be mobilized . . . for the duration of the war.'"[118] The resolution passed unanimously. King was somewhat embarrassed by the event and responded by insisting that there would be no conscription for overseas service.[119] Dissatisfied with King's response, Hepburn formed the Ontario War Resources Committee composed of himself, Lieutenant Governor Albert Matthews, and George Drew. On 3 October 1939, the committee met with King for two and a half hours "in order to

117. McKenty carefully documents the development of the bad blood between the two men. Hepburn, disappointed with broken promises, formally broke with King in 1937. "I am a Reformer. But I am not a Mackenzie King Liberal any longer. I will tell the world that, and I hope he hears me" (McKenty, *Mitch Hepburn*, 125).

118. Ibid., 188.

119. Ibid., 189.

discuss ways and means by which Ontario can best serve Canada in this great crisis."[120] King parted with them on good terms thanking them for Ontario's cooperation. It looked as though in the national hour of emergency, peace between the two men had been made. However, within days Hepburn was publicly expressing his exasperation with King's lack of leadership, because King had not immediately dropped everything else to embrace Hepburn's agenda. At the opening of the Ontario Legislature, 18 January 1940, Hepburn stunned the nation with a motion condemning the King government's war preparations. In introducing the motion Hepburn stated: "Let me say again that I stand firm in my statements that Mr. King has not done his duty to his country—never has and never will. I sat with him in the Federal House for eight years and I know him." The motion stated that the Legislature regretted that "the Federal Government at Ottawa has made so little effort to prosecute Canada's duty in the war in the vigorous manner the people of Canada desire to see." After a near revolt by the Liberal party members, Hepburn was able to get the vote passed by a count of forty-four to ten.[121] Prime Minister King's reaction was to prorogue parliament on the day it was assembled. In his throne speech on 25 January 1940, King responded to the Ontario War Resolution:

> That resolution was passed to start a political campaign, while this Parliament is sitting . . . Already the leader of the Conservative Party in Ontario speaking at a political meeting, has said the election should be held. And he gives the slogan for the election: 'King must Go.' I am quite prepared to accept that slogan and go to the people.[122]

On 26 March 1940, Canada went to the polls and renewed King's mandate. In what had to be considered a smashing defeat for Hepburn and the Conservative Leader Manion's National Government, the King government won 178 seats to Manion's 39.[123]

Throughout this national debate, Shields was not silent, and he did everything in his power to influence the outcome of events. Somewhat surprisingly, given the nature of the issue, Shields sided with King.

120. Ibid., 200.
121. Ibid., 209.
122. Ibid., 211.
123. Ibid., 218.

Driven by an animus of his own against Premier Hepburn, Shields rejected Hepburn's accusations and praised the efforts of the King government. Shields clearly discounted Hepburn's concern for the Imperial cause, and he labeled Hepburn and Drew "axis-partners" in their joint attempt to bring down the King government:

> I honour Mr. King and his government particularly for this one thing, that when Aberhart in the west and Hepburn in Ontario and Duplessis in Quebec were doing their utmost to effect the disintegration of confederation and to blow this Dominion to smithereens they wisely held the balance and by moderate control secured the unity of Canada for this great effort in the war. I believe he is a good man and honorable, an able man; that he is the experienced head of an experienced, aggressive, efficient, sane, stable, steady and dependable government, whose war effort thus far merits the confidence of the country.[124]

At an address supportive of King given Monday 11 March 1940, at Jarvis Street Baptist Church, over 1,600 people packed the auditorium to listen to Shields's message: "Hepburn—Drew—King—Manion—What Shall We Do with Them?" Copies of the address were published ahead of time, and over 1,500 were sold at the doors. The *Toronto Star* reporter noted: "They laughed at Dr. Shields' witticisms, heckled him several times and applauded vigorously when he urged them to 'join with me in voting for the government of Premier King.'"[125] He later made the claim to a Member of Parliament that copies of the speech were used by "various committees of the Liberal party in support of Mr. King and his regime."[126]

Shields interpreted King's victory as a rejection of Hepburn: "The vote of Tuesday overwhelmingly supporting the King government surely constitutes an utter repudiation of Messrs. Hepburn and Drew. The King government was overwhelmingly endorsed in the province of Ontario, while Dr. Manion was left without one supporter in Nova Scotia, Quebec, and Alberta." [127] Shields, furthermore, was less than modest in his assessment of the role he played in the election:

124. "Ontario 'Lunatic Asylum' If with Hepburn—Shields," *Toronto Star*, 12 March 1940, 3.

125. Ibid.

126. Shields, "Open Letter to McDonald," 3.

127. Shields, "Canada Has Spoken," 5. The *Star* republished this editorial as "Hepburn, Drew Telegram Played an Unworthy Part," *Toronto Star*, 29 March 1940, 6.

The recent senseless fulminations of a certain Mr. Mitchell F. Hepburn were broadcast over the world as though they were the utterances of an authoritative voice, whereas his Hitlerian ravings had less effect upon the Canadian electorate than my own moderate and considerate counsel . . . For you see, Canada accepted my advice rather than Mr. Hepburn's and elected Mr. King.[128]

Shields also viewed himself as something of an authority on the matter when he took the *Toronto Telegram* to task for an editorial in which they interpreted the results of the election as an anti-war vote:

But for any responsible journal to suggest that the vote of yesterday indicated a desire on the part of Canada generally that the war should not be fought with the utmost vigor to the end, that it was in any sense an "anti-war" vote, is a slander which every loyal Canadian will resent. The Evening Telegram is a poor looser.[129]

In his controversy with the *Toronto Telegram*, Shields also weighed in on the conscription question. When the *Telegram* argued that Manion had lost because the people feared conscription, Shields responded that "No one could have spoken more plainly in opposition to conscription than did Dr. Manion." Shields was adamant in his contention that "conscription was not at issue in this election; for both parties had most emphatically declared their opposition to it."[130]

Within weeks, however, the warmth of Shields's support for King had nearly dissipated. On Sunday 26 May 1940, Shields's evening sermon was entitled "How Can Canada Wake Up Ottawa?" The sermon was a diatribe against the government's present war effort. He discussed in some detail the deficiencies of Canada's present contribution, including a discussion of its sixteen antiquated tanks, insufficient recruitment of manpower for the army, and a paltry 169 airmen for what was supposed to be "the principal air training centre for the Empire." Shields commented that, when he read the parliamentary discussion about the formation of a third Canadian division of fifteen thousand men, he ran out of patience: "It was piffling stuff, worthy the discussion of a third-rate Ladies' Aid Society of a back-country lodge!" Shields noted that if "the Minister of Defense needs every Tom, Dick, and Harry to tell him

128. Shields, "The Inept Speech of the Ontario Attorney-General," *GW*, 11 April 1940, 5.

129. Shields, "Canada Has Spoken," 5.

130. Ibid.

how to get a unit from his neighbourhood, if he has no greater ability than that, he ought to be removed immediately, and somebody put in his place who knows how to organize men."[131] The record noted that this demand was met with "loud applause." In a move not far removed from Hepburn's recent "Ontario War Resolution" Shields now added his own voice to the "King Must Go" chorus:

> I do not suggest that the present Prime Minister of Canada is incapable of the leadership Canada requires; but I do say that in the light of that which has transpired of recent weeks, the Prime Minister ought—and must supply leadership of a different and more aggressive quality, or else, in the same way as a change was effected in Britain he should be required to step aside and give the reins to other hands.[132]

The *Toronto Telegram* was quick to note Shields's "awakening" and gloated in his reversal:

> If it is any comfort to Dr. Shields, he had lots of company on March 26th and he has lots of company now. But what is expected of a man in his position is leadership and the ability to see beyond his nose. The time for that leadership and vision was prior to March 26th. Repentance at this time may be good for Dr. Shields' soul, but it doesn't do Canada much good.[133]

Significantly, Shields's sermon of the night of 26 May 1940 appealed for several actions that would be points of contention in the days to come. In the first place, he called for national unity in the struggle towards a total war effort. "How then is such effort to be made?" he asked. "I repeat, by avoiding everything that would make for disunion and by actually grasping at everything that will tend to unite us." A second appeal was one that at times almost seemed to describe his own attitudes towards his political opponents. He demanded that Canada pursue the war effort with "all our hatred":

> I stand in this Christian pulpit and offer no apology for saying it. I should question my relationship to Christ, I should question my own moral integrity, and even my right to a place in decent, ordered, society, if I did not hate Hitler and his gang, and all that

131. Shields, "How Can Canada Wake Up Ottawa?" 3.
132. Ibid., 4.
133. "Rev. Dr. T. T. Shields Awoke Rather Late," *Evening Telegram*, 28 May 1940, 6.

they stand for, with the intensest hatred of which my soul is capable. I hate them as I hate the devil and hell; for I am sure they are the agents of both of them. And in reaction from that, I am prepared to love, or at least agree with, anyone who will help me fight them; to make every kind of allowance, to forget all grievances, all differences and join as one in this fight.[134]

As the coming days would show, the corollary was also true, and those who hindered his fight drew his deepest contempt and animosity.

The third appeal was for conscription. Perhaps remembering his appointed role as a champion of the Borden government in the conscription fight of those years, Shields once again raised the mantra of mandatory enlistment.[135] Arguing that since Britain "had adopted conscription at the beginning of the war," similar measures should be introduced in Canada. In a subtle jab at the King government, he suggested that perhaps the Canadian public should begin "by conscripting the government and the prime minister."[136]

What began as a protest for Shields soon hardened into determined opposition. In less than a year his critique of King had turned into contempt. In exaggerated fashion he minimized his earlier commendations of King and passed off his vote for King as merely voting for the "lesser of two evils." In an editorial in February of 1941, entitled "The Canadian Fuehrer Has Spoken," Shields spoke of his vote for King and quoted the Mayor of New York when he said, "When I make a mistake, it's a 'beaut.'"[137] Later, when King announced a plebiscite on the conscription question, Shields' outrage could not be contained: "I am of the opinion," said Shields, "that the Government has been guilty of the grossest dereliction of duty in its handling of the whole military situation. I doubt whether in any administration of the past, Ottawa has ever known such an aggregation of governmental ineptitude as is represented by the King administration."[138]

134. Shields, "How Can Canada Wake Up Ottawa?" 3.

135. Shields, "Censor and the Editor," 11. In 1917 Shields was invited by the Union Government "to deliver a number of addresses in support of the Government and its war measures."

136. Ibid., 5.

137. Shields, "The Canadian Fuehrer Has Spoken!" *GW*, 27 February 1941, 2.

138. Shields, *Plebiscite Speech*, 21.

To the casual observer, the intensity of Shields's opposition to Prime Minister King in his handling of the war effort might be somewhat surprising. Shields's British background certainly would have influenced his loyalties in the present struggle but that alone could not account for his fanatical denunciations of seemingly every action taken by the King government. When King refused to impose conscription, Shields voiced his vigorous opposition. When King indicated that he was prepared to reverse his stand and announced a plebiscite on the question, Shields was even more outspoken and his condemnations reached a fevered pitch. The key to understanding Shields's opposition to King was not to be found in British patriotism, nor in partisan politics, but rather in his religious convictions. Shields was a militant Protestant, and he was very quick to trace his religious lineage back to the great heroes of the Protestant Reformation: "I have only to say that I stand in a grand and glorious succession with . . . John Huss, Wycliff, Knox, Calvin, Luther; with Ridley, Latimer, and numberless others whom the Papacy did to death, and many thousands of others whose blood was shed by the Inquisition." By Shields's estimate, King, like Hepburn, had become a tool of Roman Catholic machinations. In a reference to "Popery in Quebec and Roman Catholic supremacy in the Canadian House of Commons," Shields decried that "immutable Church which Premier King defends, and to whose will he is always subject."[139]

Anti-Catholic denunciations had always been part of Shields's repertoire, but with the passing years this anti-Catholicism became more and more virulent until it became an almost singular fixation. Some might be inclined to see in Shields an increasing paranoia somehow related to his advancing years. While many of the claims Shields made at the time might seem to a twenty-first-century audience somewhat bigoted and outlandish, it must be remembered that at the time fears of Catholic intentions for Canada were not unique to Shields.[140] As noted at the outset, Shields's own take on the matter was to observe that "the menace is more imminent, the gangsters are nearer to their prey; hence their description and identity meets with a more raucous response."[141]

139. Shields, "Challenging Answer," 4.

140. Shields had a ready audience in the Orange Order and there are various references to cooperation between Shields's Canadian Protestant League and the Orange lodges in the Shields literature.

141. Shields, "Challenging Answer," 4.

The gangsters Hepburn and King, Shields charged, were guilty of selling out Ontario and Canada to Rome.

Where Hepburn was charged with selling out on the Separate School issue, King was charged with selling out on the conscription issue. Shields's almost frantic expostulations with the King government related directly to the fact that, in Shields's mind, Roman Catholicism represented a Fifth Column in Canada, and King was blindly selling out to the enemy. For Shields, Roman Catholicism was the antithesis of everything democratic and the avowed enemy of Western liberties. As a religious system, Shields argued, Catholicism should be respected and allowed its liberties like everyone else. What Shields confronted was the threat of Roman Catholicism as a political system:

> But as all Christian history attests, and as the Roman Catholic Church, by its present profession and position must acknowledge, the Roman Catholic Church is not only a religious institution but is also a powerful international political organization. The Roman Catholic Church claims the right of temporal power. It claims that its Sovereign Pontiff, as it calls him, is superior to all the kings of earth, and, by implication at least, that any ruler holding office without his permission is a usurper.[142]

He saw Catholicism as a "malignant power that has ruined every state in which it has gained the ascendency [*sic*] and will ultimately ruin us unless we check its progress."[143] With suggestive imagery he described a parasitic aspect to Catholicism that he graphically likened to a horseleech:

> It fastens itself upon every state as a leech, and sucks its very life-blood. It infects the blood-stream of every political party, and, like a deadly bacillus, destroys the red corpuscular principles by and for which the party lives, and reduces it to an anaemic mass of potential corruption. Like a cancer, Roman Catholicism insinuates itself into every government, and wraps its parasitical and strangling tentacles about every governmental organ, converts it into a banqueting house for political buzzards, and makes it a stench in the nostrils of every lover of righteousness.[144]

142. Shields, "Hepburn's Alliance with Rum and Rome," 2.
143. Shields, "Menace of Present-Day Roman Catholicism," 5.
144. Shields, *Roman Catholic Horseleach*, 5.

Not only was this parasitic behavior directed towards government, Shields contended, but also toward commerce, religion, education, and every organ of public expression. Catholicism was an all-out subversion of individual liberties and rights, rights which Shields claimed were the by-product of the gospel:

> Anyone who really knows the gospel, who has really tasted of the liberty there is in Christ Jesus, must know that Romanism is anti-Christian, contrary not only to the gospel itself, but to all the by-products of the gospel. Our individualism and the free democratic way of life have grown out of the gospel. All that you and I enjoy as free British citizens, we enjoy, not because of our British blood of whatever variety, but because of the blood of Another [Christ].[145]

The fight against Catholicism, then, was the same fight that was going on in the war in which the world was presently engaged. It was a fight for liberty and freedom. In an address given as President of the Canadian Protestant League, Shields openly wondered if Canadians were "losing at home the freedom for which they are fighting abroad."[146]

For Shields, evidence of Roman Catholic influence was written all over the government's actions since the outset of the war, particularly in its resistance to conscription for overseas service. Quoting Premier Godbout after the "no-conscription for overseas service Act had been passed," Shields repeatedly referred to his remarkable assertion: "A little handful of French-Canadians led by M. Ernest Lapointe dictated its will to the country."[147] Shields's fundamental conviction was that political subservience to Quebec was at its heart a sellout to Catholicism. Shields felt that devout Roman Catholics necessarily faced a dilemma of divided loyalties: "The Roman Catholic Church in Canada is virtually a colony

145. Shields, "Canada's Invasion," 9.

146. Ibid.

147. Shields, "Challenging Answer," 12. Lapoint was the leading French Canadian in federal politics during the King period and served as Minister of Justice and King's Quebec lieutenant. Betcherman notes: "When Ernest Lapoint was on his death bed, Mackenzie King told him, 'But for you, I would never have been Prime Minister, nor would I have been able to hold the office, as I have held it through the years.' King was dependent on Quebec. He was elected time after time because Quebec as a bloc voted for him. Yet he understood neither the province nor its language. He left that to Ernest Lapoint, his minister of justice, 'as a kind of local governor, almost autonomous in his powers'" (Betcherman, *Ernest Lapointe*, ix).

of a foreign kingdom; and the devout Roman Catholic owes a primary duty of obedience to the Church as being an authority superior to that of any merely human government."[148] This was the same allegation he had made in the East Hastings by-election and which had aroused Hepburn's particular contempt.

Now Shields pointed to this issue of divided loyalties as the underlying factor in Quebec's resistance to conscription and its general lack of support for the war effort. Complicating matters for the devout Catholic, Shields argued, was the fact that the Vatican had achieved formal statehood under Mussolini and was ostensibly allied with the Axis cause.[149] Formally, the Vatican maintained neutrality, but Shields spent a great deal of time demonstrating the Vatican's support of Mussolini and the Axis powers. Foremost was the Vatican's recognition of the Petain government, a government now openly hostile to the Allies. Shields then was dumbfounded at the King government's decision to allow "French Minister Rene Ristelhueber, representing the Petain Government to remain in Ottawa as a diplomat accredited to the Canadian Government," even though the government he represented had "severed diplomatic relations with the Government of Great Britain."[150] The ramifications for Shields were profound:

> Britain has severed diplomatic relations with Petain, but Canada maintains those relations notwithstanding Petain handed over four hundred German aviators whom our men were largely instrumental in shooting down; and did his best to hand over the French fleet to Germany—and has been manifestly anti-British throughout. Yet . . . the representative of a Government that is no friend of Britain, is at Ottawa enjoying "diplomatic immunity," free to correspond with the Government at Vichy, and with the Pope, without let or hindrance. I say that ought not to be![151]

The matter for Shields was simple: the Roman Catholic Church in Canada was a Fifth column simply because "the Roman Catholic Church is just as much at war with the British Empire as Hitler or Mussolini."[152]

148. Shields, "Hepburn's Alliance with Rum and Rome," 2.
149. Shields, "Pope's Fifth Column," 4.
150. Shields, "An Amazing Decision," *GW*, 8 August 1940, 2.
151. Shields, "More about the Pope's Fifth Column," *GW*, 5 September 1940, 1.
152. Shields, "Challenging Answer," 27.

Shields's paranoid suspicion of a government sellout to Roman Catholicism kept him fixated on every new policy King introduced. The vigor with which Shields evaluated King's every action could have led some to believe that Shields somehow imagined himself to be the leader of the opposition. Throughout the period of the war, nearly every edition of his weekly magazine the *Gospel Witness* contained a "war sermon" that attempted to assess the progress of the war and particularly Canada's role in it.

A notable example of Shields's critique of government policy came in reaction to the government's presentation of the Rowell-Sirois Report.[153] "I spent weeks of study day and night on the Sirois Report," claimed Shields. The product of that grueling work was an address entitled, "Shall the Dominion of Canada Be Mortgaged for the Church of Rome? The Religious Aspects of the Sirois Report as Symptomatic of Dangerous Trends in Canadian Life." Shields boasted that his own knowledge of the report surpassed that of at least one of the Premiers who had voted against it: "When I was at the coast last summer I found that the Premier of British Columbia had frankly admitted that he did not know what was in it. I met Premier Aberhart, of Alberta, and talked with him. He said he voted against it. He did not say he had not read it, but I fear he had not." Shields's simple assessment of the report was, "it is the most wicked document that ever was produced for the economic enslavement of free men. It proposes to mortgage the entire Dominion of Canada in the interests of the Roman Catholic Church."[154] Shields's evaluation seemed to turn every paragraph inside out to consider every possible advantage this new constitutional arrangement would give to the Roman Catholic Church in Quebec. "The indisputable fact is that the Roman Catholic Church, like a malignant parasite, has fastened itself upon the body of Quebec and is draining it of the last drop of its blood, reducing it to something little better than an emaciated political skeleton; and the Report appeals to the other eight Provincial members of

153. "The Rowell-Sirois Commission, appointed to examine the financial structure of Canadian Federalism, had recommended sweeping changes in the taxing relation of Ottawa and the provincial administrations. In return for assuming provincial debts and responsibility for unemployment relief, the federal Government would acquire sole taxing authority in the personal income, corporation, and inheritance fields." (McKenty, *Mitch Hepburn*, 225).

154. Shields, "Challenging Answer," 26.

the Dominion family to donate a blood transfusion, and generous food supplies, to maintain this parasite still further."[155]

Shields, like his nemesis Premier Hepburn, castigated King for introducing a debate on constitutional change in the middle of war. The consequences he felt could be nothing but destructive to the cause of Canadian unity. The irony of this rebuke was that Shields seemed impervious to the charges that he himself was causing deep rents in the fabric of Canadian unity. He was well aware that he was stirring up a storm of controversy in Quebec and boasted, "Now, of course, there is scarcely a paper in the Province of Quebec, either in the English or French language, that is not discussing it, [the religious aspect of the Sirois Report] and blaming me for raising the issue."[156] His excuse for violating his own call for national unity was that "It is necessary . . . that we should be on our guard always lest in seeking the removal of one evil we throw wide the door to another."[157] Clearly, the threat of Catholic subversion trumped concerns about national unity. Defending himself against charges of stirring up religious controversies, Shields explained to one Member of Parliament why his support of King had been removed and the price that could not be paid for Canadian unity:

> I believed at that time that Mr. King could do more to unite the people of Canada in a great war effort than could Dr. Manion, and I therefore supported him. I had no idea at the time of the price Mr. King intended to pay for this so-called "unity." In common with many thousands of others who voted for the King regime in the last election, I have been sadly disillusioned. My eyes have been opened, and I have learned, as I shall proceed to show, that such unity as now obtains, has been effected only by complete submission to Quebec—and to Quebec as controlled by the Roman Catholic Hierarchy.[158]

For himself and his followers, Shields professed that they would never surrender to Catholicism but would fight it to their dying breath:

> Our only reason for speaking thus to you is found in the reason for the existence of this church. It is because we believe something, and because those things we believe are so precious to

155. Shields, "Shall the Dominion of Canada be Mortgaged," 62.
156. Shields, "Abiding Menace," 8.
157. Shields, "Pope's Fifth Column," 3.
158. Shields, "Open Letter to McDonald," 2.

us, we must defend them. I believe there are hundreds of people here to-night who would rather die than surrender to Popery. It is the testimony of all history, and of recent history, that the insidious approach of these enemies of our glorious gospel need to be watched. The proper time to put out a fire is when it begins.[159]

In a matter of this gravity, then, even civil war was not out of the question for Shields. While Canada could not afford to allow itself to be dictated to by Quebec, neither could it allow Quebec to secede. Alluding to the American experience, he noted: "The Civil war was not fought primarily to liberate the slaves, but for the preservation of the Union; and if I were Prime Minister of Canada, I would preserve the unity of this Dominion at all costs, no matter what Quebec might say."[160]

For those who dared to disagree with him or to challenge his right to address these issues he reserved great contempt:

> There are not a few who would appear very superior, saying, "What does Dr. Shields know . . . about such a matter as that?" I know a little—more than the Roman Catholic politicians like me to know. Sometimes people say I speak strongly. I do not know whether you think I do, or not, but if you knew how much I restrain, you would admire my moderation. And when these little intellectual pygmies some of them call themselves preachers affect a superior air—to me they are about as dignified and impressive as "President Andrew H. Brown of the Fresh Air Taxi Company." "Intellectual?" "Intelligensia?" Ah me! I could eat a dozen of them for breakfast and not know I had eaten.[161]

In the best of times Dr. Shields'S fulminations could have been expected to provoke strong reaction. This, however, was a period in which Canada and its government were embroiled in a world war. It is not surprising then that Shields's militant diatribes against Catholicism came to the attention of governing authorities and even evoked serious questions of censorship.

The first indication of official reaction came from the National Press Censor, W. Eggleston, complaining about the 5 December 1940 issue of the *Gospel Witness*. This issue featured two inflammatory ar-

---

159. Shields, "The Protestant Samson and the Papal Delilah," *GW*, 16 January 1941, 14.

160. Shields, "Challenging Answer," 28.

161. Shields, "Abiding Menace," 9.

ticles. The first, "A Reply to Father Lanphier's Broadcast in Criticism of Our Exposure of the Pope's Fifth Column," was a defensive reaction to Lanphier's comment: "Those who attempt to set religion against religion and Catholic against Protestant by talking about the Pope's fifth column are beneath contempt."[162] In this article Shields added even more allegations of fifth column activity, claiming that every papal representative by virtue of "diplomatic immunity" was in effect spying for the enemy. He also charged the Quebec hierarchy with treason: "Call me what you will, the Hierarchy of Quebec is not loyal. It is anti-British, and Quebec is made disloyal by the Roman Hierarchy that rules her."[163] A second article was entitled, "Sundry Quotations on the Papacy and the War." It brought together quotations from many sources attempting to demonstrate "the machinations of the Pope's Fifth Column in Canada and elsewhere."[164]

Eggleston expressed serious concerns about Shields's comments, citing the "damaging effect which certain passages in your sermon as reported here may have on Canada's war effort." In a seemingly reasonable request Eggleston asked Shields to exercise restraint:

> We have every confidence in your own loyalty and zeal for victory and we feel sure that by drawing to your attention the damage which may be unwittingly done among certain important sections of the Canadian public by expressing strong views on controversial subjects in these difficult times, we shall have your wholehearted co-operation. It has been our determined policy since the outbreak of war as Press Censors to extend and maintain the freedom of the press to the greatest possible extent, consistent with the maintenance of Canadian war morale, and we do not feel that it is unreasonable to ask our public to refrain from strong expressions, which may be perfectly legitimate in peacetime but which may, on the other hand, do great damage in wartime if allowed to develop unchecked.[165]

Shields was never one to take criticism sitting down, and a perceived rebuke from an authority such as this and the demand for restraint had much the same effect as waving a red flag in front of an

162. Shields, "A Reply to Father Lanphier's Broadcast," *GW*, 5 December 1940, 6.

163. Ibid., 8.

164. Shields, "Sundry Quotations on the Papacy and the War," *GW*, 5 December 1940, 11.

165. Shields, "Censor and the Editor," 10.

enraged bull. Shields unhesitating response comprised five pages of the 2 January 1941 edition of the *Gospel Witness*, where he published the full correspondence. With a condescending air, Shields cited his credentials for his public discussion of these national issues. Noting his thirty-one year pastorate of Jarvis Street Baptist Church, he wryly commented that he might "therefore be presumed to know something of the responsibilities of public speech." Concerning his support of the war effort, he noted the two hundred and ninety men he had sent from his own church in the previous war "and not a conscript among them." As to understanding the conscription question he boasted, "In the General Election of nineteen hundred and seventeen I accepted the invitation of the Union Government Committee to deliver a number of addresses in support of the Government and its war measures."[166] His loyalty to the British cause, he bragged, was so well known that he had been granted significant privileges by the British government:

> Later, I suppose as an indirect recognition of my unreserved support of the British cause, I was invited by the British Ministry of Information to see Britain's war effort. I was the guest of the Ministry, off and on, over a period of four months. During that time, under the auspices of the Ministry, I visited Ireland, and was afforded opportunity of discussing the Irish question with leaders in the North, in Dublin, in Cork, and in London. These included John Dillon, the leader of the Irish Nationalist Party; the acting head of the Sinn Feiners, who was a Roman Catholic priest—De Valera was then in jail; the commanders of the forces in Dublin and in Cork; the Archbishops of Ireland; the principal leaders in Ulster; and later I had the privilege and honour of being Lord Carson's guest at dinner in London, spending a whole evening discussing the Irish problem—especially in relation to the Papacy.[167]

Whether the Censorship committee was cowed by their being called "intellectual pygmies," or whether they quickly recognized that efforts to silence Shields were going to have the opposite affect and only served to add fuel to the fire, the committee replied in a somewhat subdued fashion: "We have been extremely interested in learning your views and are glad to have these on record. May we thank you for so carefully and

---

166. Shields, "The Editor's Reply," *GW*, 2 January 1941, 11.
167. Ibid.

comprehensively reviewing your stand."[168] Shields was quick to publish what he called "the censor's very courteous, and shall we say exonerating? Reply!"[169]

Open condemnation on the floor of parliament finally gave the matter the national attention that Shields felt it deserved. Twice in two years, the Prime Minister expressed his personal contempt for Shields's behavior. On 4 March 1941, Mr. W. R. McDonald (Pontiac) rose to speak to a resolution concerning the suppression of newspapers and pamphlets subversive to Canada's war effort. In that context he then proceeded to read excerpts from a number of Shields's publications which condemned Catholicism: "Speaking in this house as a humble member of that church," asserted McDonald, "and, I believe, speaking in the names of four million Roman Catholics throughout this country, I protest with all the vigour of my manhood against the publication and circulation of such material." McDonald concluded his remarks with an appeal to national unity:

> Could my words reach the ears of the reverend gentleman whom I have been discussing this afternoon I would respectfully submit to him that in the interests of peace and harmony in our country, and for the sake of the cause which he claims to have at heart, he should refrain from the publication of these articles. In the event of his refusal to do so, I would suggest that the Minister of Justice, who is charged with the enforcement of the defense of Canada regulations, that *The Gospel Witness* be suppressed for the period of the war, on the ground that the articles published therein are subversive of national unity.[170]

Shields's response was to publish the Hansard report of the debate and "An Open Letter to Mr. W. R. McDonald, M. P., Pontiac." Copies of the issue were sent to all the Members of Parliament. A copy was also sent to Mr. A. Belanger, who was a member of the provincial legislature for Prescott, because of similar discussion in the Ontario Legislature. Shields included a note to the latter asking him "please to understand that it is sent to him with the Editor's compliments, and the suggestion that he read our open letter to Mr. W. R. McDonald, M. P., Pontiac, as a

168. "The Censor's Reply," *GW*, 16 January 1941, 16.

169. Shields, "Wake Up Protestants!" *GW*, 23 January 1941, 5.

170. Shields, "The Gospel Witness is Discussed in Parliament," *GW*, 13 March 1941, 1.

reply to himself as well as to Mr. McDonald."[171] Shields's letter in manner and content were much the same as that addressed to the National press censor.

A more serious challenge arose in 1943, when Prime Minister King himself entered into a parliamentary discussion of Shields. Responding to an amendment made by Mr. J. S. Roy castigating Shields and calling for suppression of "anti-Catholic propaganda,"[172] Prime Minister Mackenzie King commented: "Speaking here as a member of a Protestant church, I wish to say that I have utter contempt for Dr. Shields and his unworthy utterances."[173] The *Globe and Mail* was undoubtedly right in its assessment of the event:

> It is astonishing that Parliament would spend time debating Rev. Dr. Shields' crusade against the Roman Catholic Church and make it an issue for a vote. This is the greatest publicity the Toronto pastor and his Protestant League have ever had, and the Parliamentarians who worked themselves into a heat over the subject can be assured it will be put to full use, Dr. Shields being Dr. Shields. Moreover, Mr. King is likely to be reminded often and vigorously that it was the Prime Minister and party Leader, and not a private citizen, who poured out contempt for the clergyman and all his utterances. Such is the penalty for mixing religion with politics.[174]

King noted in the course of the two hour debate the folly of making a martyr of Shields by prosecuting him. He asked the house what might have been the consequence if "the government at Ottawa, which had a large following from the province of Quebec, at the instance of its following from Quebec province, through its new Minister of Justice from Quebec province had started a prosecution on religious matters in the province of Ontario?" He concluded, "If you want to start a religious controversy in this country that it may be impossible to control, just begin having matters of the kind affecting race and religion dealt with as between one province and another." King's advice concerning men of Shields's kind was "to ignore them and treat them with contempt." He also noted that "laws of libel and slander exist and to these laws re-

---

171. Shields, "In the Ontario Legislature," *GW*, 13 March 1941, 8.

172. *Dominion of Canada Official Report of Debates*, Vol. 1, 1943, 656.

173. Ibid., 664.

174. "Religion in Parliament," *The Globe and Mail*, 25 February 1943, 6.

course for address may be had by churches as well as other institutions and by individuals."[175]

Dr. Shields "being Dr. Shields," did indeed make the most of the opportunity that had been afforded him. On 25 February 1943, Shields discharged his first salvo in an editorial entitled, "Reply to Premier King and Other Parliamentary Critics," a title emblazoned in large bold and capitalized print. Herein he announced his intent to speak to the issue the following Sunday evening and to publish a special issue of the *Gospel Witness* and to place a copy of it "in the hands of every member of Parliament, of every member of all the Legislatures of the country, of the Prime Minister himself—and of thousands of others."[176] Making good on his promise, the following issue of the *Gospel Witness* ran to forty-eight pages, three times its normal length. If the Prime Minister was going to treat him with contempt, Dr. Shields was determined to respond in kind. Referring back to King's broadcasting of his decision to read the lesson in St. Andrew's Presbyterian Church at the time of the celebration of the Roman Catholic Mass on Parliament Hill, Shields brought his own charges of contempt:[177] "He has honored me by saying that he has only 'a supreme contempt for Mr. Shields and all his utterances.' I would not say that of the Prime Minister because he is Prime Minister; but I must say that in this particular instance, in using the Word of God, the house of God, and the day of God, to play party politics, the Prime Minister acted contemptibly!"[178]

In the manner of a modern day Luther, Shields resolved to "stand." Despite the concerns raised about the hurtful character of his diatribes against Catholicism, Shields appealed to his rights: "I stand on my rights as a British citizen, and contend that it is an element in the principle of religious freedom that I have a right to believe in and to proclaim Jesus Christ as Lord, and an equal right to denounce the blasphemous presumptions of the Papacy as representative of that 'continuous person,' the Antichrist." With an obvious allusion to Luther's famous "stand" at

175. *Dominion of Canada Official Report of Debates*, Vol. 1, 1943, 664.

176. Shields, "Reply to Premier King and other Parliamentary Critics," *GW*, 25 February 1943, 2.

177. The celebration of the Catholic Mass on Parliament Hill in September of 1941 caused a storm of protest and was the occasion of the founding of Shields's Canadian Protestant League.

178. Shields, "Challenging Answer," 10.

the Diet of Worms Shields declared: "For that I stand, and shall continue to stand; and I challenge the Premier of Canada, his minister of Justice, and the Attorney-General of the Province of Ontario, to dare to try to stop me."[179] With defiance matched only by his arrogance, Shields challenged the Prime Minister to public debate in any forum suitable: "I do not count it a display of any particular courage, nor even an example of audacity, to say that I will, singlehanded, take them all on at once—with Mr. Hepburn thrown in." His frustration at their lack of response was also evident:

> But unless and until I obtain some such consent to public debate from the bachelor hermit of Ottawa, I must waste my polemical sweetness on the desert air of this despised conventicle, or dictate my "contemptible" utterances to the pages of *The Gospel Witness*. In this one-sided gladiatorial contest, in the absence of the inspiring presence of my opponent, the Right Honourable, the Prime Minister of Canada, I cannot be expected to reach the maximum of my logical assault.[180]

In a second expression of contempt for King, Shields charged the Prime Minister with behavior violating the laws of the land: "The Premier then stooped, I think I may properly say, to a piece of 'contemptible' conduct. In his privileged position in Parliament Mr. King basely insinuated that I had committed some offence which might render me liable to prosecution under the Criminal Code. If that does not involve defamation of character I am greatly mistaken."[181] At the same time, Shields dared King and the Attorney-General of Ontario to press charges: "If they want to bring this matter of my exposure of the Roman Catholic church into court, I shall be well content. I will promise to defend myself in open court. I shall have the privilege of calling witnesses, and of cross-examining witnesses that are put in the box against me."[182] Wisely, no action was ever taken. Despite Shields's boast that he would make himself hard to ignore, the best response was to give him no added forum that could further publicize his claims.

Throughout the duration of the war, Shields continued to snipe at King. However, one last controversy is worthy of note for its impact

179. Ibid., 6.
180. Ibid.
181. Ibid., 30.
182. Ibid., 33.

upon the King government. In 1944 a second conscription crisis rocked the King Government. J. L. Ralston, the Minister of National Defense, after a visit to the war front, became convinced that the voluntary system of recruitment could no longer meet the need for reserves, particularly for the infantry divisions. Several other cabinet ministers soon supported Ralston in his demand for conscription, and King faced the specter of several resignations that would have left the Liberal government in shambles. King's attitude throughout the war had been that to invoke conscription would be to destroy Canada's unity and perhaps even incur civil war. By every means then he fought to avoid conscription. With Ralston's resignation imminent, King asked General McNaughton to replace Ralston as the Minister of National Defense. Having become suspicious of a conspiracy within his own cabinet, on 1 November 1944 King acted preemptively and demanded Ralson's resignation.[183] It was a risky move and could have resulted in the resignations of all the conscriptionist members. However, McNaughton had made the claim that he could find the necessary recruits without resorting to conscription and the decision was made to give him time to do so.

From the outset McNaughton faced setbacks. In his first public speeches he was jeered at and heckled. English Canada appeared to be becoming more and more restive under the government's continued subservience to Quebec. The press was particularly vocal in its demands for conscription. Furthermore, McNaughton's hope of raising volunteers among the NRMA men proved to be fruitless.[184] Three weeks later it had become painfully evident that Ralston was right and King was forced finally to introduce conscription for service overseas. It was only by very skillful management of his cabinet and a three hour speech to Parliament that King was able to survive a vote of confidence on the issue. Remarkably, nineteen French-speaking members of parliament voted with King.[185] However, the danger was not yet over, and King

183. Granatstein, *Canada's War*, 356.

184. NRMA men were those drafted for home defense in accordance with the National Resources Mobilization Act of 21 June 1940. Under the terms of this Act, the draft was limited to purposes of home defense and was not for "overseas service." NRMA men were known disparagingly as Zombies. The Act was a compromise between national demands for the draft and Quebec resistance to the draft. By November of 1944 approximately 40 percent of the NRMA men were French Canadian. For a full discussion see Granatstein, *Canada's War*, 201–48, 333–81.

185. Ibid., 373.

feared the consequences of the deep divisions within his party over the issue. As illustrated by a note in his diary, his hopes for healing rested on General McNaughton and the by-election in Grey North that would give McNaughton a seat in parliament:

> On top of all, there is the division that has grown out of Ralston's action in precipitating what was a real crisis in the party and might have split it for good. Altogether the whole business is little short of a tragedy for I fear it may mean a situation at the end of the campaign where no party will have a majority over all and where we may have a very floundering condition at a time when the most difficult of all the problems will arise. The one hope on the horizon is McNaughton. If he wins North Grey, it will galvanize life into the whole party. He has the personality which would help in binding the party together.[186]

However, once again Shields proved to be an effective thorn in King's side. Upon hearing of Ralston's "forced resignation" Shields was again on the warpath. With the announcement of his topic for Sunday evening 5 November 1944, the church was unusually packed. According to reports, Jarvis Street's auditorium "was crowded in every part, with people sitting down the aisles in the gallery, down the gallery steps to the platform, on the Communion platform, and a fair number of chairs . . . put in where . . . safe to put them."[187] The title of the address was posed in the form of a question: "Will 8 Provinces Consent to Bear Quebec's Blood-Guiltiness?" His address evaluated recruiting records, health standards, the Zombie army, and the Zombie 'King'. He attempted to demonstrate that present recruiting methods significantly favored Quebec's non-participation, and suggested that government policy was dictated by fear of open revolt in Quebec. The record of the address was published in the following week's *Gospel Witness*, of which an extra 13,000 issues were printed and distributed. Furthermore, the *Gospel Witness* of that date outlined plans for a preaching tour across Canada for the purpose of "rousing public sentiment in such a way as to bring increased pressure to bear upon the Government, to pass the Order-in-Council which would make nearly eighty thousand trained men immediately available for reinforcements." This tour was to take in all nine provinces and thirty six cities.[188]

---

186. Pickersgill and Forster, *Mackenzie King Record*, 2:289.

187. "Last Sunday Evening in Jarvis Street," *GW*, 9 November 1944, 2.

188. "Dr. Shields Projected Tour," *GW*, 9 November 1944, 8.

Shields also opened up an attack on General McNaughton. Dismissing the media hype for McNaughton's war service, Shields penned an editorial entitled "General McNaughton Surrenders Unconditionally to Quebec!" His immediate observation was that of all the "idiotic drivel" he had heard from politicians, "not one has surpassed General McNaughton." Shields observed, "If he had no more sense as a soldier than he has manifested as a politician within less than a week of his appointment, it is an unspeakable mercy to the Canadian army that circumstances forced his resignation as their commander."[189] In attempting to assess McNaughton's apparent sellout to Quebec, he of course had to examine the Roman Catholic connection. Having heard rumors that McNaughton had converted to Catholicism, Shields wired McNaughton asking for clarification:

> As a matter of great public interest, respectfully request advice whether I am correct in having reported you as identified with Anglican church (stop) My statement as above is disputed by many who insist that you are now a member of the Roman Catholic Church (stop) Should greatly appreciate immediate telegraphic reply

As the case soon proved, McNaughton unwisely replied, and with too much information: "Your telegram eleventh November (stop) I am and have always been Anglican (stop) My wife is and has always been a member of the Roman Catholic Church." Shields was courteous in reply, but he immediately went to the presses with the charge that McNaughton's wife was a Roman Catholic. Shields commented that "the information given by the General on that matter was wholly unsought, though very significant." It was significant because of Catholic Church policies relative to accepting mixed marriages and the arrangements the non-Catholic partner had to make. His rather tenuous conclusion was "it is neither unfair nor unkind to assume that the Roman Catholic Hierarchy well knows how to register its will effectively in the Department of Defense."[190]

Prime Minister King's first awareness of the impending storm was recorded in his diary upon reading the day's news account of Shields's address to the Canadian Protestant League in Owen Sound, 5 January

189. Shields, "General McNaughton Surrenders Unconditionally to Quebec!" *GW*, 9 November 1944, 6.

190. Shields, "Premier King Calls Parliament Protestants—Beware," *GW*, 23 November 1944, 3.

1945. King noted, "I felt incensed when I read, in this morning's paper, the account of an address by Shields at Owen Sound, raising, in the most crude and cruel fashion a religious cry." It was clear from King's comments on the matter that he held Shields responsible for setting the tone of the election and blamed him for the manner in which the Tories subsequently waged the campaign. Upon reading of Shields's comments, King commented, "It made me definitely determined to see that there will be a dissolution of Parliament before the election in North Gray [sic] takes place." Though King ultimately relented on this determination and held the by-election, he was appalled at the Tory strategies: "The whole attitude of the Tories," he reflected, "is the most unpatriotic thing I have known in my experience in public life, encouraging class hatred, race hatred, religious hatred—everything that can make for intolerance and this while we are in the midst of war and men are sacrificing their lives to save the freedom of the world. I must get out and speak to the Canadian People fearlessly on the significance of all this."[191]

Assessment of the whole situation led King to believe that a McNaughton victory was almost a foregone conclusion. Placing his hopes on a McNaughton win, King determined to go ahead with the election. However, as the 5 February 1945 election date neared, King began to express fears concerning the effects that Shields's propaganda would have: "So far as the Tories go, I have been fearful of the Orange complexion of the constituency and the use that may be made of the Orange crusade against the French and the Catholics. The fact that Mrs. McNaughton is a Catholic would be used for all it was worth among Orangemen."[192] King's fears proved to be prophetic, and McNaughton went down to defeat to the Conservative candidate.[193] Shields's attitude in the days leading up to the election was well-expressed in his delight at the report of a Quebec newspaper: "*Le Devoir* of Montreal" he noted, "prints the following note in a front page feature column. 'The intervention of pasteur Shields in the campaign in North Grey must have put General McNaughton out of countenance. No doubt he would have preferred to measure himself against Field Marshall von Rundstedt on the battlefields of the Low Countries.'"[194]

191. Library and Archives of Canada, "Diaries of Mackenzie King," entry for 5 January 1945.

192. Pickersgill and Forster, *Mackenzie King Record*, 2:290.

193. Ibid., 292.

194. "General Shields vs. General McNaughton," *GW*, 18 January 1945, 5.

CONCLUSION

Nearly three-quarters of a century later it is difficult to know how to assess Shields. T. T. Shields was the product of two world wars, and his attitudes were shared by great numbers who lived through those times. Shields himself often expressed confidence that history would vindicate him. There is little doubt that Shields was right about a number of the events that he reported. His work ethic was impressive indeed, and his research into matters that concerned him made him a dangerous foe. Few if any ever tried to dispute with him simply on the basis of facts. Even fewer could hope to best him in the art of invective. In the field of moral reform many remembered another time and saw in Shields a champion of a more righteous society. As a critic of governmental subservience to Quebec, Shields exploited resentment from broad segments of the Canadian public and found wide support for his assertions that Canada's total war effort was being compromised. With a conscription question that threatened even to split King's own cabinet, Shields had stumbled upon an emotional issue that was easy to assail. Undoubtedly, religious and ethnic factors lay behind Quebec's resistance to aspects of Canada's war effort. However, aggravating those differences with suggestions of a papal plot rightly merited the condemnation of the governing authorities. Perhaps the greatest challenge Prime Minister King faced was the very thorny issue of Canadian unity. In his expressions of contempt for Shields, Prime Minister King was a model of self restraint. Shields's determination to find Catholic machination behind every action taken by the governments of Premier Hepburn or Prime Minister King spoke of a deep-seated paranoia born of his own antagonism towards the papacy, a paranoia akin to what would be seen later in the McCarthy anti-communist purge. Though an anachronism, perhaps the best way to describe Shields's behavior could be to call it an "anti-Catholic McCarthyism." Where Roman Catholic leaders felt they were fighting a losing battle to protect their rights and their culture, Shields saw a deliberate attempt to subvert or subordinate all Canadian rights to ultramontane rule.

Not only has history failed to vindicate Shields's interpretation of events, but also circumstances have demonstrated clearly that Shields's methods were counter-productive. Shields may have armed himself with many facts and figures, but in the end he always resorted to personalities. With an overinflated view of his own abilities, he belittled his opponents, often judging and imputing motives. Comments about

Hepburn, King, and McNaughton were unkind, disrespectful, and insensitive. Furthermore, his judgments were too often untrue, because he was completely oblivious to the very real and complex political pressures that these men faced. He may have had a textbook understanding of democratic forms, but in practice, his attitude to dealing with political matters was simplistic, unrealistic, and autocratic. He was quick to condemn governmental action as dictatorial, but his own recommendations belied his democratic pretensions. It is surely significant that, though his tirades often came to the attention of governing authorities, no suggestion or recommendation coming from his soap-box ever merited consideration or produced anything other than open contempt and settled opposition.

Biblical imagery uses the preservative and savoring effects of salt as the defining characteristic of the Christian's role in society.[195] Few would suggest that Shields did not pursue the goal of being salt with unusual vigor. As a pastor and evangelist, Shields saw years of unparalleled success. As a moral reformer his record was far more questionable. He fought to preserve the moral hegemony evangelicalism once enjoyed in the broader social context. He fought valiantly against the rising tide of secularism. However, while he maintained a very outspoken voice in Ontario society, Shields's desperate fight to shape a moral consensus in the province was doomed by the lack of restraint in the manner of his struggle. Shields more commonly resembled salt rubbed in a wound than that salt that flavors the meat. To the end of his life, Shields made "good copy." However, while his outbursts were entertaining and provocative, his efforts in the social context were counterproductive. Secularization was advanced not hindered. As Charles Adler recently observed, "Too much sanctimony in the market place of ideas, renders a person and/or institution less than relevant."[196]

195. Matt 5:13.

196. Charles Adler, "Jesus Had a Human Face Too," Comment, *Toronto Sun*, 24 May 2006, 21.

BIBLIOGRAPHY

Anglin, Gerald. "The Battling Baptist." *Maclean's Magazine*, 15 June 1949.

Betcherman, Lita-Rose. *Ernest Lapointe: Mackenzie King's Quebec Lieutenant*. Toronto: University of Toronto Press, 2002.

Campbell, Lyndsay. "A Slub in the Cloth: The St. Clair Affair and the Discourse of Moral Reform in Toronto, 1912–1913." Paper presented at the 1996 Annual Meeting of the Canadian Law and Society Association, Brock University, St. Catharines, Ontario, June 1996.

Carder, W. Gordon "Controversy in the Baptist Convention of Ontario and Quebec, 1908–1928." *Foundations* 16 (1973) 355–76.

Cole, Stewart G. *The History of Fundamentalism*. New York: Harper & Row, 1931; reprint, Hamden, CT: Archon Books, 1963.

Dominion of Canada Official Report of Debates in the House of Commons; Fourth Session—Nineteenth Parliament. Vol. 1, 1943.

Dozois, John D. E. "Dr. Thomas Todhunter Shields (1873–1955) in the Stream of Fundamentalism." BD thesis, McMaster University Divinity School, 1963.

Elliot, David. "Three Faces of Baptist Fundamentalism in Canada: Aberhart, Maxwell and Shields." Unpublished paper presented at the Baptist Heritage Conference in Edmonton, Alberta on 21 May 1990.

Ellis, Walter Edmund Warren. "Social and Religious Factors in the Fundamentalist-Modernist Schisms among Baptists in North America, 1895–1934." PhD thesis, University of Pittsburgh, 1974.

Furniss, Norman. *The Fundamentalist Controversy, 1918–1931*. New Haven: Yale University Press, 1954.

The Globe, 1912–1934.

The Globe and Mail, 1936.

Goldenberg, Susan. *Snatched! The Peculiar Kidnapping of Beer Tycoon John Labatt*. Toronto: Dundurn Group, 2004.

The Gospel Witness, 1940.

Granatstein, J. L. *Canada's War: The Politics of the Mackenzie King Government, 1939–1945*. Toronto: Oxford University Press, 1975.

Hostettler, John. *Sir Edward Carson: A Dream Too Far*. Chichester: Barry Rose Law, 1997.

Hyde, H. Montgomery. *Carson: The Life of Sir Edward Carson, Lord Carson of Duncairn*. London: William Heinemann, 1953.

Library and Archives Canada "The Diaries of William Lyon Mackenzie King." 5 January 1945. Online: http://www.collectionscanada.gc.ca/databases/king/001059-119.02-e.php?&page_id_nb=20&PHPSESSID=jh7dn6d8mgh73fmc26oagf9td1.

McKenty, Neil. *Mitch Hepburn*. Toronto: McClelland & Stewart, 1967.

———. "Mitchell F. Hepburn and the Ontario Election of 1934." *Canadian Historical Review* 45, no. 4 (1964) 293–313.

Parent, Mark. "The Christology of T. T. Shields: The Irony of Fundamentalism." PhD dissertation, McGill University, 1991.

Pickersgill, J. W., and Forster, D. F. *The Mackenzie King Record*. Vol. 2. *1944–1945*. Toronto: University of Toronto Press, 1968.

Pinnock, Clark H. "The Modernist Impulse at McMaster University, 1887–1927." In *Baptists in Canada: Search for Identity amidst Diversity*, edited by Jarold K. Zeman, 193–207. Burlington: Welch, 1980.

Rawlyk, George A. *Champions of the Truth: Fundamentalism, Modernism and the Maritime Baptists.* Montreal: McGill-Queen's University Press, 1990.

Saywell, John T. *'Just Call Me Mitch': The Life of Mitchell Hepburn.* Toronto: University of Toronto Press, 1991.

Shields, T. T. "Canada's Invasion by Roman Catholic Amalekites." In *Canadians Losing at Home the Freedom for Which They Are Fighting Abroad*, 3–28. Toronto: The Gospel Witness, 1943.

———. "A Challenging Answer to Premier King and Other Parliamentary Critics." In *Three Addresses*, 3–34. Toronto: The Canadian Protestant League, 1943.

———. "England in Wartime." In Addresses, JBCA, Toronto.

———. *The Hepburn Government's Betrayal of Its Public Trust by Diverting Public School Revenue to the Support of Roman Catholic Separate Schools.* Toronto: The Gospel Witness, 1936.

———. Letter to the Deacons of Jarvis Street Baptist Church, 2 November 1918. Box 1910 to 1928, in Shields's Correspondence, JBCA, Toronto.

———. *The Plot That Failed.* Toronto: The Gospel Witness, 1937.

———. *Premier King's Plebiscite Speech in Commons Analyzed.* Toronto: The Gospel Witness, 1942.

———. *The Roman Catholic Horseleach.* Toronto: The Gospel Witness, 1936.

———. "Shall the Dominion of Canada be Mortgaged for the Church of Rome?" In *Three Addresses*, 35–62. Toronto: The Gospel Witness, 1943.

Slade, H. C. "Forward," in Tarr, *Shields of Canada*, 3.

Stackhouse, John G. Jr. *Canadian Evangelicalism in the Twentieth Century.* Toronto: University of Toronto Press, 1993.

———. "Proclaiming the Word: Canadian Evangelicalism since World War One." PhD thesis University of Chicago, 1987.

———. "Thomas Todhunter Shields." In Charles H. Lippy, ed. *Twentieth-Century Shapers of American Popular Religion*, edited by Charles H. Lippy, 393–402. Westport, CT: Greenwood, 1989.

Tarr, Leslie K. *Shields of Canada.* Grand Rapids: Baker, 1967.

The Toronto Telegram, 1934.

Wilson, Paul. "Baptists and Business: Central Canadian Baptists and the Secularization of the Businessmen at Toronto's Jarvis Street Baptist Church, 1848–1921." PhD thesis, University of Western Ontario, 1996.

———. "Caring for Their Community: The Philanthropic and Moral Reform Efforts of Toronto's Baptists, 1834–1918." Paper presented at the 2008 Annual Meeting of the Canadian Baptist Historical Society, Jarvis Street Baptist Church, Toronto, 1 March 2008.

Wilfred Currier Keirstead
in his University of New Brunswick professorial robe
(From the UNB Class Composites Encaenia Group, 1920.
Image courtesy of Archives & Special Collections,
Harriet Irving Library, University of New Brunswick)

3

The Formation of a Public Intellectual

Wilfred Currier Keirstead, Christian Personalism, and Modernity [1]

DANIEL C. GOODWIN

DESPITE ALL THAT HISTORIANS have written about the process of secularization in Canada, surprisingly little focus has been given to the changing relationship between the sacred and secular in the public sphere.[2] This void is curious given the fact that the benchmarks of a secularizing nation are often identified with decline in religious adherence, the compartmentalization or differentiation of religious organizations and thought, and the privatization of religion and its accompanying removal from public life and discourse. However, those historians who argue for an essentially secularized Canada by the 1920s have had a tendency to see the liberalism of the modern world as fundamentally incompatible with transcendence in general and Christianity in particular.[3] In response to these historians, Gauvreau and Hubert have argued that this view is far more a reflection of the historians' meta-narratives than of actual historical reality.[4] José Casanova has written in his highly

1. The biographical material in this chapter was first published as Goodwin, "Origins and Development," and is used by permission.

2. The exception to this generalization is the ground-breaking work, Van Die, ed., *Religion and Public Life*.

3. Some examples include: Cook, *The Regenerators*; Shore, *Social Redemption*; Ferguson, *Remaking Liberalism*.

4. Gauvreau and Hubert, *Churches and Social Order*, 3–45.

influential *Public Religion in the Modern World* that "the assumption that religion [in the West] will tend to disappear with progressive modernization . . . [is] a notion which has proven patently false as a general empirical proposition."[5] In fact, Casanova maintains that "forms of modern public religion . . . may be both viable and desirable from a modern normative perspective."[6]

This chapter will examine the origin and nature of W. C. Keirstead's popular and academic discourse during the first four decades of the twentieth century.[7] It will be shown that this high profile public intellectual from the Maritime Baptist tradition spoke to a number of issues while drawing upon a Christian perspective. This biographical study allows for a close analysis of Keirstead's worldview development and its expression in the public sphere. While this study does not suggest that just any Christian perspective would have been accepted in the Maritime marketplace of ideas, it does contend that Keirstead's counsel and critique concerning issues as far-ranging as global politics, regional economic disparity, education, and taxation were highly compatible with the goals of a modernizing (some might say "secularizing") Canada during the first half of the twentieth century. To use Casanova's language, Keirstead's theologically-informed views were regarded by some as both "viable" and arguably "desirable" throughout his career.

Wilfred Currier Keirstead was one of the best known social philosophers to live in Maritime Canada during the first four decades of the twentieth century. Born in Corn Hill, New Brunswick in 1871, and ordained as a New Brunswick Free Christian Baptist minister in 1896,[8] he studied at the New Brunswick Provincial Normal School in Fredericton,[9] and at the University of New Brunswick (UNB), where he received his BA in 1897 and his MA in philosophy two years later. In 1903, he earned the PhD in religion and philosophy from the University of Chicago. Five years later he became Professor of Philosophy and Economics (and later

5. Casanova, *Public Religions*, 7.

6. Ibid., 7–8.

7. The literature on Keirstead is: Williams, "Political Philosophy of Two Canadians"; Armour and Trott, *Faces of Reason*; Armour, "Four Philosophic Responses." See also Goodwin, "Origins and Development," which pays less attention to the theological nature of Keirstead's thought and public discourse.

8. Burnett, *Biographical Directory*, 119.

9. *The Daily Telegraph* [Saint John], 9 September 1889.

Education) at the University of New Brunswick and remained there un-til shortly before he died in 1944. As a leading philosopher and educator, Keirstead was a pioneer in social causes, motivated by a deep desire to institutionalize in public policy and law what can be described as a mix-ture of evangelical religion, Christian Personalism, and Christian and socially conscious liberal democratic ideals. Not surprisingly, during his career he was Administrator of the Federal Food Board (1916–1919), Chair of the New Brunswick Commissions on Mothers' Allowances and Minimum Wage Legislation, President of the Fredericton Children's Aid Society, a member of the Social Service Board of the Maritime Baptist Convention, and he prepared studies for the provincial government on railway ventures and federal subsidies, taxation, and public finance.

In order to understand the development of Keirstead's social thought it is essential to begin with the religion of his childhood and early adult-hood. Keirstead's family was associated with the Free Christian Baptist Church in Corn Hill, a rural farming community in King's County, New Brunswick. His mother, Melvina Keirstead, became an active member of the church and its Women's Foreign Missionary Aid Society, following a significant religious revival that swept through the community in 1883 under the leadership of Rev. A. C. Thompson. Sixty-seven people were added to the church roll as a result.[10] While the church records are not that revealing for this period, it is difficult to imagine that this revival did not impact the twelve-year-old Wilfred Keirstead. However, he did not experience the much coveted evangelical conversion until his early twenties. Nevertheless, it is clear that his early religious culture was that of the Free Christian Baptists in New Brunswick. When he was sixty-five, Keirstead recalled "the country home of my childhood and . . . the fathers who were leaders of the local church. They were crude simple men, strong of impulse and harsh in a sense because they were crude. But they had a tenderness, a spirit of forgiveness and a high standard of rectitude that came from their religious faith."[11] If Keirstead admired the simple Christian witness of rural Free Baptist laity in Corn Hill, he also came to appreciate the vision of a powerful group of Free Baptist minis-

10. Burnett, *Biographical Directory*, 175. Keirstead's parents' gravestone in the United Baptist Church Cemetery, Corn Hill, NB, records his father's death as 1883 and his mother's as 1887.

11. Keirstead, "Religion and World Peace" (W. C. Keirstead fonds, UA RG 63 Series 3, Box 5, item 47).

ters in New Brunswick who attempted to transform the denomination during the last three decades of the nineteenth century.[12] These preachers distanced themselves from the excesses of their radically experiential past that was rooted in the Great Awakening of the late eighteenth century under Henry Alline, and adopted orderly denominational structures that paralleled other mainline Protestant groups.[13] Leading Free Baptist leaders embraced a more formal worship style, and developed a very positive posture toward modernity. New Brunswick Free Baptist leaders such as Ezekiel and Joseph McLeod believed that their denomination's fortunes depended upon shaping their province's future, not by retreating from it. In order to accomplish this goal, an educated clergy and laity would be required so that their voices would be heard in the marketplace of ideas.[14]

If New Brunswick Free Baptists wanted to distance themselves from some of the excesses of their past, they tenaciously held to their Arminian theology that argued for the free moral agency of the individual in spiritual and temporal matters. Believing that all individuals are made in the image of God, have enormous potential to choose redemption in Christ, and can make the world a better place through the social implications of the gospel, they proceeded to encourage a new generation of leaders to take up the challenge of bringing personal and social redemption to New Brunswick and the world. Wilfred Keirstead became an important member of that new generation of leaders and he never strayed far from these essential points of Free Baptist theology. At the end of his life, Keirstead's minister captured his theological position well when he recalled:

> To Dr. Keirstead, a finely developed theology was the background of his splendid liberalism. Arminian theology, with its confidence in human nature, opened the door for his broad sympathies, his humanitarian outlook, his compassionate concern for the welfare of his students, his generosity and private philanthropy.[15]

12. About one year after his conversion experience, Keirstead preached for the Free Baptist Church in Corn Hill, which is further evidence that he was attached to the church of his youth. See *Kings County Record*, 26 April 1895, which records that he preached both the morning and evening services.

13. For a discussion of this radical evangelicalism, see Rawlyk, *Ravished*. For the shift to a more formal evangelicalism, see Bell, "Allinite Tradition."

14. Bell, "Allinite Tradition"; MacKay, "Entire Instantaneous Sanctification," chap. 4.

15. *Maritime Baptist*, 22 November 1944.

Keirstead received his first post-secondary education at the Provincial Normal School in Fredericton in 1889 when he was in his late teens. This choice for education was not uncommon for men and some women from modest backgrounds who needed a steeping-stone to the professions. The successful completion of the Normal School program yielded a teacher's license and usually a job.[16] The available evidence suggests that Keirstead taught school until 1893 when he enrolled at the Union Baptist Seminary, located in St. Martins, New Brunswick, matriculating the following spring.[17]

The Union Baptist Seminary was an experiment in Christian higher education. It had been initially established in Fredericton in 1836 by New Brunswick's Calvinistic Baptists, but by 1884 the Free Baptists had become equal partners in the school. The Seminary impacted Keirstead in two complementary ways. First, he was exposed to a variety of subjects in the humanities, the arts, and religion as well as a more systematic approach to understanding Christianity that would come to deeply inform his scholarship.[18] The school was structured to inculcate evangelical Protestant faith in implicit and explicit ways. For example, faculty, staff, and most of the students lived, studied, and worshiped together in one large building. The daily routine was designed to impact the lives of students intellectually, socially, and spiritually. In spite of the religiously motivated social control, the school promoted a free environment of intellectual and religious enquiry. The Calendar of the school stated:

> The Seminary is not a sectarian but Christian School. No narrow or sectarian elements are present within its walls. Harmony and happiness are characteristic of its life, and no bigoted or false spirit has any place or standing. The faculty and students represent many shades and forms of religious belief, yet there is no prejudice and no bigotry. The name of Jesus Christ is known and honoured, and simple trust in a Divine Savior is considered the ground work of true religion, and essential to living faith.[19]

16. Marr, "Women," 30–31.

17. Keirstead, "Rural Taxation," 685. Keirstead mentions that he taught public school from 1890 to 1892, though it is likely that he actually taught until 1893, the year he enrolled at the Union Baptist Seminary.

18. Keirstead's graduating essay was entitled "Canadian Patriotism," which suggests that even in his early years of formal education he was occupied with the individual's attachment to the emerging state. (*Religious Intelligencer*, 20 June 1894).

19. *Union Baptist Seminary Calendar 1893–94*, 23. This "mere Christianity" advocated by the Union Baptist Seminary was an expression of the "Evangelical Creed" that

Keirstead's understanding of Christianity was forged at the Union Baptist Seminary, and it continued to inform his non-dogmatic approach to questions of faith throughout his life. He came to regard an open spirit of inquiry as essential to authentic faith and the progress of civilization. The religious position of the school also promoted a generic Protestant vision for Canadian society that Keirstead would later try to realize in the public school system and economic relations. During Keirstead's time of study, this broad-minded Christianity was powerfully modelled by the school's young principal, Austen K. DeBlois, a freshly minted PhD in philosophy from Brown University.[20]

On a more affective level, the school in St. Martins provided an engaging environment that led to the evangelical conversion experience that changed the direction of Keirstead's life. Almost immediately, he set out to preach in a number of small rural churches in southern New Brunswick. He declared in a letter to the *Religious Intelligencer* (the denomination's newspaper) that he wanted to serve God for the rest of his days.[21] Around the time of his conversion, he became involved in social causes such as the temperance movement,[22] the YMCA at Union Baptist Seminary where he became its first President,[23] the Young People's Union of his denomination, and preaching in local churches.[24] Concern for his young nation's future and identity was reflected in his graduating essay entitled, "Canadian Patriotism."[25] Social and political causes informed by Christianity would preoccupy Keirstead for much of his career. At this point in his life, not even Keirstead could have imagined that he would become an important public intellectual who would speak to a host of social, economic, and political issues during his career.

---

is explored in Gauvreau, *Evangelical Century*, 6–7.

20. *The Daily Sun* [Saint John], 21 August 1894.

21. See Keirstead's letter in the *Religious Intelligencer*, 12 September 1894.

22. Keirstead was a member of his denomination's temperance committee. See the *Religious Intelligencer*, 20 October 1897.

23 Keirstead was involved in the founding of the YM/YWCA at the Union Baptist Seminary in 1893. See the school's periodical *The Bema*, 9 December 1893, 104–5. He later joined the YMCA at UNB and represented the chapter at the Northfield Conference in Connecticut in 1897. See his letter in the *Religious Intelligencer*, 30 June 1897.

24. "Letter from the President," *Religious Intelligencer*, 16 March 1898.

25. *Religious Intelligencer*, 20 June 1894.

Keirstead began his undergraduate program at UNB in 1896, while preaching in churches close to Fredericton.[26] The university at this time was small, boasting little more than one hundred students.[27] Professors tended to be poorly paid and often taught for only a few years before moving on to more lucrative positions in other universities.[28] Three years before Keirstead started at UNB, John Davidson was hired to take up the chair of mental and moral philosophy and political economy. Educated at the Universities of Edinburgh and Berlin, Davidson was committed to newer approaches to education that built not only on the classics but also stressed the social sciences as a way to understand and guide social life.[29] During his ten-year tenure, he helped UNB steer a middle course between a traditional arts curriculum and the university's growing preoccupation with "applied" programs such as engineering.[30] Shortly before leaving UNB, Davidson wrote "I hope that the University will go on prospering and that the prosperity will be communicated to the Arts course [program], which is what I value most in a college."[31]

Davidson's view of university curriculum was impressed upon Keirstead while Keirstead was an undergraduate and a Master's student in philosophy.[32] Davidson wrote in his book *A New Interpretation of Herbert's Psychology and Educational Theory* that the "highest aim of education, whether this aim includes all lower aims or not, is the foundation of character."[33] Even a cursory reading of Davidson's corpus reveals that for him, character formation was in the Judeo-Christian tradition. Keirstead maintained this view of education throughout his career as it became integral to his Personalist philosophy.

Davidson's tutelage was almost as influential as New Brunswick Free Baptist religion in Keirstead's formation. The Scottish academic tradition that Davidson represented was built upon an approach to political

26. *Religious Intelligencer*, 17 June 1896.

27. Petrie, "Obituary," 111.

28. MacKirdy, "Formation," 42.

29. Walker, "Davidson, John." See also Goodwin, *Canadian Economic Thought*, 179–83.

30. Frank, "Davidson, John."

31. *The University Monthly* 23 (June 1904) 255.

32. Keirstead, "The Light." The actual MA degree was granted in May 1900 (*Calendar of the University of New Brunswick*, 1902, 100).

33. Davidson, *New Interpretation*, 1.

economy that easily accommodated insights from philosophy, history, sociology, geography, and psychology. In English Canada during the first half of the twentieth century, this undifferentiated "social science" was committed to the unity of truth and resisted the compartmentalization of knowledge and academic disciplines.[34] For example, Davidson published articles and books on wages in the free market system, British imperial economic policy, church history, Christian ethics, Canadian history, and the findings of Canada's 1891 and 1901 censuses. This approach to scholarship was ideal for public intellectuals such as Davidson and Keirstead, who addressed a remarkably wide range of issues faced by a young Canada. It should also be remembered that the comparatively small UNB resisted overt specialization in the late nineteenth century not only because of its view of knowledge, but also because of its size. When Keirstead arrived on the scene, he was ready to embrace an education that was academically challenging, interdisciplinary, and practical. As an educator coming from a denomination whose mission was to save the individual in part by saving society, a varied approach to studying the world was attractive to the twenty-four-year-old. Although no account of Keirstead's assessment of Davidson has survived, a comparison of their written works betrays the student's debt to the teacher.[35] The most obvious similarity is seen in their wide ranging academic interests and their implicit rejection of specialization. For example, in addition to philosophy and economics, Davidson lectured on psychology, constitutional history, German, and political science. Similarly, at the end of his own career, Keirstead would be regarded as a one-man faculty of arts[36] in the tradition of Davidson. Desmond Pacey said of Keirstead that he was "a great liberal, a great humanitarian, a great teacher, occupied the chair of philosophy and related subjects (practically the field of the social sciences for a good part of the time) for over thirty years, and was beyond all doubt the dominant figure in the humanities at this uni-

---

34. Drummond, *Political Economy*, 108, makes this point implicitly in his study of political economy at the University of Toronto.

35. B. S. Keirstead, W. C. Keirstead's son, who later came to teach economics at UNB, reported in an unpublished paper that Davidson had a significant impact upon the educational trajectory of his father and UNB. See B. S. Keirstead, "John Davidson," UNB Archives, Ms.2.2.37.

36. Pertie, "Obituary," 112. It should be noted that fiscal challenges at UNB forced professors to teach a wider variety of subjects than they might have otherwise.

versity during the first half of the twentieth century."[37] Although UNB did develop more specialized academic departments during his career, Keirstead remained steadfast in his commitment to the unity and coherence of knowledge.

If Keirstead's basic interdisciplinary approach was inherited from Davidson, so too was his belief that knowledge was by definition useful for humanity. Upon his arrival in Fredericton, Davidson declared in his inaugural lecture that "Philosophy is practical . . . and the study of it is fitted to produce men and citizens able to play a strong hand in the game of life."[38] Keirstead did not find in Davidson's approach a secular alternative to his Christian faith, but rather he saw the broad contours of political economy as a way to achieve some of the social goals of his Baptist religion. Historian David Frank has noted that Davidson's "intellectual endeavours reflected the preoccupation of a generation of political economists who were trying to reconcile economic theory with empirical observation. His work addressed issues of public concern as well as academic interest and like other economists of the historical school he injected ethical and subjective elements into the analysis of economic problems."[39] In fact, Davidson was sometimes chastised in reviews of his *Bargain Theory of Wages* for infusing his discussion of employer-employee relations with "an ethical or altruistic bearing." Imbued with the confidence of Positivism the reviewer dismissively declared "every departure from the impersonal is a departure from science."[40] Another reviewer remarked, "Such a conception of theory is destructive to clear thinking."[41] Undaunted, Davidson showed no signs of changing his position, believing truth to be unified and not tied exclusively to the scientific method. While his implicit Christian perspective was unhappily acknowledged by some reviewers of his work, Davidson was also explicit about his faith when the purpose of writing called for it. In his article, "Luxury and Extravagance," he used the Bible to support his argument. Quoting passages such as 2 Sam 23:14–17, John 12:3–8, and Matt 26:13, Davidson argued that the ethical standards for modern life needed to

37. Pacey, "The Humanist Tradition," 67.

38. *University Monthly* 12, no. 2 (November 1892) 18, as cited in Lingley, "John Davidson," 11–12.

39. Frank, "Davidson, John," 242.

40. Taylor, review of *Bargain Theory of Wages*.

41. Fetter, review of *Bargain Theory of Wages*, 569.

be forged in light of the Old and New Testaments.[42] He regarded the Christian religion in its appeal to biblical authority and transcendence to be highly compatible with modernity. In fact, for him the process of modernization in Canada and the West required the moral resources of the Judeo-Christian tradition. Keirstead would spend his entire academic career drawing deeply from the well dug by Davidson, taking the findings of social science and interpreting them through a grid that betrayed Christian and liberal democratic ideals. Adopting a historical perspective on social problems and incorporating insights from the social justice tradition found in the New Testament Gospels, Keirstead would preach countless sermons, make scores of presentations and public lectures, and write many academic journal and newspaper articles. Indeed, one of Keirstead's defining features is that his distinctively Christian approach informed his work as a public intellectual.

That Keirstead found Davidson's analysis of political economy relevant is not surprising since a wave of industrialization, spawned by Sir John A. MacDonald's National Policy, was transforming many communities in Maritime Canada. Manufacturing grew dramatically in the 1880s with investments in textile mills, iron and steel plants, and a host of spin-off industries that powerfully reshaped social life, creating an identifiable working class. Increased urbanization, out-migration, and a general economic instability in the region also meant that industrial developments were at best a mixed blessing.[43] Davidson was one of the first scholars to draw on empirical sources to diagnose systematically the economic history and fortunes of the region.[44] For example, in his two articles on England's commercial policy toward her colonies in the eighteenth and nineteenth centuries, and his study of the financial relationship between Canada's federal and provincial governments to 1905, Davidson sought to outline the impact of administrative decisions on Canada, and especially the Maritimes. Analyzing policy documents and statistics, he wove together a historical narrative that demonstrated how vulnerable the Maritimes were to decisions made outside of the region,

42. Davidson, "Luxury and Extravagance," 67.

43. McCann, "The 1890s."

44. In *The Bargain Theory of Wages*, John Davidson used statistical data to compare economic trends in the region to those in selected parts of the United States and Great Britain.

a scholarly activity to which Keirstead would later dedicate himself.[45] In an attempt to bring home the stark social realities brought on by the economic changes of the period, Davidson took his UNB students to the industrial city of Saint John and to sites closer to Fredericton such as the Gibson Cotton Mill in Marysville, not far from the church where Keirstead preached as a university student.[46] Such field trips were often accompanied by lectures on business and politics. During his time at UNB, Davidson endeavored to impress upon his students that they, as educated people, had a responsibility to serve and improve society.[47] Later in Keirstead's career, the methodology and moral sensibility learned from Davidson would give him the necessary model and courage to challenge university students[48] and as a public intellectual to encourage governments and industries to foster business and social environments that would promote the positive formation of individuals in all aspects of their lives.[49]

If Keirstead grew in his ethical understanding of political economy and the transformation of Maritime society during the late nineteenth century while at UNB, he also grew as a philosopher and theologian. These developments are best seen in his Master's thesis, which was supervised by Davidson and partially written while he studied theology at Cobb Divinity School in Lewiston Maine, during the 1898–99 academic year. This first serious scholarly endeavor, entitled "The Light Which Self Consciousness Sheds upon the Existence of God," reflects his abiding concern for philosophical anthropology inherited from his Arminian Baptist religion. In this study he examined the materialist and deistic views of humanity and found them wanting. Writing in the Christian

45. Davidson, "England's Policy," "England's Policy II," and "Financial Relations." See also Keirstead, "Claims of the Maritimes," 42.

46. While Keirstead became known primarily as an educator and scholar, he was an effective minister. For example, in 1897, Keirstead's church in Gibson grew by 31 members, 10 of whom he baptized (*Religious Intelligencer*, 13 October 1897).

47. Lingley, "John Davidson," 16.

48. See the newspaper article that reported on Keirstead's address to Acadia University's graduating class: "Says Wealth Should Not Be Higher Aim: Rev. W. C. Keirstead Special Acadia Speaker," *The Halifax Chronicle*, 26 May 1930. For the full text of the address, see the untitled sermon based on Mark 10:21 in W. C. Keirstead fonds, Box 9, File 4, item 45. Keirstead, "Past and Present," 33–42.

49. For examples, see: Keirstead, "White Commission," and "Dictatorships and Democracies."

Personalist tradition established by Boston University professor Borden Parker Bowne, Keirstead embraced the position that "All knowledge is knowledge by an individual" and "Personality thus becomes a gateway through which knowledge must pass."[50] Borrowing from Bowne, Keirstead believed that all significant questions of life must be reconciled to the notion of personality. He believed that there was a recognizable relationship between a Personalistic view of reality and theism that could be acceptable to scientists, philosophers, and theologians. Keirstead has been criticised by Trott and Armour, who say that his philosophy had no internal consistency.[51] While this judgment may be understandable, it betrays a lack of appreciation for the Christian Personalism of late nineteenth-century America that meshed so well with Keirstead's Free Baptist religion.

In his remarkable Master's thesis, Keirstead treated philosophical materialism from the Personalist vantage point and declared that it "discredits personality" and "reduces mind to the level of matter."[52] As a champion of the emerging science of the day, Keirstead cautioned that "science deals purely with secondary causes and gives but provisional explanations."[53] Consequently, he did not find evolutionary science to be at odds with his own view of humanity, for he argued that science discovered raw data about the universe but could not provide explanations for its ultimate meaning.[54] His progressive worldview, so central to his social Christianity, saw in evolutionary science a description of how God had created all things and how humans were the crowning glory of that divinely directed achievement. During Keirstead's student days at UNB, Professor L. W. Bailey and others kept students abreast of developments in evolutionary thought, which can be seen in Keirstead's thesis.[55] As Jerry Pitman has shown in his study of religious periodicals in the Maritimes during the last forty years of the nineteenth century, newspa-

50. One of the best introductions to Bowne's thinking is Puls, "Personalist Theism," 1.

51. Armour and Trott, *Faces of Reason*, 396.

52. Keirstead, "The Light," 2.

53. Ibid.

54. Ibid., 1. Keirstead seems to have adopted a dynamic humanism rooted in the transformation of the Victorian understanding of the Classics. For a discussion of this intellectual development, see Jenkyns, *Victorians and Ancient Greece*, 17, 74–76.

55. Toole, "Scientific Tradition," 71.

per editors and many readers "believed reconciliation [between evolution and Christianity] was possible" and "they did not think evolution
forced Christians to abandon special creation or secularize their faith."[56]
Consequently, it is not surprising that Keirstead never saw any conflict
between his religion and his belief in evolution.[57] In fact, evolution became a permanent feature of his thought, which he used to explain how
God had created the world and humanity.[58] As he saw it, evolutionary
science did not compromise the notion of divine transcendence or necessarily imply philosophical materialism. On the contrary, the undeni-
able reality of human personality made God or transcendent personality
a necessity. Drawing on Kant and Bowne, who both argued for the moral
necessity of God, Keirstead insisted that "Materialism simply ignores
self-consciousness"[59] and therefore fails to account for all there is. "Self-
consciousness constitutes the spiritual element in man. It lifts him above
nature. He becomes supernatural. He distinguishes himself from a world
of impersonal and personal beings."[60] In his discussion, Keirstead did
not hesitate to use biblical materials to support his arguments, a method
similar to John Davidson's. Declaring the nobility of humanity, Keirstead
used passages from the Old Testament such as Genesis 1 and Psalm 8.

As an emerging social philosopher in late nineteenth-century
North America, Keirstead found it impossible to ignore the thought
and "practical agnosticism of [Herbert] Spencer," who believed that
ultimate reality "must remain absolutely unknown."[61] His sustained
treatment of Spencer is not surprising, since so much social thought in
the Victorian period drew upon this theorist.[62] He also studied Spencer
under Davidson at UNB.[63] For Keirstead, the salient question to ask of
Spencer was whether personal beings exist. Believing that Spencer must
either reject the category of person or remain uncommitted, Keirstead

56. Pittman, "Darwinism and Evolution," 43.

57. Keirstead, "The Light," 17.

58. For a brief summary of Keirstead's view of science, see Armour, "Four
Philosophic Responses," 113–15.

59. Keirstead, "The Light," 7.

60. Ibid., 11.

61. Ibid., 24.

62. See the helpful discussion of Spencer's influence in Canada in McKay, *Reasoning
Otherwise*, 31–36.

63. *University of New Brunswick Calendar 1896–97*, 45–46.

declared that he "treats man as a thing rather than a person."[64] Such a position was a violation of Keirstead's maturing Christian Personalism that synthesized his Free Baptist value of humans with his formal study of Kant and Bowne. Throughout his career, Keirstead would be unfailing in his penchant for sifting major social questions of the day through the sieve of Christian Personalism. While he accepted the theory of evolution as did Spencer, it was on a radically different basis. Upon the emergence of humans from the evolutionary process, Keirstead argued, God gave them free moral agency and a unique personality. He wrote in his thesis: "Personality to me is the most *real*, the canon of reality. Why then should I think of the final reality other than in analogy with my own personality, and believe him to be 'Ever active moral reason and purpose at the root of a divine sustained physical order.'"[65] Although Keirstead the philosopher would rely upon the Kantian notion of the "moral necessity" and a modified Hegelianism that often seems to be little more than theistic evolution, to argue for God's existence, Keirstead the theologian would conclude his thesis by stating that "God is Creative Reason, conscious will revealing himself progressively in space and time. God is Infinite Love discipling and developing man, whom He has made in His own image, till he shall become perfected in him."[66]

At the completion of his studies at UNB in 1899, Keirstead knew how to frame philosophical arguments to support his optimistic view of humanity and had grasped the tools of the social scientist from Davidson to craft the right environment for the material, social, and spiritual progress of the individual. In short, Keirstead believed he had been empowered through education to advance the Kingdom of God. As a Christian Personalist, Keirstead would always find the individual to be the starting point for his thought. His formal theological studies at Cobb Divinity School and at the University of Chicago buttressed his liberalism at that point. In a revealing letter to the *Religious Intelligencer* in 1899 he wrote, "Religion is not mere acceptance of doctrine. God is not found at the end of a syllogism, so that if the logic be shown defective, God is taken away. Religion is one's experience of God coming, in Jesus Christ, in personal contact with one. Doctrine is but an attempt to

64. Keirstead, "The Light," 25.

65. Ibid., 17.

66. Ibid., 64. Keirstead is inconsistent in capitalizing the divine pronouns in the original.

interpret that experience. Life is first, and the views of it afterward. The outer form may change . . . but the inner life abides."[67] While this view of Christianity reflected Liberal Protestant influences, it resonated with Keirstead's Free Baptist religion that stressed personal religious experience as essential to authentic Christianity. Religion that was mere cognitive assent was little more than an ideal yet to be realized personally. In short, all truth by definition is personal, a point he made repeatedly in his Master's thesis.[68]

Keirstead's two semesters at Cobb Divinity School in 1898–1899 were a preparatory period for his PhD studies.[69] It should be remembered that UNB did not offer theology courses per se, and was not in the business of preparing anyone for church ministry. While Keirstead benefited greatly from a broad range of courses at UNB, he still had not studied theology formally, even though he had been ordained in 1896 and had pastoral experience. Cobb Divinity School was a logical choice for Keirstead as New Brunswick Free Baptists regarded the Free Will Baptists in New England as a sister denomination.[70] The school was founded in 1840 by the Free Will Baptists in Maine, and in 1870, the Divinity School became the *de facto* department of theology at Bates College.[71] New Brunswick Free Baptists regularly sent their young aspiring ministers to receive theological training in Lewiston with a view to producing a more cultured and better educated leadership that could increase the denomination's influence in society.[72]

When Keirstead began his studies at the University of Chicago in the fall of 1899, he was motivated in part by a desire to continue his learning trajectory. Bates College and Cobb Divinity School had a close relationship with the University of Chicago, as professors and former students often went to Chicago to teach and study. For example,

67. *Religious Intelligencer*, 22 November 1899.

68. Keirstead, "The Light," 1, 7–9, 12, 16–18, 26–28.

69. Although personal information about Keirstead is wanting for this period of his life, especially, the records at the Cobb Divinity School indicate that by 1898, both of his parents were dead. See "Faculty Meeting Minutes," 16 September 1898.

70. For a historical survey of Cobb Divinity School and Bates College, written by a New Testament professor admired by Keirstead, see Anthony, *Bates*, 188–205.

71. *Cobb Divinity School Catalogue, 1898–99*, 4.

72. Free Baptists from New Brunswick and Nova Scotia attended Bates College and Cobb Divinity School. See, for example, "Commencement at Bates," *Religious Intelligencer*, 10 July 1895.

Shailer Mathews was both an alumnus and former professor of Bates College before accepting the position in New Testament and later Dean of Theology at the University of Chicago.[73] Keirstead's friend and New Brunswick Free Baptist contemporary, Shirley Jackson Case, also made a similar transition, leaving Bates College to teach at the University of Chicago in 1908.[74]

The new university, bankrolled by John D. Rockefeller, was an exciting environment for the twenty-eight-year-old Keirstead. Its ethos appealed to him as it had been shaped by the compelling vision of its president, William Rainey Harper, who believed that "Protestant Christianity was commissioned by God to transform the world through democratic institutions and veneration of the individual."[75] Change was to be thoughtful and incremental, not radical or revolutionary. This approach appealed to Keirstead's Personalism, which held that change should be evolutionary so that it did not violate or stifle human potential and personality, even if attempts were made to address injustice. The University of Chicago was also broadly Baptist in its orientation, with almost its entire divinity faculty being leading Baptist scholars.[76] According to theologian Victor Anderson, these scholars were

> intellectually intoxicated by the march of human creative intelligence conceptually moving from its reliance on a metaphysical chain of being grounded on the apriority of absolute Mind. They wanted a theology that would contribute to the advancement of learning, guiding human intelligence creatively, spiritually, and ethically through the age of positive science.[77]

While Keirstead never fully embraced his mentors' modification of metaphysics, he was shaped by their conservative progressivism which

73. Hinson, "Baptist Contributions," 46.

74. Nicols, "Shirley Jackson Case," 55–56.

75. Cherry, *Hurrying toward Zion*, 2.

76. See Hinson, "Baptist Contributions," 39, 40, 45–47. He suggests in his article that the Baptist faith was especially compatible with the rise of liberal theology that stressed, among other things, free moral agency, personalism, the centrality of Jesus Christ, and the use of reason in accommodating Christianity to the explosion of knowledge at the end of the nineteenth century. W. C. Keirstead clearly held to these points by the time he completed his Master's thesis at UNB. Nevertheless, he still held to the need for personal faith and conversion throughout his life, a testimony to his New Brunswick Free Baptist roots.

77. Anderson, "Pragmatic Theology," 162.

sponsored a "gospel of improvement" rather than one of "sweeping reconstruction."[78]

A number of New Brunswick Baptists were already students when Keirstead arrived, and over thirty students were involved in a "club" for Canadians at Chicago.[79] While doctoral students had to declare their major area of study, there was a great deal of freedom to take courses in other departments. This appealed to Keirstead's commitment to the unity of knowledge and his dual interest in theology and social science. He registered for the PhD in systematic theology and took courses in biblical and theological studies from leading Liberal Protestant scholars such as George Burman Foster and Ernest De Witt Burton.[80] He took social science and ethics courses from John Dewey, whose fame was growing at that time.[81] Keirstead had been introduced to Dewey's thought while at UNB, as it was a regular part of the BA program in the mid-1890s.[82] From the theology faculty at Chicago, Keirstead developed a more sophisticated approach to the historical and literary study of the Bible, believing that biblical criticism could determine more fully the "original meaning" of the text. As well, the scholars under whom he studied also stressed the transformative value of critical Bible study for lay people.[83] This approach resonated with Keirstead's belief in the democratization of biblical knowledge and its relation to individual formation and societal progress.[84] Since he held that all knowledge is useful, he believed it must be pressed into service for the benefit of the masses.[85] Much of Keirstead's vocation as a public intellectual was directed to that end.

78. Cherry, *Hurrying toward Zion,* 11.

79. *Religious Intelligencer,* 25 September 1901.

80. *Religious Intelligencer,* 3 April 1901.

81. See Keirstead's typed notes taken from a course he took at the University of Chicago from John Dewey, "The Sociology of Ethics," University of Chicago, 1902–1903 (UNB Library).

82. *University of New Brunswick Calendar, 1896–97,* 45–46.

83. This influence can be seen in a letter Keirstead wrote to his New Brunswick Free Baptist constituency extolling the value of the historical-critical method of Bible study for churches. *Religious Intelligencer,* 14 November 1900.

84. See Keirstead's sermon, "The Importance of Bible Study"(W. C. Keirstead fonds, UA RG 63 Series 3, box 5, item 1). This address seems to have been given to fellow students at Bates College, Maine.

85. For a helpful discussion of this theme, consult Carter, "Higher Criticism," 5–68. Keirstead continued to teach and preach the Bible as a "layman" at the George Street United Baptist Church throughout his time at UNB. See the many entries in the

At Chicago Keirstead researched the thought of Albrecht Ritschl,[86] the German Protestant theologian who stressed that the "object of God's love is the organic community, the church" and that "human faith was not passive but expressed actively: toward God in humility, patience, and prayer and toward others in love—in an ethical vocation aimed at the Kingdom of God."[87] That he should select to work on Ritschl was not a temporary change of direction in Keirstead's intellectual concerns, as Armour and Trott suggest in their study on Canadian philosophers.[88] In fact, Keirstead was following a predictable path of scholarly enquiry. As Richard Allen has argued, "Ritschl's thought, usually unsystematically appropriated, provided the implicit theological foundations of much of the social gospel" in Canada.[89] Ritschl's thought came to influence in North America in the 1890s, and Keirstead found it attractive as it took historical developments and ethics seriously. The German theologian attempted to refashion Christianity in a way that could "carry out a mission of reform and renewal." The Ritschlian school of thought was optimistic about recovering the religion of Jesus or at least the moral formulation of the gospel in the apostolic age.[90] Keirstead and others of his generation found in Ritschl a way to employ biblical higher criticism to uncover timeless moral principles they believed were desperately needed in a changing North America. In this line of thought, Christianity was not regarded so much as a list of doctrinal statements but as a living movement or a way of life. More than many social gospellers of his day, Keirstead was closer to Ritschl's conviction that change should be incremental and not revolutionary.[91]

From his doctorial research Keirstead wrote an article entitled, "Theological Presuppositions of Ritschl," that praised the German theologian for conceiving of supernatural revelation as one "of values which are possessed by the community and appropriated by the individual by

---

Church Records, George Street United Baptist Church, 1908–1944. (Acadia University Archives, Wolfville, NS).

86. See the two articles that were published from his dissertation research: Keirstead, "Theological Presuppositions of Ritschl" and "Metaphysical Presuppositions of Ritschl."

87. Jodock, "Ritschl," 137.

88. Armour and Trott, *Faces of Reason*, 394.

89. Allen, *Social Passion*, 4.

90. Dorrien, *Making of American Liberal Theology*, 26.

91. Ibid., 24–25.

faith."[92] Keirstead would spend much of his academic career writing and speaking about the necessity of integrating the ethics of Jesus into the social and political fabric of modern Canada. He declared with confidence that in Ritschl the "religious, scientific, and philosophic thought of the age meet . . . and they all move in the practical direction."[93] A fair reading of Keirstead's corpus would suggest that Keirstead tried to live up to the example of Ritschl, though as a Maritime public intellectual.

From his studies with John Dewey at Chicago, Keirstead came to understand more fully how social institutions in a democracy, such as governments, public education, the church, and the economy, could be fashioned so that individuals would achieve their social, moral/spiritual potential, which fused nicely with his Free Baptist Arminianism, John Davidson's approach to political economy, Christian Personalism, and Ritschl's vision of ethics. While Clifford Williams,[94] whose Master's thesis is the only sustained study of Keirstead's thought to date, states that the New Brunswick philosopher never maintained a consistent metaphysical position, it may be argued that unity is nevertheless found in his thought. It simply turns on his Arminian Baptist view of humanity and his belief that structures must continually be adapted to ensure the progress of humanity. To expect a tightly crafted and consistent philosophy from Wilfred Keirstead is to misunderstand the passion that drove much of his thinking, writing, and speaking. He was committed to clear forms of ethical thinking that could be pressed into action and transform the individual and society, not in fashioning an overarching philosophical system in the Kantian or Hegelian tradition. In fact, Keirstead's studies in Chicago impacted his overall method of inquiry far more than any particular aspect of his theological beliefs. This is not surprising in light of recent developments in the historiography of North American Liberal Protestantism. Kathryn Lofton has compellingly argued that modernist theologians, such as those under whom Keirstead studied, advanced an "aggressive, demanding process of cross-examination and inquiry, a process that transformed the terming of biblical narrative and Christian faith within universities, Protestant churches, and American culture." For these scholars the "*process* of believing is emphasized over and above the definitive dogma. How you believe, for the modernists, was your

92. Keirstead, "Theological Presuppositions of Ritschl," 450.

93. Ibid.

94. Williams, "The Political Philosophy of Two Canadians," 66–107.

belief,"[95] an approach that was reinforced by his reading of Bowne and Ritschl.

From 1903 to 1906, Keirstead was the minister at First Baptist Church, Rockford, Illinois, during which time the church achieved numerical growth, much needed repairs to its buildings, and financial stability.[96] Keirstead also became a popular lecturer in the city, giving a series of talks on topics such as "Dowie and Dowieism" and temperance.[97] Even though brief, his pastorate indicates that Keirstead took seriously the notion of the educated and professional clergyman as social reformer and public educator that was being advanced at the University of Chicago Divinity School. Growing the Kingdom of God required that the laity be educated on a host of topics informed by the latest scholarship. Although Keirstead was much loved as a pastor by the Rockford church and was praised in the church records for bringing "vigor and enthusiasm" to the position,[98] frequent letters and visits to the Maritimes during his sojourn in Illinois suggest that he had a particular attachment to the place of his birth and early formation as a Christian and scholar. Consequently, it is not surprising that he not only resigned his very successful position at First Baptist Church, Rockford, but also declined an offer of a teaching position at the University of Chicago in order to become the Baptist minister in Woodstock, New Brunswick.[99] There were many highly educated Baptist preachers and educators in the greater Chicago area, but there were relatively fewer educated Baptists in the Maritimes who might bring to bear the benefits of a University of Chicago doctorate. In fact, Baptist preachers who left the region for graduate theological education in the United States tended not to return

95. Lofton, "Methodology of Modernists," 378.

96. From October 1903 to November 1906, Keirstead was the pastor of First Baptist Church, Rockport, Illinois (Church Records, First Baptist Church Rockford, IL, 1903–1906 [copies]). I am grateful to Shirley Smith, church secretary at First Baptist Church, Rockford, for sending me copies of relevant material from the minute books during Keirstead's pastorate.

97. *The Rockford Republic*, 28 January 1905.

98. Church Records, First Baptist Church Rockford, Illinois, 4 November 1906.

99. Church Records, Woodstock United Baptist Church, 1907–1908. (Acadia University Archives, Wolfville, Nova Scotia). This decision was probably wise as Ritschlianism at the University of Chicago was eclipsed by the socio-historical method in studying the Bible and Christianity by the second decade of the twentieth century. Interestingly, this shift was due in large part to the influence of Shirley Jackson Case, another New Brunswick Free Christian Baptist.

to the Maritimes.[100] It should be pointed out as well that Keirstead did not have any immediate family living in the Maritimes by this time. His parents were both dead by 1898, and his brother was a minister in New England. Consequently, W. C. Keirstead's attachment to the Maritimes should be seen, in part, as an expression of his commitment to fostering "Christian progress" in his geographical and spiritual home.

Keirstead's notions of progress meshed well with the church union movement that was sweeping Maritime Baptists in the late nineteenth and early twentieth century. In 1905, the Maritime's Calvinistic Baptists and New Brunswick's Free Christian Baptists merged to create the United Baptist Convention of the Maritime Provinces. The following year, Nova Scotia's Free Christian Baptists joined the union. During the critical meetings among the Calvinistic Baptists during the summer of 1904, Keirstead was invited to speak to the issue of Baptist union while on vacation from Rockford, Illinois. The Free Christian Baptist newspaper reported with pride that he "made a deep impression. We heard it spoken of on every hand as a strong and clear presentation of the truth."[101] Ecumenical cooperation and denominational mergers had become commonplace in late-Victorian Canada with a series of Methodist and Presbyterian unions that culminated in the formation of the United Church of Canada in 1925.[102] Keirstead, and Maritime Baptists more generally, shared the national reformist impulse that swept progressive Protestants throughout Canada. Wilfrid Laurier had said that the twentieth century was to be Canada's century, and in the minds of many Protestants, denominational mergers would contribute toward this vision by providing a more united voice and coordinated efforts in making Canada "His Dominion."[103] Keirstead believed that Baptists were especially well positioned to contribute toward Christianizing society, because they were among the most democratic and non-creedal denominations that celebrated the freedom and unlimited potential of individual personality. In his view, and that of the Baptist scholars of the Chicago School, Baptists did not carry the burden of tradition, complex doctrinal systems, and hierarchical authority structures that frequently played havoc with adapting to modernity.

100. See the editorial in *Religious Intelligencer*, 31 December 1902.

101. *Religious Intelligencer*, 31 August 1904.

102. Goodwin, "Maritime Baptist Union"; see also Cameron, "Garden Distressed."

103. Kiesekamp, "Presbyterian and Methodist Divines."

Not surprisingly, the prospect of becoming the Baptist minister in Woodstock, New Brunswick was attractive to Keirstead because he would become the first pastor of a congregation comprised of former members of the Main Street Free Christian Baptist Church and the Albert Street [Calvinistic] Baptist Church.[104] He began his official duties in December of 1906, and although he resigned his position within twenty months to teach at UNB, he continued to take a keen interest in the church and was often a guest preacher.[105] During this short ministry in Woodstock, Keirstead continued his role of community educator and social reformer. Shortly after his arrival he declared in a sermon that was published in the local newspaper:

> The enemies of religion are not education and investigation. Religion has nothing to fear from intellectual freedom and nothing to gain from intolerance and bigotry and prejudice. But the spirit of commercialism and self seeking; the mad rush for material wealth; the desires [sic] for pleasure which has intoxicated us and the sensuality of our nation are the deadly foes of the religious values.[106]

As a Christian thinker committed to modern forms of thought and organization, Keirstead in his sermon reflected not only the "Chicago School" that resisted the compartmentalization of religion but also John Davidson's commitment to the unity of knowledge. That Keirstead's approach to theological questions seemed to be different from that of previous generations of preachers did not go unnoticed. Two months after he resigned his position, the Woodstock church held a congregational meeting to discuss finding a new minister. A motion was made "that this church refuse to call as pastor any minister who was known to hold doctrinal views commonly known as 'the new theology.'"[107] The motion was seconded though soundly defeated with only two voting in its favor. However, the discussion does suggest that there was awareness among the congregants that Keirstead approached the faith in a new way.

104. See Keirstead's "Church Dedication," which he presented 24 May 1908 (Woodstock UBC Records, 1908).

105. Ibid., 24 November 1908; "History of the United Baptist Church of Woodstock, New Brunswick," n.d., 2 (Woodstock UBC Records).

106. *Carleton Sentinel*, [December, 1906]. This sermon may have been his inaugural address to the newly united congregation. Similar themes can be found in his Baccalaureate sermon published in the *Carleton Sentinel*, 16 August 1907.

107. Woodstock UBC Records, 7 September 1908.

Nevertheless, the essential nature of the Maritime Baptist faith of his childhood remained intact. At the formal dedication of the new Baptist church building in Woodstock on 24 May 1908, Keirstead prayed that "saints may be edified, sinners converted, and little children instructed in the Word and brought into the fold."[108] It would have been difficult for anyone in a church meeting to argue that such a prayer commitment did not reflect the experiential faith of the previous century, the "new theology" notwithstanding.

Exactly how far Keirstead would have developed his thought in the direction of the Chicago School's "new theology" is uncertain, since after his appointment to UNB in 1908, he concentrated almost exclusively on injecting Christian ethics and theological insights into social policy and criticism in order to promote his version of progress that was first fleshed out in his Master's thesis.[109] While his Chicago mentors were committed to accommodating Christianity to modern sensibilities—something Keirstead himself applauded—the minister-turned-professor was more interested in embedding Christian thought into the economic and social order.

While it is beyond the scope of this study to provide a full exposition of Keirstead's public writings from 1908 to 1944, it is appropriate to provide a few representative examples of how his worldview shaped his thought. Keirstead continued to publish in religious periodicals until the late 1920s; however, his efforts became increasingly taken up with the social order. In 1912, he wrote an article entitled "Some Essential Facts of Social Progress" that captured the tension between the individual and society that is seen throughout his corpus. He argued that individuals have always existed in groups with prescribed social habits. Change or "social progress means the modification or reconstruction of the existing customs, institutions, or beliefs through the originative, inventive intelligence of the individual."[110] The engine of progress, ac-

108. Woodstock UBC Records, "Church Dedication," [1908].

109. According to theologian Creighton Peden, scholars of the Chicago School became so enamoured with accommodating Christianity to modern thought that they came to deny transcendence itself. See his *Chicago School*, chaps. 1–3. Also consult Dean, *American Religious Empiricism*, 19–40. That Keirstead was invited to be a professor at UNB is not surprising since he "formed an intimate friendship" with the president, Cecil C. Jones, when they were both undergraduates at UNB and graduate students at the University of Chicago. See Keirstead's memorial reflections on Jones in *Daily Gleaner*, 15 August 1943.

110. Keirstead, "Some Essential Facts," 39.

cording to Keirstead, was the individual, a position consistent with his Christian Personalism, which regarded human personality as the image of the Divine. Societies become enlightened when they realize that freedom for individuals is necessary to unleash the creative potential of humans. While the individual has been shaped by custom and tradition, he maintained that progress would only occur when individuals challenged the very tradition that had shaped them and brought stability to their society. Freedom, then, was an essential ingredient in his recipe for progress. In an almost Hegelian style, Keirstead declared: "The conservative and radical, the priest and the prophet, the orthodox and the heretic, the legalist and the anarchist, the capitalist and the socialist, the persecutor and the reformer—each is impotent without the other, and each, checked by the other, may make a contribution toward genuine social welfare."[111]

Keirstead's thought was permeated by the assumption that progress was incremental and that "reconstruction" of every period required that the ideals be applied to all aspects of life so as to create the new "custom." As the traditions are realized, society "must give a higher appreciation to the function and worth of the individual. For the pivot of progress is the soul of man."[112] He argued that since the dynamics of progress were now known, it was possible to guide the process through the deliberate refashioning of societal institutions. He regarded the process of "modernization" through state formation, urbanization, and industrialization as an opportunity to expand the Kingdom of God. Christian principles were needed to negotiate the new paradigm.[113] The ideals that were essential to progress were to be found in the Western tradition, in the "arts, the sciences, the literature, the hymns and psalms and prayers, the social institutions of our race."[114] For Keirstead, this understanding of progress did not imply a journeying away from Christianity, but was rather the result of "the living spirit of God which binds humanity into a unity and conditions the development of today . . . enabling us to carry forward the onward march of the Kingdom of God."[115] Modernization was not

111. Ibid., 40.

112. Ibid., 43.

113. For a stimulating discussion of the "Liberal Order," that Keirstead regarded as highly compatible with Christianity, consult McKay, "Liberal Order Framework."

114. Keirstead, "Some Essential Facts," 46.

115. Ibid.

an evil to be resisted by the public intellectual but rather a divinely appointed opportunity to be taken.[116] This had been the position of the Free Christian Baptist leaders of his youth as well as the sophisticated scholars with whom he studied at the University of Chicago.

In a sermon delivered in 1910, Keirstead confidently affirmed that the public sphere of business and politics

> can be changed and must be changed. Don't mistake this fact, they can be made Christian and that is our task as Christian men and women. The ethics of the profession must be rationalized and widened into the ethics of the Christian life. The ethic of statesmanship must be the ethics of the Christian man. There is only one standard and it is the task of the Christian man to uphold and stand for this standard in public and social life.[117]

Keirstead's scholarship in economics and business exemplified his desire to bring "the Golden Rule" into the public sphere. Rejecting Adam Smith's notion that the laws of supply and demand would prove to be universally beneficial, he argued for state regulation of business activities to keep "injustice and social injury" in check.[118] Even those who benefited from unrestrained capitalism were in danger of injuring their own "moral character." Drawing on his background in political economy gained from John Davidson, he believed that proper scientific evaluation of the economy would provide a course of action that would promote the ethic of the "Golden Rule." For him, this biblical principle stood for "the Christian valuation of personality and requires of industrial enterprises as of other institutions such organization and functioning as shall enrich personal life and promote the common happiness and progress."[119] Far from advocating the revolutionary dismantling of capitalism that he identified with the Soviet Union's form of communism, Keirstead argued predictably for an evolutionary approach that gradually and scientifically regulated the industrial order, moving closer to the ideal though never fully realizing it because the ideal itself was always gradually changing.[120] Even in the 1930s, when notable Maritime

116. Gauvreau and Hubert, *Churches and Social Order*, 3–45.

117. Keirstead, untitled sermon (W. C. Keirstead fonds, AU RG 63 Series 3, box 5, Item 27).

118. Keirstead, "The Golden Rule in Business," 142.

119. Ibid., 147.

120. Ibid., 149.

Baptist ministers were calling for the dismantling of the capitalistic system, Keirstead maintained his "evolutionary" position.[121] In the end, those involved in business needed to take up their responsibility to act ethically for the sake of society as well as their own spiritual well being. The grand socializing institutions properly constituted on Christian principles, such as the family, local churches, and schools were needed to balance any tendency in the individual to compete for selfish gain. Indeed, influenced by John Dewey on this point, Keirstead believed that competition was not innate in humans and that proper socialization could reduce or remove it.[122]

So central was public education to Keirstead's vision for a modern and Christian New Brunswick that his important study on rural taxation in his beloved province focused primarily on how the collection of public revenues impacted the funding of schools. Published in the *Journal of Political Economy* in 1926, Keirstead's article showed how unjust, inefficient, and outdated the taxation system was in New Brunswick's rural parishes. Modernization of the taxation system was not the enemy but the way out of the "evils and inequalities of parish underassessment."[123] A fully coordinated province-wide approach to collecting revenues at the municipal and parish levels in line with modern bureaucratic models would promote biblical justice. With passionate frankness, he stated that when "the administration of a general property tax is in the hands of an untrained, arbitrary, and autocratic official, ignorant of modern methods of taxation and lacking any high sense of justice, citizens may be robbed of the equality of treatment which is regarded a birthright in modern society."[124] Those being "robbed" were children and families in rural areas that had inadequate funding for schools. Consequently, individuals and rural communities were disadvantaged in realizing their full potential, an affront to his Christian Personalism. "Modern" methods of taxation had the potential to usher in greater justice and

121. Crouse, "Capitalism under Fire." In spite of the fact that Keirstead would have been a well known "Baptist economist" in the region, he failed to enter the debate over capitalism that raged in the *Maritime Baptist* in the 1930s. Instead, he busied himself with less contentious activities such as serving as a judge in Acadia University's essay competition on Maritime economics, which awarded S. A. Saunders $1000 for his *Economic Welfare* (Saunders, *Economic Welfare*, 3).

122. Keirstead, "The Golden Rule in Business," 154.

123. Keirstead, "Rural Taxation," 682.

124. Ibid., 677.

progress. Having grown up and been educated in rural Kings County, New Brunswick, Keirstead would have empathized with rural folk trying to secure an education from an inadequately funded school system. His former student, the economist J. R. Petrie, said of Keirstead, "As a student of regional economic problems, he was instrumental in clarifying many issues for both the provincial and Dominion governments. Happily he lived to see many of his proposals incorporated into government policy."[125]

Keirstead's commitment to justice and opportunity for those marginalized, seen in his call to reconstruct New Brunswick's taxation methods, was expressed in a variety of contexts during his career. For example, in his detailed assessment of the Report of the White Commission, published in the *Canadian Journal of Economic and Political Science*, he identified methodological problems that might lead policy makers to ignore the Commission's findings. In addition, he was critical of the study's findings. While the Report sought to address the unresolved issues of "Dominion-Provincial relations" in Canadian Confederation, he counseled his readers that "Neither the federal nor provincial government is one with society" and that they were simply "associations of citizens" who were charged with the responsibility to achieve "good ends."[126] He concluded his article by suggesting that more decision-making power and subsidies based on need should go to the provinces. Even though Keirstead was not an advocate of social engineering per se, he believed that proper recognition of the sacred nature of human personality could not be advanced apart from an equitable, just, and modern system of checks and balances.

As professor of Philosophy and Education at UNB from 1932 to 1944, Keirstead became involved in a number of committees that made recommendations for changes to New Brunswick's public education system. In an undated document, probably from 1937, entitled "Introduction: Educational Aims" is found a variety of ideas and statements that reflect Keirstead's sentiments even if they were not actually written by him. For example, the committee refused to present society in a dualistic fashion that posited the secular over the sacred, but rather saw it as an organic whole where public education combined with the "home, the church, [and] the community at large" to produce "good

---

125. Petrie, "Obituary," 111.
126. Keirstead, "White Commission," 378.

citizenship."[127] Thirty years earlier, Keirstead had made the same point in a two-part article published in the *Maritime Baptist*.[128] For Keirstead and the committee, education was fundamentally a moral exercise. They declared:

> We must supply experiences and direct activities in such a way that the children will grow up with a social and moral consciousness. The spirit of Christianity should be ever present in the school—not the teaching of a particular religious dogma, but rather the exemplifying of those beliefs and the practice of those virtues which are the common heritage of the Christian world.[129]

It should be remembered that Keirstead's experience at the Union Baptist Seminary in the mid-1890s exposed him to a non-dogmatic and generically "Christian" approach to education where the goal was the moral and spiritual formation of the individual regardless of denominational affiliation. That these notions showed up in a document designed to provide general principles for the public education system in New Brunswick is not surprising, given the presence of UNB's professor of education and the widely held notion that society was essentially Christian in its outlook, a view likely shared by many on the committee. As an "expert" Keirstead was responsible for "setting up the background" of the committee's report, which was logical since he had carried out an extensive study of provincial systems of education throughout the nation and had studied with John Dewey who was one of the architects of public education in the United States.[130] Even though there are similarities between the thought of Dewey and Keirstead, it would be a mistake to assume that the latter adopted the program of the former. It is more accurate to say that Keirstead found great compatibility between his New Brunswick Baptist view of public education and that of the famous American philosopher because he regarded the modern liberal program

127. Keirstead, "Educational Aims."

128. Keirstead, "Baptists and Public Schools," *Maritime Baptist*, 3 and 10 December 1906.

129. Keirstead, "Educational Aims."

130. Glimpses of Keirstead's involvement on this committee can be seen in "Curriculum Committee Meeting" (W. C. Keirstead fonds, Series 1, Number 1). For his studies on the state of Canadian public education, see his more than twenty-five newspaper articles published in 1937. (W. C. Keirstead fonds, UA RG 63 Series 5, Item 9). Similar themes are also developed in his unpublished address, "Religious Education in the Public Schools" (W. C. Keirstead fonds, UA RG 63 Series 5, Item 42).

as the best medium through which to propagate the Christian religion in the twentieth century.

During the rise of Western totalitarian regimes in the 1930s, Keirstead became increasingly convinced of the need to protect democracy in order to encourage a social context in which individuals could develop to their fullest. He declared that freedoms, including of "conscience or of worship" and of "teaching in schools and colleges," among others, were essential for the broader public discussion needed to counter propaganda and pursue the truth.[131] In order to have a society that was thoughtful and informed, improved educational institutions were going to be needed. "What stands in the way of providing an education that will expose prejudice and privilege and that will develop objective and impartial thinking?" In typical fashion, Keirstead concluded that there needed to be a symbiotic relationship at work to preserve human progress. "Until we get a better social order we cannot get the education we need and until we get a better system of education we cannot get a better social order."[132] Again, change was required but needed to be implemented with careful precision.

In June of 1929, the Royal Commission on Radio Broadcasting held hearings in Fredericton and Keirstead advised that the federal government should allow private ownership because this would be responsive to the desires of the listening public. But he also advised that it should be regulated in a way that allowed for the public to be educated. Creating a new social order was going to require media that took seriously their moral responsibility to educate the populace in a democracy.[133] So tireless was Keirstead in promoting educational reform that one of his colleagues declared, "No man of his time has exerted a greater influence in New Brunswick's educational circles, and that influence has spread beyond provincial boundaries."[134]

Keirstead's discussions never strayed far from his Christian Personalism that saw the ideal of human personality as "a heritage from our Christian religion," maintaining that it was "Jesus who taught the

---

131. Keirstead, "Discussion," 377.

132. Keirstead, "Discussion," 378.

133. National Archives RG 33, 14, Royal Commission on Radio Broadcasting Papers, Vol. 2, file 227–10–7 to 227–12–5, Public Hearings Fredericton, 13 June 1929, 8, as quoted in Nolan, "Infant Industry," 504

134. Petrie, "Obituary," 111.

infinite worth of personality, and who declared that to offend one of his little ones was to commit an unpardonable sin."[135] In his study of political systems at the close of the Great Depression, he criticized totalitarian and communist regimes for denying the value of individuals in favor of a forced collectivist state. "Values inhere not in individuals but in the state; truth, science, justice, the rule of law are not human and universal, but are national. The infinite worth of personality and the common brotherhood of man are denied by this conception of the state."[136] Democracy, on the other hand, allows humans to flourish, and by definition leads to progress. That Keirstead would unapologetically build his argument on a Christian view of humanity in a public forum, such as the *Dalhousie Review* in 1939, suggests that Christian discourse was not only welcomed but acceptable as an authority in thinking about the nature and future of Canada in the modern world.

While it has not been the purpose of this study to measure the degree to which Keirstead's Christian Personalism was accepted and influential in public discourse, it has been shown that his perspective was welcomed on a myriad of issues in Canadian life. He believed throughout his career that his view of the world was highly compatible with a modernizing Canada and the structure of his thought suggests that he was right. The value Keirstead placed on the individual—a value that emerged from his New Brunswick Free Baptist faith and was later supplemented by other sources—was easily accommodated to the Canadian liberal experiment. His religious and early philosophical formation not only provided an effective way for him to understand and appropriate change, they combined to become a vehicle for advancing many aspects of modernity in what Keirstead surely thought was a Christian Canada.

135. Keirstead, "Dictatorships and Democracies," 41.

136. Ibid., 42.

BIBLIOGRAPHY

Allen, Richard. *The Social Passion: Religion and Social Reform in Canada*. Toronto: University of Toronto Press, 1971.

Anderson, Victor. "Pragmatic Theology and the Natural Sciences at the Intersection of Human Interests." *Zygon* 37 no. 1 (March 2002) 161–73.

Anthony, Alfred Williams. *Bates College and Its Background: A Review of Origins and Causes*. Philadelphia: Judson, 1936.

Armour, Leslie. "McCulloch, Lyall, Schurman and Keirstead: Four Philosophic Responses to Science, Religion and the Unity of Knowledge." In *Profiles of Science and Society in the Maritimes Prior to 1914*, edited by Paul A. Bogaard, 101–16. Fredericton, NB: Acadiensis Press and the Centre for Canadian Studies, Mount Allison University, 1990.

Armour, Leslie, and Trott, Elizabeth. *The Faces of Reason*. Waterloo, ON: University of Waterloo Press, 1981.

Bell, D. G. "The Allinite Tradition and the New Brunswick Free Christian Baptists 1830–1875." In *An Abiding Conviction: Maritime Baptists and Their World*, edited by Robert Wilson, 55–82. Hantsport, NS: Lancelot, 1988.

Burnett, Frederick C. *Biographical Directory of Nova Scotia and New Brunswick Free Baptist Ministers and Preachers*. Hantsport, NS: Lancelot, 1999.

Cameron, James. "The Garden Distressed: Church Union and Dissent on Prince Edward Island, 1925." *Acadiensis* 21 no. 2 (Spring 1992) 108–31.

Carter, Robert Lee. "The 'Message of the Higher Criticism': The Bible Renaissance and Popular Education in America, 1880–1925." PhD dissertation, University of North Carolina at Chapel Hill, 1995.

Casanova, José. *Public Religions in the Modern World*. Chicago: University of Chicago Press, 1994.

Cherry, Conrad. *Hurrying toward Zion: Universities, Divinity Schools, and American Protestantism*. Bloomington and Indianapolis: Indiana University Press, 1995.

Cook, Ramsay. *The Regenerators: Social Criticism in Late Victorian English Canada*. Toronto: University of Toronto Press, 1985.

Crouse, Eric. "Capitalism under Fire: Voices of Baptist Social Protest in New Brunswick and Nova Scotia during the Great Depression." *Journal of the Canadian Church Historical Society* 43 no. 1 (Spring 2001) 39–56.

Davidson, John. "Luxury and Extravagance." *International Journal of Ethics* 9 no. 1 (October 1898) 54–73.

Davidson, John. "England's Policy toward Her Colonies since the Treaty of Paris." *Political Science Quarterly* 14, no. 1 (March 1899) 39–68.

Davidson, John. "England's Policy toward Her Colonies since the Treaty of Paris II," *Political Science Quarterly* 14 no. 2 (June 1899) 211–39.

Davidson, John. "The Financial Relations of the Dominion of Canada and the Provinces." *The Economic Journal* 15 no. 58 (June 1905) 164–85.

Davidson, John. *A New Interpretation of Herbart's Psychology and Educational Theory through the Philosophy of Leibniz*. Edinburgh: Blackwood, 1906.

Dean, William. *American Religious Empiricism*. Albany, NY: State University of New York Press, 1986.

Dorrien, Gary. *The Making of American Liberal Theology: Idealism, Realism, and Modernity*. Louisville: Westminster John Knox, 2003.

Drummond, Ian M. *Political Economy at the University of Toronto: A History of the Department, 1888–1982.* Toronto: University of Toronto Press, 1983.

Ferguson, Barry. *Remaking Liberalism: The Intellectual Legacy of Adam Shortt, O. D. Skelton, W. C. Clark and W. A. Mackintosh.* Montreal and Kingston: McGill-Queen's University Press, 1993.

Fetter, F.A. Review of *The Bargain Theory of Wages* by John Davidson. *Political Science Quarterly* 13 no. 3 (September 1898) 566–69.

First Baptist Church Rockford, Church Records, IL, 1903–1906.

Frank, David. "Davidson, John." In *Dictionary of Canadian Biography*. Vol. 13, 241–42. Toronto: University of Toronto Press, 1994.

Gauvreau, Michael. *The Evangelical Century: College and Creed in English Canada from the Great Revival to the Great Depression.* Montreal and Kingston: McGill-Queen's University Press, 1991.

Gauvreau, Michael, and Ollivier Hubert. *The Churches and Social Order in Nineteenth- and Twentieth-Century Canada.* Montreal and Kingston: McGill-Queen's University Press, 2006.

Goodwin, Craufurd D. W. *Canadian Economic Thought: The Political Economy of a Developing Nation 1814–1914.* London: Cambridge University Press, 1961.

Goodwin, Daniel C. "Maritime Baptist Union and the Power of Regionalism." *Journal of Ecumenical Studies* 41 no. 2 (Spring 2004) 125–46.

———. "The Origins and Development of Wilfred Currier Keirstead's Social and Political Thought." *Acadiensis* 37 no. 2 (Summer/Autumn 2008) 18–38.

Hinson, E. Glenn. "Baptist Contributions to Liberalism." *Baptist History and Heritage* 35 no. 1 (Winter 2000) 39–47.

Jenkyns, Richard. *Victorians and Ancient Greece.* Cambridge, MA: Harvard University Press, 1980.

Jodock, Darrell. "Ritschl, Albrecht Benjamin." In *Biographical Dictionary of Christian Theologians*, edited by P. W. Carey and J. T. Lienhard, 136–38. Peabody, MA: Hendrickson, 2002.

Keirstead, Wilfred Currier. "The Claims of the Maritimes." *McLean's Magazine*. February 15, 1934.

———. "Discussion in Democracy." *The Canadian Forum* 18, no. 218 (March 1939) 377.

———. "Educational Aims." W. C. Keirstead Fonds, UA RG 63 Series 1, Number 12.

———. "The Golden Rule in Business." *Journal of Religion* 3 no. 2 (March 1923) 142–56.

———. "Ideals in Dictatorships and Democracies." *Dalhousie Review* 19 no. 1 (April 1939) 41–48.

———. "The Light Which Self Consciousness Sheds upon the Existence of God." MA thesis, University of New Brunswick, 1899.

———. "Metaphysical Presuppositions of Ritschl." *American Journal of Theology* 10, no. 3 (July 1906) 677–718.

———. "The Report of the White Commission." *Canadian Journal of Economics and Political Science* 1 no. 3 (August 1935) 368–78.

———. "Rural Taxation in the Province of New Brunswick." *Journal of Political Economy* 34 no. 6 (December 1926) 669–90.

———. "Some Essential Facts of Social Progress." *Biblical World* 39, no. 1 (1912) 38–46.

———. "Theological Presuppositions of Ritschl." *American Journal of Theology* 10, no. 3 (July 1906) 423–51.

————. "The University of New Brunswick: Past and Present." *Dalhousie Review* 22, no. 1 (1942) 33–42.

Kiesekamp, Burkhard. "Presbyterian and Methodist Divines: Their Case for a National Church in Canada, 1875–1900." *Studies in Religion* 2 (1973) 280–302.

Lingley, Darren S. "John Davidson: Political Economist." MA thesis, University of New Brunswick, 1990.

Lofton, Kathryn. "The Methodology of the Modernists: Process in American Protestantism." *Church History* 75, no. 2 (June 2006) 374–402.

MacKay, Garth. "'Entire Instantaneous Sanctification' and New Brunswick Free Christian Baptists, 1832–1888." MA thesis, Acadia University, 2007.

MacKirdy, Kenneth A. "The Formation of the Modern University, 1859–1906." In *The University of New Brunswick Memorial Volume*, edited by A. G. Bailey, 33–46. Fredericton, NB: University of New Brunswick, 1950.

Marr, Lorna J. "Women and the New Brunswick Normal School, 1890 to 1910: Society's Untapped Resource?" MA thesis, University of New Brunswick, 2002.

McCann, Larry. "The 1890s: Fragmentation and the New Social Order." In *The Atlantic Provinces in Confederation*, edited by E. R. Forbes and D. A. Muise, 119–54. Toronto: University of Toronto Press, 1993.

McKay, Ian. "The Liberal Order Framework: A Prospectus for a Reconnaissance of Canadian History." *Canadian Historical Review* 81 no. 4 (December 2000) 617–45.

McKay, Ian. *Reasoning Otherwise: Leftists and the People's Enlightenment in Canada, 1890–1920*. Toronto: Between the Lines, 2008.

Nicols, Robert Hastings. "Shirley Jackson Case." *Church History* 17 no. 1 (March 1948) 55–56.

Nolan, Michael. "An Infant Industry: Canadian Private Radio 1919–36." *Canadian Historical Review* 70, no. 4 (1988) 496–518.

Pacey, Desmond. "The Humanist Tradition." In *The University of New Brunswick Memorial Volume*, 57–68. Fredericton, NB: University of New Brunswick, 1950.

Peden, Creighton. *The Chicago School: Voices in Liberal Religious Thought*. Bristol, IN: Wyndham Hall, 1987.

P[etrie], J. R. "Obituary: Wilfred Currier Keirstead, 1871–1944." *Canadian Journal of Political Science* 11, no. 1 (February 1945) 111–14.

Pittman, Jerry N. "Darwinism and Evolution: Three Nova Scotia Newspapers Respond, 1860–1900." *Acadiensis* 22, no. 2 (Spring 1993) 40–60.

Puls, Mary Sarto. "The Personalist Theism of Borden Parker Bowne." PhD Dissertation, Marquette University, 1965.

Rawlyk, George. *Ravished by the Spirit: Religious Revivals, Baptists, and Henry Alline*. Montreal: McGill-Queen's University Press, 1984.

The Religious Intelligencer and Bible Society, Missionary and Sabbath School Advocate. Denominational Newspaper of the New Brunswick Baptist Conference (Free Christian Baptist Church), published in St. John, NB.

The Rockford Republic & *Carleton Sentinel*.

Saunders, S. A. *The Economic Welfare of the Maritime Provinces*. Wolfville, NS: Acadia University Press, 1932.

Shore, Marlene. *The Science of Social Redemption: McGill, the Chicago School, and the Origins of Social Research in Canada*. Toronto: University of Toronto Press, 1987.

Taylor, W. G. L. Review of *The Bargain Theory of Wages* by John Davidson. *The Journal of Political Economy* 7 no. 1 (December 1898) 125–26.

Toole, Francis J. "The Scientific Tradition." In *The University of New Brunswick Memorial Volume*, edited by A. G. Bailey, 69–74. Fredericton, NB: University of New Brunswick, 1950.

Van Die, Marguerite, ed. *Religion and Public Life in Canada: Historical and Comparative Perspectives*. Toronto: University of Toronto Press, 2001.

W. C. Keirstead Fonds, University of New Brunswick Archives and Special Collections. Harriet Irving Library, Frederickton, New Brunswick.

Walker, Francis C. "Davidson, John." In *Standard Dictionary of Canadian Biography*, 142–43. Toronto: Trans-Canada, 1934.

Williams, Clifford. "The Political Philosophy of Two Canadians: John Watson and Wilfred Currier Keirstead." MA thesis, University of Western Ontario, 1952.

Woodstock United Baptist Church, Church Records. Acadia University Archives, Wolfville, Nova Scotia.

Tommy Douglas making one of his many speeches.
Used by permission of Douglas-Coldwell Foundation www.dcf.ca.

4

"One Here Will Constant Be"

The Christian Witness of T. C. "Tommy" Douglas

SANDRA BEARDSALL

I N THE SPRING OF 1911 a pregnant Scottish woman arrived in Winnipeg on a colonist train, her six-year old son and four-year old daughter in tow. There, Anne Douglas reunited with her husband, Tom, an iron molder who had journeyed to Canada a few months before to find work. The Douglases and their children settled into their rented home in north Winnipeg, one more anonymous family in the great surge of immigrants flocking to western Canada in search of jobs and secure futures. The life of that migrant family's son, Thomas Clement "Tommy" Douglas, however, would be anything but ordinary. He would eventually evoke a gamut of emotions as one of the best known political figures in Canadian history. Celebrated by many and disdained by some, T. C. Douglas became a preacher and politician unafraid of either gospel or left-leaning rhetoric and passionate in defense of his principles and actions.[1]

---

1. A 1,142-page report on Tommy Douglas, compiled in secret by the Royal Canadian Mounted Police over the several decades Douglas served as an elected representative, is now retained by the Canadian Security Intelligence Service (CSIS), which defended its refusal to release the document by arguing that its content could still jeopardize national security. Journalists and political scientists, however, suggested that the revelation of these intrusions into Douglas's life, which included wire-tapping and other forms of spying, would embarrass the government and security officials. For details of the CSIS dossier, and the court challenge to unseal it, see http://www.cbc.ca/canada/story/2010/02/10/csis-tommy-douglas-.html.

On the one hand, Douglas was "Tommy," a beloved hero. Canadians cherish him as the "Father of Medicare" and selected him in a nation-wide popular poll in 2004 as "The Greatest Canadian" of all time, ahead of hockey players, entertainers, founding political leaders, and other prominent individuals.[2] His radiant smile, his ringing oratory (with its lingering hint of a Scots brogue), his sincere Christian faith grounded in his Baptist ordination and lifelong church membership, and his legacy of accomplishments, have placed him above reproach in the national mind. Although he was small of stature, it seemed fitting that a 2006 television miniseries about Douglas was titled *Prairie Giant: The Tommy Douglas Story*.

On the other hand, T. C. Douglas was also a self-declared socialist. "Capitalism hasn't the answer," he declared early and often.[3] He consort-ed with peace activists, labor organizers, and leftist thinkers. He spoke in vivid terms of the ways that private control of resources exploits others. He advocated for public ownership of "anything that affects the public."[4] He took principled but risky positions throughout his career, from chas-tising the Allied Forces for their refusal to let the Red Cross ship food to children behind enemy lines in 1943[5] to opposing the imposition of the War Measures Act during the 1970 "October Crisis" in Canada. The CBC withdrew *Prairie Giant* from further broadcast after its initial air-ing, following strong accusations of inaccuracy in the film's presentation of a Liberal politician, James G. Gardiner, who sparred with Douglas. Even after his death, Tommy Douglas has remained a dangerous figure in the contested realm of Canadian identity and myth-making.

These diverging portraits make Douglas an intriguing figure. Although Douglas did not write his own memoirs, many of his speeches were recorded. Douglas also gave extensive interviews later in his life, and he is the subject of several detailed biographies.[6] Born near Glasgow,

2. Waiser, *Tommy Douglas*, 69.

3. Title of a 1944 radio broadcast, reprinted in Lovick, *Tommy Douglas Speaks*, 82.

4. Radio broadcast on CKCK, Regina, 14 September 1943 (Saskatchewan Archives, Saskatoon, Tape S-67a).

5. Radio broadcast on CKCK, Regina, 22 December 1943 (Saskatchewan Archives, Saskatoon, Tape S-67a).

6. The most comprehensive study is that of McLeod and McLeod, *Tommy Douglas*, who conducted extensive interviews with Douglas and others. See also Shackleton, *Tommy Douglas*. Another key work is Thomas, *Making of a Socialist*, consisting of extensive interviews with Douglas. Lovick, *Tommy Douglas Speaks* records some of

Scotland, raised in Winnipeg, educated at the Baptists' Brandon College and through summer studies at the University of Chicago, and called to pastor at Calvary Baptist Church, Weyburn, Saskatchewan, Douglas became increasingly convinced that his evangelistic message demanded a public social witness. First elected as a federal Member of Parliament for the Cooperative Commonwealth Federation (CCF) in 1935, his greatest impact arguably came in the years he spent as CCF Premier of Saskatchewan (1944–1961). He went on to lead the federal New Democratic Party (1961–1971), remained a sitting federal member until 1979, and died in 1986, at age 81 in Ottawa.

All his biographers grapple to varying degrees with Douglas's religious faith and its impact on his political life. A few scholars have focused on his theology.[7] The purpose of this study is to draw together some of those threads to demonstrate the ways that Tommy Douglas's Christian faith and political commitment were inextricably linked throughout his years in congregational work and in government, and to suggest that a significant part of his contribution to Canadian public life relates to his Christian formation and Baptist identity. Douglas's spiritual life is divided chronologically into two parts: his years of personal spiritual formation and Baptist congregational ministry, and his long public career. The passage from the first era to the second did not represent a breach, a change of heart, or a capitulation to "mainline" Protestantism beyond what his own Baptist denomination was embracing in his day. Rather, evangelism and the public good lay at the heart of both his pastoral and his political callings, but with differing emphases. In the first part of his life Douglas became a "politicized evangelist," while he lived the second part as an "evangelizing politician." The purpose of this chapter is to explore Douglas's faith and witness through both these eras, in order, finally, to confirm that Tommy Douglas remained true to his early religious heritage, and that it is reasonable to claim that he "really was," throughout his life, a Baptist: he was loyal to the Baptist church that he encountered in his time and place and faithful to the core distinctives of a western Canadian Baptist "identity."

Douglas's speeches. Margoshes, *Tommy Douglas,* and Stewart, *Life,* offer commentary, but not much new data. Johnson with Proctor, *Dream,* focuses on the Saskatchewan years. Tyre, *Douglas in Saskatchewan,* brings an anti-socialist perspective to a study of Douglas's political life to that date.

7. Oussoren, *Baptist Preacher;* Ban, "Case Study"; Ellis, "Baptists and Radical Politics," esp. 173–78.

THE "POLITICIZED" EVANGELIST

The influences on Tommy Douglas's worldview began early and persisted. The lenses through which Douglas learned to observe and assess society before his election in 1935 would shape his thought and his action throughout his political career. Such influences were not simply a series of persons, events, and ideas, however. The manner by which Douglas encountered this network of impressions also molded his character from his early life through his Brandon years to his Weyburn pastorate and Chicago studies.

Tommy Douglas was born in Falkirk Scotland on 20 October 1904, and he was always fiercely proud of his Scottish heritage. His father, Tom, was a trained and employed ironworker. Tom Sr. nurtured his young son in a cradle of staunch Labor Party views, Robert Burns's egalitarian poetry, and the belief that Tommy could and should aspire to a life beyond the ironworks. Douglas remained emphatic about his father's effect on his perspective. Tom Douglas Sr. was not formally educated, but he was honest and forthright. He despised hypocrisy. He urged his son to learn and perform the poetry of Robert Burns, a talent Tommy would exercise over and over, from adolescence on. Tommy considered Burns "the first apostle of human equality," a champion of the laboring classes and their rights.[8] Tommy also learned from Burns to distinguish contempt for the "establishment church" from reverence for a "benevolent Creator . . . and a conviction that God's sacred nature pervaded the whole of his Creation."[9] Tom Sr. reflected that view in his own life, having quit the Presbyterian Church in Scotland after a row with the minister. But he did not discourage his family from practicing their Christian faith.

The Baptist influence came from Tommy's mother, Anne. Her father, Andrew Clement, drove a Glasgow delivery wagon. He had been an alcoholic, but was converted to Christianity—and sobriety—by the Plymouth Brethren. However, he left the Brethren for the Baptists, among whom he found "more room to breathe," and his family, including Tommy's mother Anne, remained in the Baptist fold.[10] Baptists were a small minority in Scotland's religious culture. Although some had arrived with Cromwell's armies in the 1640s, enduring Baptist communities

8. Tyre, *Douglas in Saskatchewan*, 62.

9. McLeod and McLeod, *Tommy Douglas*, 9.

10. McLeod and McLeod, *Tommy Douglas*, 8.

had emerged only in the nineteenth century, generally among disaffected Scots Presbyterians. Divergent Baptist groups had come together in the Baptist Union of Scotland in 1869, around common concerns for temperance, education, and youth work.[11] The Baptist Women's Auxiliary, formed in 1909, had as its motto "By love serve one another."[12] It was among these moderate activist Baptist women that Tommy Douglas first encountered Baptist faith. This Baptist influence was reinforced in the years of Tommy's childhood that Anne and her children spent living with her parents in their Glasgow flat while Tom Sr. served in a Scottish unit in the First World War. These were difficult times. Tommy left school at age thirteen to supplement the family income by working in a Glasgow cork factory. "I didn't rebel, because there was no one to rebel against," he reflected.[13] However, the young Douglas emerged from that Glasgow crucible with an identity grounded in Scottish egalitarianism and a Christianity nurtured in early twentieth-century evangelical faith. Each of these perspectives would continue to mark his life and work.

The Douglas family returned to Winnipeg in 1918. Canada's third-largest city boomed with railway business and industry. For two decades immigrants from the British Isles, Poland, Germany, Russia, and Scandinavia had been pouring in, seeking, as did the Douglases, opportunities for economic and social advancement. By 1911, 19 percent of the city's population was European immigrant. Despite some economic clouds on Winnipeg's horizon, and the labor strife that was sweeping the nation, there was employment for both father and son: Tommy worked as a messenger and then a printer's apprentice, eventually becoming the youngest linotype operator in Canada.[14]

Roman Catholics, Anglicans, Methodists, and Presbyterians had been planting churches in Winnipeg and other parts of western Canada since the mid 1800s, but the Baptists had been slow to act in this region. The Regular Baptist Missionary Convention of Ontario had sent Thomas Davison and Thomas Baldwin to western Canada in 1869. When they returned to report that they had encountered "severe weather, limited

11. Stepp, Review of *The Search for a Common Identity*, 107–8.

12. See a brief history of the Baptist Union of Scotland at http://www.scottish baptist.org.uk/history.htm.

13. Interview with Ian McLeod, 26 April 1985. McLeod and McLeod, *Tommy Douglas*, 14.

14. Margoshes, *Building*, 22.

resources, and the presence of native inhabitants" the Convention took no further action in the west for the time being.[15] It was when "Pioneer" Alexander McDonald arrived from Ontario in 1873 that western Baptist work began in earnest. Initially, McDonald founded or shared preaching points with other Protestant denominations. By 1875, he had established First Baptist Church, Winnipeg with fourteen members. By 1880, four churches had joined the Red River Association. The first Baptist church in Saskatchewan was founded at Moose Jaw in 1883.[16]

Baptist missions in western Canada were complicated by several factors. The "new Baptists" of the west tended to be merchants and professionals, which meant that Baptist influence stayed mostly in the urban centers.[17] Furthermore, a small nucleus of self-supporting congregations constantly strove to support a large number of immigrant missions. Immigrant churches also affiliated with Baptist associations of their ethnic heritage, rather than seeking union with other Baptists in their area. However, the bulk of western Baptists came together in 1907 to form the Baptist Union of Western Canada.

Beulah Baptist Church, Winnipeg, was a logical destination for Anne Douglas and her children. Located on Kelvin Street, near their north Winnipeg home, it was also where the other neighborhood teenagers attended church and a host of youth programs. It seems likely that Beulah maintained the combination of evangelical piety and social activity that was common to North American Protestant churches of the time.[18] Along with Sunday morning and evening worship and afternoon Sunday School, Tommy was at Beulah for Scouts on Tuesday nights, Prayer Meeting on Wednesdays, Young People's Meeting on Fridays, and on Christian Endeavour youth group outings on Saturdays.[19]

Anne and her children had also found a welcome at the Methodist All People's Mission, which, during the family's earlier sojourn in Winnipeg, had been pastored by the Methodist Social Gospeller James S. Woodsworth. Douglas later reflected on Woodsworth: "in the part of

15. Chan, "Recovering a Missing Trail," 21.

16. McDonald, *Baptist Missions*, 28.

17. Ellis, "Baptists and Radical Politics," 164.

18. Diana Butler-Bass describes North American congregations 1870–1950 as "social congregations," gathered around family and parish hall: the church "*is* a civic organization" (Butler-Bass, *Practicing Congregation*, 17).

19. McLeod and McLeod, *Tommy Douglas*, 17.

society we moved in, he was a little god . . . My mother had a great regard for him."[20] There is a tendency in scholarship to label the Social Gospel movement as defunct by the First World War.[21] In Canada, however, while its theologians had been somewhat marginalized, its message was thriving. Its language of "Kingdom building" and the value of "personality" were central to the nascent political parties that Social Gospellers such as Woodsworth were striving to develop.

Douglas began to learn this language in his Winnipeg youth, and it affected how he viewed church life in the Beulah congregation. He did not resist or reject Beulah—he became a Scout leader and was deeply connected to the church's life and programs—but he and his friend, Beulah Scout leader Mark Talnicoff (later Talney), according to Talney saw themselves as "young rebels." Talney stated that the issue was the preacher's "total emphasis on the after-life" and the fact that he never preached on the "vicious problems and the evils which plagued the people of Canada." Douglas and Talney saw themselves as Christians, but they sought a Christianity committed to embracing the "social side" of the gospel. The two young men began to believe that they could "best work for Christian improvement through the Christian ministry."[22]

While Beulah and its Christian message were central to Douglas's life, he received them through the filter of other experiences that perhaps fed and enhanced his dissatisfaction with an "after-life-oriented" Baptist faith. His father, Tom, continued to espouse an egalitarian philosophy, which he extended to his view of his culturally diverse Winnipeg neighborhood. In an era when even progressive Anglo-Protestants spoke in condescending terms of eastern European and Asian immigrants, Tom delighted in the ethnic plurality of his neighbors. Tommy recalls him saying: "You're playing with the Kravchenko kid. This is marvelous; this is what the world should be like. Sure, I can't understand the family next

20. Interview with Ian McLeod, 25 April 1985, in McLeod and McLeod, *Tommy Douglas*, 10.

21. George Hoffmann asks if Douglas was really affected by the Social Gospel, when its "strength had failed" (Hoffmann, Review of *Tommy Douglas: The Road to Jerusalem*, 125). Other historians make similar claims. See, for example, Marshall, *Secularizing the Faith*.

22. Mark Talney, taped interview, 1986, quoted in McLeod and McLeod, *Tommy Douglas*, 17.

door, but you kids are growing up together, and you'll work for the same kinds of things, and you'll build the same kind of world."[23]

The young Douglas's worldview was also affected by the people and books he encountered in his work at the print shop and by those he met while boxing at the One Big Union gym and in the DeMolay (Masonic Lodge) youth group. Co-workers and youth leaders encouraged him to read, to speak, and to aspire to further education. He began to delve into the books he was helping to print, including *The Farmer in Politics*, by the former Methodist minister, now Calgary Labour politician, William Irvine.[24] On 23 June 1919, Douglas watched the deadly events of that "Bloody Saturday" in the Winnipeg General Strike from the roof of a downtown building. To witness firsthand the shooting of strikers and to learn of the arrest and jailing of the estimable J. S. Woodsworth (who had left Methodist ministry but was in Winnipeg on a speaking tour) reinforced Douglas's dawning conviction that the world was out of sorts, and that faith could not be separated from the task of setting the social order right.

As a youth, Tommy Douglas experienced his Christian faith in a matrix of social and political realities and commitments. "A man's a man, for a' that" he learned from Robbie Burns, as he formed friendships with children from struggling families of all backgrounds. At Beulah Baptist Church he learned devotion and personal commitment, but he also gained a sense of belonging and a call to leadership, as he was offered opportunities to work with youth groups and to plan Sunday evening services. In 1922, Douglas preached his first service as a lay minister there,[25] marking the beginning, one might say, of his astonishing career in public oratory. In Winnipeg's labor struggles he saw faith leaders laying down their lives for the oppressed. William Irvine's words struck a chord that would continue to reverberate, perhaps for the rest of Douglas's life: "The line between the secular and the sacred is being rubbed out."[26] Tommy's Christian faith would be deep and sincere, but it could not be world-hating.

---

23. Tommy Douglas, interview with Ian McLeod, 26 April 1985, in McLeod and McLeod, *Tommy Douglas*, 10.

24. McLeod and McLeod, *Tommy Douglas*, 16.

25. Thomas, *Making of a Socialist*, 39.

26. McLeod and McLeod, *Tommy Douglas*, 16.

Tommy Douglas's decision to save money to study for Baptist ministry would forever alter the direction of his life, for it would take him to Brandon College. Preceded (and predeceased) by the populist Prairie College, Brandon College, with its motto "Education Crowned with Reverence" opened its doors in 1899. As Margaret Thompson has noted, Brandon was "committed to the same educational standards for ministry as was McMaster."[27] In other words, it was focused on a "church-type" seminary model that put strong emphasis on a grounding in liberal arts. As Walter E. Ellis describes it, "prairie Baptist educational policy was dominated by a liberal spirit and eastern orientation."[28] This educational commitment reflected the fact that Canadian Union Baptists were immersed with other mainline Canadian Protestants in the project of nation-building. This common cause led Baptists to early participation in the talks that would lead to the formation of the United Church of Canada in 1925. Baptists left those conversations, but they did not sever their inter-church connections.[29]

However, the Fundamentalist-Modernist debates of the early twentieth century found their way into the Baptist Union of Western Canada in the 1920s. In 1920–1921, Professor Harris Lachlan MacNeill, professor of New Testament, Greek, and Latin, underwent a heresy trial. MacNeill, an Ontario-born Baptist with a PhD from Chicago, a scholar of "outstanding ability,"[30] was accused of "undermining historic Christianity." The investigating church commission exonerated MacNeill, but the coalition that had laid the charge continued to batter the college.[31] Brandon College eventually bowed under the weight of dissent and the economic distress of the 1930s. It was sold to the citizens of Brandon in 1938.[32]

Although he arrived at Brandon in 1924 just two years after the heresy trial, the young student Douglas was not unsettled by these conflicts. In this intellectually rich setting his natural talents blossomed. He completed the equivalent of his missed high school education and then a Bachelor of Arts. He was an excellent student, a natural leader, and

27. Ellis, "Place to Stand," 35, quoting Margaret E. Thompson, *The Baptist Story in Western Canada* (Calgary: BUWC, 1974), 405.

28. Ellis, "Baptists and Radical Politics," 165.

29. Ellis, "Place to Stand," 44.

30. Ban, "Case Study," 258.

31. Brackney, *Baptists in North America*, 165.

32. Wilson, "Patterns of Baptist Life," 39.

a fine orator and debater. These years also confirmed the spiritual lessons of Tommy Douglas's early youth. Despite the challenges of the fundamentalists, and the generally more conservative nature of Baptists,[33] Douglas continued to encounter the progressive Christianity and Social Gospel rhetoric of the early twentieth century. The college President, John Evans, was active in Baptist circles, but he "championed the cause of freedom of inquiry in all matters, including Christian doctrine." He helped the budding orator Douglas learn how to write a speech.[34]

It was during the Brandon years that Douglas began to experience interdenominational ministry. To earn much-needed funds, Douglas took on student supply ministry work at Knox Presbyterian church in Carberry, Manitoba. In so doing, he was following a well-established pattern among prairie Baptists. As far back as the venerable "Pioneer" Alexander McDonald, Baptists had cooperated with other Protestants in preaching and mission. At Knox, Douglas had his first encounter with Anglo-Protestant rural Canada, where "their politics were blue, their lodge Orange."[35] He also met a Methodist teenager, Irma Dempsey, who began attending the Presbyterian church and whom he would marry in 1930. Douglas would maintain an easy and cordial relationship with other Christian denominations for the rest of his life.

The main effect of the Brandon years, however, was to affirm Tommy Douglas's gifts for ministry, and this was done in the context of a supportive Baptist learning community. Douglas was particularly influenced by Professor Harris MacNeill. Near the end of his life, Douglas would claim: "Any intellectual curiosity I have came from [MacNeill]. . . . He recognized that you have to have answers to the questions about what we are here for, what we are supposed to be doing . . . How do you work with your fellow man to build the Kingdom of God?"[36]

During his final year at college, Douglas and his friend and fellow student Stanley Knowles[37] alternated as supply preachers in Weyburn, Saskatchewan. The congregation was supportive of Brandon College

33. Ban, "Case Study," 258.

34. Thomas, *Making of a Socialist*, 50.

35. McLeod and McLeod, *Tommy Douglas*, 25.

36. Tommy Douglas, interview with Ian McLeod, 24 April 1985, in McLeod and McLeod, *Tommy Douglas*, 23.

37. Knowles went on to be ordained in the United Church of Canada, and then to serve as a CCF/NDP Member of Parliament for 38 years between 1942 and 1984.

and its theological perspective, and they were impressed with both of its student ministers. They decided to issue a call to Douglas because of his interest in youth work. Douglas was ordained, and in 1930, Irma and Tommy began their life and ministry at Calvary Baptist Church, Weyburn. Douglas brought enormous energy to his pastoral work. He conducted extra Sunday preaching services in communities outside Weyburn that lacked ministers, held weeklong revival meetings at Calvary, and engaged the youth in dramatic productions.[38] He met with community leaders, and helped raise money for the local swimming pool. He started a boys' group, and he developed a first-year-university level course in economics to offer at the community level.

Supply preaching during his years at Brandon had helped Douglas shape his ministry style: energetic, deeply engaged with all aspects of community life, and especially attracted to work with youth—in both the congregation and the wider community. These were patterns he had learned at All People's Mission and Beulah Baptist, and that Brandon College had reinforced for him. A resident of Weyburn noted: "Of course Mr. Douglas was never political in church. But he was always for the underdog. That was clear whenever he spoke."[39] Another parishioner described his preaching as relevant, practical, and understandable: "He took quotations from the Bible, but he tailored them to fit the conditions of the 1930s. . . . He preached a practical sort of Christianity that everybody understood because it was down-to-earth and it took heed of our physical needs as well as our spiritual."[40] The Calvary Baptist Board of Deacons enthused about Douglas's effective revival preaching,[41] but it also supported him in his community efforts. Calvary was known as a tolerant congregation,[42] but no doubt some of the warm reception of Douglas's socially engaged ministry stemmed from the fact that he wove word and world together seamlessly in what he said and did.

Douglas also worked on his Master of Arts program in sociology, offered by McMaster University through Brandon College by correspondence, completing his thesis on "The Problems of the Subnormal

38. Shackleton, *Tommy Douglas*, 47.
39. Ibid., 49, quoting Mrs. Jack Clark.
40. Tyre, *Douglas in Saskatchewan*, 65.
41. McLeod and McLeod, *Tommy Douglas*, 30.
42. Ban, "Case Study," 265.

Family" in 1932.[43] At the same time, he began a PhD program at the University of Chicago Divinity School, and in 1931 he took a summer leave of absence from the Weyburn congregation to attend courses in "Religious Drama" and "Christian Sociology" in Chicago.[44] The Chicago experience helped him clarify his attraction to the word "socialist," and it introduced him to the staggering poverty of the thousands of young drifters (hobos) who had been displaced by the Great Depression in this huge urban centre.

The Great Depression was also striking southern Saskatchewan with a vengeance. Drought added to the economic misery, and Weyburn was in one of the driest and hottest parts of the province. Douglas worked with the local Ministerial Association on relief efforts, as well as with teachers, cooperative organizations, and labor groups in an attempt to confront the growing desperation. In 1931, Tommy and Irma were shaken by a coalfields strike at nearby Bienfait and Estevan, where a peaceful motorcade of striking miners was brutally suppressed by the RCMP, resulting in the death of three miners and many injuries.[45] Douglas's sermons, always topical and socially-oriented, would become increasingly so. "Jesus the Revolutionist: Would Jesus revolt against our present system of graft and exploitation?" Douglas asked his congregation.[46] He began to recognize that local efforts were not enough; the situation, he believed, required a larger political organization to confront the socioeconomic problems facing his region. He wrote to J. S. Woodsworth, and asked what "ought to be done."[47] Woodsworth put him in touch with M. J. Coldwell, the Regina-based leader of the Independent Labor Party (ILP). Coldwell visited Douglas in his church study, recognized his talent, and recruited him for the party. Through Coldwell, who would remain a lifelong friend, Douglas began his life in organized politics.

This turn to organized political action did not mark a departure for Douglas from his faith or theological commitments. His MA studies and his summer in Chicago were seminal in introducing Douglas to

43. Douglas's thesis suggested the use of "eugenics" to curb reproduction in families with intellectually or "morally" low-functioning parents. He abandoned this interest when Nazi atrocities around eugenics surfaced.

44. Oussoren, *Baptist Preacher*, 31.

45. See Endicott, *Bienfait*.

46. McLeod and McLeod, *Tommy Douglas*, 35.

47. Thomas, *Making of a Socialist*, 67, 71.

the devastating global nature of the crisis, but also in giving him a conceptual theological framework to take back to the desperate southern Saskatchewan situation. As John Oussoren states, these studies "enabled Douglas to reflect upon and analyze the poverty and hopelessness from sociological, economic, and political perspectives. His pastoral and religious education skills and Social Gospel theology enabled him to respond imaginatively, effectively, and compassionately."[48]

In Chicago, Douglas interacted with prominent socialist and Marxist academics, and while he became impatient with what he experienced as a preference for talk over action, these discussions helped him to formulate his socialist stance. In a shanty town visit he met a homeless man who, when Douglas asked if he could do anything for him, replied: "No! Young man, there is nothing you can do for us. You and your friends go back to university, get an education and change conditions so that future generations will not have to exist as those of us here are doing." Douglas resolved to "do everything within his power" to follow the hobo's advice.[49] Significantly, when he grasped for answers, Douglas turned to theologians: the Baptist Walter Rauschenbusch's clarion Social Gospel call in *Christianity and the Social Crisis* (1907) and some writings of J. S. Woodsworth provided him with answers. As he matured intellectually, Douglas continued to conceive his political identity within the context of his Baptist faith.

When his quest for a faithful approach to economic ruin took him into organized politics, Douglas found himself helping to form a political party whose agenda was explicitly based on Social Gospel principles, and whose very name had featured in the writings of Walter Rauschenbusch: the "Cooperative Commonwealth."[50] Thus, when Tommy Douglas became a candidate for the Farm-Labour (soon to be CCF) Party in the 1934 provincial election, it was not a break from, but an extension of, his pastoral work in Weyburn. As he put it: "At no time did I make a definitive decision to go into politics. It was a cumulative conclusion."[51] The party could not find a candidate, and Douglas agreed to run, he said, "purely with the idea that it was an education campaign."[52] He did not

48. Oussoren, *Baptist Preacher*, 24–25.
49. Clements, "Chicago Shanty Town," 13.
50. McLeod and McLeod, *Tommy Douglas*, 47.
51. Thomas, *Making of a Socialist*, 67.
52. Ibid., 76.

realize that in a few years' time, all of Canada would be introduced to this pastor-educator's Gospel-driven vision.

TRANSITION: THE PASTOR AS A POLITICAL CANDIDATE

Tommy Douglas had entered the realm of political organization at an eventful moment. Coldwell's ILP merged with the farmers' party to form the Farm Labor Party (FLP), which then joined with parties in the four western provinces to create the Cooperative Commonwealth Federation (CCF) in 1932, with J. S. Woodsworth as leader. Its first convention, at Regina in 1933, produced the "Regina Manifesto," with its detailed plan of economic and social reconstruction and its famous closing statement: "No CCF Government will rest content until it has eradicated capitalism."[53]

In June 1934, Tommy, with the agreement of the Calvary Baptist congregation, ran as an FLP/CCF candidate in the Saskatchewan provincial election. In his nomination speech he stated: "We have a sacred obligation before God" to provide for children, the old, and the disabled. "Must children starve while big interests take their pound of flesh?"[54] On election night the Liberals regained government after a Tory interlude. However, the new CCF party became the official opposition. Despite his party's strong result, Douglas finished third in his riding, behind the winning Liberal and incumbent Tory. Handling the defeat with grace, Tommy resumed his pastoral work at Calvary Baptist, and he considered continuing to work for political change from within his pastoral role, or perhaps pursuing university teaching, rather than offering to run in the looming federal election.

Two events helped to change Douglas's mind. One was a visit from the Baptist Union superintendent for the West, who met with the congregation, acknowledged that most of the members supported Douglas's political activities, but then told Douglas that if he were to run, he must make this campaign his last one. Douglas replied that he had "seen the party build up" and hated to "walk out and leave it." Then the superintendent issued a threat: "Leave it. If you don't leave it, and if you don't stay out of politics, you'll never get another church in Canada, and I'll see to it. The Board has given me authority." Douglas replied: "You've

<hr>

53. Waiser, *Saskatchewan*, 14–15.

54. McLeod and McLeod, *Tommy Douglas*, 49.

just got the CCF a candidate." The same week, Douglas received a letter from Stanley Knowles, now ministering in Winnipeg, who wrote that it was Douglas's "duty" to run for office. Tommy discussed the situation with Irma, and he ran in the 1935 federal election.[55] In October 1935, Douglas won the Weyburn federal constituency with 44 percent of the vote. He resigned as minister of Calvary Baptist Church, and the family moved to Ottawa. The politicized pastor would spend the rest of his life as an evangelizing politician.

In the years leading to his long sojourn in political life, Tommy Douglas had experienced saving faith and social engagement as one indivisible reality. Faith without society and the good of the soul without the good of the world—such views were inconceivable to the young believer and then pastor. Gradually Douglas developed the language of the Social Gospel and democratic socialism to describe the relationship between faith and social activism. Eventually, one kind of work overtook another in his quest for the Kingdom.

THE EVANGELIZING POLITICIAN

If Tommy Douglas's pastoral formation and ministry work was consistently rooted in the socio-economic sphere, the converse also applies: Douglas's political life bore the constant imprint of his Baptist theology and ministry. "In a sense," say his biographers, "he stayed in the ministry all his life."[56] The Baptist Union of 1935 decided—despite the superintendent's threat—to retain Douglas on their rolls as a minister in good standing,[57] and he declared himself to be a Baptist minister all his life. One can group the evidence of Douglas's "ministry" into three areas: his parties' platforms and policies, his political practices, and most famously, his rhetoric.

In the 1944 Saskatchewan election campaign, with Douglas at the helm as CCF party leader, the Liberals attempted to equate the CCF platform with the National Socialism of Nazi Germany. In fact, the CCF platform carried the stamp of the Social Gospel agenda. It described an orderly, accountable society, where individuals would retain their private property, but there would be public ownership of natural resources—

55. Thomas, *Making of a Socialist*, 80–81.
56. McLeod and McLeod, *Tommy Douglas*, 26.
57. Ibid., 82.

with no benefits for "promoters, investors, or absentee capitalists," and the economically vulnerable would be protected.[58] "Personality"—the Social Gospellers' understanding that all society must coalesce around practices that allow the individual to thrive[59]—would be achieved through socialized health services, financing for students in post-secondary education, free school text books, penal reform, and freedom of speech, elections, and religion.

These issues would continue to dominate Douglas's political agenda throughout his career. Most of them would eventually become legally enshrined rights for all Canadians. State-funded universal health care, or "Medicare," would come to the fore, given its complexity and the power and wealth of the interests that sought to prevent its enactment. But the championing of "personality" also occurred in small ways. Early in its mandate, for example, the Saskatchewan CCF amended the Vital Statistics Act: the province would no longer register children born out of wedlock as "illegitimate."[60]

Douglas's federalist perspective, which came sometimes at the expense of the goodwill he had won provincially, had a Social Gospel foundation. McLeod and McLeod argue that "He believed that just as the strong should help the weak in the local community, the rich should bear the burdens of the poor in the nation." As Douglas stated in 1961, "If Saskatchewan has newfound riches it cannot share with the rest of Canada, there is no longer room in the party for me."[61]

Some observers cannot reconcile the fact that Tommy Douglas was, and remained, an ordained minister within the rough and tumble world of party politics. Assuming that Christians are docile and inoffensive, and that the Christian clergy are doubly so, such critics see a contradiction in Douglas's political "boldness" and "cockiness."[62] When Douglas thundered at an opponent during a political debate, such behavior is criticized for being a "far cry" from his pastoral calling.[63] This shallow view of pastoral integrity did not faze Douglas. He knew that the Kingdom of God would not be won without battles. He was, after all, a

58. The platform is summarized in Thomas, "CCF Victory," 9.
59. See, for example, the sermon by Fosdick, "When Life Goes All to Pieces."
60. Saskatoon *Star-Phoenix*, 27 March 1945, 4.
61. McLeod and McLeod, *Tommy Douglas*, 134.
62. Hoffmann, Review of *Tommy Douglas: The Road to Jerusalem*, 125.
63. Tyre, *Douglas in Saskatchewan*, 99.

trained boxer who stated, "I think you avoid fights if somebody knows that you're willing to fight."[64]

The Christian marks of Douglas's political practices were his loyalty, his honesty, and his integrity. His lifestyle was disciplined, even ascetic (tales of his devotion to oatmeal and prunes abound). His abundant, if corny, jokes were wholesome and usually self-deprecating. A legislative reporter described him as "warm, plain, sympathetic and principled."[65] His steadfast faith helped him take lonely stands. Yet he was also gracious and welcoming. Eleanor McKinnon, who served as his personal assistant for forty-two years, stated: "He was always willing to see people—especially if they had a problem."[66] Douglas also sought persons of conscience and expertise to do the work of governance, even if they were not political allies.[67] He joked: "It's easier to make a socialist out of an engineer than an engineer out of a socialist."[68] He used his pastoral skills to build collaborative networks. Said fellow NDP MP Grace MacInnis, "I think he always believed genuinely in cooperation, and I think he lived that way, and that's why people loved him."[69]

Above all, Tommy Douglas's faithful continuity of his pastoral ministry was evident in his public rhetoric. In the words of a senior Saskatchewan civil servant: "The essence of Douglas lay in his idealism and his capacity to inspire others with his sense of mission."[70] He used his rhetoric to inspire in various ways. In emulation of the Gospels' Jesus, Douglas created parables, brief tales based on familiar objects, to explain complex realities like the Canadian economic system and why it was failing. His two most popular parables were "The Cream Separator" and "Mouseland," the latter of which included the famous line: "Watch out for the little fella with an idea!"[71] In the late 1940s he began Sunday

64. McLeod and McLeod, *Tommy Douglas*, 17.

65. Schreiner, "Always Accessible," 24.

66. McKinnon, "Open Door Policy," 25.

67. See, for example, the story of civil servant John Shaw, who had worked for the Tory administration, but was retained and granted a raise by the CCF. Whalen, "Tommy Kept His Word," 66.

68. Al Johnson interview with T. H. McLeod, 6 February 1987, in McLeod and McLeod, *Tommy Douglas*, 166.

69. Grace MacInnis, interview with Ian McLeod, 21 April 1985, in McLeod and McLeod, *Tommy Douglas*, 234.

70. Waiser, *Tommy Douglas*, 42.

71. "Douglas Campaigning: Two Socialist Parables, (1944)" in Lovick, *Tommy Douglas Speaks*, 78–81. Both are also available as audio files on-line on YouTube.

evening "Fireside Chats" on radio, where he attempted to recreate the Sunday evening gatherings he had enjoyed with the church youth of Weyburn. These "chats" were folksy, with humanistic themes and religious overtones, although Douglas kept the Christianity subtle: "We can never all agree on what religion means—we can only know what it means for us. . . . Judge not, that ye not be judged."[72]

Sometimes Douglas quoted biblical texts to ease or define a situation, as a preacher would. After the hard losses of the 1962 federal election, he quoted 2 Corinthians: "We are troubled on every side, but not distressed; we are perplexed, but not in despair."[73] At the post-electoral defeat CCF provincial convention in 1964, he compared the scattering of the persecuted disciples in Acts with the need for the party to scatter into the corners of the province to rebuild trust and membership. "Instead of sitting around holding hands and saying what a wonderful group they were," he said of the early Christians, "they were forced to go out and talk to other people."[74]

Douglas's most frequent use of theological rhetoric was to evoke themes of the Social Gospel. In a 1943 radio address, he spoke directly to the Christian community, lifting up statements from each of the Roman Catholic, Anglican, and United Churches to argue that "the various branches of the Christian church are unanimous in their condemnation of the capitalist economy." He then explained the need for a new economic system based on "the supreme worth of human personality," concluding with a statement he would reiterate throughout his life: the new economic system is but a means to an end. "Life at its best," he said, "consists of spiritual values, such as regard for truth, a love of beauty, and a seeking after righteousness . . . We in the CCF have stressed the need for economic change because we have seen how pagan our economy is . . . [But] changing our economic status is not enough in itself. Improving our economic status is only a first step in man's upward climb toward a higher destiny."[75] In a similar vein he would tell a teachers' convention, "Education must be concerned with the formation of character, because in the final analysis, democracy depends on human character."[76]

72. McLeod and McLeod, *Tommy Douglas*, 182–83.
73. Ibid., 229.
74. Ibid., 204.
75. Radio Broadcast on CKCK, Regina, 3 November 1943 (Saskatchewan Archives, Saskatoon, Tape recording S-67b).
76. Douglas, "Teachers' Convention, Swift Current."

Douglas often used "pilgrimage" language in speeches to the political faithful. He told the 1963 national NDP convention, "I do not offer you easy victories or personal gain. I offer you only the chance to save your day and your generation. I offer you the comradeship of being a partner in the great crusade to uplift humanity."[77] And in his final address as federal NDP leader in 1971, Douglas quoted J. S. Woodsworth: "May we be the children of the brighter and better day which even now is beginning to dawn. May we not impede, but rather cooperate with the great spiritual forces which we believe are impelling the world onward and upward. For our supreme task is to make our dreams come true and to transform our city into the Holy City—to make this land in reality 'God's own country.'"[78]

It is worth pondering why Douglas's Social Gospel message was so effective in an era when, as we have noted, the Social Gospel's moment was considered to have passed, its idealism choked out by the clouds of world wars and the intervening dust of economic depression. Scholars generally argue that by the 1940s Reinhold Niebuhr's theology of "Christian Realism," with its more limited view of human capacity and a strong sense of human sinfulness, had repudiated and replaced the hopeful vision of the Social Gospel.[79] A simple explanation would be that nobody had bothered to tell Tommy Douglas that. He did not find the Social Gospel's optimism naïve, or its expectation that humanity could reach for the Kingdom of God unrealistic or hubristic.

In Douglas's world, however, the Social Gospel was not simply an attractive theory. It came attached to a plan, a blueprint for achieving the human solidarity it promised. The soaring rhetoric of Douglas's speeches was always wrapped around a careful explanation of the socioeconomic situation and the possibilities for changing it. As in his "practical" sermons in Weyburn, he asked his listeners to explore both their physical and their spiritual identities. As one observer put it, "He made converts by letting people find out about themselves."[80] Or as United Church minister Ross McMurtry eulogized at the Weyburn memorial service for Douglas: "To him it was not an option, but a solemn obliga-

77. McLeod and McLeod, *Tommy Douglas*, 232.

78. Ibid., 282, quoting Thomas C. Douglas Papers, Ottawa, v. 148, convention speech, 21 April 1971.

79. See an early Canadian example of this view in Crysdale, *Industrial Struggle*, 47.

80. Archer, "Thinking Class Farmers," 43.

tion to leave this world better than he found it . . . To him it was not an idle dream or a pious hope. For him it was the way it was meant to be."[81]

Tommy Douglas used his wide-ranging political pulpit to invite his listeners to share that holy responsibility and to show them how it might be done. He asked them to convert, not to his specifically Christian faith, which was real, but to the powerfully humanistic vision that emerged from that faith. For over forty years, he preached that sermon to a large and sympathetic public congregation. When Thomas Clement Douglas died on 24 February 1986, aged 81, Parliament suspended its sitting so that its members could be among the thousand persons who attended the funeral.[82] Social Gospelers, friends, foes, and strangers, all in some way affected by this preacher who had guided Canadians through peril and promise to that "retreating horizon"[83] which he had kept ever in view.

CONCLUSION

In 1965, a conservative journalist opined: "As much as any man, it was Douglas who turned Canada into the most highly socialized country in the Western world without anybody really noticing what was happening."[84] Could that sort of left-wing public trickster behavior really be the work of a *Baptist*? Observers might be forgiven for their confusion. While there has never been unanimity among Canadian Baptists about their theological positions, Canadian Baptist identities have undergone particularly dramatic shifts in the decades since Tommy Douglas's ordination in 1930. Historian Walter Ellis argued in the late 1980s that the Baptist Union of Western Canada was suffering an "identity crisis."[85] Since then Baptists in Western Canada have continued to evolve[86] to the point that some scholars consider North American Baptist tradition to be in "disarray."[87] As we have seen, Tommy Douglas lived in a very differ-

81. *Regina Leader Post*, 3 March 1986, A4.

82. *Regina Leader Post*, 4 March 1986, D13.

83. "You're moving toward the horizon, and it's a retreating horizon." (Douglas in radio interview, 1985), quoted in McLeod and McLeod, *Tommy Douglas*, 4.

84. McLeod and McLeod, *Tommy Douglas*, 234, quoting Charles Lynch, *Canadian Annual Review*, 1965, 72.

85. Ellis, "Place to Stand," 48.

86. See Ellis, "Fragmented Baptists."

87. Brackney, *Baptists in North America*, 257.

ent denominational milieu than do contemporary Canadian Baptists. Both in the context of his own time and by wider definition, we can claim Douglas, trickster or not, to be truly a Christian of the "Baptist" tradition.

The Baptist churches on the prairies were in many ways at their zenith as Tommy Douglas entered their fold. During Douglas's student years, Brandon College was a small but vibrant Baptist school. It reflected the progressive social Christianity it had come by honestly from the American Baptist Walter Rauschenbusch and those who had studied and worked with him or who had studied in Chicago and other centers that had embraced the Social Gospel movement.[88] Douglas might represent what Ontario fundamentalist T. T. Shields would dismiss as "a baptized pagan of the Fosdick type,"[89] but he was in good Baptist company.

The collegial attitudes Douglas encountered among prairie Protestants, coupled with Baptists' long-standing commitment to religious liberty, created a sense of denominational fluidity that allowed Douglas to affiliate as a Baptist, yet consider the Methodist J. S. Woodsworth "our minister."[90] While he remained a self-proclaimed Baptist, Douglas easily and naturally moved among various churches. In the late 1950s he noted that he would conduct twelve to fourteen services a year, in Baptist, United, Lutheran, and Salvation Army churches, and in Jewish synagogues.[91] Douglas was obviously not of the "come-outer" Baptist strain.

While it can be argued that Douglas, in his context, was and remained a faithful Baptist minister, his link to the Baptist heritage runs deeper than that affiliation. Any attempt to define a "Baptist spiritual identity" is fraught with peril, but some marks might include: an orientation in the Scriptures, an independent spirit, a concern for order, a passion for evangelism, and a sense that the believer is called to "ceaseless effort."[92] These characteristics resonate with the portrait gleaned of Tommy Douglas. Biographer Doris Shackleton notes that Douglas was hard to probe, perhaps because he was "layered with teaching and self-discipline."[93] It was this sincere, yet careful, construction of identity—

88. Ellis, "Baptists and Radical Politics," 165.

89. Shields, "Minutes of Jarvis Street Baptist Church," 504.

90. Thomas, *Making of a Socialist*, 32.

91. Ibid., 352.

92. This list combines features of Hinson, "Puritan Spirituality," and Brackney, *Baptists in North America*, 6.

93. Shackleton, *Tommy Douglas*, 316.

this arguably Baptist identity—that permitted Douglas to speak truth to power, and to speak truth while *in* power. RCMP wiretaps notwithstanding, his authenticity was not in question. Douglas was not interested in being mysterious or complicated. He did not waste time on vanity and self-pity. He wanted to be clear to let his message take center stage.

Baptists, states William Brackney, "have historically exercised exemplary forms of dissent."[94] Surely Tommy Douglas was an "exemplary dissenter." Rejecting the prevailing political worldview, he caught a scriptural vision, committed every ounce of his passion to that mission, and pursued it with the singular resolve of John Bunyan's famous pilgrim, "Christian." And surely no hymn better describes Douglas's life and quest than Bunyan's own, set on the lips of that virtuous spiritual traveler, "Valiant-for-Truth":

> Who would true valour see?
> Let him come hither;
> One here will constant be,
> Come wind, come weather.
> There's no discouragement,
> Shall make him once relent,
> His first avowed intent
> To be a pilgrim.[95]

Tommy Douglas was indeed a pilgrim, determined to invite everyone he met to journey with him from the City of Destruction to the shimmering Celestial City, whose contours resembled the Social Democracy he had learned, from church and from society, to embrace with his whole being. T. C. Douglas was a pilgrim, and his was a pilgrimage that would change Canada forever.

94. Brackney, *Baptists in North America*, 260.
95. Bunyan, *Pilgrim's Progress*, 263.

BIBLIOGRAPHY

Archer, John H. "Thinking Class Farmers." In *Touched by Tommy*, edited by Pemrose Whelan and Ed Whelan, 43. Regina: Whelan, 1990.

Ban, Joseph D. "Tommy Douglas: A Case Study of the Conscientious Pastor." *American Baptist Quarterly* 2, no. 3 (1983) 256–68.

Brackney, William H. *Baptists in North America*. Oxford: Blackwell, 2006.

Bunyan, John. *The Pilgrim's Progress*. Edited by Roger Sharrock. Toronto: Penguin, 1987.

Butler-Bass, Diana. *The Practicing Congregation: Imagining a New Old Church*. Herndon, VA: Alban Institute, 2004.

Chan, Chung-yan Joyce. "Recovering a Missing Trail in Canadian Baptist Footprints in the Northwest: Stories of Chinese Baptists in Western Canada." *Baptist History and Heritage* 39 (Summer-Fall 2004) 20–35.

Clements, Gareld K. "Chicago Shanty Town." In *Touched by Tommy*, edited by Pemrose Whelan and Ed Whelan, 13. Regina: Whelan, 1990.

Crysdale, Stewart. *The Industrial Struggle and Protestant Ethics in Canada*. Toronto: Ryerson, 1961.

Douglas, Tommy. "Teachers' Convention, Swift Current." On *Tommy Douglas*, LP Recording (NDP, 1971).

Ellis, Walter E. "Baptists and Radical Politics in Western Canada (1920–1950)." In *Baptists in Canada: Search for Identity amidst Diversity*. Edited by Jarold K. Zeman, 161–82. Burlington ON: Welch, 1980.

———. "Fragmented Baptists: The Poverty and Potential of Baptist Life in Western Canada." In *Memory and Hope: Strands of Canadian Baptist History*, edited by David T. Priestly, 111–21. Waterloo, ON: Wilfred Laurier University Press, 1996.

———. "A Place to Stand: Contemporary History of the Baptist Union of Western Canada." *American Baptist Quarterly* 6 (1987) 31–51.

Endicott, Stephen L. *Bienfait: The Saskatchewan Miners Struggle of '31*. Toronto: University of Toronto Press, 2002.

Fosdick, Harry Emerson. "When Life Goes All to Pieces." In *The Power to See It Through*. New York: Harper, 1935.

Hinson, E. Glenn. "Puritan Spirituality." In *Protestant Spiritual Traditions*, edited by Frank C. Senn, 165–82. New York: Paulist, 1986.

Hoffmann, George. Review of *Tommy Douglas: The Road to Jerusalem*, in *Saskatchewan History* 40 (1987) 125.

Johnson, A. W., with Proctor, Rosemary. *Dream No Little Dreams: A Biography of the Douglas Government of Saskatchewan, 1944–1961*. Toronto: University of Toronto Press, c. 2004.

Lovick, L. D. *Till Power Is Brought to Pooling: Tommy Douglas Speaks*. Lantzville, BC: Oolichan Books, 1979.

Margoshes, Ed. *Tommy Douglas: Building the New Society*. Montreal: XYZ Society, 1999.

Marshall, David B. *Secularizing the Faith: Canadian Protestant Clergy and the Crisis of Belief, 1850–1940*. Toronto: University of Toronto Press, 1992.

McDonald, J. R. *Baptist Missions in Western Canada, 1873–1948*. Edmonton: BUWC, 1948.

McKinnon, Eleanor. "Open Door Policy." In *Touched by Tommy*, edited by Pemrose Whelan and Ed Whelan, 25. Regina: Whelan, 1990.

McLeod, Thomas H., and McLeod, Ian. *Tommy Douglas: the Road to Jerusalem*. Edmonton: Hurtig, 1987, re-released 2004.

Oussoren, John. *From Baptist Preacher to Social Gospel Politician: T. C. Douglas' Transition.* Vancouver: Chalmers Institute, 1998.

Prairie Giant: The Tommy Douglas Story. Toronto: CBC Mini-Series, 2006.

Schreiner, John. "Always Accessible." In *Touched by Tommy*, edited by Pemrose Whelan and Ed Whelan, 24. Regina: Whelan, 1990.

Shackleton, Doris French. *Tommy Douglas.* Toronto: McLellan & Stewart, 1975.

Shields, T. T. "Minutes of Jarvis Street Baptist Church, 14 October 1926." In *Baptist Life and Thought*, edited by William H. Brackney, 504. Valley Forge, PA: Judson Press, 1998.

Stepp, Eddie. Review of *The Search for a Common Identity: The Origins of the Baptist Union of Scotland*, by Brian R. Talbot. *Baptist History and Heritage* (Spring 2005), 107–8.

Stewart, Walter. *The Life and Political Times of Tommy Douglas.* Toronto: McArthur, 2003.

Thomas, Lewis H. "The CCF Victory in Saskatchewan, 1944." *Saskatchewan History* 34, no. 1 (1981) 1–16.

————. *The Making of a Socialist: the Recollections of T. C. Douglas.* Edmonton: University of Alberta Press, 1982.

Tyre, Robert. *Douglas in Saskatchewan: The Story of a Socialist Experiment.* Vancouver: Mitchell, 1962.

Waiser, Bill. *Saskatchewan: A New History.* Calgary, AB: Fifth House, 2005.

————. *Tommy Douglas.* Markham, ON: Fitzhenry & Whiteside, 2006.

Whalen, Ed. "Tommy Kept His Word." In *Touched by Tommy*, edited by Pemrose Whelan and Ed Whelan, 66. Regina: Whelan, 1990.

Wilson, Robert S. "Patterns of Baptist Life in the Twentieth Century." *Baptist History and Heritage* 36 (Winter-Spring 2001) 27–60.

5

"A Very Present Help in Trouble"

The Canadian Baptist*'s Response*
to the Fenian Invasion of 1866

JAMES TYLER ROBERTSON

O N THE MORNING OF 1 June 1866, under the leadership of General
John O'Neil, the Fenians landed some troops and successfully
invaded Canada.[1] Launching from Pratt's Iron Furnace Dock, Buffalo,
troops landed at approximately half-past three in the morning just south
of Fort Erie. Although initially caught unaware, the Canadian volunteer
militia soon sprang into action. Toronto, Montreal, Hamilton, and countless small villages along the Niagara Peninsula saw young Canadian men
grab coat and shoes and run to help defend their land. Although there
were numerous invasions, "Ridgeway was the most serious encounter
which the Canadian militia had with the Fenians."[2]

Major-General Napier ordered troops dispatched to Port Colborne
and St. Catharines in order to prevent the Fenians from capturing the
Niagara Peninsula. The *Canadian Baptist* reported some of the events at
Ridgeway for its readers:

---

1. For further information regarding the Fenian invasion, see Senior, *Last Invasion*
and *Fenians and Canada*. For an eyewitness account, see MacDonald, *Troublous
Times*. For reading on the Fenians as an organization, see Kenny, *Fenians*; Newsinger,
Fenianism, and Jenkins, *Fenian Problem*.

2. Campbell, *Fenian Invasions*, 16.

[The Hamilton Volunteers] had proceeded only a few miles when they encountered Fenian skirmishers, whom they drove in, and also the supporters for more than a mile. All at once, the brave Volunteers found themselves in the face of a superior force, supposed to be fully 1,500 strong. The Canadians did not hesitate, but continued to advance.[3]

Despite this positive report, the Canadian advance was thwarted. Although the day was won for the Fenians, they were not in high spirits for long. The evening meal had depleted the food supply, and the ferocity of the defenders they had faced during the day led them to believe that they needed significant help. They believed that the break of the next day would bring a substantial Canadian assault, and if they were captured, the hangman's noose would be next. It was decided to cross back to Buffalo in order to gather reinforcements and supplies. On the trip across, the USS Gunboat "Michigan" caught and captured the Fenians. And with that the invasion of Fort Erie concluded.

Although the Fenians fell woefully short of their intended goals of assaulting British territory and acquiring land, and many of their people were captured and sent to trial, they were able to earn the respect and fear of a number of Canadians. The threat of a Fenian return loomed large over Canada for the remainder of the year, as constant reports came from various places that Fenians were ready to make good on their promise of taking Canada. As reported in the *Canadian Baptist*: "The rumored concentration of Fenians at St. Albans, Malone, Ogdensburg, and other points, are [*sic*] doubtless well-grounded; but up to this time we have not learned that they have crossed the lines in force."[4]

This chapter will explore the *Canadian Baptist* response to the Fenian invasion of June 1866. The manner in which the newspaper navigated its own cultural influence at a tumultuous period such as that which surrounded the Fenian invasion is worth examining, for how the *Canadian Baptist* interpreted and reacted to the invasion allows modern readers to gain a better understanding of how this denominational paper attempted to shape public life in Ontario. Such a study reveals

---

3. "Engagement near Ridgeway Station," *Canadian Baptist*, 7 June 1866, 3. For more information and anecdotes from the front lines printed in the religious press, see "Americans Moving."

4. "Americans Moving," 3.

valuable insights into the theology and national identities of Baptists within Ontario.[5]

This chapter examines three aspects of the *Canadian Baptist's* views related to the Fenians in order to illustrate the political views of Baptists, as extolled by their public press, and how such teachings in the *Canadian Baptist* related to other Protestant denominational literature of the time.[6] Such reporting in the press is especially important for a study of Baptists in public life because the primary goal of the Fenians was nationalistic. Consequently, each opinion put forward by the *Canadian Baptist* contained arguments based on a growing sense of Canadian nationalism, written in what would prove to be the year before Confederation.

The first section will focus on the *Canadian Baptist's* condemnation of the Fenian moral character to illustrate the Ontario Protestant understanding that Christian character directly contributed to, and determined the success of, public governance. The next section will look at how this group of "dissenters" utilized Canada's relationship with England to undermine the Irish notion of self-rule as well as to propel Canada's own bid for the same. Finally, the *Canadian Baptist* reserved most of its space and vitriol to attack both the American character of the Fenians as well as the American democratic system. This section is saved for last, because it speaks to the fear in Ontario of an imminent American assault that some historians have argued actually propelled Confederation.[7] In addition, it also serves to show the *Canadian Baptist's* desire to distance itself from any American "taint" that might have become attached to the denomination on account of its American connections.

---

5. This research is the "further research" envisioned by John Moir. In his study of nineteenth-century Baptists and the Social Gospel, Moir leaned exclusively on the *Canadian Baptist*. He stated that it had remained virtually unexamined "despite its obvious importance," but that it was useful to introduce scholarship to some trends within Baptist circles that he hoped would "point the way for further research" (Moir, "Canadian Baptist," 147).

6. I hope to inspire others to use Protestant denominational literature as excellent sources revealing the "public voice" of churches. The obvious weakness of such a study is that all forms of media are inherently edited and written with a mass appeal in mind and the question of how effective they actually were in reflecting their denomination's views must remain in view. However, I agree with Moir that a study of literature like the *Canadian Baptist* is important because, "certain tendencies [within the *Canadian Baptist*] will point the way for further research" (ibid).

7. Waite dedicates an entire chapter to the impact the Fenian invasion had on Confederation. See Waite, *Life and Times*, 263–82.

The problems of official denominational literature as primary sources are numerous. Naturally, one must be suspicious of anything that condenses something as complex as a denominational ideology into redacted and edited segments fit for publication in a newspaper.[8] However, because this chapter is about Baptists in the public sphere, it is those traits that make such a source particularly relevant. The *Canadian Baptist* was the public voice for the small Ontario Baptist denomination at a time when, as William Westfall and Michael Gauvreau have clearly demonstrated,[9] Protestantism was arguably the dominant cultural landscape of Ontario. The Baptist Associations of Ontario were uniform in their praise for the *Canadian Baptist*, "as a means of spreading our distinctive gospel principles"[10] and the Central Canada Baptist Association took it even further by stating that the paper filled a vital educational goal, "as an important auxiliary in the great work of religious instruction" for Baptists in the province, as well as "in the family and other circles."[11]

The *Canadian Baptist* from 1865 to 1867 features prominently throughout the chapter but, when applicable, denominational literature like the *Canadian Churchman* (Anglican) and the *Christian Guardian* (Methodist) will be quoted to help locate the *Canadian Baptist* along the Protestant spectrum. Also, Association minutes and sermons from around Ontario will be offered to supply either contrast or support to the articles found in the press and to give a richer insight into Baptist culture. Finally, the so-called secular press will be used sporadically,

8. For more discussion on this and the use of other religious writings as historical sources, see: Hume, "Historical Methods"; Carlson, "English Funeral Sermons"; Chesebrough and McBride, "Sermons as Historical Documents"; Heath, "Passion for Empire"; Knudson, "Late to the Feast"; Franzosi, "Press as a Source"; Hennessy, "Press and Broadcasting." In his work on Confederation, Waite defends the use of newspapers as effective sources specifically because of their nature. Waite writes, "The newspapers reported and informed; they condemned and criticized; and in the broadest sense they revealed the diversity not only of men and politics but of life itself" (Waite, *Life and Times*, 4).

9. Westfall, *Two Worlds*, and Gauvreau, "Protestantism Transformed."

10. "The Canadian Baptist," *Canadian Baptist Convention, East, 1867*, 42.

11. "This Association recognize[s] the value of a good religious paper in disseminating the truth in the family and other circles . . . we heartily recommend the *Canadian Baptist* to the support of our Churches as an important auxiliary in the great work of religious instruction" ("Canadian Baptist," Minutes of the Central Canada Baptist Association, 1866, 5).

although only in cases when secular papers are referenced by the denominational literature. Unless otherwise noted, all Baptist sources were found at the Canadian Baptist Archives located at McMaster Divinity College in Hamilton, Ontario.

A THEOLOGY OF CITIZENSHIP

There was no instrument more powerful for shaping popular thought in English-speaking Canada in the nineteenth century than the Bible. As Michael Gauvreau notes: "The Bible, which all Protestant Christians regarded as a sure and trustworthy record of God's revelation, supplied the data of faith and the moral principles which directed the conduct of both Christian believers and societies."[12] In order to justify support for state-sanctioned violence, the *Canadian Baptist* asserted the idea that those who fought against the Fenians did so with the blessing of God. What emerged was a multifaceted understanding of how certain types of war were antithetical to Christianity, while others enjoyed the blessing of divine sanction. Thus, when the Baptist press condemned the Fenians and praised the Canadian soldiers who fought them, they did so not just from an understanding that certain wars were "just" and, therefore, praiseworthy, but also for the more materialistic reason that Ontario was a good and beneficial land for its inhabitants and, as such, worth fighting to defend.[13] Such nuanced arguments illustrate that for the Protestants of the time, the Bible and theology were not private tools that had no place in the realms of political policy but were the very guidelines that underpinned any good government.

In the wake of the Battle of Ridgeway, the *Canadian Baptist* appealed to the gospel of Jesus Christ to support its stance against the violent intentions of the Fenian mission. One article claimed, "It is true that war is diametrically opposed to the spirit of the gospel."[14] However, the Baptists were not universally condemning violent conflict but argued that there was a theological difference between the actions of an invader,

12. Gauvreau "Protestantism Transformed," 54. See also Airhart, "Ordering," 98–100; John Strachan, "Letter from the Bishop of Toronto to the Duke of Newcastle, 19 March 1853," in Moir, *Church and State*, 238; Grant, "Impact."

13. "Our Late Troubles," 2. See also "Fenianism in Rome," *Canadian Baptist*, 29 March 1866, and "The Fenian Invasion"; For the idea that the dead from Ridgeway were "victims" of the Fenians, see Stewart, *Country's Trouble*, 8–13.

14. "Our Late Troubles," 2.

who killed for an immoral cause, and those of the invaded, who killed in self-defense and out of a sense of duty and responsibility to their country. In late June of 1866, W. T. Janson of the Central Canada Baptist Association passed the following resolution:

> [T]his Association feels thankful to God for the preservation of our Government, liberties and peace, when threatened by invasion by numerous bodies of armed men calling themselves "Fenians," and . . . we would beseech the great giver of all Blessings to grant to our rulers wisdom to take such steps as shall bring to confusion the lovers of anarchy and violence.[15]

Such a statement was not one of pacifism but one that sought to high-light the Fenians' reported immoral character for the members of the Association, as well as for any who might read their minutes. For the *Canadian Baptist*, it was also essential that the Fenians be seen simply as "a lawless band of men," and not as romantic heroes.[16] Perhaps out of a growing fear that the Fenians might find support for their position among the Irish in Canada, the paper consistently called into question the moral integrity of the movement and the men involved. As the pos-sibility of armed conflict grew stronger, the *Canadian Baptist* struggled to show that the Canadian side was biblically and spiritually superior to that of the Fenians. To accomplish this, the Canadian people were cast as law-abiding and peaceful citizens who had violence thrust upon them by scurrilous and immoral foes.[17] In alignment with that, one writer for the *Canadian Baptist* stated:

> Uncalled for aggression is at all times a crime, by whomsoever committed; and disturbers of the public peace forfeit their lives the moment they enter upon their errand of iniquity and blood . . . The path of peace is the path of safety, and, for all legitimate purposes, the road to honor.[18]

---

15. W. T. Janson, "State of the Country," Minutes of the Central Canada Baptist Association, 1866, 5.

16. "The Fenian Invasion," 2. See also "Our Late Troubles," 3; Stewart, *Country's Trouble*, 13–14; Ganust, *Fenian Invasion*, 5.

17. William Stewart claimed: "On the principles of the New Testament, [war] can be defended and tolerated, only when it is physical might sustaining moral right" (Stewart, *Country's Trouble*, 6).

18. "Fenianism and Patriotism," 3; "The Canadian Volunteers," *Canadian Baptist*, 6 June 1866, 90.

In such a setting, the Christian male citizen's duty, lamentably, became one of violence in order to defend the land and structures where he and his family lived and worked and worshiped. The North Grand River Association recorded a "grateful sense of the gallantry, patriotism, and selfdenial [*sic*] displayed by our Volunteers and other brave defenders in repelling the foe and guarding the Institutions of our beloved Province."[19]

In celebrating the cessation of hostilities, the Huron Association stated that "it is a point of public duty devolving on our Country, to make suitable provisiou [*sic*] for [the wounded men's] wants, as a reward of justice for their valor and patriotism."[20] And William Stewart provides another example of this stance as he preached to his flock only days after the invasion:

> When a territory is openly invaded, and the inhabitants of a peaceful country are ruthlessly plundered, armed resistance and opposition to the invaders becomes an imperative necessity. No doubt every true Christian loves peace, and will ever pray for it; but every true Christian loves justice too, and will ever assert it. War is a tremendous evil, a last and terrible resort.[21]

Although war was considered a last resort, the published Baptist opinion was that the Fenians were violent criminals who must be resisted should they ever enter into Canadian territory.[22] Thus, military success was determined not by the prowess of the soldiers but by the blessing of the Lord and the "power in right and the love of order" that, the *Canadian*

---

19. Minutes of the Tenth Annual Meeting of the Grand River (North) Association, 1866, 10.

20. Minutes of the Seventh Annual Meeting of the Huron Association, 1866, 6.

21. Stewart, *Country's Trouble*, 6.

22. It should not be overlooked how important national purity was at this time in the Protestant mindset. Although an idea of national sin was not prevalent in Baptist writings related to the Fenian invasion (this will be covered in a subsequent section of the chapter) Canadians had inherited from Britain the belief that Christian nations were responsible for the conversion of their neighboring nations. Therefore, the believers of each nation were called upon to live pious lives in order to influence their nation and, in turn, the world. A large amount of Christian rhetoric surrounding the importance of the British Empire hinged on the necessity of a Christian Empire for the good of the entire world. The *Baptist Register* commented on this when it wrote, "Patriotism and piety alike unite their voices in demanding, that those who have the light of truth shall let it shine upon the nations, while they themselves walk in the light as the children of the light, holding it fast and showing it forth." See the "Fifteenth Annual Report," 17.

Baptist argued, gave the readers every "hope to rely upon the strength afforded by being placed in a just and truly defensive position."[23]

William Westfall has noted how prophecy and promised lands were "central to interpretation of Canadian history,"[24] and the Canadian Baptist commentary on the invasion was no exception. To reiterate the spiritual significance of the skirmish, Stewart called the young soldiers in his church "Davids,"[25] and by uniting the battle with the biblical narrative he encouraged these men to see themselves as servants of God with their divine King aiding them in the conflict.[26] Also implied in such language was the idea that the land being fought for was, like the Promised Land of the Bible, a place that housed godly beliefs and godly people. According to the *Canadian Baptist Register*, "Christianity is the great civilizer and pacificator of the nations of the earth," and thus it was imperative that the people retain their piety because the divine presence, "does more to secure the stability of human governments than ever was or ever will be done by fleets on sea or armies on land."[27]

However, there was a small but vocal group of people within the Methodist and Anglican camps that saw the Fenian invasion as evidence of God's displeasure. To this group, Canada was no less guilty than the Fenians for the national distress. E. Stephens wrote, "we shall have *no occasion* to go to war *if* we observe and do, as a nation, all the commandments of God thus sustaining the character of the nation that is specially protected and exalted on account of its righteousness."[28] The Anglican Synod of Huron was audience to a similar sentiment as expressed by Rev. E. Softley at the 1866 gathering:

23. "Passing Events," *Canadian Baptist*, 12 April 1866, 2.

24. Westfall, *Two Worlds*, 5.

25. Stewart, *Country's Trouble*, 6.

26. See Westfall, *Two Worlds*, 4, for the following quote: "buried beneath this materialistic ethos [of Canada] rests a deeply spiritual vision. The biblical passages foretell a new type of society on the earth when the wilderness of sin and injustice will become the dominion of the Lord." Westfall does masterful work communicating how the Protestant church viewed the intertwining of both the secular and the sacred. The call to pray and spiritually prepare for something as carnal as war would seem to support Westfall's claims about the tensions that existed within Canadian Protestant culture of the time of an under-girding of spirituality in most aspects of Canadian life.

27. "Fifteenth Annual Report," 19.

28. Stephens, "Short Way of Dealing with Fenians," 78. Italics part of the original quote.

> [T]his Synod cannot separate without recording its solemn ap-
> prehension of the present critical position of our country. That
> while we have confidence, under God . . . we humbly recognise
> [*sic*] herein a deserved chastisement at the hands of Almighty
> God for our ingratitude as a people, for religious benefits, and
> our unfaithfulness to religious duties.[29]

To these religionists, the Fenians were nothing more than instruments
of God's divine judgment and there was little point in condemning the
men or their ideologies, since "Fenian raids etc. will pursue a people
just so far and no farther than God is pleased to permit, but that they
are special scourges in the hands of a just God, which he brings upon
a people as a punishment for their sins, and which, but for their sins,
would never have known."[30]

　　While such thinking was present in other denominations it did not
appear in Baptist literature of the time. The *Canadian Baptist* contained
no such condemnations and as it pertained to the Fenian invasion, the
South Grand River Association, "express[ed] sincere thanks to Almighty
God for the prospects of deliverance from the ruthless band of invaders."[31]
And the Haldimand Association "earnestly pray[ed] for the continuation of our present privileges both civil and religious."[32] However, it was
the North Grand River Association that either echoed, inspired, or in-
dependently arrived at sentiments identical to those of William Stewart
when it resolved: "we give thanks to Him 'from whom all blessings flow,'
that the plans of the marauders have been so effectually frustrated and
defeated, and would earnestly exhort the members of our churches still
to pray that 'God would be our refuge and our strength, a present help in
trouble.'"[33] Thus, despite the existence of the Fenians, the public Baptist
opinion remained unshaken in its belief that their country was blessed.

　　Why Baptists considered Canada West and later Ontario to be
blessed will be the subject of the next section, but here one must note
that the Christian nature of the government and the prosperity of the

29. Softley, "Notices of Motions by the Rev. E. Softley," 206.

30. Stephens, "Short Way of Dealing with Fenians," 59.

31. "Saturday Afternoon," Minutes from the Tenth Annual Meeting of the Grand
River (South) Association, 1866, 4.

32. Minutes of the Forty-Eighth Annual Meeting of the Haldimand Association,
1866, 5.

33. Minutes from the Tenth Annual Grand River (North) Association, 1866, 10.

late nineteenth century provided Baptists with ample evidence of God's pleasure with the province. With that in mind, the *Canadian Baptist* assaulted the leadership of the Fenians in order to contrast them with the blessed leadership that had led Canada West and its citizenry to construct a garden of the Lord out of a howling wilderness.[34]

The *Canadian Baptist* attacked the Fenians's financial stewardship to further denigrate their character and ability to govern.[35] Seeing in the printing of Irish bonds by the Fenian organization a sinister plot to bleed the already struggling Irish immigrant dry for nothing more than a fictitious pipedream, the *Canadian Baptist* stated: "To obtain money from these people is swindling pure and simple."[36] In case such an argument was too subtle, the paper also reported evidence from within the Catholic Church accusing the American center[37] of using donations to support a lavish lifestyle rather than the cause he professed to serve so whole-heartedly.[38]

By exposing Fenian financial mismanagement, the *Canadian Baptist* was able to accomplish two important ends. First, it helped deflect any suspected Irish-Canadian anger away from England and Canada, and aimed it towards the Fenians. If it could be shown that the Fenians had mismanaged funds, then their role would be transformed from being the saviors of Ireland to being just another corrupt oppressor of the poor Irish peasantry. The *Canadian Baptist* declared that "Ireland has the greatest reason to cry 'Save me from my friends!' The boastful Fenians are doing more damage than long years of prosperity will repair."[39] Second, the discrediting of the Fenians afforded the *Canadian Baptist* an opportunity to proclaim its support for the Irish on the northern side of the border. Articles like these made it known that the Irish

34. For use of this metaphor in Baptist publications of the time, see Robertson, "Go Up and Possess."

35. Such statements were in publication as early as 1865.

36. "Tough Nut to Crack," *Canadian Baptist*, 29 March 1866, 3.

37. The Fenians called their leaders in various cities "centers," as they were to act as the hubs or centers of the organization.

38. "O'Mahony and his executive officers were having a fine time, spending the money which had been forwarded them from the various circles in the United States and Canada." See "The Fenian Brotherhood," *Canadian Baptist*, 21 December 1865, 2. See also "The Fenians: Archbishop Cullen's Letter," 3.

39. "Feniana," 2. See also Clarke, *Piety and Nationalism*, 171.

were respected in Canada West and that their peaceful existence within the province would improve their financial and social lot in life more than if they joined sides with a shameful, financially and morally irresponsible rabble like the Fenians.[40] The invasion somewhat forced the question of whether or not Canada West would be better off with someone like Colonel William R. Roberts, the President of the new republic declared by the Fenians, in charge.[41] According to the *Canadian Baptist*, the moral laxity of his men provided strong indication that Fenian leadership would be substantially inferior to the existing system.[42]

In conclusion, the *Canadian Baptist*'s belittling of the Fenians simultaneously decried the invader and extolled the defender. In the first issue after the invasion, the reader was comforted by realizing that "It is natural for a peaceable people, unaccustomed to seasons of commotion like the present, to be deeply moved." According to the *Baptist*, it was assumed that the reader was, like the nation, peaceable and distressed by such a violent disturbance. Such a statement spoke of the idea that Canada was a sanctuary for those who desired a non-violent life. The *Canadian Baptist* then continued to comfort its readers by assuring them that "a very short time will suffice to show that the war tempest has subsided" before explaining that the successful termination of the Fenian threat meant "the triumph of liberty and peace more perma-

40. "Whatever may be the motives of the advocates of Fenianism, and of those who claim to be in favor of an Irish Republic, one thing is likely to prove true, and that is an increase of the want and destitution of the poorer classes at home." See "The Effects of Fenianism," *Canadian Baptist*, 29 March 1866, 3. See also "The Fenian Invasion," 3; "American News," *Canadian Baptist*, 7 November 1865, 3; "The Fenian Demonstrations," *Canadian Baptist*, 15 March 1866, 3.

41. In September of 1865, the Fenian Senate met in Cincinnati and Roberts was unanimously named as the President of the new republic. He then chose Colonel T. W. Sweeny to be his Secretary of War. Almost immediately the two started gathering money for their enterprise into Canada by issuing bonds for the Irish Republic. The Roberts/Sweeny wing was fervent and immovable in its intentions to invade Canada. Roberts believed that the invasion of Canada would achieve two necessary and desired results for the Fenian movement. First, it would be an actual assault on British ground; second, the acquisition of land in Canada was fundamental to the future legitimacy of the Fenian venture. According to Fenian reasoning, if they could secure even a small territory in Canada, they could then legally declare war, attack British ships without fear of being charged with piracy, and print Irish Republican currency.

42. Gauvreau does comment that for evangelicals of the later nineteenth century, poverty was "the penalty for immoral or 'irresponsible' conduct" (Gauvreau, "Protestantism Transformed," 92). That idea translated to governments as well and adds another spiritual dimension to the condemnation.

nently restored."[43] Thus, while the corrupt actions of immoral men had shattered Canada West's serenity, the downfall of such men would signal the return to the material and spiritual prosperity that Protestants of that time had worked so hard both to define and defend.[44]

LOYAL CANADIAN SUBJECTS

The Protestant culture of Ontario largely depended on the British Empire for many of its traits.[45] However, Bartlet Brebner's "North Atlantic Triangle" is useful in this instance because it offers a picture of how Canadians viewed their culture as both British and American, and of how perceptions related to which nation exercised greater influence changed periodically.[46] In Ontario, Baptists were one of the four domi-

43. "The Fenian Invasion," 3.

44. The following articulates the *Canadian Baptist Register*'s views related to the role of God and evangelical Christianity in the development of a country: "It is 'righteous-ness that exalteth a nation,' and this inspired declaration is fortified by the history of all those free and enlightened nations, where the inhabitants possess an open Bible, an unfettered press, and an evangelical ministry" ("Fifteenth Annual Report," 18). The Grand River (North) Association also lamented the commercial interruption the skirmish created when it stated: "Our country has lately been invaded by a lawless horde of miscreants, whose efforts have been directed towards the subversion of our civil and religious liberties, and have resulted in the temporary *interruption of commerce*, the disturbance of national peace, and the loss of valuable lives." Minutes from the Tenth Annual Grand River (North) Association, 10.

45. With relation to government, the Anglican Church was especially supportive of the British constitution. However, the Methodist reformers of the late nineteenth century would also use Britain as their model for the forms of government they espoused. Jane Errington has done excellent work showing how it was not an American versus British system that created Tory and Reform tensions but how the two groups interpreted what it meant to be British. Whereas the Tories feared any change to the British system, the Reformers feared letting the Tories have a monopoly on defining what a British system looked like. Therefore, both used England as their model but in different ways. See Errington, *Lion*, 20–34, 97–118, and 166–85. However, it should be noted that, of the four Protestant denominations, the Baptists were always the most removed from any form of church-state alliance. In fact, whereas the Anglicans, Presbyterians, and Methodists all received money from the clergy reserves from 1841–1854, the Baptists did not because they "explicitly eschewed any connection between church and state" (Gauvreau, "Protestantism Transformed," 88).

46. "To an extraordinary extent the history of Canada is the history of relations with two other communities: the United Kingdom and the United States. . . . The extraordinary thing about the North Atlantic Triangle—the phrase coined by the late Bartlet Brebner—is what a remarkably flexible figure it is: so much depends on the point of it at which you find yourself" (Stacey, *Canada and the Age of Conflict*, 1:7).

nant Protestant denominations that existed throughout the province[47] but whereas Anglicans had traditionally enjoyed the support of the crown, even possessing clergy reserves until 1854, the Methodists and Baptists were frequently criticized for being entirely too American in their methods, origins, and influence.[48] Therefore, when the staunchly anti-British Fenians invaded the colony of Canada West, the issue of British loyalty was brought to the foreground. While the *Canadian Baptist* never supported the Fenian's political stance in relation to England, neither was it as overt as the Anglican *Churchman* in its support of the crown. For the *Canadian Baptist*, the solution was neither in violent insurrection nor blind loyalty, but in the very Canadian trait of combining both British governance and self-governance.

There is little indication that any of the Protestant denominations held anything but high esteem for the government of England, especially when compared to the notion of Irish rule. The Anglican paper, *The Churchman*, expressed its English sympathies by writing, "If those fanatics would only look at the present position of Ireland, under the glorious flag of our noble queen, they would possibly discover their native land was better off than they could make her."[49] Although the Fenians hoped to be greeted as liberators aiding Canada in its separation from the tyranny of England,[50] the Methodists saw them as mercenaries sent to

47. Donald Akenson has done masterful statistical work on Irish population information, including religious affiliation, in Ontario. However, his final census is from 1842 (Akenson, *Irish*, 392–93). Therefore, this chapter will use Michael Gauvreau's table at the end of "Protestantism Transformed," 96–97. In his chart, which stops in 1861, the Baptists of Ontario are fourth largest at 5.2% of the total population, which is up from being 3.9% of the Protestant population of Ontario in 1842. The other three denominations are: Church of England at 26.4% (1861); Methodists at 29.7% (1861) and Presbyterian at 25.7% (1861). Although in the top four, the Baptist church was far and away the smallest group in the Protestant majority at that time.

48. One example among many is the 1828 Legislative debates between the Anglican John Strachan and Marshall Bidwell (who was Methodist but not representing the Methodist churches at the time) over the issue of provincial education. Strachan argued that the faculty of King's College should have only Anglican faculty due to the potentially disastrous influence of American ideas should Methodists or any of the other leaders of "American" denominations become eligible to teach.

49. "Orange Soiree," *The Canadian Churchman*, 7 March 1866, 2.

50. "I have often been asked what right we had to invade Canada, a people who had never injured us. We had no intention to invade the Canadian people or to interfere with their rights, but we desired to aim a blow at our ancient enemy where it would be done most effectively and Canada was that point. I maintain that we had as much right

steal Canada from England and "invade our soil and wrest our country from the British crown."[51] Although it should be noted that while the Baptists showed themselves at least somewhat understanding of Irish (not necessarily Fenian) frustration with England,[52] they remained in line with the other Protestants in their scorn of the Fenian attack on Britain. Considering it sheer folly that such "wild looking"[53] men could defeat the acknowledged super-power of the day, the *Canadian Baptist* accused the Fenians of being delusional "Giant Killers":

> The plans and boasted strength of Fenians to humble British pride, and break up British Empire, remind us of the exploits of Jack, the Giant Killer. . . . How can they administer soporifics to Great Britain, so that she will remain inactive while their plans are being consummated?[54]

The *Canadian Baptist* went even further and warned that America should take care not to align itself too closely with the Fenians out of fear for how Britain might respond.[55] Furthermore, the *Canadian Baptist* frequently reprinted articles from England that allowed the Canadians to see that their "Mother Country" would not abandon them in this time of need:

> I feel the fullest confidence that these men of British North America, who have proceeded from our loins . . . know well how to defend their homes, their wives, and children; and if, unhap-

as Washington to send troops there during the Revolution. The Fenians went there to meet the soldiers who upheld the power of the British people, even the Queen's Own Rifles" (O'Neill, *Speech to the Nashville Circle*, 2). This is probably the best quotation for understanding the motives of the Fenian Brotherhood in their choice of Canada as the target.

51. "Miscellaneous Resolutions: State of the Country."

52 "No matter what sympathies we may have with the wrongs of Ireland no invasion of Canada by people like these Fenians can be anything but brigandage on a great scale" ("America and the Fenian Raids," 2).

53. *Canadian Baptist*, 7 November 1865, 2.

54. "The Fenians," *Canadian Baptist*, 8 February 1866, 2.

55. "But should the resources of the North be called into active requisition in carrying on war with a first class power like Great Britain, then would the dismemberment of the Union be probable" ("Mistaken Policy," 3). C. P. Stacey comments that during this time the exact opposite was true and that it was England who feared America. He cites the following comment: "There is a craven fear of the United States on the part of England" (Goldwin Smith, *The Treaty of Washington*. Ithaca: Cornell University Press, 1941, cited in Stacey, *Canada and the Age of Conflict*, 25).

pily, the need arose, there is no resource possessed by [England] that she would not freely spend to assist them in their holy work. (Cheers).[56]

With such statements issuing from across the Atlantic, the *Baptist* reiterated its allegiance to England from the belief that the might of the British military would keep Canada safe.

The Fenian desire for independent rule prompted the *Canadian Baptist* to devote considerable time and space to critiquing the legitimacy of Irish self-governance. In essence, the public voice of Ontario Baptists called into question the Irish ability to live successfully without supervision from England: "It is quite a natural thing for [the Fenians] to get into difficulty; and we have no doubt that their leaders will leave them in handsome style, should their lives be placed in jeopardy, or failure attend their plans."[57] Unfortunately, the *Canadian Baptist* did not always clearly delineate which of its comments were meant for the Fenians and which were intended for the Irish people as a whole. Therefore, less than a year after the invasion, the *Canadian Baptist* expressed the opinion that the Irish, as a race, were incapable of self-governance and any victory towards that end should actually be viewed as a failure for the Irish people.[58] As early as 1865, the *Canadian Baptist* printed an article from an American church that espoused this position, and it compared the Irish troubles to recent conflicts between Black and White Americans:

> [T]he majority of the American people do not deem (the Irish people) fit for self-government. The same objections to granting the elective franchise to the colored population of the South will hold good with reference to the question of Irish independence. . . . Their destiny is involved in that of Great Britain, and all who have at their heart the best interest will prefer to have their condition ameliorated under English rule to deluding them with the hope of an Irish republic, which is sure to be blasted at the first attempt to realize it.[59]

---

56. "Mr. Gladstone and the Fenians," 2. Note the understanding that Canada came from the "loins" of Great Britain.

57. *Canadian Baptist*, 12 April 1866, 2.

58. "The onlooking world cannot forget that as Irishmen have never shown capacity for self-government, were the revolution to triumph, its very success would be its worst defeat" ("What They Think of the Fenians," *Canadian Baptist*, 28 March 1867, 2).

59. *Canadian Baptist*, 16 November 1865, 3. Italics part of the original quotation.

These sentiments, which are abhorrent to twenty-first-century readers, reveal the nineteenth-century Protestant idea that certain races were simply better off allowing the British to rule over them.[60] Great Britain's constitution was built on Scripture, and many colonial Protestants argued that despite the Empire's possession of potentially despotic power, it had acted with benevolence.[61] Therefore, any political or social group that challenged English supremacy did so to the detriment of God's kingdom on earth.[62] Thus, the comment that Great Britain was in control of the Irish destiny found its legitimacy within a Protestant concern for the stability of the Empire as well as the destiny of the Irish themselves should the Fenian plan, which was seen as folly based on the assumed inability of the race to responsibly govern itself, succeed.[63] It is fortunate for Canada that these writings did not actually win some Irish-Canadians over to the Fenian cause.[64]

The lack of Canadian support proved to be a bitter disappointment for the Fenian movement. Their goal to overthrow English rule

---

60. In the early nineteenth century, Anglican clergy like the Rev. John Strachan used the hierarchy present in nature to argue for the necessity of church establishment in the colony of Upper Canada. Such arguments were used to minimize the influence of other more evangelical denominations like the Methodists (predominantly) but also the Baptists, due to the inroads such denominations were making into the frontier communities. However, as Gauvreau and Westfall have convincingly argued, what separated Anglicans, Presbyterians, Methodists, and Baptists in the first half of the 1800s dissolved in the changing landscape to the point that an identifiable, and much more united, Protestant culture was in place by the later nineteenth century.

61. That theology should influence political policy was a more common and not controversial idea in the Baptist mind at this time.

62. Although referencing the so-called Boer War at the turn of the century, Gordon L. Heath's work on the British Empire's missionary activity speaks to such sentiments. One of Heath's arguments is that the success of the British Empire was directly linked to the spread of God's word under the protection of a Christian empire. Heath writes, "This confidence that missionary work would be better off under British rather than Boer rule was rooted in the conviction of the relative superiority of the British Empire. . . . Under British rule, missionary work would have a better chance of success" (Heath, *Silver Lining*, 137).

63. "It is a pity that failure should attend every step in favor of Irish independence; but as blunders are very frequently associated with a national tendency towards the ridiculous as well as the sublime, we find the same characteristics cropping out on American soil" ("The Fenian Stock Market," 2).

64. Although the fact that it did not win any Canadian Irish to the Fenian side may be an argument for how widely held such a belief was even within the Irish community.

proved to be an unpopular objective that won them few friends.[65] While Irish nationalism thrived in the United States, it never found the same prominence north of the border.[66] All the way up until the Battle of Ridgeway, the Ontario Protestants continually proclaimed their allegiance and loyalty to England from a belief in "the strong British arm that we were assured, if need be, would be raised in our defense."[67] It was the Canadian pride at being a jewel in the British crown that proved to be the doom of the Fenian hopes for Canadian assistance. The Ontario Protestant churches were "profoundly loyal to [England's] government and institutions, and entirely satisfied with its relation to the British Empire."[68] Only days after the invasion, the Niagara Baptist Association commented on their identity within the Empire when they made the official declaration that

> we deeply deplore the recent troubles through which our beloved country has recently passed, express our grateful admiration of the gallantry and patriotism of our brave defenders, extend our heartfelt sympathy to the bereaved and wounded, and earnestly pray that peace may be maintained, and that the integrity of the great empire to which it is our happiness to belong, may be preserved and unimpaired.[69]

65. For an interesting explanation, offered by a former Fenian who was to play a prominent role in Canadian politics, as to why Fenianism did not catch on in the predominantly Catholic Montreal, see McGee, *Account*.

66. This statement is simplistic it must be admitted. Brian Clarke's sensitive treatment of the development of an Irish-Canadian cultural identity in Toronto is well worth examining because it presents a more nuanced understanding than the sentence above. In *Piety and Nationalism* he does make a compelling argument that divisions that separated people in Ireland disappeared once Irish immigrants found themselves awash in a sea of numerous other ethnic groups. Therefore, people from Cork and Limerick found greater alliance in Canada than they would have enjoyed in Ireland. Of particular relevance to the topic at hand would be the chapter "The Irish in Toronto," 13–30. However, the point does stand that Irish nationalism took on a different flavor in British North America than it did in the United States.

67. Stewart, *Country's Trouble*, 14. However, an author by the name of Stephens also commented about the Canadian tendency to trust more in Britain than in God. He reminded the readers of *The Christian Guardian* that a true Christian finds security in the presence of God: "It is better to trust in the Lord than to put confidence in princes . . ." (Stephens, "Short Way of Dealing with Fenians," 59).

68. "St. Patrick's Day and the Fenians," *The Christian Guardian*, 21 March 1866, 46.

69. Stewart, "Canadian Troubles," 7.

The Fenians could hope for nothing but failure because their very presence gave the religious papers the fodder to create fear among the masses that, in turn, drove them deeper under Britain's wings.

Although the Toronto Hibernian Society[70] enjoyed some support in the Irish Catholic community of Toronto, it was greeted with suspicion and contempt by the Baptist press, which suspected the group of harboring ideas that were contrary to the health and prosperity of Ontario.[71] The *Canadian Baptist* was scathing in its assessment that "the Hibernian Society—affirmed to be professedly benevolent in its objects and purposes—is little else than a nursery of treason . . . the conclusion is all but unanimous that the Society is both anti-British and anti-Canadian."[72] The *Canadian Baptist* also appealed to the laws of the land that afforded Irishmen the same rights as any other citizens of Canada. The *Canadian Baptist* argued that the Fenians "have not a shadow of grievance against the Canadians. Their countrymen enjoy equal rights with others in our land."[73] Canada's strength, so the *Canadian Baptist* argued, was in the clemency and respect it granted to all of its citizens. Since the second decade of the nineteenth century, Canada had received numerous immigrants from the United Kingdom, and believed in its ability to welcome all such people and offer them hope for a life in the new world tied to their role within the larger British Empire.[74]

Although the churches were growing in the "New World" they seemed to remain attached, in spirit at least, to their parent churches in England.[75] However, within the spirit of Canadian loyalty to Britain

---

70. Considered by some as the legitimate front for Fenianism in Canada.

71. For an excellent look at the Irish community of Toronto during this time see Clarke, *Piety and Nationalism*.

72. "Feniana," 3.

73. "Our Late Troubles," 2. See also "Mr. Gladstone and the Fenians," 2; "The Fenian Stock Market," 2; "Our Situation," 2.

74. For more information on the growth and development of the four major denominations in Ontario, see Grant, *Church in the Canadian Era*, 2–23; for a look at the same during the late nineteenth century, see Westfall, *Two Worlds*, 9–12; Wilson, *Church Grows*, 63–80. Also Akenson's *Irish*, 390–91, for the township of Johnstown's 1842 National Origins, which are outdated for the time this chapter focuses on but does highlight the role of immigration in the development of Canada.

75. The existence of strong American ideologies forced ministers and preachers working in Canada to increase their "Britishness" in order to portray their loyalty at a satisfactory level. In so doing, many of them became "as British as the British themselves, if not more so." See Webb, "Canadian Methodists," 171.

lay a growing sense of a unique Canadian nationalism. As Carl Berger states, "While [Canadians] admired many aspects of English society, they neither saw it as an unblemished model nor did they believe that Canada was a pallid transcription of it."[76]Although a distinct national identity was far too illusive to assert dogmatically, it would be equally incorrect to say that Canada was simply a British Province at this time. Some historians argue that throughout the latter half of the nineteenth century, the Protestant churches found greater impetus than before for ecumenical movements like temperance, Sunday School, and Sabbath observance, things that united them and helped form a less denominationally fractured and more united Protestant culture.[77] Although Protestants are frequently considered to have been "apathetic"[78] in regards to the act of Confederation, the Fenian crisis highlights one pre-Confederation event that forced the Protestant press to rally behind the cry of "Our country."[79] And that country had traits that separated it from both America and England.

Loyalty to Britain changed again in the months following the invasion as the Canadians realized that when the Fenians attacked, it was Canadian volunteers—not British troops—that took to the field. The *Canadian Baptist* articulated frustration over the lack of British support, and it reminded its readers that the Fenian threat only existed "on account of our connection with Britain. The real or imaginary grievances of the Fenians have not been authorized in Ottawa, but in England."[80]

76. Berger, *Sense of Power*, 260. Once again, Errington, *Lion*, is useful in her examination of how Canadian culture developed. Gauvreau uses the term "Canadianization" to describe the way in which Canadians borrowed from both England and America in order to suit their situation. In so doing, he argues, they formed something new and uniquely Canadian. See Gauvreau, "Protestantism Transformed," 67–68.

77. "For once the establishment had disappeared, the old battle between church and dissent had little meaning: former enemies became allies, if not friends" (Westfall, *Two Worlds*, 83).

78. "Apathy is a word chosen often to describe the attitude of the Protestant churches to the proposal that the British North American provinces form the nation of Canada" (Airhart, "Ordering," 98).

79. "'Our Country' has been the watchword; and 'our country's safety' has been the wish of every man worthy of being called a Canadian citizen" (Stewart, *Country's Trouble*, 4).

80. "It is not because we are Canadians that we are threatened, but on account of our connection with Britain. The real or imaginary grievances of the Fenians have not been authorized in Ottawa, but in England" ("Our Situation," 2). Also note that the difference is between Ottawa and England. The Canadians were aware that they had their

While that statement was not overly inflammatory in nature, it was in-dicative of a sense among the *Baptist* editors that the proximity of poten-tially hostile forces in the United States might outweigh the benefits of ties with a distant England. The failure of the "British arm" to materialize during the Fenian invasion helped the *Canadian Baptist* articulate home rule as necessary to the public safety of Canadians.

The performance of Canadian soldiers provided a source of mili-tary pride, and although the press was loyal to the Crown, it was also be-ginning to express more distinctly national aspirations. William Stewart included in his sermon the growing awareness that it was in joining with their eastern neighbours that Canadian citizens would find their hope in this, and any future, situation that might trouble the shores or borders of the Canadian nation. He stated:

> [C]an we not already see, that as one of the best results of the present commotion, a sentiment of nationality that will shortly bind the Provinces of British North America in one grand Confederation, and a feeling of loyalty and love to British Institutions and Britain's Gracious Queen . . . these will prove to be the best sheet-anchor to our country in all future storms.[81]

In this sermon one can see the hope of Confederation coupled with the love of England and it was in the mixing of those desires for self-sufficiency and loyalty that the nation of Canada was created.

The Fenian invasion provided a shared story of pride and injustice that Canadians rallied around and used to distinguish fellow Canadians as "us" and the American Fenians as "them."[82] However, one of the more interesting aspects of the burgeoning Canadian identity as described in the *Canadian Baptist* was a move away from Britain and towards home rule for Canada. The close proximity of the Fenians only reinforced the distance between Canada and Great Britain, and with that came the

---

own policies and own system of government that could stand separately from England. While this was not an overt statement for independence, which would not have existed in the Canadian mindset at this point in history, it was one of the earlier hints that a new form of Canadian independence was on the horizon.

81. Stewart, *Country's Trouble*, 10.

82. William Stewart captured this sentiment in his sermon when he said: "But that the best and bravest of *our* young country's sons should be shot down by an armed bunch of desperadoes—it is this thought that renders our indignation all the more in-tense, and our sorrow all the more heart-rending" (Stewart, *Country's Trouble*, 9; italics added for emphasis).

awareness that England's troubles were more than likely to find their way to Canada's doorstep if the Canadians did not start distancing themselves from their "motherland."[83] Although Canada was remarkably diverse in its population and lacked a "dominant national group,"[84] the *Canadian Baptist*, along with the rest of the Protestant press, came down squarely on Britain's side on the issue of "The Irish Question."[85] Therefore, as the case of the invasion illustrates, late nineteenth-century loyalty lived in a tension between its English roots and its American neighbors and, as Jane Errington has asserted, attempted to "maintain a distinctively British society while living in the shadow of an aggressive Republican giant."[86]

ANTI-AMERICAN SENTIMENT

With the growth of Canadian nationalism came the awareness that to be Canadian meant, above almost anything else, not to be American.[87] Historians P. B. Waite, Carl Berger, and Brian Clarke all report that there was a distinct feeling of distrust held by the Canadians towards their counterparts to the south at this time.[88] This section will explore the

83. The failure of the Americans to act honorably in the months leading up to the attack further increased the desire to remain separate from the United States. It was also a setback for the pro-annexation party in the United States. While the notion of annexation to the United States did not appear with any prominence in the Baptist writings before the invasion, it is an entirely different story in the weeks following. *The Baptist* recorded the following comment: "Peaceable annexation is now entirely out of the question" ("Mistaken Policy," 3). The lawlessness of the invasion brought a sense of outrage in the press: "The Canadians found the 1866 raids to be a boost to their nationalism. Their pride increased, and they more rapidly received home rule of their country from England" (Bertuca, *Fenian Invasion*, 18). See also Stacey, *Canada and the Age of Conflict*, 17.

84. Clarke, *Piety and Nationalism*, 176.

85. This was the term used in English circles when talking about the foreign policy with relation to Ireland. It also encompassed the Irish revolutions and, often violent, rejection of English sovereignty.

86. Errington, *Lion*, 191.

87. For a review of the multiple reasons why Canada saw itself as distinct from America, see Berger, *Sense of Power*, 153–76.

88. Clarke, *Piety and Nationalism*, 168–98. Waite believed that the Fenians were simply tools used by the American Government to help perpetrate their own national ideals, something that made Canadians just as uncomfortable: "By 1866 part of the [Fenian] movement in the United States had taken up aims directly consistent with American continental ambitions: the conquest of British North America" (Waite, *Life*

growing anti-American sentiment in the *Canadian Baptist* as well as illustrate the different reasons why the Americans were chastised in the
press. However, in an attempt to demonstrate the nuanced relationship
with the United States and despite the fact that the lion's share of the
literature was decidedly anti-American, this section will conclude with
a look at the more favorable published opinions about America during
this time.

The first—and most common—criticism was the failure of the government to take any action to prevent the Fenian invasion, even though
the Fenian plans were well known.[89] In the months leading up to the
attack the churches speculated about American intentions, and while
some denominations were cordial,[90] the *Canadian Baptist* was deeply
suspicious of the United States' motives. Early on the *Canadian Baptist*
was confident that the Americans, not wanting to incur the wrath of
Great Britain, would not allow the Fenians' plot to materialize. One article stated the matter plainly:

> However deeply Americans may sympathize with the people of
> Ireland touching the injuries received at the hands of the English
> Government, they are not such fools as to encourage open re-

---

and Times, 28–35). Carl Berger states that the Canadian dislike of America was indicative of nationalism more than anything else: "Canadians also could most effectively describe those possessions which they felt made them a distinctive people by contrasting
them with what existed in another country, especially since that country was founded
upon principles diametrically opposed to everything they held dear" (Berger, *Sense of
Power*, 176).

89. "'The government does not regard the evidence sufficient to warrant interfer-
ence.' If this be true the Washington Government is not disposed to do its duty"
(*Christian Guardian*, 7 March 1866, 38). See also "News," *Christian Guardian*, 7
February 1866, 22; "The News," *Christian Guardian*, 14 March 1866, 42; "The News,"
Christian Guardian, 18 April 1866, 62. The Baptist perspective on this is found in
"The Fenians in America," 2; "American News," *Canadian Baptist*, 21 December
1865, 2; "Fenianism and Patriotism," 2; "Mistaken Policy," 2; "The Fenian Invasion,"
2; "Americans Moving," 2.

90. While suspicious of its validity, the Methodist paper of the American movement
was no more than evidence of a keen interest in jurisprudence and a desire to collect
enough evidence to insure that the Fenians would get away with nothing: "It is believed
that the American Government is only apparently an indifferent spectator of the Fenian
manifestations; that it will be ready to prevent the first movement towards the invasion
of any of the British Provinces. . . . We therefore think that the policy of waiting by the
American Government for more active demonstrations by the Fenians may have all
the effects of connivance, if not collusion" (*Christian Guardian*, 7 February 1866, 22).

sistance on the part of the poor peasantry of the Emerald Isle against the gigantic military power of Great Britain.[91]

Incredulous and feeling betrayed by the American Government, the *Canadian Baptist* then printed, "We have been at a loss to account for the apathy with which the American Government has viewed the preparations and menacing attitude of the Fenians towards Canada."[92] The *Canadian Baptist* appeared frustrated that Canada was forced to assemble volunteers and train young men to fight because, had the American Government done its duty, such actions would not have been necessary.

One of the chief criticisms of America was the willingness of the politicians to openly court any group, regardless of their moral repugnancy, if such courting could attain votes.[93] Such behavior invited severe criticism from the *Canadian Baptist*: "Considering the character of electioneering tactics in the neighboring Republic, where any convenient *ruse* is adopted to obtain increased party support, we were not surprised at some men of influence giving countenance to the Fenian banditti."[94] The American offense, from the *Canadian Baptist* perspective, was not only political irresponsibility, but also moral and spiritual failure. The *Canadian Baptist* was especially adamant on the point that "Where high

91. "A Nut for the Fenians to Crack," *Canadian Baptist*, 16 November 1865, 2. Note this is an example of Canada's acknowledgement of British culpability in Ireland's suffering. See also "The Fenians in America," 2; "Correspondence," *The New York Times*, 25 September 1866, 1. During his sermon following the Fenian raid William Stewart could not contain his disbelief at the actions of the United States government: "[The Fenians] have done all [their planning] throughout the length and breadth of the territory, and with the full knowledge of the government of a professedly friendly nation. . . . Senators of the nation harangued the unwashed mob, the very scum of their cities and offscouring of their society; magistrates and officials presided at their meetings and merchants subscribed of their wealth to their cause. . . . What wonder that the misguided men, surrounded by such helpers and sympathizers, should imagine that they had on their side, both the material and moral support of the nation?" (Stewart, *Country's Trouble*, 4–5). The perceived support for the Fenians within America was also addressed in the article "The Fenian Invasion," 2.

92. "Americans Moving," 3. See also "Political Morality," 2; "The Fenians: Archbishop Cullen's Letter," 2; McGee, *Account*, 10; Stewart, *Country's Trouble*, 4–5.

93. "The major component of the Canadian image of the United States was the idea that the British constitution was superior to republicanism" (Berger, *Sense of Power*, 155). Berger correctly goes on to explain that the Canadians viewed the American system as greatly inferior to the British model. This will be dealt with more completely later in this section.

94. "Fenian Sympathy," *Canadian Baptist*, 28 June 1866, 2.

christian [*sic*] principle might reasonably be expected to be blended with civilization and progress, we are disappointed in finding men willing to make shipwreck of the former for the sake of party strength and advantages."[95] Such perceived moral failings by the Americans only strengthened the *Baptist* claim that Canada was the morally superior victim forced to combat immoral people in order to maintain its own sense of decency and freedom.

However, American politicians were not the only ones charged with pandering to violent Fenians. The *Canadian Baptist* consistently expressed its displeasure at the attitudes of the American people and wondered throughout the year whether or not the United States was allowing the Fenians to attack out of some desire for retribution against Canadians who took sides during the Civil War or even for the St. Alban's Day Raid.[96] The *Canadian Baptist* questioned whether or not their southern counterparts desired a more successful outcome for the Fenians in order to bolster their own economy.[97] The general sentiment within the *Canadian Baptist* was a growing suspicion that the American people had immeasurably aided the invasion, because "[t]he Fenians would be powerless for evil were it not for sympathy and material aid extended to them by American citizens and officials."[98]

95. "Political Morality," 2. Other churches also commented on how such behavior would reflect on America's international reputation. The Methodist paper, the *Christian Guardian* wrote, "the tolerance and harbouring of such an unparalleled conspiracy as that of the Fenians, will disgrace them for ever, and prevent any nation ever trusting to their good faith" ("Attacks at Other Points," *Christian Guardian*, 6 June 1866, 90).

96. In 1865, some Confederate soldiers held up three banks in the Vermont town of St. Albans and then made their way across the Canadian border with approximately $200,000. They were arrested in Canada and charged with the robbery. However, their lawyer represented them so well that the charges were dropped and the Canadian bank that was holding the money returned it to them. This caused outrage in the United States and the Canadian government was forced to re-arrest the men. Troops were also ordered to the border to make sure that some American officials did not make good on their threats of crossing the border and taking the men by force. For more on this event, see Phelan, *Ballad of D'Arcy McGee*, 68–71.

97. "There is a growing conviction in the public mind of this country, that the American people have an object in giving encouragement to the Fenians in their attempts at invasion" ("Correspondence: Supposed Sympathy with Fenianism," *New York Times*, 25 September 1866, 1).

98. "Our Situation," 2.

The *Canadian Baptist* also seemed to fear that a Fenian victory would be viewed as a ticket to more land for the Americans.[99] According to P. B. Waite, the imminence of Confederation struck a chord within the American mind as the independent United States wondered whether or not a unified nation loyal to Britain for a neighbor could be a threat to their way of life. Some American journalists wrote that the Fenians could be an excellent tool to disrupt Canadian unity:

> [I]t will be well for our government to watch this confederation movement in Canada, and see whether it does not portend evil . . . It will, however, only be necessary to utter a word of encouragement to the thousands of Fenians who are eagerly awaiting an invitation to invade Canada, for our government to settle the question of a Canadian monarchy with an English Guelph upon the throne, promptly and forever.[100]

Sentiments such as these strengthened the *Canadian Baptist* argument that the Fenians received much of their encouragement and hope for the success of their mission by reading articles like this written in various newspapers. Although it was not mentioned very frequently in the Baptist publications and correspondence, one article in the *Canadian Baptist* did lay some of the blame at the feet of American newspapers.[101]

However, it must be stated that even the ardently anti-American musings of the *Canadian Baptist* took a break every once in a while. Although the articles and editorials opposing the Americans greatly outweighed the pro-American ones, it is worth noting that the *Canadian Baptist* did reprint this article from an issue of the *New York Nation*. In this article the *Nation* instructed its readers that there was nothing good to be gained in siding with the Fenians:

> We are a Christian people, and no matter what the Canadians have left done or undone, we owe it to our own souls not to let bands of ruffians leave our shores for the purpose of killing their

99. Although this thought was countered in the following quotation, "The Americans don't want Canada, although the English think we do. We have enough soil already" ("The Fenian Brotherhood and the Independence of Ireland," *New York Herald*, 24 October 1865). Berger also discusses the idea that Canadians feared Americans were always going after land. See Berger, *Sense of Power*, 175.

100. Waite, *Life and Times*, 264, quoting *New York Herald*, 15 March 1866. The irony of this is that Waite saw the Fenian invasion as one of the greatest catalysts to bring about confederation in Canada.

101. *Canadian Baptist*, 15 March 1866, 3.

young men and desolating their homes. There are some forms of retaliation to which we cannot descend without guilt, and connivance at or sufferance of Fenian raids is one of them. No matter what sympathies we may have with the wrongs of Ireland no invasion of Canada by people like these Fenians can be anything but brigandage on a great scale.[102]

This article, though not wholly complimentary to Canada, did show an awareness of the fact that Canada was not responsible for the woes of Ireland.

Throughout the Ontario Baptist denomination, good relations with America endured throughout the trial of the Fenian invasion. The Huron Association, in contrast to the earlier condemnations of the *Canadian Baptist*, thanked God in their annual meeting for the work of the American government in "rightly us[ing] their power and authority to restrain the Fenians from invading Canada, and hope God will guide them to suppress finally the Fenian rebellion, as regards the civil authorities of the United States, and of the British Empire."[103] In the September following the troubles, the Amherstberg Association assigned delegates to travel to the Michigan, Illinois, and Ohio Associations,[104] and the *Canadian Baptist Register* opened its Foreign Missions section of the report in 1867 with the following: "[We] give grateful thanks to the God of Missions for the great work of the American Baptist Missionary Union . . . and pledge ourselves, as Canadian Baptists, to renewed interest, greater liberality, and closer cooperation in the Foreign Missionary enterprise."[105] That same *Register* even commented on concerns among Ontario Baptists that too many able ministers were finding greener ecclesiastical pastures on the southern side of the border.[106] All such writings

---

102. "America and the Fenian Raids," 2. It is interesting to note that this paper also references an American desire for revenge against Canada for things "done or undone" without specifically mentioning what those things might be.

103. Minutes of the Seventh Annual Meeting of the Huron Association, 1866, 6.

104. Minutes of the Prudential Committee of the Amherstburg Association, 14 September 1866. The adopted motion sent delegates to Ohio in order to support the Anti-slavery Association.

105. "Foreign Missions," in *Canadian Baptist Register, 1867*, 10.

106. "Some have supposed that [the lack of missionary ministers] arose from the migration of Baptist ministers from Canada to the States . . . [but] as many have returned from the States to labor again in Canada"("The Demand for Men and Money," *Canadian Baptist Register, 1867,* 37).

indicate that, irrespective of the *Canadian Baptist*'s vitriol towards the United States, cross-border relations remained prevalent and friendly.

According to the *Canadian Baptist*, the relationship between Canada and the United States was greatly strained because of the Fenian invasion. The paper issued numerous articles lamenting the American involvement in the incident and questioning the integrity of a nation that could allow pirates such free reign. However, while the official denominational literature rarely showed anything but animosity towards the United States, the denomination itself continued its relationship with their American co-religionists unimpeded. Such a discrepancy could argue against the efficacy of the *Canadian Baptist* as a voice for its church, but another explanation is just as plausible. Within the Baptist writings and the Association minutes there was a tension that, in a way, defined Canada at that point in time. Whereas the *Canadian Baptist* was in harmony with the literature of other denominations regarding loyalty to Britain and outrage over the Fenian audacity, the reality of the situation was that no matter how much blame could be placed at the feet of America, pragmatism dictated that a relationship be maintained.

One of the defining traits of Canada at this early stage of the country's history was the awareness that Canadians and Americans were fundamentally different but linked together nonetheless. It is easy to see why the attack deeply offended the people, but geographically, socially, culturally, and even religiously the two nations were (and remain) too close to abandon relations with the other. However, given the Ontario Baptists' close association with the United States and the rancor that such a connection created with some of their fellow Canadian Protestants, it was likely very wise of the official denominational literature to explicitly state its disappointment even if such sentiments never developed beyond the level of rhetoric.

CONCLUSION

In conclusion, the *Canadian Baptist* is one of the few sources of information for most Ontario Baptists in the nineteenth century. It was not simply a collection of sermons, children's stories, advertisements, or Bible studies, but a portal to the world. The religious press reported on events that were occurring around the globe, and the writers gave their thoughts and helped shaped the tone and content of the papers. Since not everyone read the denominational reports, and published sermons were not always easy to come by, the religious press had the widest sphere of influence within church writings. The attitudes and opinions recorded in the *Canadian Baptist* had considerable power in shaping the way the average Ontario Baptist thought about the world in which he or she lived.

As the Baptist press reported on the Fenian invasion, several widely shared opinions came through. Baptists did not approve of the moral character of these "freedom fighters" and did not hold them up as noble heroes but as villains, who stole from the poor, engaged in war mongering, and were untrustworthy as leaders. Such attacks on the morality of the Fenians echoed the Protestant understanding that the Bible, and biblical character, were foundational to the successful governance of any nation.

The *Canadian Baptist* consistently called on its readers to remember their ties to Mother England and to honor their country's proud heritage of fidelity to the Crown. Despite its origins as a dissenting sect in England, in Canada, where there was no established church, "dissenting" lost its meaning and the public Baptist voice was unwavering in its desire to remain within the British Empire. It applauded the young men who took to the field of battle and risked life and limb in order to combat a group that so publicly decried Britain, because the *Canadian Baptist* saw "Britishness" as definitive to the Canadian Protestant identity. However, such loyalty came with the reality that Canada was too far removed from England to rely wholly on the mother country's governance, and so the Fenian invasion became one more piece of evidence that Canada needed more power to control its own national destiny.

Finally, the attitude of the *Canadian Baptist* towards the United States is crucial in defining how this small Protestant group had carved out a unique identity for itself. Publicly distancing itself from the social and political realms of America could only help this relatively tiny denomination as it attempted to garner more of a foothold in Ontario. Throughout the century, the Methodists had been forced to embrace their more "Wesleyan" roots in order to downplay their own American origins, and the Baptists were in a similar situation. Even as the denomination continued cross-border relations with Baptists in the United States they did so as "Canadian Baptists," distinct and unique from their American counterparts.

Thus, by looking at the *Canadian Baptist's* response to the Fenian invasion of Canada in 1866 one can grasp how this denomination's literature interpreted the traumatic event for its readership. Noting the issues on which the *Baptist* focused helps modern readers understand how the paper attempted to guide the denomination and, in so doing, helped construct its identity within the larger Protestant culture. In fact, despite a couple of differing ideas related to national sin and the merit of the Irish cause, it was the *Canadian Baptist's* alignment with its fellow Protestant newspapers that is most noticeable.[107] Whether or not such uniformity was based on a fear of stepping out of line or was simply indicative of the Protestant culture's influence at that time is a matter for another study. What can be seen is that the Baptists, along with other Protestants, breathed life into a burgeoning sense of Canadian identity, and the public response to the Fenian threat to that identity provided one more avenue to extol the virtues that the *Canadian Baptist* believed defined both its church and its nation.

107. W. Gordon Carder echoed such a sentiment when he examined the Christian newspapers of the time. He wrote: "The Baptist responses to current events noted in this paper show identity and sensitivity to the Canadian culture of the time. The expressed feelings and ideas were in harmony with the Canadian Protestant sentiments" (Carder, "Headlines," 143).

BIBLIOGRAPHY

Airhart, Phyllis D. "Ordering a Nation and Reordering Protestantism, 1867–1914." In *The Canadian Protestant Experience, 1760–1990*, edited by George Rawlyk, 98–138. Burlington, ON: Welch, 1990.

Akenson, Donald Harman. *The Irish in Ontario: A Study in Rural History*. Montreal: McGill-Queen's University Press, 1984.

Berger, Carl. *The Sense of Power: Studies in the Ideas of Imperialism 1867–1914*. Toronto: University of Toronto Press, 1970.

Bertuca, David J. *The Fenian Invasion of Canada, 1866*. Ridgeway: Ridgeway Battlefield Museum, [n.d.].

Campbell, Francis Wayland. *The Fenian Invasions of Canada of 1866 and 1870 and the Operations of the Montreal Militia Brigade in Connection Therewith*. Montreal: John Lovell and Son, 1904.

The Canadian Baptist, 1865–67.

Carder, W. Gordon. "A View of Some Canadian Headlines, 1860–1912." In *Baptists in Canada: A Search for Unity amidst Diversity*. Edited by Jarold K. Zeman, 137–47. Burlington, ON: Welch, 1980.

Carlson, Eric Josef. "English Funeral Sermons as Sources: The Example of Female Piety in Pre-1640 Sermons." *Albion: A Quarterly Journal Concerned with British Studies* 32, no. 4 (Winter 2000) 567–97.

Chesebrough, David B., and McBride, Lawrence W. "Sermons as Historical Documents: Henry Ward Beecher and the Civil War." *The History Teacher* 23, no. 3 (May 1990) 275–91.

The Christian Guardian, 1866.

Clarke, Brian P. *Piety and Nationalism: Lay Voluntary Associations and the Creation of an Irish-Catholic Community in Toronto, 1850–1895*. Montreal: McGill-Queen's University Press, 1993.

Errington, Jane. *The Lion, the Eagle, and Upper Canada: A Developing Colonial Ideology*. Montreal and Kingston: McGill-Queen's University Press, 1987.

Franzosi, Roberto. "The Press as a Source of Socio-Historical Data: Issues in the Methodology of Data Collection from Newspapers." *Historical Methods* (1987) 5–16.

Ganust, Doscen. *History of the Fenian Invasion of Canada, with Numerous Illustrations*. Hamilton: Wm. Brown, [n.d.].

Gauvreau, Michael. "Protestantism Transformed: Personal Piety and the Evangelical Social Vision, 1818–1867." In *The Canadian Protestant Experience 1760–1990*, edited by George Rawlyk, 48–97. Burlington, ON: Welch, 1991.

Grant, John Webster. "The Impact of Christianity on Canadian Culture and Society, 1867–1967." *Theological Bulletin* 3 (January 1968) 40–50.

Grant, John Webster. *The Church in the Canadian Era*. Burlington, ON: Welch, 1988.

Heath, Gordon L. "Passion for Empire: War Poetry Published in the Canadian English Protestant Press during the South African War, 1899–1902." *Literature and Theology* 16, no. 2 (2002) 127–47.

———. *A War with a Silver Lining: Protestant Churches and the South African War, 1899–1902*. Montreal and Kingston: McGill-Queen's University Press, 2009.

Hennessy, Peter. "The Press and Broadcasting." In *Contemporary History: Practice and Method*, edited by Anthony Seldon, 17–29. Oxford: Blackwell, 1988.

Hume, David. "Historical Methods: The Case of Miracle Stories." In *Philosophies of History: From Enlightenment to Postmodernity*, edited by Robert M. Burns and Hugh Rayment-Pickard, 42–45. Oxford: Blackwell, 2000.

Jenkins, Brian, *The Fenian Problem: Insurgency and Terrorism in a Liberal State, 1858–1874*. Montreal and Kingston: McGill-Queen's University Press, 2008.

Kenny, Michael. *The Fenians*. Dublin: The National Museum of Ireland, 1994.

Knudson, Jerry W. "Late to the Feast: Newspapers as Historical Sources." *Perspectives* (October 1993) 1–3.

MacDonald, John A. *Troublous Times in Canada: A History of the Fenian Raids of 1866 and 1870*. Toronto: Johnston, 1910.

McGee, Thomas D'Arcy. *An Account of the Attempts to Establish Fenianism in Montreal*. Montreal: Post, 1882.

"Miscellaneous Resolutions: State of the Country." In *Minutes of Several Conversations between Ministers of the Wesleyan Methodist Church in Canada at Their 43rd Annual Conference*, 76. Toronto: Samuel Rose, 1866.

Moir, John S. "The Canadian Baptist and the Social Gospel Movement, 1879–1914." In *Baptists in Canada: A Search for Unity amidst Diversity*, edited by Jarold K. Zeman, 147–60. Burlington, ON: Welch, 1980.

———, ed. *Church and State in Canada 1627–1867: Basic Documents*. The Carleton Library 33. Toronto: McLelland and Steward, 1967.

Newsinger, John. *Fenianism in Mid-Victorian Britain*. London: Pluto, 1994.

O'Neill, John. *Speech to the Nashville Circle of the Fenian Brotherhood upon His Return from Buffalo, New York (12 June 1866)*. Pamphlet. N.p. Copy accessed in the Ridgeway Museum.

Phelan, Josephine. *The Ballad of D'Arcy McGee: Rebel in Exile*. Toronto: MacMillan, 1967.

Robertson, James Tyler. "Go Up and Possess the Garden of the World: The Ontario Baptist Mission to the North West Territories, 1869–1880" *McMaster Journal of Theology and Ministry* 10 (2008–2009) 140–73.

Senior, Hereward. *The Last Invasion of Canada: The Fenian Raids, 1866–1870*. Toronto: Dundurn, 1991.

———. *The Fenians and Canada*. Toronto: Macmillan Company, 1978.

Softley, E. "Notices of Motions by the Rev. E. Softley." In *Minutes of the Ninth Session of the Synod of the Diocese of Huron*. London: "Free Press" Office, 1866, 206.

Stacey, C. P. *Canada and the Age of Conflict*. I. *1867–1921*. Toronto: University of Toronto Press, 1984.

Stewart, William. *The Country's Trouble and the Christian's Consolation: A Discourse Suggested by the Late Lawless Invasion of Canada and Preached in the Baptist Chapel, Brantford*. Brantford, ON: Brantford "Courier" Office, 1866.

Stewart, William. "Canadian Troubles." In *Minutes of the Forty-Seventh Annual Meeting of the Niagara Association, 1866*, 7.

Waite, P. B. *The Life and Times of Confederation: 1864–1867*. Toronto: University of Toronto Press, 1962.

Webb, Todd. "How the Canadian Methodists Became British: Unity, Schism, and Transatlantic Identity, 1827–54." In *Transatlantic Subjects: Ideas, Institutions, and Social Experience in Post-Revolutionary British North America*, edited by Nancy Christie, 159–98. Montreal and Kingston: McGill-Queen's University Press, 2008.

Westfall, William. *Two Worlds: The Protestant Culture of Nineteenth Century Ontario*. Montreal: McGill-Queen's University Press, 1989.

Wilson, Douglas J. *The Church Grows in Canada*. Toronto: Ryerson, 1966.

6

Traitor, Half-Breeds, Savages, and Heroes

Canadian Baptist Newspapers and Constructions of Riel and the Events of 1885 [1]

GORDON L. HEATH

"IT APPEARS THAT LOUIS Riel is the leader of some dissatisfied half-breeds in the North-West. It is a pity that this fellow—a leader in sedition and a murderer—had not received his deserts years ago. He was dealt with all too leniently. Of course the movement which he now heads will be quickly squelched."[2] So begins the Canadian Baptist newspaper commentary on the events of 1885 regarding Louis Riel and conflict in the Canadian prairies. That commentary continued off and on until Riel's execution in the fall of the same year.

Over twenty years ago, Thomas Flanagan noted that the "literature on Riel is immense."[3] Since that statement was made, the literature on Riel has continued to grow, and contemporary studies of his life, religious convictions, sanity, and trial have continued to provoke and provide new interpretations of his life and impact.[4] The recent publishing of his entire written works is a boon for historians who seek first-hand

---

1. I would like to thank the Acadia Center for Baptist and Anabaptist Studies (ACBAS) for its financial assistance and Pat Townsend for her help in the research of Maritime Baptist attitudes to Riel.

2. *Religious Intelligencer*, 27 March 1885, 2.

3. Flanagan, "Riel."

4. A recent biographer notes that "no figure in Canadian history has been the subject of more biographical study than Riel" (Bumstead, *Riel v. Canada*, 7).

knowledge of the convictions of such an enigmatic figure in Canadian history.[5] However, despite the hundreds of works on Riel, there have been no works devoted solely to a study of what the Canadian Protestant churches had to say about Riel and the events of 1885. This is startling, since religion played such an important role in late-Victorian Canada, and surprising, since Canadian Baptist newspapers, for instance, had a great deal to say about Riel.[6]

This article is concerned with four inter-related issues. First, while the attitude of the churches towards Confederation was ambivalent,[7] by the turn of the century the English Protestant churches had captured a vision for the new Dominion and had taken it upon themselves to be "nation-builders." As Phyllis Airhart notes, this nation-building ethos was widespread among the leaders and far-reaching in its application.[8] The question this article asks is: were the Baptists acting as nation-builders this early on? Second, it is evident that newspapers played a critical role in shaping public opinion in the late-Victorian English-speaking world.[9] What has been neglected until recently is that the "late-Victorian Protestant denominational press [also] needs to be seen as an important factor in the development of not only religious convictions, but also political values and opinions."[10] Consequently, what role did the Baptist press play in supporting (or not) the government's role in the

5. Stanley, *Writings*.

6. As Northrop Frye has argued, "religion has been a major—perhaps the major—cultural force in Canada, at least down to the last generation or two." See Frye, "Conclusion," 832. While Baptist papers had a great deal to say about Riel, histories of the Baptist churches in the west make only a few comments about the events of 1885. McLaurin mentions that the conflict led to difficulties for Baptist mission work. See McLaurin, *Pioneering*, 102–3. Thompson provides brief commentary on Baptist attitudes during the events of 1869–70 and 1885. See Thompson, *Baptist Story*, 11–12, 16–17, 100–101.

7. Preston Jones argues that the churches had a wide variety of responses to Confederation, and that "there was no true religious consensus to be found" (Jones, "His Dominion"; see also Grant, *Canadian Era*, 24–45).

8. Airhart, "Ordering," 99.

9. In the late nineteenth century the press was a significant factor in the formation of public opinion. For instance, the "New Journalism" was linked to the "New Imperialism." John A. Hobson, one of the most prominent late-Victorian opponents of imperialism, was concerned about the power of the press in creating imperial sentiment. See Hobson, *Imperialism*, 216–17. Bourinot claimed that the influence of the press played a key role in educating the "masses" about the important issues of the day. See Bourinot, *Intellectual Development*, 83.

10. Heath, "Forming."

events of 1885? Third, while much is stated about the Protestants (especially in Ontario) and Riel, there is no published work specifically on the Canadian Protestant churches and Riel. This article will begin the task of determining the churches' response(s) to Riel and the events of 1885.[11] Fourth, since the breakup of European empires, post-colonial analysis has paid particular attention to the creation of the "Other" and the formation of myth.[12] For instance, Albert Braz notes that Riel is "simultaneously one of the most popular and most elusive figures in Canadian literature, and culture in general."[13] He goes on to say that he has been "depicted variously as a traitor to Confederation, a French-Canadian and Catholic martyr, a bloodthirsty rebel, a New World liberator, a pawn of shadowy white forces, a Prairie political maverick, an Aboriginal hero, a deluded mystic, an alienated intellectual, a victim of Western industrial progress, and even a Father of Confederation."[14] This fluidity of meaning suggests that depictions of Riel and the events of 1885 are primarily influenced by the perspectives and needs of the depicters. In fact, Braz argues that depictions of Riel are "less about him than about their authors and their specific social reality."[15] This research is concerned with how the Canadian Baptist denominational newspapers portrayed the events of 1885. Leaning upon the assumptions of Braz, and others such as Douglas Owram[16] and Wolfgang Klooss,[17] it will explore what these representations tell us about Canadian Baptists (or at least the Canadian Baptist press),[18] mythmaking, and the creation of the "Other" during the tumultuous events of 1885.

11. This research is the beginning of a larger project that will study the Protestant churches' reaction to Riel. For a paper on Riel in 1867–1870, see Robertson, "Possess."

12. Edward Said's *Orientalism* is a "classic" in post-colonial studies.

13. Braz, *False Traitor*, 3.

14. Ibid.

15. Ibid.

16. Owram has noted how the myth of Riel changed over time based on the "perceived need in the minds of the community or because . . . [it was] thought useful to those creating the myth." See Owram, "Myth of Louis Riel," 315–16.

17. Klooss, "Stereotyping," demonstrates how the nineteenth-century images of Riel fulfilled a specific ideological function.

18. In regards to this use of newspapers as primary sources, Glenn Wilkinson has noted that the late-Victorian newspapers are an "excellent source" of information for cultural and social historians. Because a newspaper needs to connect immediately with its readership there is a "form of two-way communication" between the paper and its readers, reflecting in its pages the immediate events and perceptions of the period.

What this research reveals is the Baptist press's unabashed loyalty to the nation, a commitment to a (Protestant) Christian Canada and support for the inevitable advancement of Christian civilization into the Canadian West—a growth that necessitated conversion and assimilation of everyone in its path. Riel and his followers did not fit within any of these assumptions about the nation, its identity, and its inevitable (and necessary) growth, and consequently the press constructed a Riel and a rebellion that needed to be crushed.

Canadian Baptists were one of the four largest Protestant denominations in Canada in 1885, comprising just less than 7 percent of the Canadian population.[19] They arrived in the Canadian West in the 1870s, but by the time of the events of 1885 they still had no significant presence in the prairies (except for Manitoba, where they accounted for roughly 14 percent of the population).[20] Canadian Baptists were a significant but small percentage of Ontario Protestants (over 5 percent), having arrived much earlier (1790s) and had time to build and organize churches and institutions. Baptists arrived even earlier in the Maritimes (1760s) and were one of the dominant Protestant denominations. In the later part of the nineteenth century they comprised roughly 5 percent of the population of Prince Edward Island, 19 percent of the population of Nova Scotia and 25 percent of the population of New Brunswick.[21]

Wilkenson writes "images in newspapers had to conform to the perception of war that readers already held. In this regard, newspapers had little or no thought for posterity or future reputations of their creators, and they needed to create and foster an immediate connection with their reader audiences. This makes the newspapers a form of two-way communication, with readers more than 'blank slates' awaiting to be etched with how to think about the world by the press" (Wilkinson, "To the Front," 203–4). Of course, there are also pitfalls in using newspapers as primary sources. Peter Hennessy has noted that one of the most significant issues related to the use of newspapers as primary sources is editorial bias. He writes that the "value of any report or piece of commentary has to be judged in the light of a paper's editorial predilections as well as the writer's own bias. The fair-mindedness which ought to characterize the historian's work cannot be assumed to govern that of journalists" (Hennessy, "Press and Broadcasting," 20). For another helpful discussion on the potential and pitfalls of using newspapers for research, see Franzosi, "Press."

19. Roughly 60 percent of Canada was Protestant and 40 percent Roman Catholic. The four main Protestant denominations at the time were Methodists (over 17 percent of the Canadian population), Presbyterians (over 15 percent), Anglicans (over 13 percent), and Baptists. See Airhart, "Ordering," 102–4.

20. This figure would drop to just over 3 percent by 1901 (Airhart, "Ordering," 103).

21. Airhart, "Ordering," 102–4.

Like the other larger Protestant denominations in Canada, Baptists had a fairly extensive network of newspapers.[22] Not counting various and numerous missionary publications, Maritime Baptists had two weekly newspapers (the *Religious Intelligencer* and the *Messenger and Visitor*),[23] Central Canada had one weekly (the *Canadian Baptist*)[24] and Western Baptists had a monthly paper (the *North-West Baptist*, that began publication in the summer of 1885).[25] For many, these newspapers were the only source (or just one of a few sources) of information on regional, national, and international affairs. And consequently, as noted above, these papers played an important role in the formation of political opinions.

The Baptist press followed the events in the Northwest closely. For instance, the *Religious Intelligencer* had a weekly column entitled "The North-West Rebellion" devoted to the developments in the west, whereas the *Messenger and Visitor* had weekly commentary on events in its "News Summary" section. Along with such columns, various articles and editorials addressed the conflict, and key events such as the arrest, trial, and execution of Riel were noted and commented on. The week-to-week news was often re-printed from daily papers such as the *Mail* or the *Globe*, or from reports by military expedition leaders such as General Middleton. As A. I. Silver notes, the varied (and often second-hand) sources of information that newspapers drew upon during the conflict made accurate reporting difficult, and certainly impacted the formation of how events were portrayed to the readers of various papers.[26] The differences between the various papers' coverage were subtle: the *North-West Baptist* tended to emphasize policies of immigration and assimilation, the two Maritime publications focused on blow-by-blow accounts of the battles as well as on the departure, performance, and return of their "local boys" who fought, and the *Canadian Baptist* spent

22. For a complete summary of late-Victorian Protestant publications, see Heath, "Forming."

23. Both the *Messenger and Visitor* and *Religious Intelligencer* (editor, Rev. Joseph McLeod) were published in Saint John, NB. The former was a publication of the Baptist Convention of the Maritime Provinces and the latter a publication of the Free Baptists.

24. For a helpful history of the *Canadian Baptist* see Trinier, *Century of Service*. In 1885 the *Canadian Baptist* was published in Toronto, and the editor was E. W. Dadson. Circulation was between 4,000 and 5,000.

25. The *North-West Baptist* began publication in Winnipeg in the summer of 1885.

26. Silver, "Fanaticism," 23–25; Silver, "Nineteenth Century News Gathering."

a great deal of time criticizing the government for its culpability in the events.

PATRIOTISM AND IMAGES OF THE COMBATANTS

The central and eastern Canadian Baptist weekly press (and to a much lesser degree the monthly *North-West Baptist*) provided extensive commentary on military events. Not surprisingly, Britain's imperial conflicts were reported on extensively. The rising tensions between Britain and Russia were an ongoing concern—and at times seemed to eclipse the events in the Canadian West.[27] Smaller conflicts such as the war in (what was then called) Burma were also noted—and approved of.[28] When the troubles in the Canadian West flared up, the press was unanimous in its conviction that the rebellion needed to be put down as soon as possible.

Commenting on the power of the secular press, Paul Rutherford notes that, although there were limitations on what influence the press could have on its readers, the press did have the power to set agendas, mobilize, stereotype, confer status, manipulate, socialize, and legitimize.[29] That argument holds for the religious press. As shown below, readers of the press were presented with a number of subtle and not-so-subtle images that portrayed what true patriots did and supported during the crisis of 1885. For instance, the positive portrayal of the Canadian soldiers was striking, and their character and role was extolled. By the time of the South African War (1899–1902) the image of Canadian (and British) soldiers as distinctly Christian soldiers would be much more fully developed.[30] However, even at this early stage in the development of the young nation, Canadian soldiers were portrayed in idealized terms.

In the opening stages of the conflict, the *Messenger and Visitor* devoted an entire article to the sending of troops to the "war in the Northwest." It was with pride that it declared:

27. "War"; "Jottings from Toronto," *Messenger and Visitor*, 29 April 1885, 4; "What Shall the End Be?"; "Wars and Rumours," *Religious Intelligencer*, 17 April 1885, 2; "Russia Growing More Arrogant," *Religious Intelligencer*, 17 April 1885, 3; "England and Russia," *Religious Intelligencer*, 1 May 1885, 3.

28. "Missionary News," *Canadian Baptist*, 3 December 1885, 1.

29. See Rutherford, *Victorian Authority*, 7–8.

30. For comments on the idea of Christian Canadian soldiers, see Heath, *Silver Lining*, 38. For comments on the idea of a good Christian soldier, see Anderson, "Christian Militarism," 48–49.

From what we hear they are right brave fellows who will give a good account of themselves, if called upon to have a "baptism of fire." It is the first time in this generation that the threat of serious war has come so near to us, and it is well that our volunteers show themselves worthy sons of plucky ancestors, and are ready to present their breasts to the foe that would harm their country or their countrymen and women.[31]

The noble character and mission of the soldiers was repeated in many different papers and articles, and the willingness of many to sign up was considered to show a commendable and hopeful degree of patriotism in the new Dominion. For instance, the *Religious Intelligencer* declared that the number of volunteers, and the speed at which they signed up, was a "convincing declaration of the National spirit of the country."[32]

There was an understandable degree of pride over how local volunteers performed on the battlefield. But in every case, regardless of the point of origin, the Canadian soldiers' virtues and performance were extolled with descriptors such as "manly and patriotic enthusiasm,"[33] "grit and bravery,"[34] "courage in battle" and "humaneness after the battle."[35] They had been tested in battle and had shown themselves as "men to be depended upon."[36] They were enthusiastically described, in the jingoistic language of the day,[37] as ones who had the "blood of warlike ancestors in their veins . . . [who would do] no discredit to the brave men from whom they have sprung."[38] One of the most enthusiastic displays of myth-making was a message delivered to the officers and men of the 62nd Battalion on 15 May 1885. The address was printed on the front page of the *Messenger and Visitor* and portions of it read,

> [The] daring and coolness of our volunteers at the recent battles of Fish Creek, Cut Knife Hill and Batouche Landing serve to show we have the materials of which heroes are made. . . .

31. "Our Young Soldiers," *Messenger and Visitor*, 15 April 1885, 4.

32. *Religious Intelligencer*, 3 April 1885, 2.

33. *Religious Intelligencer*, 15 May 1885, 2.

34. "News Summary," *Messenger and Visitor*, 29 July 1885, 8.

35. "News Summary," *Messenger and Visitor*, 22 July 1885, 8.

36. *Canadian Baptist*, 30 April 1885, 4.

37. Braz provides descriptions of some of the jingoistic descriptions of soldiers in other literary genres. See Braz, *False Traitor*, 52–53.

38. "News Summary," *Messenger and Visitor*, 20 May 1885, 8.

[Y]ou go forth on the most sacred mission that ever enlisted the service of men. You go to uphold constituted authority. You go to preserve law and order and to protect the home of the pioneer on the outposts of civilization and to save his helpless children and wife from the tomahawk and scalping knife of the merciless Indian. You go *sub sacre causa umbra*, and success must crown your mission . . . The life of the state is worth more than the life of the individual, of many individuals, and to preserve it, a Latin poet has sung, It is sweet to die . . . Officers and men, you have heavily responded to the call of duty, the noblest word in our language. Our poet Laureate tells us, the line of duty is the path to glory.[39]

Such glory and nobility of purpose was, it seems, even more glorious and noble when the behavior of the idealized soldiers was contrasted with the evil other—the "merciless Indians."

The papers did lament the loss of life. For instance, in June the *Canadian Baptist* noted the recent burial of two of Toronto's "brave sons" who had been "laid away as heroes in the presence of sorrowing thousands" and expressed thanksgiving for the fact that there were only two deaths.[40] There was also concern expressed over the impact that the war would have on the character of the soldiers and the militarization of Canadian society.[41] Nevertheless, the soldiers were still praised for their duty and devotion. Upon their return from the front it was considered "eminently fitting" that the returning soldiers be met with "honourable recognition" by the waiting crowds.[42] They had made a "noble record" in the west, and citizens should do all that they could to show appreciation for their bravery and sacrifice.[43]

Of course, the glorious character and victory of the patriotic soldiers was in stark contrast with the many images of Riel, the "half-breeds," and the "Indians." While a few articles identified and praised

39. "Address Delivered by Dr. Alward."

40. *Canadian Baptist*, 4 June 1885, 4. Other papers noted the total loss of life. See "News Summary," *Messenger and Visitor*, 3 June 1885, 8.

41. The *Canadian Baptist* made it clear that the "stimulation of the military spirit" in Canada would be a great evil, and the introduction of military drills in schools would not be a good idea. See "Effects of the Rebellion."

42. "Notes by the Way," *Religious Intelligencer*, 7 August 1885, 2.

43. *Canadian Baptist*, 23 July 1885, 4. See also "News Summary," *Messenger and Visitor*, 29 July 1885, 8.

some actions of the "Indians" as brave and commendable,[44] the majority of battlefield images were negative. It was claimed that Riel misused prisoners on the battlefield and threatened other "half-breeds" with death if they did not fight for him.[45] He was, "at best," a cowardly villain.[46] The Métis were referred to as "simple-minded half-breeds."[47] Atrocity stories and accounts of wanton destruction of property by "red-skins" were noted, and Riel and his followers were even described as "creatures" that should be "hunted down as a wolf would be that had torn to pieces little children."[48] Perhaps one of the most offensive images to contemporary readers would be the reference already noted above: the soldier's duty to defend the "helpless children and wife from the tomahawk and scalping knife of the merciless Indian."[49]

When referring to this period, Myra Rutherdale declares that it was "an age of classification" and that the "discourse of difference" was an everyday occurrence.[50] Terms like "race," "breed," "stock," "Indian," "half-breed," and the like were quite common and, for most, were considered to be inoffensive. (For instance, even a socially progressive leader such as J. S. Woodsworth used such racial categories.)[51] Rutherdale's work indicates that such terms were an everyday part of the Canadian missionary's experience within the Canadian West.

As noted above, Braz argues that depictions of Riel are "less about him than about their authors and their specific social reality."[52] What the contemporary reader glimpses with these racially loaded depictions of the combatants is that the Baptist press supported and propagated the alleged racial, religious, and cultural supremacy that was so much a part of Anglo-Saxon imperialism and civilization.

---

44. "The Indians and their squaws fought with coolness and bravery." See "News Summary," *Messenger and Visitor*, 13 May 1885, 8.

45. "News Summary," *Messenger and Visitor*, 6 May 1885, 8.

46. "The Northwest Rebellion." See also *Religious Intelligencer*, 15 May 1885, 2.

47. "The Rebellion."

48. See "News Summary," *Messenger and Visitor*, 6 May 1885, 8; "Riel's Rising," *Religious Intelligencer*, 3 April 1885, 3; "The North-West," *Religious Intelligencer*, 19 June 1885, 3; "The Northwest Rebellion."

49. "Address Delivered by Dr. Alward."

50. Rutherdale, *Women*, 152–53.

51. See chapter on "the orientals" in Woodworth, *Strangers*.

52. Braz, *False Traitor*, 3.

AN EXPANDING CIVILIZATION
AND CHRISTIAN NATION

Upon closer examination, there were significant tensions and contradictions in the papers. While no paper had anything good to say about Riel (he was portrayed to be a pathetic figure, a law-breaker, or a trouble-maker), some of the images of the Métis and First Nations people are both surprising and ironic. There were comments published that presented them in a positive light. The two Maritime papers were the most consistently hostile in their portrayals of the Métis and the First Nations peoples. For instance, the article in the *Messenger and Visitor* that described the alleged reasons for Anglo-Saxon racial superiority expressed well the attitudes towards Riel and his followers during the conflict.[53] However, the central and western-based papers included articles that were much more sympathetic towards to the First Nations peoples. One article (sadly, entitled "Our Canadian Savages") spoke of the need to care for the "Indians" and to protect them from injustice.[54] Another article decried the conditions that led to what it coined "the Indian Problem" and wished to see a "great searching of hearts and consciences throughout all the Christian churches of Canada, and a simultaneous uprising of all who love their fellow-men to undertake a great work for the North-West Indians."[55] Yet another article declared that the heart of an Indian was the same as a white man's and that the "Indian is your brother."[56]

What is ironic is that even in these positive statements of equality the First Nations people were portrayed as savages, pagans, untamed, and pathetic.[57] For instance, consider the following statement of charitable intentions that is filled with paternalism and negative racial assumptions:

> What to do with the untamed Indians is a question which should weigh heavily upon the Christian conscience of Canada as upon that of the United States. The late uprising may evolve some good if it leads us as a people to a sense of our duty in the premises.

53. "The Anglo-Saxon Mission," *Messenger and Visitor*, 8 July 1885, 1.

54. "Our Canadian Savages."

55. "The Indian Problem."

56. "North West Missions."

57. Here the press was similar to other contemporary descriptions of the "Indians" and "half-breeds." See Klooss, "Stereotyping," 134–38; Braz, *False Traitor*, chap. 2.

> The day is, it may be hoped, past when any man with a head
> and a heart can believe that a civilized nation can do its duty
> to tribes of conquered savages by shutting them up on reserva-
> tions, and doling out to them a scanty subsistence, even though it
> should not permit adventurers to crowd them off their lands, or
> dishonest agents to rob them of their land. One can but wonder
> at the supineness of our churches and the people in regard to the
> North-west Indian. With what apparent coolness do we abandon
> them to their filthy paganism and give them over to gradual ex-
> termination by disease and starvation.[58]

Sadly, this very compassion for the First Nations peoples would lead
to even more grief for the First Nations—for the solution to their ills
was shaped by assumptions about race, and even more so by assumptions about the necessary, inevitable, and providential advancement of
"civilization." The solution was understood to be either extermination or
assimilation.

Quite naturally, the *North-West Baptist* printed a variety of articles
that dealt with the larger question of the assimilation of the varieties of
non-British immigrants that settled in the west.[59] The concern was for
the various peoples to become Christians (and hopefully Baptists). The
role of the churches in this process of nation-building was critical, for
it was felt that the "power of the gospel . . . [would] be no unimportant
factor in the assimilation."[60] In other words, as the churches converted
people to Christianity, the diverse peoples would also become a part of
a universal "Brotherhood of Faith" and be united together as fellow citizens of a Christian Canada. Rather than lament the arrival of the new
immigrants, one article in the *North-West Baptist* claimed that the new
immigrants were a providential fulfillment of prophecy:

> By divine decree a union of races is taking place on this side of
> the globe. God made all the nations from one, and He is now
> converging them all into one, so His grand purpose is being ful-
> filled on this continent . . . We shall gain a great deal if we see God

58. "Our Canadian Savages."

59. Airhart notes that this concern over immigrants and the need to "Canadianize"
and "Christianize" them would continue into the twentieth century, and be a concern of
the four major Protestant denominations. See Airhart, "Ordering," 129–30.

60. "Are We to Be One People?" The *North-West Baptist* also provided a summary
of a sermon preached at the Baptist Convention in Winnipeg. In this sermon the role of
Christianity in shaping and uniting nations was emphasized. See "Baptist Convention
of Manitoba and the North-West Territories," *North-West Baptist*, 1 July 1885, 2–3.

as the chief immigration agent of this country; its future will then be lifted up above the sphere of uncertainty; we shall recognize the rapid settlement of these vast prairies as part of God's plan for establishing the bounds of the habitations of the people on all the face of the earth. God has foreordained the peopling of this land. For the last three hundred years the peoples of Europe have been coming to this continent. This great Northwest constitutes about His last survey to make room for the nations of the earth. The people must come; the text prophecies that they must come.[61]

In light of such inevitability, the only solution was, as one article put it: "yield to assimilating influences or agree to extermination."[62]

Articles in the *Canadian Baptist* did not share the same language of providence, but they did assume the inevitable advance, and blessing of, Western civilization. Such articles presented the same choice: assimilate or be exterminated. Of course, extermination was not considered to be an option. The only Christian solution, it was argued, was for a process of assimilation that would allow for the survival of the First Nations peoples. The role of the churches in this process was not to be under-estimated, for it was felt that the politicians had made such a mess that the churches needed to salvage the situation.[63] The solution proposed in the pages of the *Canadian Baptist* was a system of what they called "industrial schools" that would begin the process of assimilation. The example of such schools in the United States was noted,[64] and it was felt that the American model would work well in Canada:

> Shall not the Christian people of Canada imitate their example by inaugurating some such institution in the North-West on a worthy scale? . . . The whole work should be done under posi-tive Christian influence. Hence, as well as for other good reasons, it cannot be left to the State. . . . But why cannot the Christian people of all of Canada arise in their might, cast aside all sectar-ian fetters, and gird themselves for the great work of giving an industrial Christian education to the largest possible number of young Indians in the North-West?[65]

61. "North West Missions," 3.
62. "Are We to Be One People?"
63. "The Indian Problem."
64. Ibid.; *Canadian Baptist*, 4 June 1885, 4; "Our Canadian Savages."
65. "The Indian Problem."

With such an education, it was argued, the people would be safe, civilized, Christianized, and fully assimilated into Canadian life, with the added bonus of Canada avoiding future troubles in the west.[66] As this commentary reveals, one outcome of the troubles of 1885 was the perceived need to solve the "Indian problem," and that solution would become what today is more commonly known as the Residential School system. Sadly, as the recent accounts of abuse at Residential Schools in Canada indicates, this well-meaning and hoped-for assimilation resulted in tragedy for thousands of First Nations people.

MAKE WAY FOR PEACE AND PROGRESS—RIEL MUST GO

While Riel was certainly seen to be the leader of the unfortunate troubles in the west, the image of Riel presented to readers varied from paper to paper. Surprisingly, in Orange Ontario, the image of Riel portrayed in the *Canadian Baptist* was less severe than in the Maritime papers (in this regard, the *Canadian Baptist* mirrored attitudes in other Ontario-based papers).[67] The emphasis in the *Canadian Baptist* was more on the culpability of the Canadian government than on the crime of Riel. In the opening days of the conflict it declared:

> No one who knows anything of the half-breeds of the Territories has hitherto doubted that they are naturally disposed to be quiet, peaceable and tractable. Those are, probably, very wide of the mark who think that Riel is the head and front of the whole uprising. Riel has no doubt applied the match, but he did not prepare the combustibles. Had not the suspicions and fears of the half-breeds been thoroughly aroused, had they not, wrongly or rightly, believed that they were being unjustly treated, that their complaints were disregarded, their grievances unredeemed, half a dozen Riels could not have driven them to take up arms.[68]

This emphasis on the guilt of the Canadian government repeatedly showed up in reporting on the western events. The rebellion was blamed on Canada's national sin of mistreating those in the west.[69] It was a na-

66. The *North-West Baptist* noted a Baptist Convention presentation in Winnipeg that declared that had the "Indians" been "enlightened and educated" they would not have followed Riel into rebellion. In other words, one tangible benefit of assimilation was that it would solve political unrest. See *North-West Baptist*, 1 August 1885, 6.

67. Silver, "Fanaticism," 27.

68. "The Rebellion."

69. "What Shall the End Be?"

tional disgrace that could have been avoided by compassionate and just rule, and was a "monument of unwisdom and unrighteousness on the part of our rulers."[70]

The events surrounding Riel and his followers' arrest and trial were also faithfully reported on in the Maritime papers.[71] However, as noted above, the Maritime reaction to Riel was somewhat less sympathetic than the central Canadian reaction, but, as J. M. Bumstead notes, similar to many other newspapers and even the Canadian government's official position.[72] The opening remarks on the unrest in the west portrayed Riel as a "leader in sedition and a murderer" who should have been punished for his first rebellion.[73] He was also portrayed as "villainous" for inciting his followers to "great crimes."[74] Upon his capture, the *Religious Intelligencer* described him in a manner that, in many ways, would become a standard description in English Canada in the decades that followed:[75]

> He is evidently a cowardly villain at best.... Such creatures should not be treated as combatants treat each other when engaged in what is called "honorable" warfare. A rebel and a murderer years ago was treated with a degree of leniency that was more and worse than a mistake. Now he is doubly a rebel and a multiplied murderer of the most heartless and cruel sort, and it does not become the military representative of an outraged people to treat such an [sic] one at all. He should have been hunted down as a wolf would be that had torn to pieces little children. Now that he is a prisoner he must, of course, receive trial as provided for the

70. "Effects of the Rebellion."

71. For instance, see "News Summary," *Messenger and Visitor*, 3 June 1885, 8; "News Summary," *Messenger and Visitor*, 8 July 1885, 8; News Summary," *Messenger and Visitor*, 15 July 1885, 8; "News Summary," *Messenger and Visitor*, 22 July 1885, 8; "News Summary," *Messenger and Visitor*, 5 August 1885, 8; "News Summary," *Messenger and Visitor*, 12 August 1885, 8; "News Summary," *Messenger and Visitor*, 26 August 1885, 8; "News Summary," *Messenger and Visitor*, 9 September 1885, 8; "News Summary," *Messenger and Visitor*, 7 October 1885, 8; "The North-West," *Religious Intelligencer*, 22 May 1885, 3; "The North-West," *Religious Intelligencer*, 19 June 1885, 3; "The North-West," *Religious Intelligencer*, 17 July 1885, 3; "The North-West," *Religious Intelligencer*, 24 July 1885, 3; "The North-West," *Religious Intelligencer*, 31 July 1885, 3.

72. Bumstead, *Riel v. Canada*, 269–71.

73. *Religious Intelligencer*, 27 March 1885, 2.

74. *Religious Intelligencer*, 15 May 1885, 2.

75. For similar literary descriptions in the decades that followed, see Klooss, "Stereotyping," 140–45; Braz, *False Traitor*, chap. 2.

worst characters. There ought not, though, be any unnecessary delay nor any possibility of influences interfering in his behalf such as prevailed for him when he should have been hanged years ago.[76]

One brief article judged that the responsibility of the rebellion was Riel's, and prophesied (quite incorrectly it would seem) that in Canada, Riel would forever be labeled "the rebel of the Dominion."[77]

Despite these differences, all three papers in Ontario and the Maritimes agreed upon the necessity of the death sentence for Riel (the *North-West Baptist* did not report on the trial or execution). Despite contemporary claims to the contrary, Riel, it was argued, was a rebel, clear and simple, and a rebellion could not go on or even worse things would happen.[78] The solution for such unrest was first to put Riel to trial. While some late-twentieth-century commentators have come to different conclusions,[79] the press at the time was convinced that the trial had been fair, and Riel had legitimately been found guilty. Upon a guilty verdict, the press supported his execution. The *Canadian Baptist* declared that "the shedding of his blood was demanded," asked for mercy for his followers, and then stated that the need was to deal with the injustices that led to rebellion in the first place.[80] The *Religious Intelligencer's* perspective was much more polemical.[81] As the trial concluded it stated that the court had no real option other than to execute Riel:

> It now remains for the sentence of the Court that convicted him to be carried out. Of course there is the talk that has been from the beginning of the case about the possibility of his sentence being changed to imprisonment, &c. We incline to the belief,

76. "The Northwest Rebellion."

77. "The North-West," *Religious Intelligencer*, 24 July 1885, 3.

78. For instance, there were numerous comments on how a larger more generalized "Indian War" could arise out of the rebellion. See "The Rebellion"; "What Shall the End Be?"; "War"; "News Summary," *Messenger and Visitor*, 6 May 1885, 8; "News Summary," *Messenger and Visitor*, 20 May 1885, 8; "News Summary," *Messenger and Visitor*, 27 May 1885, 8; "News Summary," *Messenger and Visitor*, 17 June 1885, 8; "News Summary," *Messenger and Visitor*, 5 August 1885, 8.

79. For instance, see the introduction in Morton, *Queen v. Louis Riel*; Goulet, *Trial of Louis Riel.*

80. *Canadian Baptist*, 19 November 1885, 4. The concern for justice was echoed in other Ontario-based newspapers. See Silver, "Fanaticism," 32–34.

81. For the announcement in the other Maritime paper, see *Messenger and Visitor*, 18 November 1885, 8.

however, that he will be executed. He ought to be. No criminal in Canada ever more deserved the extreme penalty of the law for his many and bloody crimes. If he is allowed to escape because of the clamoring of any class, then law is a farce.[82]

Once Riel was executed, the *Religious Intelligencer* noted its approval by declaring that he should have been executed after the first rebellion, but was satisfied with the execution this time around.[83] The execution or imprisonment of other alleged accomplices went relatively unnoticed.[84]

Despite the outrage in Quebec over the trial of Riel,[85] minimal commentary was provided on the opinions of the French support for Riel.[86] In Ontario there was no anti-French rhetoric in the *Canadian Baptist*. The most extensive commentary on French opinion was in the *Religious Intelligencer*. Like its other reporting on the situation in the west, its language was inflammatory. Its reporting was also naïve when it came to French Canadian sensibilities.[87] It argued that the English would not have complained if Riel had been English and had been executed, so why should the French be upset? It stated that the French concern for Riel was a "silly craze, unworthy [of] people [with an] average intelligence,"[88] and it was hoped that the French rulers would calm things down. There was, however, the recognition that there was a threat to Canada if the French-English tensions continued:

> If however, the race feeling is kept alive and increased till it becomes so impudent that it cannot be borne patiently, it will likely receive a very summary and emphatic rebuke from the country at large. The people of this country are not of the temper to submit to the domination of any class whose action has its origin in sym-

82. *Religious Intelligencer*, 30 October 1885, 2.

83. *Religious Intelligencer*, 20 November 1885, 2. For other commentary on Riel's trial, see "The North-West," *Religious Intelligencer*, 7 August 1885, 4.

84. *Messenger and Visitor*, 14 October 1885, 8; *Messenger and Visitor*, 2 December 1885, 8. For a contemporary criticism of the government's treatment and trial of the First Nations and Métis prisoners, see Stonechild and Waiser, *Loyal till Death*.

85. For a brief description, see Bumstead, *Riel v. Canada*, 311–12.

86. *Religious Intelligencer*, 20 November 1885, 2; "The News of the Week," *Religious Intelligencer*, 20 November 1885, 3; "News Summary," *Messenger and Visitor*, 9 September 1885, 8; "News Summary," *Messenger and Visitor*, 23 September 1885, 8; "News Summary," *Messenger and Visitor*, 18 November 1885, 8.

87. *Religious Intelligencer*, 27 November 1885, 2.

88. Ibid.

pathy with a miserable, scheming, self-seeking rebel and cold-blooded murderer. If the country is to be periodically threatened with this kind of trouble the sooner the testing comes the better. We shall continue to believe, however, that wiser counsels than those given by the hot-headed demagogues who have stirred up this excitement will prevail, and that our French citizens will see that their interest and that of the country are promoted by the punishment of such creatures as Riel rather than by blind and frenzied sympathy with them . . . [The] leaders and best men of all parties and of no party will stand together for the country against the insane and destructive course of a section whose race-feeling leads it to sympathy with a hanged murderer to the extent of jeopardizing the country's welfare.[89]

Such fears of French-English tensions during military conflict would be addressed by the religious press in Canada's first overseas war (the South African War, 1899–1902),[90] but would be addressed in a much more sympathetic and less harsh tone than this example in 1885.

Based on the reactions throughout the conflict, and specifically to Riel's trial and execution, one can see that in the opinions of the press there was no other option but to execute what they deemed to be a dangerous rebel. To let Riel free was to jeopardize peace, order, justice, and the advancement of western settlement. As one commentator stated, had "he been allowed to escape from the country, or been punished with less than the extreme penalty, justice would have been burlesqued, property and life in the North-west been altogether insecure and the settlement and development of the country been greatly retarded."[91]

CONCLUSION

It is clear that by 1885, the various Canadian Baptist papers saw the churches as having a critical role to play in the nation-building process. From the Christianizing and Canadianizing (in their minds, the same thing) of new immigrants to the assimilation of the First Nations peoples, the churches were understood to have a role to play in the formation of a distinctly Christian Canada. Through its commentary on events, the Baptist press also played a significant role in the nation-

---

89. Ibid.

90. Heath, *Silver Lining*, 83–86.

91. *Religious Intelligencer*, 20 November 1885, 2.

building process, and, in the case of the events of 1885, supported the Canadian government's decision to crush any dissent.

As for constructions of the events of 1885, it is obvious that this research sheds more light on the Canadian Baptist press than on the actual person of Riel, or on what the Métis or First Nations people were really like. Like much of the writing on Riel, personal and corporate biases tended to shape how he was perceived and constructed. In the case of Riel, he stood in the way of what the Baptist press deemed important: advancement of the nation westward, racial/cultural superiority and assimilation, law and order, and patriotism and pride in their soldiers. Consequently, it was inevitable that the press would construct Riel and his followers in such a negative way, especially since the sources used for information were already so biased.

There were some surprises in this research. Perhaps the greatest surprise was the response of the Ontario-based *Canadian Baptist*. Bumstead argues that Riel was executed to satisfy the expansionist interests of Protestant Ontario.[92] While there may have been pressure from Orange Ontario to execute Riel, the Maritime press was far more jingoistic than the *Canadian Baptist*. Nevertheless, the convictions of the Baptist press in general worked against Riel. As Owram notes, "A man who stood in the way of that expansion, even if with some reason, was not the sort of figure to become a Canadian folk hero. . . . Louis Riel was ultimately on the wrong side of history not because he lost but because he had misunderstood the forces around him."[93] Patriotism, racial superiority, an inevitable and even providential expansion of the new nation westward (with the necessary assimilation that followed such growth), these were the assumptions that shaped the Baptist press's response to Riel. Or as Braz puts it, this was the "specific social reality" that shaped the constructions of Riel.

92. Bumstead, *Riel v. Canada*, 319.
93. Owram, "Myth of Louis Riel," 320–21.

BIBLIOGRAPHY

Airhart, Phyllis D. "Ordering a Nation and Reordering Protestantism, 1867–1914." In *The Canadian Protestant Experience, 1760–1990*, edited by George Rawlyk, 98–138. Burlington, ON: Welch, 1990.

Anderson, Olive. "The Growth of Christian Militarism in Mid-Victorian Britain." *English Historical Review* 85 (January 1991) 46–72.

Bourinot, George. *The Intellectual Development of the Canadian People: An Historical Review*. Toronto: Hunter, Rose & Company, 1881.

Braz, Albert. *The False Traitor: Louis Riel in Canadian Culture*. Toronto: University of Toronto Press, 2003.

Bumstead, J. M. *Louis Riel v. Canada: The Making of a Rebel*. Winnipeg: Great Plains Publications, 2001.

The Canadian Baptist, 1885.

Flanagan, Thomas. "Louis Riel: A Review Essay." *Journal of Canadian Studies* 21, no. 2 (1986) 157–66.

Franzosi, Roberto. "The Press as a Source of Socio-Historical Data: Issues in the Methodology of Data Collection from Newspapers." *Historical Methods* 20, no. 1 (1987) 5–16.

Frye, Northrop. "Conclusion." In *Literary History of Canada: Canadian Literature in English*, edited by Carl F. Klinck, 821–49. Toronto: University of Toronto Press, 1965.

Goulet, George R. D. *The Trial of Louis Riel: Justice and Mercy Denied*. Calgary: Tellwell, 1999.

Grant, John Webster. *The Church in the Canadian Era*. Burlington, ON: Welch, 1988.

Heath, Gordon L. "'Forming Sound Public Opinion:' The Late Victorian Canadian Protestant Press and Nation-Building." *Journal of the Canadian Church Historical Society* 48 (2006) 109–59.

———. *A War with a Silver Lining: Protestant Churches and the South African War, 1899–1902*. Montreal and Kingston: McGill-Queen's University Press, 2009.

Hennessy, Peter. "The Press and Broadcasting." In *Contemporary History: Practice and Method*, edited by Anthony Seldon, 17–29. Basil: Blackwell, 1988.

Hobson, John A. *Imperialism: A Study*. London, 1902; reprint, Ann Arbor, MI: Ann Arbor Books, University of Michigan, 1967.

Jones, Preston. "'His Dominion'? Varieties of Protestant Commentary on the Confederation of Canada." *Fides et Historia* 32, no. 2 (Summer-Fall 2000) 83–88.

Klooss, Wolfgang. "Stereotyping in Canadian Literature: The Métis in Anglo- and Francophone Writing." In *Images of Louis Riel in Canadian Culture*, edited by Ramon Hathorn and Patrick Holland, 131–74. Lewiston: Edwin Mellon, 1992.

McLaurin, C. C. *Pioneering in Western Canada: A Story of the Baptists*. Calgary: self-published, 1939.

The Messenger and Visitor, 1885.

Morton, Desmond. *The Queen v. Louis Riel*. Toronto: University of Toronto Press, 1974.

The North-West Baptist, 1885–86.

Owram, Douglas. "The Myth of Louis Riel." *Canadian Historical Review* 63, no. 3 (1982) 315–36.

The Religious Intelligencer, 1885.

Robertson, James Tyler. "Go Up and Possess the Garden of the World: The Ontario Baptist Mission to the North West Territories, 1869–1880." *McMaster Journal of Theology and Ministry* 10 (2008–2009) 140–73.

Rutherdale, Myra. *Women and the White Man's God: Gender and Race in the Canadian Mission Field*. Vancouver: University of British Columbia Press, 2002.

Rutherford, Paul. *A Victorian Authority: The Daily Press in Late Nineteenth-Century Canada*. Toronto: University of Toronto Press, 1982.

Said, Edward. *Orientalism*. New York: Vintage, 1979.

Silver, A. I. "Nineteenth Century News Gathering and the Mythification of Riel." In *Images of Louis Riel in Canadian Culture*, edited by Ramon Hathorn and Patrick Holland, 63–92. Lewiston: Edwin Mellon, 1992.

———. "Ontario's Alleged Fanaticism in the Riel Affair." *Canadian Historical Review* 69, no. 1 (March 1988) 21–50.

Stanley, George F. G., ed. *The Collected Writings of Louis Riel*. 5 vols. Edmonton: University of Alberta Press, 1985.

Stonechild, Blair, and Waiser, Bill. *Loyal till Death: Indians and the North-West Rebellion*. Calgary: Fifth House, 1997.

Thompson, Margaret. *The Baptist Story in Western Canada*. Calgary: Baptist Union of Western Canada, 1976.

Trinier, Harold U. *A Century of Service: The Story of the* Canadian Baptist, *1854–1954*. Board of Publication of the Baptist Convention of Ontario and Quebec, 1954.

Wilkinson, Glenn R. "'To the Front': British Newspaper Advertising and the Boer War." In *The Boer War: Direction, Experience and Image*, edited by John Gooch, 203–12. London: Frank Cass, 2000.

Woodworth, J. S. *Strangers within Our Gates*. Toronto: Stephenson, 1909.

Elizabeth McMaster
Founder of the Hospital for Sick Children in Toronto.
Used by permission of Hospital and Libary Archives
of the Hospital for Sick Children, Toronto.

7

Caring for Their Community

The Philanthropic and Moral Reform Efforts of Toronto's Baptists, 1834–1918

PAUL R. WILSON

THE CURRENT CALLS FOR a revival of compassionate social action by those North American evangelicals who support the "emerging church" movement are nothing new.[1] Central to the English Canadian evangelical experience that dominated the Victorian and Edwardian Protestant religious landscapes in central Canada was the value that all Christians had a duty to be involved in charitable works that "put right the wrongs of the world around them."[2] For many of Toronto's most notable middle class Baptists in the nineteenth and early twentieth centuries, involvement in their city's public life included a commitment to philanthropy and moral reform. Long before some more liberal-minded Canadian Baptists accepted the social gospel, Toronto's Baptists were on a Christian mission to care for their community by converting less fortunate citizens to Christ and addressing the material, social, and moral ills that plagued their city. For Toronto's Baptists in the period from 1834 to 1918, philanthropy and moral reform served a dual purpose as both a practical application of religious altruism and a socio-cultural pathway to acceptance and respectability within the public life of Toronto's middle class anglo-Protestant evangelical community. To support this

1. Campolo, "Missing the Point." See also Webber, *Younger Evangelicals*, 227–36.
2. Walvin, *Victorian Values*, 96.

claim, this chapter will uncover and analyze the beliefs, assumptions, and values at the heart of Baptist efforts, the contributions of Baptists to Toronto's public life, and the motives, trends, and patterns related to the purposes that characterized Baptist activism in three different periods. But before the present study begins, a brief discussion of the existing historiography is in order.

Thanks to the work of Canadian Baptist and religious historians such as George Rawlyk, Charles Johnston, Donald Goetz, and John Stackhouse we have a preliminary understanding of Baptist philanthropy in support of some local church and denominational causes. In particular the contributions of Baptists to higher education have received considerable attention from historians.[3] This research seeks to take their work a step further and examine Baptist benevolent and moral reform activities within Toronto's interdenominational context.

Historians such as Sara Posen, Cathy James, and Xiaobei Chen, who have already studied evangelical philanthropy in nineteenth- and early twentieth-century Toronto, have examined many of the key initiatives and institutions, and the religious, socio-economic, and cultural character and motivations of Toronto's philanthropists and moral reformers.[4] On the subject of Baptist philanthropic contributions to Toronto's public life, however, much less is known. Recognizing that for Baptists, as for other evangelicals, it was assumed that one's religious beliefs and values would be carried into one's public life, the emphasis here is on Baptist philanthropic activities that promoted both evangelism and moral improvement in the wider Toronto community.

Canadian social historians, such as Mariana Valverde, have examined the push for moral reform in English Canada from 1885–1925.[5] Nancy Christie, Michael Gauvreau, and Phyllis Airhart have persuasively argued that Canadian Protestantism became more socially active

3. See, for example, Donald Goertz on the Memorial Institute, in his *Century for the City*, 40–46; The standard work on Baptists and higher education is Rawlyk, *Christian Higher Education*. For information on William McMaster's financial contributions to Baptist higher education in Ontario, see Johnston, *McMaster University*, 1:26, 32, 34, 44, 54; On the leadership provided by Elmore Harris in the founding of Toronto Bible College, see Stackhouse, *Canadian Evangelicalism*, 53–70.

4. See, for example, Posen, "Examining Policy"; James, "Reforming Reform"; Chen, *Tending the Gardens*.

5. Valverde, *Age of Light*.

and engaged in the early twentieth century.[6] While these studies have
made a valuable contribution to our understanding of patterns and
trends at the national and provincial levels, the philanthropic and moral
reform efforts of smaller religious groups, such as Baptists, at the municipal level have remained largely overshadowed or ignored. There is
a tendency among such historians to assume or claim, without much
sensitivity to the various Baptist socio-cultural identities or much supporting evidence, that all Baptists simply followed the motives, trends,
and patterns of larger evangelical Protestant denominations.[7] While
such a view may well be accurate, a careful examination of the available
evidence for Baptist philanthropic and moral reform efforts is needed to
provide a solid historical basis for such claims. This chapter offers both
arguments and evidence that enables one to understand better Baptist
belief and behavior.

CONTEXTUALIZING BAPTIST PHILANTHROPIC
AND MORAL REFORM EFFORTS

The terms philanthropy and moral reform both require definition.
Philanthropy is defined here as benevolent acts intended to help hu-
mankind. In practice this meant that one could offer money, time, or
energy in support of a particular charitable cause that sought to meet
a perceived social or physical need of the recipient.[8] Moral reform refers to what Mariana Valverde has called "the effort . . . to reshape the
ethical subjectivity of both immigrants and native-born Canadians."[9] By
these definitions, many of Toronto's middle class Baptists were heavily
involved in philanthropy and moral reform.

For historians everywhere, defining the "middle class" is still problematic. While numerous Canadian historians freely use the term "mid-

6. Airhart, *Serving the Present Age*, 24–26, 74–77, 103–11; Christie and Gauvreau,
Full-Orbed Christianity, 15–16, 62–63, 106–8, 136–42.

7. This is the case, for example, in Christie and Gauvreau, *Full-Orbed Christianity*,
where the focus is on a few Baptist intellectuals such as A. L. McCrimmon and C. A.
Dawson and their views of social reform and social welfare in Canada. In an apparent
effort to compensate for the "undue weight" given by historians "to the protests" of T.
T. Shields, the views of these intellectuals are mistakenly presented as representative of
Baptist views. See, for example, pp. 84, 132, 180, 188, 233.

8. For a discussion of the "eccentric" of nineteenth century philanthropy, see James,
"Reforming Reform," 62–63.

9. Valverde, *Age of Light*, 17.

dle class" in their studies of philanthropy and moral reform, few actually provide a definition. In his study of the emerging American middle class, Stuart Blumin has drawn our attention to the problems, perils, and debates surrounding attempts to arrive at a definitive definition.[10]

Blumin correctly points out "that the concept of the middle class, historically and in the present, is both pervasive and elusive; indeed, that it is elusive precisely because it is pervasive."[11] Obviously, the purpose of this research is not to address all of the issues raised by historians like Blumin in their attempts to come to terms with the development and definition of the middle class. In this study the term "middle class" refers to an ever-expanding and ever-changing social group of Baptist professionals and businessmen and their families who shared similar beliefs, values, assumptions, and aspirations and who earned incomes above those of workingmen and women but below that of the Upper Canadian gentry.[12]

Respectability is a term that also requires definition. In this chapter respectability means that one uses certain characteristics, behaviors, wealth, and position as the means of gaining acceptance by those who are already members of a particular social class.[13] In this case, Baptists were seeking to become respectable within Toronto's middle class. Consequently, it was the socio-cultural ethic of the middle class with its values of industry, duty, charity, and purity that Baptists sought to exemplify.

Another important contextual issue is gender. British, American, and Canadian historians and sociologists have focused considerable attention on the questions of gender definitions and roles within the social

10. Blumin, *Emergence of the Middle Class*, 1–16.

11. Ibid., 2.

12. For a detailed discussion and analysis of the complexities related to wages and incomes for the working class and middle class professionals in Ontario, see Gidney and Millar, *Professional Gentlemen*, 400–405. For discussion and analysis of living standards in Ontario from 1784–1945, see McCalla, *Planting the Province*, 21–22, 179–96, 245–47; Drummond, *Progress without Planning*, 10–14, 37–44, 224–31. Though there are numerous problems with municipal assessments throughout the period covered here, I have used Toronto's Assessment Rolls as a basis for establishing who qualifies as a member of the middle class. As Gidney and Millar point out, the amount to qualify as middle class changes over time.

13. My definition is based on Thompson, *Rise of Respectable Society*, and Prentice, *School Promoters*, 66–87. For specific marks of respectability in Toronto's middle and upper classes, see Careless, *Toronto to 1918*, 124, 128, 161–72.

and political domains. Many historians and sociologists argue that the nineteenth century was dominated by a "cult of domesticity" that put men and women in "separate spheres," where women were responsible for the home and childrearing and men were the breadwinners and governors of social and political life.[14] This over-arching ideology was reinforced by the cults of true womanhood and manhood. The Victorians assumed that women possessed a nature that was morally superior to men. Women were innately more loving, caring, and nurturing. In contrast, men were naturally more aggressive, confrontational, and competitive. As Mangan and Walvin have noted, this "neo-Spartan ideal of masculinity was diffused throughout the English speaking world with the unreflecting and ethnocentric confidence of an imperial race."[15]

The reality of "separate spheres," however, did not mean that women were barred from engaging in philanthropic and moral reform activities outside the home. In fact, as Mary Kinnear has noted, by the end of the nineteenth century the "cultural expectations for educated middle class women" in the public domain "included an obligation of service to the community."[16] Women of wealth and privilege were to be exemplars of their Christian faith by helping "those less fortunate than themselves."[17]

Toronto's Baptists, of course, shared the assumptions and views of gender held by other Victorian evangelicals. Early Baptist journals based in Toronto continually exhorted parents to fulfill their parental and other domestic obligations. In February 1851, for example, *The Christian Observer* ran an article entitled "A Mother's Influence" that underscored the primacy and importance of a mother's childrearing role: "The influence of a mother upon the manners and salvation of her children, especially the latter, is probably greater than that of all other beings united. On you chiefly depends, under God, what your children shall be in both worlds."[18] Similarly, instructions and guidance given to Baptist men

14. Morgan, *Public Men*, 3–5; Mandell and Momirov, "Family Histories"; Muir and Whiteley, "Canadian Women's Christian Work." For an interpretation that challenges the conventional wisdom about "separate spheres," see Hughes, "Madness of Separate Spheres."

15. Mangan and Walvin, "Introduction," 3.

16. Kinnear, "Shaping of 'Public Woman,'" 197.

17. Ibid.

18. "A Mother's Influence," *The Christian Observer* 1, no. 2 (February 1851) 6. For evidence that some Baptists stayed committed to the notion of separate spheres, see the articles by Joshua Denovan, "Women's Sphere and Work," *The Canadian Baptist*,

regarding their role in the public domain were equally forthright. For example, in a letter to the editor of *The Christian Observer* concerning the Clergy Reserves question, dated 23 November 1851, one concerned Baptist noted, "There is nothing incompatible between the maintenance of a consistent Christian profession and the discharge of civil offices; for in becoming Christians, we do not cease to be *men*; and cannot, on this ground, therefore, claim exemption from those duties and responsibilities which are common alike to *all men*."[19] For many Baptists, men and women had clear and distinct roles in the home and in the world.

Finally, charity and social purity were considered essential hallmarks of true "Christian character." For central Canadian Baptists, these "goods works" provided evidence of personal "salvation" from the ravages of sin, and "sanctification," the gradual process by which a believer was transformed into the likeness of Christ. Baptists also believed that social purity, the moral regeneration of society, was only possible if the believer chose to live a "sanctified" and "separated life." One had to practice discipline and self-restraint in order "to keep himself unspotted from the world." In the Baptist mind, the living of a morally pure and separated life gave one the moral credibility, authority, and responsibility to advocate for policies and practices that brought about greater social purity. A final point of connection to Baptist belief was the concept of "stewardship." According to Baptist teaching, all of one's possessions belonged to God. The individual believer had a duty and responsibility to manage his/her time, money, and abilities for the "glory of God." Placed in this context, philanthropy and moral reform were expressions of religious altruism intended to advance the kingdom of God on earth.[20]

---

15 June 1893, 1; 22 June 1893, 1. For an argument in favor of gender equality, see Alexander Campbell's response to Denovan, "Women's Sphere," *The Canadian Baptist*, 29 June 1893, 1.

19. "Communications: Religion and Politics," *The Christian Observer* 1, no. 12 (December 1851) 186. The italics are in the original article.

20. The information given in this paragraph regarding the central Canadian Baptist view of salvation, sanctification, separation, and stewardship is a summary based on the material covered in my doctoral dissertation. See Wilson, "Baptists and Business," 53–87; The phrase "to keep himself unspotted from the world" is taken from James 1:27. For a discussion of social purity, see Cook, *Through Sunshine and Shadow*, 90–99.

BAPTIST PHILANTHROPIC AND MORAL REFORM EFFORTS IN EARLY VICTORIAN TORONTO, 1834–1848

Early Baptist efforts in Toronto, between the city's incorporation in 1834 and the typhus epidemic of 1847, were shaped by certain religious and socio-cultural beliefs, assumptions, and values that addressed the social and political realities of the new city. The process of establishing the infrastructure necessary to address major social issues such as immigration, disease, education, and poverty was only in its infancy. Despite bouts of cholera in the 1830s and a typhus epidemic in 1847, Toronto had no public health or adequate sanitation systems to deal with such problems. The temporary Board of Health that was set up to deal with periodic outbreaks of disease lacked sufficient resources and expertise.[21]

Similarly, in the areas of education, poor relief, and settlement, Toronto still relied heavily on the efforts of individual citizens and private voluntary religious charities to provide its social services. This pattern would begin to change in the 1830s as voluntary charities and societies were gradually replaced by civic institutions that assumed responsibility for providing services to the citizenry.[22] Large scale immigration meant that Toronto experienced a population explosion from 9,765 persons in 1835 to 21,000 by 1848.[23] In the political arena, the earlier spirit of co-operation that had dominated the relationships between the Tories and the Reformers in the 1820s was replaced by bitter rivalry and division that characterized much of civic political life in the 1830s.[24] It was in these contexts that a small number of Baptists sought to work their way into Toronto's middle class circles and provide spiritual and social assistance through their church and public activities. Philanthropy and moral guidance were tools used by such Baptists for personal socio-economic advancement and for the evangelization and education of the city's most vulnerable and impressionable citizens.

21. For information on the cholera and typhus outbreaks and the Board of Health, see Careless, *Toronto to 1918*, 51, 59, 71–73; On the lack of medical expertise, see Gidney and Millar, *Professional Gentlemen*, 85–86; See also Splane, *Social Welfare*, 199.

22. For an explanation of this pattern and process, see Baehre, "Paupers."

23. These population statistics are taken from Armstrong, *City in the Making*, 42, and Careless, *Toronto to 1918*, 73.

24. For further detail concerning the political dynamics of this period, see Armstrong, *City in the Making*, 42, 191, and Romney, "A Struggle for Authority."

Even though their numbers were small at incorporation and their church was still struggling in the early 1840s, Toronto's Baptists were already involved in a number of philanthropic and moral reform efforts designed to reach the lost, aid the unfortunate, and protect the vulnerable.[25] Of course, such efforts were informed by the belief that every Christian had a duty not only to spread the gospel of Christ, but also to devote a portion of his or her time, energy, and earnings to support both church and community charities that promoted the social welfare and moral purity of the city. In this period, Baptists who sought middle class respectability and status showed a tendency to blame poverty on systemic deficiencies and the spiritual and moral shortcomings of the poor. For example, on 14 November 1834, the well-connected Toronto Baptist preacher, John Eglington Maxwell, recorded in his diary beliefs and perceptions shared by many of his coreligionists: "Indolence and ignorance are parents of poverty. A great deal of misery arises to families for want of domestic economy; no proper system of teaching females has yet been introduced and the misery running through the length and breadth of society has been great."[26] The socio-cultural assumption held by Baptist middle class men like Maxwell was that those in need of help should help themselves. Solutions for poverty and distress were found primarily on self-help, namely, spiritual and moral reformation, hard work, and education. Voluntary charitable societies certainly had a role to play, but only in cases of extreme hardship or deprivation for persons "deserving" of assistance.

Another important socio-cultural factor that informed Baptist philanthropic and moral reform efforts was the stigmatization of Toronto Baptists as uneducated low class dissenters and socio-cultural outsiders. In the 1820s, many Baptists were insulted by having to go before a magistrate and produce proof of ordination and proof of their fitness for ministry. They also resented having to take the Oath of Allegiance before

25. The church had 13 members in 1840 and 77 members in 1846. See "Reminiscences of the Baptists of Toronto," *The Canadian Baptist*, 29 April 1886, 3; also Bond Street Baptist Church Minute Book, 1845–55, 2 April 1846, in Jarvis Street Baptist Church Archives.

26. John Eglington Maxwell, Diary, 14 November 1934. Baldwin Room, Toronto Reference Library. Maxwell was married to Johanna Carfrae, the daughter of Thomas Carfare Sr., a prosperous general merchant located on King Street. For information on the rise of the Carfraes, see Armstrong, *City in the Making*, 164–91.

they could perform marriages.[27] At the time of the 1837 Rebellion, some Baptist sympathizers were imprisoned or mistreated. William and James Lesslie had their house "invaded by the militia," and they "were detained without warrant for two weeks."[28] Both men were charged with sedition but found not guilty. A similar fate befell the early Baptist stove manufacturer, David Van Norman.[29]

Also, in 1832, the Presbyterian minister William Proudfoot offered a scathing socio-cultural assessment of pastor Alexander Stewart: "Was considerably disappointed to day in Mr. Stewart. I have been now several times in his house, but never heard any thing that could indicate his possessing a literary turn. He is always working as a labourer, covered with mud or lime. His manners the manners of a man of *work*."[30] Some Baptists were obsessed with refuting and counteracting such characterizations. Well into the 1870s, Baptists, particularly in the rural areas of Central Canada, continued to voice their complaints and concerns about "denominational bigotry," and many remained convinced that they were "the sect everywhere spoken against."[31] Viewed in this context, Baptist philanthropic and moral reform efforts were actions intended to counter these perceptions and place Toronto's Baptists, in this case, within the middle class evangelical mainstream.

Despite the pressing demands of leading and growing their local church and their involvement in wider Baptist causes, Toronto's few middle class Baptists devoted significant resources to establishing voluntary societies that sought to meet the spiritual and social needs of their city. In 1830, for example, bookseller James Lesslie and hardware merchant David Patterson helped to establish the York Mechanics' Institute. Modeled after similar institutions begun in Scotland in 1823, the initial aim of the Institute was to provide an education in "practical arts and sciences" for workers who desired to improve their skills.[32]

27. See Riddell, "The Law of Marriage"; *Journals of the House of Assembly for the Province of Upper Canada*, 14 January 1826, 78; Gibson, *Fyfe*, 68, 69, 91, 97.

28. Lesslie Papers, James Lesslie File, MU 1720, Archives of Ontario, Toronto.

29. Fraser, *History of Ontario*, 743.

30. William Proudfoot, Diary, 5 December 1832, Regional Collection at the University of Western Ontario.

31. See, for example, *The Canadian Baptist Register for 1872*, 30, and *Eastern Ontario Association Minutes, 1877*, 15, both found at McMaster University, Canadian Baptist Archives, Hamilton, Ontario.

32. Careless, *Toronto to 1918*, 58. For information on the early social role of books, bookstores, and libraries, see Fleming et al., *History of the Book*, 132–37.

Unfortunately, the Institute failed to flourish in its early years. Consistently driven by his desire for moral and political reform, a frustrated James Lesslie blamed the suspicion "by some of our local gentry" for the early struggles of the Institute. According to Lesslie, the gentry thought that the "lower classes" could be kept in their place so long as they remained ignorant.[33] Lesslie's laying of the blame for failure at the feet of his Tory political adversaries testifies more to the highly charged and adversarial nature of Toronto's political arena than it speaks to the ineffectiveness of the Mechanics' Institute. Whatever caused the slow response, J. M. S. Careless has rightly noted that the Institute "soon became a middle class institution" that sponsored talks on a wide variety of subjects, ran classes in the fine arts, and "began collecting a library more suited to entertain well-to-do subscribers than meet the technical needs of artisans."[34] As a consequence, the Mechanics' Institute attracted more shop clerks and apprentices than workingmen, and its initial objective to provide technical education for the working class was never fully achieved.

Beyond an interest in the education of the lower classes, Toronto's Baptists were also concerned about the growing numbers of urban poor. In the pre-Rebellion atmosphere of 1837, the City Council granted funds to establish a House of Industry to provide poor relief on the English workhouse model.[35] This action effectively anticipated and implemented the House of Industry Act passed by the Upper Canada Legislature in the same year. While the provincial legislation failed to have much practical effect, efforts in Toronto went forward despite the animosity and uncertainty created by the 1837 Rebellion.[36] Essentially, the adoption of the English workhouse model meant, as Richard Splane has noted, that "as well as being a house of refuge," such an institution, "was to have something of the character of a house of correction."[37] Rules and regulations concerning cleanliness, maintenance of those receiving assistance

33. I have used the quotations as given in Glazebrook, *Story of Toronto*, 67.

34. Careless, *Toronto to 1918*, 58.

35. Toronto City Council Minutes, 19 January 1837, Toronto City Archives.

36. For a discussion of the provincial legislation and its effects, see Splane, *Social Welfare*, 70–73.

37. Ibid., 71. See also *Report of the Committee for the Relief of the Poor and Destitute of the City of Toronto, and Rules and Regulations of the House of Refuge and Industry Established under Their Care, January 1837*, 6–12.

both inside and outside the institution, and the moral and religious improvement of inmates were strictly enforced.

Among those who founded Toronto's House of Industry were Baptist pastor Alexander Stewart, pastor John E. Maxwell, and bookseller James Lesslie. All were "acting members" of the General Committee that provided oversight of the institution.[38] This early involvement set in place a pattern of becoming, as soon as possible, part of a philanthropic society's management and donor base. In the case of the House of Industry, other notable Baptists such as Robert Cathcart, David Patterson, Thomas Lailey, A. T. McCord, and William McMaster provided both financial support and management expertise.[39] In fact, the House of Industry would remain a staple of Baptist philanthropic and moral reform efforts throughout the nineteenth century.

Another philanthropic and moral reform effort, closely related to the House of Industry, was the Toronto City Mission. Founded in 1845, the Mission's leadership included prominent Baptists Reverend R. A. Fyfe (pastor of Bond Street Baptist Church), Andrew Taylor McCord (the city's Chamberlain), and dry goods merchant William McMaster. The Second [Annual] Report of the Mission in 1848 clearly shows that each of these men contributed time, energy, and money to support the mission's evangelistic and moral reform efforts.[40] Numerous other Baptists such as merchant Robert Cathcart, bookseller James Lesslie, merchant Thomas Lailey, and hardware merchant David Patterson also generously supported this mission endeavor.[41]

A particular focus of Mr. Stewart, the Missionary hired by the Mission, was to reform the intemperate. In one case a man who "was an excellent tradesman, but had been reduced to poverty by habitual drunkenness . . . promised [along with his wife] to give it up, and to

---

38. Ibid., 2.

39. *Report of the Trustees of the House of Industry, Toronto, for the Year 1851*, 1, 17–18. Robert Cathcart is listed as a Manager while all of the others are listed as subscribers or donors.

40. *Second [Annual] Report of the Toronto City Mission*, 2, 17–18. McCord, McMaster, and Fyfe were active members of the Committee. The subscriptions and donations of these Baptists are given on pages 17–18.

41. Ibid., 17–18. For evidence of ongoing financial support and involvement in the leadership of the Mission see, for example, *Sixth Annual Report of the Toronto City Mission*, 2–3, 13–16; *Tenth Annual Report of the Toronto City Mission*, 3–4, 12–14.

take the Temperance pledge."[42] In some cases the Missionary faced dangerous circumstances. In one instance the Missionary walked in on twenty-three people engaged in drinking "liquor." Before the Missionary arrived, "one woman had risen with an axe to cut her father, a man of 83 years of age; she missed him but inflicted a severe blow on the hand of another female." The Missionary "got order restored" only to witness another disturbance that "compelled" the Missionary "to abandon the house."[43] The Missionary also had to contend with the effects of cholera, "the emigrant fever," the presence of "false doctrine," and "procrastination" in the "things of religion."[44] Both the enormity and extent of Toronto's spiritual, social, and moral needs prompted A. T. McCord to second a motion calling for "an additional Missionary employed as soon as funds can be provided for that purpose."[45] Clearly, for early middle class Toronto Baptist men, the City Mission served as a primary venue through which philanthropy could be dispensed and the moral reform of the city could be advanced.

In the forefront of Baptist philanthropic and moral reform efforts in this period was Toronto's Chamberlain and a member of Bond Street Baptist Church, Andrew Taylor McCord. A man of seemingly boundless energy and strong commitment to the social and moral improvement of Toronto, McCord took an active role in numerous societies and institutions. The list of his accomplishments in the public life of Toronto, beyond his many church and denominational commitments, is both extensive and impressive. McCord held the posts of secretary and vice-president in the Upper Canada Religious Tract and Book Society. He was also prominent and active in the Upper Canada Bible Society, the Toronto City Mission, and the Toronto Temperance Reformation Society. McCord also held leadership positions in a number of other charitable ventures including the Toronto Athenaeum, the Toronto General Burying Grounds, the Irish Protestant Benevolent Society, the Toronto House of Industry, the Newboys' Lodging and Industrial Home, and the Home for Incurables. By the time of his death in 1881, McCord's reputation as a leading philanthropist and public servant was firmly established. His obituaries were filled with accolades that noted among

42. *Second [Annual] Report of the Toronto City Mission*, 4.
43. Ibid., 5.
44. Ibid., 9–14.
45. Ibid., 2.

many other qualities "the sterling honesty of his character," and his death was said to leave "a vacancy not readily filled" in Toronto's charitable enterprises. As one who lived out his faith and also acquired respectability within Toronto's middle class through his social activism, McCord and Baptists like him set the standard and example for others to follow.[46]

While A. T. McCord was setting the example for his fellow Baptists in his philanthropy and participation in moral reform, other Baptists were busy working to provide education in Toronto. For example, Alexander Stewart, who came to York (= Toronto[47]) in 1818 and became the first pastor of March Street Baptist Church once it was organized in 1829, supported himself for two years as the headmaster of the first "common school" in York. In the late 1820s, Stewart again founded a school north of York and appears to have taught there for a short time.[48] Another individual involved in education was John Eglington Maxwell. Although the evidence is slight, an entry in Maxwell's Diary for 20 October 1834 noted, "Rose about 7—taught as usual—taught spelling, geography, Latin grammar et latin . . ."[49] The location of Maxwell's teaching activities is not clear. But obviously he was involved in some teaching capacity in early Toronto, and his services may well have been used by his friend and the founder of a private school in Toronto, Thomas Ford Caldicott.

Like Stewart and Maxwell, Caldicott took an interest in education during his early days in Toronto. In the early 1830s, he built on his earlier experience as Regimental Schoolmaster for the 79th Highland regiment and opened Caldicott's Classical and Commercial Academy on Market Street. According to William Stewart, one of Caldicott's early biographers, the school was "where several who afterwards rose to considerable eminence in the city and province, received part of their early training."[50]

---

46. The biographical material and quotations in this paragraph are taken from: Houston, "McCord"; "The Late Mr. A. T. McCord," *Globe*, 6 September 1881, 7; E. O. White, "The First Baptist Church in Toronto," *Canadian Baptist*, 16 August 1906, 3.

47. York took back its more original name Toronto at its incorporation as a city in 1834.

48. Gibson, *Fyfe*, 25, 88–89. See also Hodgins, *Documentary History*, 1:251.

49. Maxwell, Diary, 20 October 1834. Baldwin Room, Toronto Reference Library.

50. See Stewart, "Thomas Ford Caldicott," 147. For a description of private academies, see Houston and Prentice, *Schooling and Scholars*, 40–45.

Perhaps the most outstanding example of one committed to the establishment of a public education system based on the principles of voluntarism, non-sectarianism, and religious freedom and equality was Robert Alexander Fyfe, the reform-minded activist pastor of the March Street Baptist Church from September 1844 to June of 1848. While Fyfe was an advocate for Baptists in many areas of public life in the 1830s and 1840s, his efforts to establish an education system that granted access to people of all classes and Protestant denominations put him at the forefront of those who pressed all levels of government on, as Theo Gibson has stated, "the root issue" of "equality of all persons before the law, regardless of religion."[51] Although it is impossible to assess the extent of Fyfe's influence, on issues such as the establishment of an elementary public education system and the King's College controversy of the late 1840s, his devotion to the educational cause opened a path for Baptist interest and participation in this area of the province's public life. Also, a number of Fyfe's cogent arguments in support of liberty and equality were eventually reflected in the legislative measures that established public education in the Upper Province.[52]

Baptist leaders like Fyfe were quick to embrace the values and aspirations of Toronto's emerging Baptist middle class. While Fyfe advocated for fair access to education, he simultaneously pushed his Toronto congregation to seek new quarters for worship away from the "miserable houses" and "vicious and miserable kind of people" living on March Street.[53] "Getting the church away from March Street and its surroundings was, humanly speaking," Fyfe later recalled, "the first step towards permanent prosperity."[54] Walter Ellis has argued that Fyfe's account stresses that "the church had been forced to move from March Street in 1848."[55] There is, however, another interpretation that more accurately addresses Fyfe's agenda and motives. Middle class respectability was behind the move from March Street. For Fyfe, and the prominent businessmen like Robert Cathcart and William McMaster who supported him, middle class respectability demanded that the church relocate to the more socially acceptable surroundings of Bond Street. Baptists could

---

51. This quotation is taken from Gibson, *Fyfe*, 162.

52. For information on these issues, see ibid., 134–45.

53. Fyfe, *Forty Years' Survey*, 12, 26.

54. Ibid., 18.

55. Ellis, "Gilboa to Ichabod," 110.

not sustain the claim that they belonged to Toronto's middle class if their primary house of worship remained in one of the worst socio-economic locations in the city.

Eventually, the relocation of the church to fashionable Jarvis Street in 1875 and the moves of wealthy Baptists like William McMaster to his "Rathnally" estate on Avenue Road Hill, and William Davies to "Lorne Hall" in Rosedale, would entrench two important patterns for Toronto's middle class Baptists.[56] Walter Ellis and Donald Goertz have previously noted that migration to northern suburbs like Rosedale and the Annex, away from poor neighborhoods in the South, was one pattern that characterized the middle class Baptist experience in Toronto.[57]

Also, a pattern of impersonal service to the poor characterized the efforts of many Baptists. While middle class Baptists would donate money to charities that helped the poor or provided service from a distance, they would seldom go to poor areas to minister or associate with the poor beyond those who were already members of their own church. All of this reveals the underlying assumption that, for many middle class Baptists, there was, as Mariana Valverde has argued, a direct correlation between poverty, uncleanliness, and the presence of evil.[58] Middle class Baptists feared that personal contact would breed moral contamination. This supposed reality provided Baptists with a rationalization for keeping a safe distance from the poor by moving to the suburbs and for serving the needs of the less fortunate from the comfortable confines of Jarvis Street, Rosedale, or the Annex. These basic patterns would not be fundamentally altered before 1918.

Middle class Baptist women were also active in doing what they could to spread the gospel and serve the less fortunate. In 1846, for example, middle class Baptist women, such as Mrs. James Lesslie and Mrs. William Lesslie, were involved in the formation and activities of the Toronto Ladies' Bible Association. Founded in 1846, the mission of the Association was to increase "the circulation of the Word of God in Toronto and its vicinity."[59] In contrast to the men's Bible Society that

56. For more information about McMaster's residences and his accumulation of wealth, see Wilson, "Baptists and Business," 254–63. For information about the Rosedale residence of William Davies, see Crawford, *Rosedale*, 118–19.

57. Ellis, "Gilboa to Ichabod," 109–10, 113–14; Goertz, *Century for the City*, 40–42.

58. Valverde, *Age of Light*, 19–33.

59. *First Report of the Toronto Ladies' Bible Association*, 5, Microform Collection, University of Western Ontario.

employed a full time missionary, the work of Bible distribution, evangelism, spiritual care, and poor relief was done voluntarily by "collectors" assigned to one of twenty "districts" in the city. Like other collectors, Mrs. James Lesslie and Mrs. William Lesslie undoubtedly carried their middle class assumptions and perspective with them as they vigorously pursued their mission to bring salvation and aid to the poor. The report of one collector in 1847 captured both the middle class perspective and the spiritual priorities of the women involved: "Our frequent visits give us an excellent opportunity of judging who are objects worthy of relief, and of interesting others in their behalf. We have in this way been able to assist a number of poor persons, in our district, who might never otherwise have been found out. Above all, we have opportunities afforded us of conversing with them on those subjects which belong to their everlasting peace."[60]

Beyond the obvious personal religious benefits of such activity, the women of the Bible Association were quick to stress the potential collective benefits of inter-denominational co-operation: "We feel that great advantages are likely to arise from Association. It is common ground, on which Christians of all denominations may meet; and we trust that it will go far to break down the sectarian spirit there has been so much cause to deplore."[61] For Baptist women, participation in such an enterprise gave them both access to and association with other middle class evangelical women. Also, as part of their collection duties, Baptist women had the obligation to solicit subscriptions and donations from everyone in their district. This activity brought them into contact with people of every class and occupation. It also meant that, unlike many of their male counterparts, some middle class Baptist women had direct contact with the poor. The benefits of both an expanded social network and a heightened social awareness would have far-reaching implications for Baptist involvement in Toronto's middle class religious, business, and political life.

The philanthropic and moral reform efforts of Toronto's Baptists in the period from Toronto's incorporation in 1834 to the great typhus epidemic of 1847–48 were limited by numbers, the demands of local church development, and available resources. Still, an emerging middle class of Baptists helped where they could in establishing religious soci-

60. Ibid., 7–8.
61. Ibid., 8.

eties and civic institutions that sought to meet the spiritual and social needs of their community. While women were involved in activities that paralleled those of their male counterparts, the Baptist belief that women were responsible for the domestic sphere limited female philanthropic and moral activity in the public domain. As the Baptist middle class became more established and affluent, and Toronto's social welfare needs grew in size and severity, the pressures on city government and Toronto's wealthier citizens to respond in a more systematic, organized, and effective manner also increased.

For the city's Baptists, a number of important patterns were in place by 1848. Baptists had established the pattern of using philanthropic and moral reform activities as a means of working their way into Toronto's respectable middle class circles. Migration away from poor neighborhoods to middle and upper middle class areas was underway but in its infancy. Social service to the poor from a distance was also an observable trend, with men creating the greatest separation while women worked both on the front lines and behind the scenes. Also, the high level of evangelistic zeal in this period was a reflection of the religious altruism that characterized so many of the Baptist endeavors. Dissatisfied with their achievements thus far, Baptists would continue their quest for middle class respectability and stay committed to their religious beliefs, values, and ideals.

BAPTISTS AND THE MAKING OF "TORONTO THE GOOD" 1849–1883

Mid-Victorian Toronto was a city in transition. Although the basic machinery of municipal government was in place by 1848, the city's social welfare system was a mess. A hodge-podge of voluntary societies and civic services struggled to address the ever-expanding settlement, healthcare, poverty, and spiritual needs of the burgeoning city. Successive waves of Irish immigrants in the late 1840s and early 1850s swelled the population and overwhelmed the available social services.[62] This was also the period in which Toronto first experienced the effects of industrialization after the coming of the railways in the 1850s, the arrival of trade unionism in the late 1850s and the creation in 1867, by the wealthy Baptist entrepreneur William McMaster, of an aggressive

62. Careless, *Toronto to 1918*, 71–76.

commercial enterprise named the Canadian Bank of Commerce, that was founded to rival its counterpart in Montreal.[63]

This was also a period of sweeping political change at both the provincial and national levels. After confederation in 1867, Canada experienced all of the challenges associated with the establishment and early development of a new nation. In Ontario, increasing industrialization and urbanization put pressure on the new provincial government to assist municipalities in their attempts to provide adequate social services to the citizenry.[64]

For Toronto's Baptists, philanthropic and moral reform efforts that served both religious altruism and vertical social mobility were even more vigorously undertaken in the period after the typhus epidemic in 1847 and before the appointment of Toronto's first medical officer in 1883. The extent and significance of these efforts is impressive when one considers that the number of Toronto's Baptists lagged behind both the Ontario and Canadian figures in the last half of the nineteenth century. In 1861, for example, Baptists accounted for only 2.9 percent of the city's populace, while the number for the province stood at 4.4 percent. By 1881, Baptists in Toronto were 4.2 percent of the city's population, while in the same year Baptists were 5.5 percent of the population in Ontario and 6.8 percent of the Canadian population.[65] Despite their low numbers, Toronto's Baptist community worked tirelessly on behalf of a myriad of charitable and moral reform causes. The result of these efforts was that Baptists were able to carve out a place for themselves within the city's respectable middle class circles. Having worked their way into the middle class mainstream, Baptists now sought to work their way up by exercising more leadership within the philanthropic and moral reform organizations in which they were involved or by initiating new social service ventures in which they held the top leadership positions.

One area of social concern and action in which Toronto's Baptists took a serious interest was the vulnerability and well-being of the young.

63. For the rise of the Bank of Commerce and McMaster's role in it, see *The Canadian Bank of Commerce Charter and Annual Reports*; Bliss, *Northern Enterprise*, 256–82; Careless, *Toronto to 1918*, 86, 117–18.

64. For an analysis of this process see Splane, *Social Welfare*.

65. The conclusions here are based on the numbers found in the *Census of Canada, 1851–1921* and the Tables found in Grant, *Profusion of Spires*, 224. Other helpful statistics are found in Gauvreau, "Protestantism Transformed," 96–97, and Airhart, "Ordering a New Nation," 102–4.

Many Baptists were fearful that without proper moral guidance, the young, and particularly young men, might fall prey to worldly temptation and vices of every kind. In response to this fear, Bond Street's pastor, Thomas Ford Caldicott, and a group of young Baptist laymen from middle class families, started the Bond Street Baptist Church Young Mens' Christian Association in 1864. The "object" of the association was the "improvement of the spiritual, intellectual and social condition of young men, and the advancement of the cause of Christ."[66] The "exercises" for a meeting held on 6 December 1864 included the reading of an essay on the character of Apollos, an original poem on the revision of the Bible by the American Bible Union, and conversations about the "progressive tendencies of the nineteenth century."[67] Conversations about science, literature, education, and religion were led by members of the association. Underlying the activities of the Young Mens' association was a number of important assumptions about age and gender. Baptists, like Caldicott, assumed that the activities of societies like the Young Mens' Association at Bond Street provided some protection from "worldliness" and "sin," while at the same time promoting and reinforcing respectable Protestant middle class values and morality. The Young Mens' Association was a perfect venue for Toronto's Baptists to call their young men to practice Christian character and commitment.

The lack of healthcare for children also captured the attention of Toronto's Baptists. In this sphere the efforts of Elizabeth McMaster stand out. Born in 1847 and raised in a well-to-do Anglican family, Elizabeth Wyllie married Samuel Fenton McMaster, a nephew of William McMaster and a junior partner in the prosperous dry goods firm of A. R. McMaster and brother in 1865, at the tender age of seventeen.[68] As Gina Feldberg has noted, this "marriage positioned her [Elizabeth] firmly on the second rung of the city's [Toronto's] social ladder." The match also provided the young Elizabeth with "financial security and extensive family network" where she had the opportunity to join "the women of this group in charitable work."[69] On 1 November 1866, Lizzie

66. "Bond Street Baptist Church," *Canadian Baptist*, 18 February 1864, 2; "Bond St. Young Men's Christian Association," *Canadian Baptist*, 14 October 1869, 2.

67. "Young Men's Christian Association," *Canadian Baptist*, 15 December 1864, 2.

68. For other details related to the McMaster and Wylie families, see Braithwaite, *Sick Kids*, 11.

69. Feldberg, "Wyllie, Elizabeth Jennet (McMaster)."

and Samuel F. McMaster were baptized and received into membership
of the Bond Street Baptist Church.[70] Now officially Baptist, Lizzie would
join her Baptist peers in their philanthropic and moral reforms efforts,
which included visits and ministrations to the poor through organizations such as the Ladies Bible Association and the Toronto Home for
Incurables.[71]

In 1874 the first meeting was held in the McMaster home located at
26 Clover Hill to discuss the organization of a Ladies Committee to work
on the establishment of a hospital for sick children [hereafter HSC].[72]
The subsequent Ladies Committee included twenty-two women, many
of whom were wives of middle and upper class citizens of Toronto. The
committee included Mrs. Edward Blake, Mrs. W. H. Howland and Lady
Macdonald.[73] By March of 1875, a house at 31 Avenue Street was rented
to serve as the first premises of the hospital. By July of 1876 the hospital
had treated one hundred and eleven patients.[74] Relying solely on free-
will donations from the public, Elizabeth McMaster and her committee had, by 1878, succeeded in securing from Edmund Osler and James
Lamond Smith a lot forty feet wide and one hundred and fifty feet deep
on Elizabeth Street. A two storey brick building on the site was used as
the location for the hospital until 1890.[75]

By all accounts, Elizabeth McMaster was the quintessential female
evangelical philanthropist. Her religious zeal and evangelistic fervor
were always at the forefront of her efforts. Believing that she was "led
by the Spirit of God to found the Hospital for Sick Children in Toronto,"
McMaster brought her religious beliefs and values to every aspect
of the work.[76] While Elizabeth McMaster was President of the Ladies

70. Jarvis Street Minute Book, 11 November 1866; See also [Bond Street/Jarvis
Street Baptist Church] Members Roll Book, 39. Both of these sources are in the Jarvis
Street Baptist Church Archives.

71. Elizabeth McMaster was involved in these activities, but she did not hold any
leadership role. See, for example, Fourth Annual Report of the Toronto Home for
Incurables, March 1878, 11, Microform Collection, University of Western Ontario.

72. Young, "A Divine Mission," 75; Braithwaite, Sick Kids, 10.

73. A list of the women on the committee is given in ARHSC 1 January to 31
December 1878, 6.

74. ARHSC, 1876, 5.

75. Braithwaite, Sick Kids, 17.

76. Ladies Committee Minutes, 2 November 1883. Hospital for Sick Children
Archives.

Committee, a post she held until 1889, their meetings always began with prayer and a hymn, and ladies on the committee were expected to visit the Hospital in shifts to offer care and teach the children hymns and Bible reading.[77] All of these activities were intended to provide spiritual instruction, guidance, and comfort. Such efforts also reveal that McMaster followed and perpetuated the earlier pattern of Baptist women of providing both direct assistance and indirect care through management.

The serious attention paid to the religious needs of the children did not prevent some committee members from regularly evaluating the extent and effectiveness of such efforts. For example, in 1879, one committee member asked if "the spiritual culture kept pace with the physical treatment."[78] And on one of her visits, that same committee member interviewed some of the boys concerning the moral lessons found in one of their books, *Ernest's Schooldays*.[79] Such actions testify to the fact that McMaster and her committee were vigilant in their efforts to instill and uphold their religious beliefs and values.

Compassion and direct contact with patients was also evident in the philosophy and practices of McMaster and her committee. As Judith Young has noted and demonstrated, "they were intensely concerned with the welfare and daily lives of the children."[80] Long stays at the hospital were common, and to help the children cope with this reality, the children were "provided with some occupation and amusement" in the boardroom.[81] To prevent "mischief and idleness" a workroom was established for the boys.[82] Furthermore, children from poor families who were in need of treatment were given this service for free by the attending physician who was on duty that day.[83]

Beyond her commitment and practice of religious altruism, Elizabeth McMaster extended the Baptist social network through the

77. Braithwaite, *Sick Kids*, 15; Young, "A Divine Mission," 73.

78. Young, "A Divine Mission," 77.

79. Ibid.

80. Ibid.

81. Ladies Committee Minutes, 10 October 1877. Hospital for Sick Children Archives.

82. Ladies Committee Minutes, 9 November 1876. Hospital for Sick Children Archives.

83. ARHSC, 1877, 4.

exercise of her considerable leadership and organizational and interpersonal skills. For example, she displayed an ability to persuade others to donate to her cause that few of her male Baptist counterparts could match. In the midst of a financial crisis in 1878 and in desperate need of a new furnace for the hospital, McMaster sent an honest, direct, and persuasive letter of appeal and Annual Report to a Toronto heating contractor on 19 October 1878. The letter emphasized, "we [the Ladies Committee on behalf of the hospital] get our money only as the Lord sends it, and that is only in answer to believing prayer."[84] McMaster then put the matter frankly to the contractor: "We consider it right to make this statement to you before you commence work, that you might either work, trusting God for the money, as we do, or not all." She then called for a decision by "Wednesday noon" and concluded with a final plea: "May God lead you to a decision that will be for His glory, and your good."[85] The letter achieved a significant result, and the contractor ordered the furnace, agreed to install it and wait "patiently" for payment "until your Committee are in funds to pay me."[86] A fervent appeal for funds went forth, and the public responded generously. At a subsequent meeting of the Ladies Committee held on 30 October 1878, McMaster expressed her belief in God's provision: "God has sent us a large gift this month—total $274.95."[87] By 5 August 1879, the "last payment of $65 was made" for the furnace.[88] This challenge was one among many, and it demonstrates the effectiveness and extensiveness of Elizabeth McMaster's leadership and faith.

The endeavors of Elizabeth McMaster beg for analysis on many levels. Clearly, McMaster used her religious altruism as a basis for moving beyond the social constraints placed on her gender by her church and society at large. As American historian Susan Hill Lindley has claimed, a woman like Elizabeth McMaster was in the category of one who "stepped out" of her "culturally assigned subordination" to achieve her religious and humanitarian objectives.[89] Her efforts also illustrate the trend to-

---

84. ARHSC, 1878, 17.

85. ARHSC, 1878, 17.

86. Ibid., 18.

87. Ibid.

88. For this fact and another account of these events, see *The Hospital for Sick Children Toronto: A Retrospect*, 19–20.

89. Lindley, *You Have Stept out of Your Place*, x.

wards the feminization of religion that was becoming evident in central Canada by the late nineteenth century. While men might continue to exercise the "lion's share" of power over Baptist philanthropic and moral efforts, women were asserting their influence to great effect in a number of areas. In Toronto at least, the efforts of middle class Baptist women were seldom intended to be a direct challenge to male authority but did seek to expand the role of women within both the church and the community. Elizabeth McMaster's efforts also reveal that patterns once set were slow to change. Clearly, she continued the practice of earlier middle class Baptist women of having some direct engagement with those they served and also serving in management roles that created more distance between client and philanthropist.

Of course, the list of other middle class Baptist women engaged in similar philanthropic and moral reform efforts in Toronto is considerable. Susan Moulton Fraser McMaster, for example, the second wife of William McMaster, "was one of the foremost promoters" of the Toronto Women's Medical College, which began in 1883.[90] Similarly, an examination of the activities of Mary Oliphant Elliot, wife of the prominent chemical and drug manufacturer William Elliot, reveals a strong commitment to many of Toronto's philanthropic and moral reform endeavors. Particularly noteworthy was her support and promotion of the Girls' Home and Public Nursery.[91] By 1873, Mary Elliot was the only "Honorary Member" on the Executive of the Home.[92] Mary Elliot was joined in this effort by her daughters Violet Elliot and Mary Scott. Mary was the wife of J. G. Scott, a prominent lawyer from Jarvis Street Baptist Church. Both daughters would hold high positions in the management hierarchy of the Home.[93]

While Baptist women like Elizabeth McMaster, Susan McMaster, and the Elliots were exhibiting their religious altruism and extending the Baptist social network, middle class men were also doing their part to enhance their philanthropic and moral reform activities in the com-

90. This is the view given in Morgan, *Canadian Men and Women*, 785. For more information on Susan Moulton Fraser McMaster, see Hall, *Per Ardua*, 15–18.

91. For a description of the Home, see Careless, *Toronto to 1918*, 100, 145.

92. See, for example, ARGH, 1873, 2.

93. Mary Scott held the positions of Corresponding Secretary in 1879, Second Directress in 1890, and First Directress in 1894. See ARGH, 1878; ARGH, 1889; ARGH, 1893. Violet Elliot held the posts of Secretary in 1879 and Treasurer in 1900. See ARGH, 1878; AGHR, 1899.

munity. A survey of various charitable societies in which middle class
Baptist men were involved between 1834 and 1883 reveals that they
often moved up in their positions within these societies. For example,
within the Upper Canada Bible Society [hereafter UCBS] and its local
expression in the Toronto Auxiliary Bible Society, the status of Baptist
men grew considerably. In 1818, when few Baptists were in York, the
Upper Canada Bible Society was founded and dominated by the town's
Anglican elite; no Baptist held a leadership position.[94] As already noted,
in the 1830s and 1840s, a few middle class Baptists, like A. T. McCord,
Robert Cathcart, and William McMaster, were able to obtain lesser
positions such as Secretary, Depository, and Committee Member in
the Auxiliary Society's leadership hierarchy.[95] These positions testified
to Baptist entry into the respectable socio-cultural world of Toronto's
middle class.

By 1880, however, one sign that Baptists were successfully moving
to the higher rungs within Toronto's middle class circles was reflected
in the posts they occupied within the Upper Canada Bible Society.
Both William McMaster and A. T. McCord were Vice-Presidents of the
Society. William McMaster also held the position of Treasurer. The list
of Directors for the Society included Rev. J. H. Castle (pastor of Jarvis
Street Baptist Church), Rev. E. M. C. Botterill (pastor of Parliament
Street Baptist Church), and hatter and furrier George Lugsdin.[96] A similar pattern of advancement is evident in the Annual Reports of the Upper
Canada Religious Tract and Book Society.[97] This evidence suggests that
Baptists took advantage of their participation in philanthropy and moral
reform to enhance their place and reputation within Toronto's middle
class community.

94. *First Report of the Bible Society of Upper Canada*. The list of subscribers on pages
42–44 reads like an Anglican Who's Who of Toronto.

95. See, for example, *Sixth Report of the City of Toronto Auxiliary Bible Society for
1834; Eleventh Report of the City of Toronto Auxiliary Bible Society for the Year Ending
30 April 1840*.

96. *Fortieth Report of the Upper Canada Bible Society*.

97. In *Twentieth Report of the Upper Canada Religious Tract and Book Society*, 1 June
1853, William McMaster is listed as Vice-President, A. T. McCord as a Secretary, and
David Buchan as a member of the Committee. By 1876, Toronto Baptists held more and
higher leadership positions. William McMaster, A. T. McCord, and Rev. R. A. Fyfe were
Vice Presidents, while William Elliot was a Director at the same level as the Committee
Members of earlier years. See, for example, *Forty-Third Report of the Upper Canada
Religious Tract and Book Society*, 2 May 1876.

One must be careful, however, not to create the false impression that upward social mobility and respectability were inevitable or easily achieved. Baptist aspirations within the UCBS, for example, did not go unchallenged. Rumours and accusations that William McMaster, the Treasurer of the UCBS, "frequently" used "$15,000 to $20,000 of the Society's funds" for his own purposes and that he "sought to saddle" the Society with a bad mortgage that he had initially underwritten, produced a serious and protracted two year conflict, from 1873 to 1875, between the Senator and the well-connected Anglican John George Hodgins. Believing that the best defense was a strong offence, McMaster responded in his customary forthright manner and blamed Hodgins for the "whispering, insinuations and shaking of heads" concerning the Senator's involvement in the financial affairs of the Society. McMaster further charged Hodgins with the "misapplication and misappropriation of the Society's funds." Hodgins retorted that he had no knowledge of the "gossip" about the senator and that his charges were completely "unfounded." The longstanding dispute between McMaster and Hodgins was finally resolved at a Board Meeting held in April of 1875, when after Hodgins threatened to resign, McMaster "apologized . . . and withdrew all his charges" against the Secretary.[98]

Apart from the obvious personality clash between the two men, this war of words was clearly intended to impugn the reputation and undermine the respectability of the other man. Such competition and challenges were not uncommon. As Baptists sought higher posts within a given philanthropic society, they sometimes had to prove that they were worthy of such authority and leadership.

Beyond greater social status and respectability there were other driving forces behind the philanthropic and moral reform activities of Baptist men in this period. Commitment to the promotion of Christian morality, biblical literacy, and evangelism remained staples as motives for such efforts. For example, the response of Thomas Dixon Craig, the Sunday School Superintendent at Jarvis Street Baptist Church, to a debate over the purpose and objectives of the Toronto Sabbath School Association in 1871 provides evidence that Baptists remained firmly

98. All of the quotations in this paragraph are taken from Hodgins, Letter to the Directors of the Upper Canada Bible Society, 7 April 1875. John George Hodgins Collection, MG 17 F3 Volume IX, Document 313, National Archives of Canada. The underlining of some text is as it appears in the original document.

committed to their religious altruism. Essentially, Craig argued that the Sabbath School should serve a dual purpose. The "great object" was "the training of all Christians, young and old in the knowledge of the Sacred Scriptures." The "other great part of the work" was "the bringing of these to Jesus." Still, Craig stressed that in his view "the great necessity of the present" was "the study of the Bible."[99] For Craig and his fellow Baptists, religious beliefs, values, and practices related to salvation and sanctification remained at the core of their philanthropic and moral reform activities.

Another moral reform issue that garnered serious attention from Baptists in this period was temperance. While a considerable number of Toronto's middle class Baptist men and women were involved in the promotion and support of this moral crusade, the work of Ezekiel Francis Whittemore, the son-in-law of A. T. McCord, stands out. In the spring of 1853, Whittemore used his influence as a former city alderman and councilman to rally support for the temperance cause in York County.[100] At the organizational meeting of the League held in May 1853, Whittemore was appointed President of the Temperance League for the County of York.[101] Along with James Ryrie Sr. and James Lesslie, Whittemore advocated for the passage of legislation similar to that of the Maine Law in the United States, which effectively banned the sale and distribution of all liquor in the state.[102] Among Whittemore's many efforts on behalf of the temperance cause was his presiding over a breakfast at the American Hotel in July of 1853. This meal was part of a weekend that featured the Honourable Neal Dow, who was the author and primary sponsor of the Maine Law.[103] In addition to his role

99. All of the quotations in this paragraph are taken from the minutes of an annual meeting of the Sabbath School Association. See *Toronto Sabbath School Association Second Sabbath School Teachers' Institute*, 21. Thomas Dixon Craig died 4 April 1905. He had a prosperous wholesale leather business, and he became an outspoken and well-respected philanthropist and Conservative politician. He served as the MPP for East Durham in 1886 and was elected to the House of Commons in 1891. For more details on his life, see his obituaries: "T. Dixon Craig Ex. M.P., Dies in Port Hope," *Toronto Daily Star*, 5 April 1905, 7; "Death of Mr. T. Dixon Craig," *Globe*, 5 April 1905, 8; "Obituaries, Craig," *Canadian Baptist*, 13 April 1905, 11; "The Late T. Dixon Craig," *Canadian Baptist*, 20 April 1905, 11.

100. Russell, *Mayors of Toronto*, 141–42.

101. "Temperance League." For a biographical sketch of Whittemore, see "Whittemore."

102. "Temperance League."

103. "The Hon. Neal Dow," *The Examiner*, 13 July 1853, 2.

with the Temperance League, Whittemore served alongside his fellow Baptists Joseph Lesslie and A. T. McCord as a committee member of the Temperance Reformation Society of Toronto.[104] Clearly, Whittemore was a leading Baptist temperance reformer.

By the time Dr. William Canniff was appointed Toronto's first medical health officer in 1883, Toronto's Baptists had used their philanthropic and moral reform efforts to practice their religious altruism and secure a firm grip on their place within the city's middle class. Moving beyond mere participation, some Baptists initiated new social services or rose to prominence in existing charitable societies. At the same time, these Baptists formed powerful social networks that would serve them well in the wider business and social worlds of mid-Victorian Toronto. Furthermore, the efforts of these Baptists had established a socio-cultural pathway for the next generation of Baptists to follow.

TORONTO BAPTISTS IN SOCIAL SERVICE, 1883–1918

Late Victorian and Edwardian Toronto experienced all of the social challenges and changes associated with a city undergoing rapid industrialization and commercialization. The population continued to increase at breakneck speed from 56,092 in 1871 to 521,893 by 1921.[105] The result was an ever-growing population of urban poor, many of whom were new immigrants from Eastern Europe. The moral reform impulse that had always given Toronto its own unique identity gained even more prominence and attention as local politicians ran for Mayor on a platform of moral reform. For example, the reform-minded Methodist, W. H. Howland, succeeded in the municipal elections of 1886 and 1887, much to the delight of some Baptists.[106]

Moreover, the professionalization of health and human services redefined the role of volunteers and private charitable organizations. The evangelistic zeal of earlier times was gradually relegated to second place or cast aside altogether, as a particular society or institution focused more attention on physical suffering and left the spiritual needs of the

104. See, for example, *Eighth Report of the Temperance Reformation Society of the City of Toronto, 11 October 1847.*

105. Careless, *Toronto to 1918*, 109, 149, 201.

106. For two discussions of Howland's personality, political regime, and reform agenda, see Morton, *Mayor Howland*, and Russell, *Mayors of Toronto*, 112–15.

individual for the churches to address.[107] There were, of course, exceptions to this trend, and the efforts of Toronto's Baptists, from the start of public health in 1883 until the end of the First World War in 1918, were somewhat paradoxical. Some Baptist endeavors showed a remarkably high level of religious altruism, while other, usually older, initiatives lost some of their religious zeal and evangelistic thrust as a particular society or institution was transformed into a public humanitarian entity that followed the trend to embrace the more secular ideas and professional methodologies of the social and health sciences. Also, the roles taken by middle class Baptist women were sometimes challenged or changed.

At the same time, the influence of the social gospel on some Baptists like Henry Moyle and Pastor John MacNeill of Walmer Road Baptist Church, and the creation of the Social Service Committee by the Baptist Convention of Ontario and Quebec in 1912, signaled the arrival of a greater social consciousness and a growing desire within progressive quarters for coordinated and comprehensive denominational participation in social action.[108] Still, as Richard Allen has noted, when compared to the efforts of Methodists and Presbyterians, "Baptists . . . seldom found their way beyond secondary leadership positions" in the wider social gospel movement.[109] Nevertheless, at the local level, and particularly in large urban centers like Toronto, the social gospel served to stimulate greater social service.

A classic example of the pressures and challenges faced by middle class Baptist women because of the trend towards professionalization and negative male reaction to feminization, is found in the experience of Elizabeth McMaster. In 1889, McMaster faced a number of challenges. She lost her husband in 1888, still had a young family to raise, and endured a very stressful debate with hospital Trustee and owner of the *Toronto Telegram*, John Ross Robertson, over the site for a new hospital building. Despite these challenges, McMaster decided to pursue nurse's training to "qualify herself more fully for the duties of Presiding Officer of the Hospital."[110] As Judith Young has observed, "the role of the trained

107. For an analysis of professionalization and its effects on an evangelical Toronto charity, see Graham, "The Haven."

108. For the changing forms and focus of the Committee, see *Baptist Year Book 1906*, 165–66; *Baptist Year Book 1908*, 25, 205; *Baptist Year Book 1912*, 21, 25–26, 28–29, 236–37.

109. Allen, *Social Passion*, 15.

110. ARHSC, 1889, 16.

nurse was becoming increasingly important" as hospitals like the HSC were transformed "from a home for the sick and destitute to a modern temple of science."[111] Moreover, the push for a new modern hospital brought with it an increased demand for the trustees to take on more financial liability and a greater say over the management affairs of the new institution. Such circumstances set the stage for wealthy and powerful men like John Ross Robertson, the owner and editor of the *Toronto Telegram* and a major donor to the HSC, to wrest control away from the Ladies Committee and its President, Elizabeth McMaster. In 1891, while McMaster was in nurse's training in Chicago, a "happy arrangement" was reached between the Ladies Committee and the Trustees "whereby a large part of the burden of care . . . was transferred from the shoulders of a few weak women to those of strong and capable business men."[112] Although on its public face the new "arrangement" was amiable, the deal effectively ended female control over the HSC and established a new regime of male dominance over its affairs.

Though McMaster returned to the HSC for about a year as Lady Superintendent, she and Robertson clashed continually over a variety of management and development issues, and McMaster finally decided to resign from her position early in 1892. While the Ladies Committee begged the Trustees to reject the resignation, it was accepted, and the official reasons given for McMaster's departure were "ill health" and "family obligations."[113] McMaster was given the opportunity to speak briefly at the opening of the new hospital on 5 May 1892, but the era of her leadership and participation in the affairs of the HSC was at an end.[114]

The experience of Elizabeth McMaster highlights the risks, rewards, and losses associated with the philanthropic and moral reform efforts of Toronto's Baptist women. Whatever her shortcomings, McMaster, through her devotion and sacrifice to the cause of the HSC, was a model of Baptist middle class respectability and wholehearted religious altruism. Her efforts helped to firmly entrench Baptists in the wider circles of Toronto's middle class and expanded Baptist involvement in community social service. But all of these benefits for Baptists came at a high personal price for McMaster. In the end, she was a victim of her

111. Young, "A Divine Mission," 82.
112. ARHSC, 1891–92, 12.
113. Young, "A Divine Mission," 85.
114. ARHSC, 1891–92, 13.

own success, her gender, and changes beyond her control. The takeover of the HSC by the male trustees exposed the ugly side of the assumption that men were to dominate within the public domain. Obviously, a "weak" woman like Elizabeth McMaster was incapable of running a philanthropic enterprise as large as the HSC. Also, the establishment of this new male regime clearly set the institution on a course that favored the medical professional over the untrained health worker, fundraising through promotion instead of prayer, and scientific research for cures over sharing the gospel with patients.

Beyond the efforts of individuals, Toronto's Baptist churches also started innovative philanthropic projects that combined a high level of evangelism and practical social service. The Memorial Institute, begun by Walmer Road Baptist Church and members of the former Memorial Baptist Church in 1911, for example, was born out of a growing and genuine concern for the spiritual and social health of Toronto's downtown. In particular these Baptists were concerned about the growing numbers of young immigrants and urban poor that populated sections of the city's core. Included in this concern was the area around Tecumseh Street located southwest of Queen and Bathurst, where the Memorial Baptist Church was situated. After a protracted period of negotiations in late 1910, an agreement between the Memorial Baptist Church and Walmer Road Baptist Church was concluded. Under the terms of the agreement, all members of Memorial became members of Walmer, Walmer took over control of the new mission venture known as "The Memorial Institute," and the property of the former Memorial Baptist Church was deeded to Walmer.[115] As Goertz has noted in his examination of how and why the Institute was created, "A ministry of this magnitude required significant financial resources."[116] Walmer certainly had both the financial and human resources needed to launch and sustain the mission.

The growth, extent, and effects of the Memorial Institute were impressive. In 1913, the second year of its operation, the Institute had a total attendance at its religious services of 37,238 and a total of 33,098 at its various institutional meetings. On a monthly basis the Institute

---

115. For resolutions and decisions related to the new Institute see, for example, Walmer Minute Book, 27 September 1911; 3 January 1912; Memorial Minute Book, 1910–1912. Both sources are in the Canadian Baptist Archives at McMaster University.

116. Goertz, *Century for the City,* 42.

served 5,851 people.[117] After two weeks of "special gospel services" early in 1913, there were some seventy-five who "professed conversion" and "the effects" were "felt all through the year."[118] Without doubt evangelism was a central emphasis in the activities of the Institute.

Equally impressive was the wide range of social services that the Institute provided. Basic social work and healthcare were provided through the work of fellow Baptist Nellie MacFarland, the Institute's first full-time non-professional nurse and home visitor. Eventually, various volunteer clubs, circles, and clinics run by the Institute promoted moral reform causes such as prohibition through "house to house" canvassing, provided skill development training through "industrial classes" in garment-making, conducted summer camps for poor women and children, supplied milk to malnourished children, opened settlement houses for immigrants, and offered free healthcare and social assistance to poor families in the community.[119]

The staff at the Institute also worked hard on developing relationships with other "social workers" in the area. The Institute's workers attended the bi-weekly meetings of the West Social Conference to advise "one another on individual cases and general methods."[120] The Director of the Institute, Awdrey L. Brown, served as chairman of the Conference in 1912 and 1913, and he also served as chairman of the "Joint Executive" and as president of Toronto's "Social Workers' Club."[121] Beyond these efforts, the workers had an even larger vision to see "a School of Civics and Philanthropy" opened in Toronto.[122]

Of course, sustaining such a large effort was challenging. For example, faced with a need for $2,300 to run the mission in 1916, a joint meeting of the Deacons, Finance Committee, and Memorial Committee held on 29 November 1915, engaged in a "free discussion on the various aspects of the work." Apparently some on the Finance Committee objected to the sum proposed, and members of the Memorial Committee were required to explain and defend "the different phases of the work." The

117. The Annual Reports for the Memorial Institute are included in Walmer's Annual Reports. For the statistics mentioned here see WRBCAR 1913, 9–10.

118. Ibid., 9.

119. Ibid., 9–13.

120. Ibid., 13.

121. Ibid.

122. Ibid.

debate concluded with an injunction to all to "recognize and remember that the Memorial Institute was a part of the church, the work there essentially a responsibility of the church and the financial problems there a part of the financial problems of the church."[123] This incident brings to light the stresses and tensions associated with such an effort.

Still, the Memorial Institute was in many ways the quintessential expression of philanthropy and moral reform by Toronto's Baptists in this period. The strengths of the effort were many. The dual emphasis on evangelism and social service made the Institute a model of how Baptists could effectively minister to both the spiritual and physical needs of others. Also, the fact that the Institute was a church-sponsored effort, as opposed to an individual effort, initiated a new pattern for other Baptists to follow. Finally, the revival of middle class interest and concern for poor downtown neighborhoods after years of migration to the suburbs was also encouraging.

But, as Goertz has astutely pointed out, there were also several flaws that characterized the mission. Certainly, control over the course and character of the Memorial Institute remained firmly in the hands of Walmer's "wealthy Anglo-Saxons," and they were often insensitive and unwilling to address the needs expressed by those who had previously been part of Memorial Baptist Church. While "merger" and "partnership" were professed, "take over" was the reality. Another weakness was the lack of integration between Memorial and Walmer. While Walmer's middle class members were willing to donate money and time to support the Memorial Institute, the negative pattern of "arm's length" ministry to those in the poor areas of the city remained intact. This meant that although Memorial Institute housed a church of immigrants, little effort was made to connect these new Canadians with Walmer's congregation.[124] Despite these weaknesses, the Memorial Institute was the premier Baptist philanthropic and moral reform mission of its day.

The Memorial Institute, however, was not the only venue for Toronto's middle class Baptists concerned about moral reform. Through their participation in the activities of the Toronto Vigilance Association, Baptists such as T. T. Shields (the fundamentalist pastor of Jarvis Street Baptist Church), Andrew Imrie (pastor of the Indian Road Baptist

---

123. All of the quotations in this paragraph are taken from Walmer Deacons Minutes, 29 November 1915, Canadian Baptist Archives, McMaster University.

124. Similar conclusions are presented in Goertz, *Century for the City*, 42–46.

Church), the wealthy jeweler from Jarvis Street James Ryrie, the box manufacturer John Firstbrook, MPP W. K. McNaught (editor of the *Canadian Baptist*), Dr. W. J. McKay, and many others saw themselves as the city's moral reformers and watchdogs. In her discourse analysis of "The St. Clair Affair" of 1912–1913, Lyndsay Campbell examines the events that followed Rev. Robert B. St. Clair's conviction on a charge of circulating obscenities in Toronto following his publication of a graphic pamphlet intended to prompt the police to shut down the burlesque show called "The Darlings of Paris" staged at the Star Theatre.[125]

Both Shields and Ryrie were outraged by St. Clair's conviction and the tepid nature of the actions taken by Inspector Kennedy of the Toronto Police Department. Shields and Imrie preached sermons in late September 1912 denouncing "The Darlings of Paris" in Imrie's words, as "vicious, devilish and pernicious."[126] Shields went even further and accused Inspector Kennedy of mishandling and misrepresenting the case, and he argued that an "open cesspool in front of the City Hall would be less injurious to the public health than that place of so-called entertainment is to the moral health of those who frequent it."[127] Kennedy promptly accused Shields of "seeking notoriety by attacking the [morality] department" but argued that "he [Shields] will not get it through me."[128] Kennedy then expressed his confidence that "the majority of clergymen in Toronto and Ontario" would, in the face of an investigation into how his department had handled the situation, "strongly commend from the pulpit the good work we are doing."[129] He moved on to vigorously defend the actions of the department's "censors" and their enforcement of the law.

This public battle between the police and moral reformers like Shields was the first salvo in an ongoing war over who would control the moral reform agenda in Toronto. The response of Canada's Chiefs of Police to outspoken clergymen at their convention later in 1912 revealed

125. Campbell, "A Slub in the Cloth." For an understanding of those who took a completely different approach to moral and social reform in this period, see Chunn, *From Punishment to Doing Good.*

126. A brief summary of Imrie's sermon is given in "Clergymen Condemn Way Police Censors Do Work," *Toronto Daily Star,* 30 September 1912, 15.

127. "Theatre Worse Than Open Cesspool," *Globe,* 30 September 1912, 8.

128. "Staff Inspector Defends Department," *Globe,* 1 October 1912, 8.

129. Ibid.

a widening division and sense of alienation between the police and the more conservative elements within Toronto's moral reform movement. A pointed resolution criticizing the sermon content and misguided tactics of moral reformers like Shields and Imrie argued "that the cause of moral reform is not likely to be helped by such senseless tirades, even when delivered from church platforms, by those whose methods are only sensational and denunciatory and whose only policy seems to be a vindictive condemnation of immoral people and unreasoning abuse of the police."[130] Such criticism did little to make conservative and fundamentalist Baptist reformers take stock.

By early October 1912, James Ryrie was the chairman of a committee struck for the express purpose of gaining greater regulation or outright closure of the Star Theatre. At a meeting held in Massey Hall on 1 November 1912, Ryrie used his keynote address to compare the Star Theatre to an "open cesspool," and he claimed that "the hand of politics and the hand of the various societies were too prominent at the City Hall." In later speeches by others, as Inspector Kennedy sat and listened, it was alleged that the police did not share the moral standards of the community and that they were negligent in their enforcement of the Criminal Code. The meeting concluded by passing a resolution that the Board of Police Commissioners should be enlarged by two who would serve unpaid for a term of three years and hold no other municipal office. Also, a "Committee of Forty," which included Shields, Ryrie, and other Baptists, was struck and charged with the duty of pursuing the specific objectives decided at this meeting.[131]

The moral reform activities of mainly conservative and fundamentalist Baptists through the Toronto Vigilance Association were a more direct and militant form of social activism. Dissatisfied with simply calling for moral reform, these Baptists saw themselves as Toronto's moral change agents who could bring about the moral reform of their city through the pressure they exerted on local politicians, the police, and the public. By using their pulpits and the press to expose vice, injustice, and lax enforcement, these Baptists sought to raise the ire of Toronto's

130. Quoted in Campbell, "A Slub in the Cloth," 4.

131. For accounts of the 1 November 1912 meeting, see "Great Gathering in Massey Hall Condemns Police, Demands a Change," *Toronto Daily Star*, 2 November 1912, 6, 9. "Clean House Demand of 4,000 Citizens," *Globe*, 2 November 1912, 1, 8; "Reorganize Police Force Demand of Mass Meeting," *Evening Telegram*, 2 November 1912, 30.

citizenry by shaming reluctant local officials into action and creating a sense of moral outrage, crisis, and scandal within the city's precincts. Their efforts sometimes achieved the desired end, but at the same time the militant nature of such efforts created a rift between some middle class Baptist moral reformers and those who held the responsibility to enforce the vice laws. Both the confrontational methods they employed and the level of judgmentalism found in their message served to discredit these Baptists in the eyes of Toronto's police.

Many middle class Baptists in this period were also found in less noisy but no less noteworthy philanthropic and moral reform endeavors of all kinds. For example, Mrs. R. W. Laird of Jarvis Street helped to found "The Haven" in 1878.[132] This charity for women addressed a wide variety of social problems. Also, the list of Baptists who worked with the Children's Aid Society was long. In 1897, for example, Rev. E. T. Fox, Mrs. C. C. Van Norman, Mrs. James Ryrie, and Mrs. John Lillie all served on the Management Committee of the Society.[133] Finally, the family of William Davies gave generously of their money, time, and energy to support the Children's Aid Society.[134]

CONCLUSION

The philanthropic and moral reform efforts of Toronto's Baptists had a profound effect on their community. From the time of the city's incorporation in 1834 until the end of the First World War, Baptists deemed participation in charitable work, evangelistic outreach, and moral reform campaigns as some of the best means to realize their religious and socio-cultural objectives. Through their many mission endeavors, Toronto's Baptists gave witness to their faith and practical expression to their religious altruism. Such interdenominational activities also provided a socio-cultural pathway for Baptist entrance and establishment within the cadre of Toronto's Anglo-Saxon Protestant middle class. In addition, such efforts effectively redefined Toronto Baptist identity by moving them from outsiders to insiders within the public life of their city.

132. See Graham, "The Haven," 289 n. 32.

133. *Sixth Annual Report of the Children's Aid Society of Toronto, September 1897.*

134. In Ibid., both William and Emily Davies are listed as "Life Members" of the Society. This title was only given to the most ardent and generous supporters of this charity.

While they engaged in their evangelical good works, middle class Baptists consistently followed a number of important patterns. They moved to Toronto's suburbs, particularly in the north and west of the city. This pattern created a geographical and physical distance between middle class Baptists and the poor. Beyond establishing a geographical separation from those they sought to serve, Baptist men in particular also created a relational distance between themselves and those less fortunate or immoral individuals who needed social assistance and salvation. Carrying with them certain assumptions and beliefs about the relationship between cleanliness and godliness, the need for social purity, and the requirement that one be separated from this present evil world, middle class Baptists often isolated or insulated themselves from possible social and spiritual contamination. To be fair, Baptist women were more relational in their philanthropic pursuits. Finally, the nature of Baptist efforts shows some significant change over time. In two periods between 1834 and 1883, individual effort characterized much of the Baptist involvement in philanthropy and moral reform. In the late nineteenth and early twentieth centuries, as the Memorial Institute and the Toronto Vigilance Association illustrate, Baptists began to take a more collective approach to their social activism.

Obviously, this chapter has only begun the process of uncovering and analyzing the complex social networks that formed the basis of Baptist involvement in Toronto's public life. Among the many issues that have not been covered is the interplay between reform politics and moral reform, and the Baptist role in this dynamic. Also, while the trends towards more professionalization and away from religious altruism have been noted in this chapter, their impact on Baptist efforts still needs a much fuller and more textured exploration and analysis. The same can be said for the role of women. While this research uncovers and analyzes some of the efforts of a few middle class women, and briefly discusses their challenge to some social conventions and behaviors, far more work is needed to gain a more complete picture of their activities and a fuller appreciation of the influences that shaped their lives. Furthermore, we know almost nothing about working class Baptist women who often did the frontline hard work of caring for the poor and ailing.

This chapter has argued that through their philanthropic and moral reform efforts Toronto's Baptists gave witness to their faith, demonstrated a commitment to humanitarianism, and followed a certain socio-cultural pathway to respectability within Toronto's middle class. Whatever our perception of their deficiencies may be, the fact remains that between 1834 and 1918 Toronto's middle class Baptists made significant and lasting contributions to their city's public life.

BIBLIOGRAPHY[135]

Airhart, Phyllis D. "Ordering a New Nation and Reordering Protestantism 1867–1914." In *The Canadian Protestant Experience 1760–1990*, edited by George Rawlyk, 98–138. Burlington, ON: Welch, 1991.

————. *Serving the Present Age: Revivalism, Progressivism, and the Methodist Tradition in Canada*. Kingston and Montreal: McGill-Queen's University Press, 1991.

Allen, Richard. *The Social Passion: Religion and Social Reform in Canada*. Toronto: University of Toronto Press, 1971.

ARGH = Annual Reports of the Girls' Home of the City of Toronto. Toronto: Rowsell & Hutchinson. MUWO.

ARHSC =Annual Reports of the Hospital for Sick Children. Toronto: Hunter, Rose & Co. MUWO and HSCA.

Armstrong, Frederick H. *A City in the Making: Progress, People and Perils in Victorian Toronto*. Toronto: Dundurn Press, 1988.

Baehre, Rainer. "Paupers and Poor Relief in Upper Canada." In *Historical Essays on Upper Canada: New Perspectives*, edited by J. K. Johnson and Bruce G. Wilson, 305–39. Ottawa: Carleton University Press, 1989.

The Baptist Year Book, 1906–12.

Bliss, Michael. *Northern Enterprise: Five Centuries of Canadian Business*. Toronto: McClelland & Stewart, 1990.

Blumin, Stuart M. *The Emergence of the Middle Class: Social Experience in the American City, 1760–1900*. Cambridge: Cambridge University Press, 1989.

Braithwaite, Max. *Sick Kids: The Story of the Hospital for Sick Children in Toronto*. Toronto: McClelland and Stewart, 1974.

Campbell, Lyndsay. "A Slub in the Cloth: The St. Clair Affair and the Discourse of Moral Reform in Toronto, 1912–1913." Paper presented at the 1996 Annual Meeting of the Canadian Law and Society Association, Brock University, St. Catharines, Ontario, June 1996.

Campolo, Tony. "Missing the Point: Social Action." In *Adventures in Missing the Point: How the Culture-Controlled Church Neutered the Gospel*, edited by Brian D. McLaren and Tony Campolo, 103–14. Grand Rapids: Zondervan, 2003.

The Canadian Bank of Commerce Charter and Annual Reports 1867–1907, Vol. 1. Toronto: Canadian Bank of Commerce, 1907. Weldon Library, University of Western Ontario.

The Canadian Baptist Register for 1872. Toronto: Canadian Baptist Office, 1872. CBA.

Careless, J. M. S. *Toronto to 1918: An Illustrated History*. Toronto: James Lorimer & Co. and the National Museum of Man, 1984.

Chen, Xiaobei. *Tending the Gardens of Citizenship: Child Saving in Toronto, 1880s–1920s*. Toronto: University of Toronto Press, 2005.

Christie, Nancy, and Gauvreau, Michael. *A Full-Orbed Christianity: The Protestant Churches and Social Welfare in Canada, 1900–1940*. Kingston and Montreal: McGill-Queen's University Press, 1996.

135. Reports etc. accessed in various archives are labeled thus: CBA = Canadian Baptist Archives, McMaster University, Hamilton, Ontario; HSCA = Hospital for Sick Children Archives, Toronto, Ontario; MUWO = Microform Collection, University of Western Ontario, London, Ontario.

Chunn, Dorothy E. *From Punishment to Doing Good: Family Courts and Socialized Justice in Ontario 1880–1940.* Toronto: University of Toronto Press, 1992.

Cook, Sharon Anne. *"Through Sunshine and Shadow": The Woman's Christian Temperance Union, Evangelicalism, and Reform in Ontario, 1874–1930.* Kingston and Montreal: McGill-Queen's University Press, 1995.

Crawford, Bess Hillery. *Rosedale.* Erin, ON: Boston Mills, 2000.

Drummond, Ian M. *Progress without Planning: The Economic History of Ontario from Confederation to the Second World War.* Toronto: University of Toronto Press, 1987.

Eastern Ontario Association Minutes, 1877. Toronto: Baptist Publishing Company, 1877. CBA.

Eighth Report of the Temperance Reformation Society of the City of Toronto, 11 October 1847. Toronto: Published by Order of the Society, 1847. MUWO

The Eleventh Report of the City of Toronto Auxiliary Bible Society for the Year Ending 30 April 1840. Toronto: Printed for the Society, 1840. MUWO.

Ellis, Walter E. "Gilboa to Ichabod: Social and Religious Factors in the Fundamentalist-Modernist Schisms among Canadian Baptists." *Foundations* 20 (1977) 109–10, 102–26.

The Examiner, 1853.

Feldberg, Gina. "Wyllie, Elizabeth Jennet (McMaster)." In *Dictionary of Canadian Biography,* edited by Ramsay Cook, 13:1118–19. Toronto: University of Toronto Press, 1994.

The First Report of the Bible Society of Upper Canada, with a List of Subscribers and Benefactors. York: Printed for the Society, 1818. MUWO.

The First Report of the Toronto Ladies' Bible Association, 31 March 1847. Toronto: Ladies' Bible Association, 1847. MUWO.

Fleming, Patricia Lockhart et al. (eds.). *History of the Book in Canada.* Vol. 1, *Beginnings to 1840.* Toronto: University of Toronto Press, 2004.

The Fortieth Report of the Upper Canada Bible Society, for the Year Ending 31 March 1880. Toronto: Hunter, Rose & Co., 1880. MUWO.

The Forty-Third Report of the Upper Canada Religious Tract and Book Society, 2 May 1876. Toronto: Dudley & Burns, 1876. MUWO.

Fourth Annual Report of the Toronto Home for Incurables, March 1878. Toronto: Bell & Co., 1878. MUWO.

Fraser, Alexander. *A History of Ontario: Its Resources and Development.* Toronto and Montreal: The Canada History Company, 1907.

Fyfe, R. A. *A Forty Years' Survey from Bond Street Pulpit.* Toronto: Dudley and Burns, 1876.

Gauvreau, Michael. "Protestantism Transformed: Personal Piety and the Evangelical Social Vision, 1818–1867." In *The Canadian Protestant Experience 1760–1990,* edited by George Rawlyk, 48–97. Burlington, ON: Welch, 1991.

Gibson, Theo T. *Robert Alexander Fyfe: His Contemporaries and His Influence.* Burlington, ON: Welch, 1988.

Gidney, R. D., and Millar, W. P. J. *Professional Gentlemen: The Professions in Nineteenth-Century Ontario.* Toronto: University of Toronto Press, 1994.

Glazebrook, G. P. de T. *The Story of Toronto.* Toronto: University of Toronto Press, 1971.

Goertz, Donald. *A Century for the City: Walmer Road Baptist Church, 1889–1989.* Toronto: Walmer Road Baptist Church, 1989.

Graham, John R. "The Haven, 1878–1930: A Toronto Charity's Transition from a Religious to a Professional Ethos." *Social History* 25, no. 50 (1992) 283–306.

Grant, John Webster. *A Profusion of Spires: Religion in Nineteenth Century Ontario.* Toronto: University of Toronto Press, 1988.

Hall, Alfreda. *Per Ardua: The Story of Moulton College Toronto 1888-1954.* Oshawa, ON: Tern Graphics, 1987.

Hodgins, George J. *Documentary History of Education in Upper Canada.* Vol. 1. Toronto: Warwick Bros. & Rutter, 1894.

The Hospital for Sick Children Toronto. A Retrospect. Toronto: Dudley & Burns, 1881. MUWO.

Houston, Susan E., and Prentice, Alison. *Schooling and Scholars in Nineteenth Century Ontario.* Toronto: University of Toronto Press, 1988.

Houston, Susan. "McCord, Andrew Taylor." In *The Dictionary of Canadian Biography*, edited by Francess Halpenny, 11:542–43. Toronto: University of Toronto Press, 1982.

Hughes, Jon Starrett. "The Madness of Separate Spheres: Insanity and Masculinity in Victorian Alabama." In *Meanings for Manhood: Constructions of Masculinity in Victorian America*, edited by Mark C. Carnes and Clyde Griffen, 53–66. Chicago: University of Chicago Press, 1990.

James, Cathy. "Reforming Reform: Toronto's Settlement House Movement, 1900–20." *Canadian Historical Review* 82, no. 1 (March 2001) 55–90.

Johnston, Charles Murray. *McMaster University.* Vol. 1, *The Toronto Years.* Toronto: University of Toronto Press, 1976.

Kinnear, Mary. "Religion and the Shaping of 'Public Woman': A Post-Suffrage Case Study." In *Religion and Public Life in Canada: Historical and Comparative Perspectives*, edited by Marguerite Van Die, 196–216. Toronto: University of Toronto Press, 2001.

Ladies Committee Minutes. HSCA.

Lindley, Susan Hill. *"You Have Stept out of Your Place": A History of Women and Religion in America.* Louisville: Westminster John Knox, 1996.

Mandell, Nancy, and Momirov, Julianne. "Family Histories." In *Canadian Families: Diversity, Conflict and Change*, edited by Nancy Mandell and Ann Duffy, 31–63. 3rd ed. Nashville: Nelson, 2005.

Mangan, J. A., and Walvin, James. "Introduction." In *Manliness and Morality: Middle-Class Masculinity in Britain and America, 1800-1940.* Manchester: Manchester University Press, 1987.

McCalla, Douglas. *Planting the Province: The Economic History of Upper Canada, 1784–1870.* Toronto: University of Toronto Press, 1993.

Morgan, Henry James, ed. *The Canadian Men and Women of the Time: A Handbook of Canadian Biography of Living Characters.* 2nd ed. Toronto: William Briggs, 1912.

Morgan, Cecilia. *Public Men and Virtuous Women: The Gendered Languages of Religion and Politics in Upper Canada, 1791-1850.* Toronto: University of Toronto Press, 1996.

Morton, Desmond. *Mayor Howland: The Citizen's Candidate.* Toronto: A. M. Hakkert, 1973.

Muir, Elizabeth Gillan, and Whiteley, Marilyn Fardig. "Introduction: Putting Together the Puzzle of Canadian Women's Christian Work." In *Changing Roles of Women within the Christian Church in Canada*, edited by Elizabeth Gillan Muir and Marilyn Fardig Whiteley, 3–16. Toronto: University of Toronto Press, 1995.

Posen, Sara. "Examining Policy from the 'Bottom Up': The Relationship between Parents, Children, and Managers at the Toronto Boys' Home, 1859–1920." In *Family Matters: Papers in Post-Confederation Canadian Family History*, edited by Lori Chalmers and Edgar-Andre Montigny, 3–18. Toronto: Canadian Scholars' Press, 1998.

Prentice, Alison. *The School Promoters: Education and Social Class in Mid-Nineteenth Century Upper Canada*. Toronto: McClelland & Stewart, 1988.

Rawlyk, George A., ed. *Canadian Baptists and Christian Higher Education*. Kingston and Montreal: McGill-Queen's University Press, 1988.

Report of the Committee for the Relief of the Poor and Destitute of the City of Toronto: and Rules and Regulations of the House of Refuge & Industry Established under Their Care, January 1837. Toronto: J. H. Lawrence, 1837. MUWO,

Report of the Trustees of the House of Industry, Toronto, for the Year 1851. Toronto, Henry Roswell, 1852. MUWO.

Riddell, W. R. "The Law of Marriage in Upper Canada." *Canadian Historical Review* 2 (1921) 226–48.

Romney, Paul. "A Struggle for Authority." In *Forging a Consensus: Historical Essays on Toronto*, edited by Victor L. Russell, 14–27. Toronto: University of Toronto Press, 1984.

Russell, Victor L. *Mayors of Toronto*. Vol. 1, *1834–1899*. Erin, ON: Boston Mills, 1982.

Second [Annual] Report of the Toronto City Mission, 3 July 1848. Toronto: Brown's Establishment, 1848. MUWO.

Sixth Annual Report of the Children's Aid Society of Toronto, September 1897. Toronto: R. G. McLean, 1897. MUWO.

The Sixth Report of the City of Toronto Auxiliary Bible Society for 1834. Toronto: W. J. Coates, 1835. MUWO.

Sixth Annual Report of the Toronto City Mission, 6 April 1853. Toronto: Globe Job and Printing Office, 1853. MUWO.

Splane, Richard. *Social Welfare in Ontario 1791–1893: A Study of Public Welfare Administration*. Toronto: University of Toronto Press, 1965.

Stackhouse, John Jr. *Canadian Evangelicalism in the Twentieth Century: An Introduction to Its Character*. Toronto: University of Toronto Press, 1993.

Stewart, William. "Thomas Ford Caldicott." *McMaster Monthly* 4 (1895) 147.

Tenth Annual Report of the Toronto City Mission, 18 November 1858. Toronto: Globe Book and Job Office, 1859. MUWO.

Thompson, F. M. L. *The Rise of Respectable Society*. London: Fontana, 1988.

Toronto Sabbath School Association Second Sabbath School Teachers' Institute, Toronto, 4–8 December 1871. Toronto: Dudley & Burns, 1872. MUWO.

The Twentieth Report of the Upper Canada Religious Tract and Book Society, 1 June 1853. Toronto: Geo. E. Thomas, 1852. MUWO.

Valverde, Mariana. *The Age of Light, Soap, and Water: Moral Reform in English Canada, 1885–1925*. Toronto: McClelland & Stewart, 1991.

Walvin, James. *Victorian Values*. London: Penguin, 1987.

Webber, Robert E. *The Younger Evangelicals: Facing the Challenges of the New World*. Grand Rapids: Baker, 2002.

Wilson, Paul R. "Baptists and Business: Central Canadian Baptists and the Secularization of the Businessman at Toronto's Jarvis Street Baptist Church, 1848–1921." PhD dissertation, University of Western Ontario, 1996.

"Wittemore, Ezekiel Francis." In *Commemorative Biographical Record of the County of York, Ontario*, 342–43. Toronto: J. H. Beers, 1907.

WRBCAR =Walmer Road Baptist Church Annual Reports. CBA.

Young, Judith. "A Divine Mission: Elizabeth McMaster and the Hospital for Sick Children, Toronto, 1875–92." *Canadian Bulletin of Medical History* 11 (1994) 71–90.

A Postcard from 1910 showing McMaster University in Toronto
(Public Domain)

8

"Sheep Not of This Fold"

Case Studies of Non-Baptist Student Populations at McMaster University, 1890–1929 [1]

C. MARK STEINACHER

THROUGHOUT THE FIRST FOUR decades of McMaster University's existence, substantial numbers of non-Baptist students matriculated. There is no single obvious reason why a denominationally-founded and sponsored institution should prove attractive to "outsiders." Employing an analytical framework from Chaos-Complexity Theory,[2] this chapter will argue that McMaster University acted as a specific type of attractor within the intellectual basin of late nineteenth- and early twentieth-century Ontario tertiary education. A particular fusing of Baptist educational philosophy grounded in a commitment to religious voluntarism with pragmatic fiscal concerns resulted in McMaster's serving as a locus of a broadly inviting evangelical pedagogy, a foil for the scientifically-oriented and secular instruction provided by the state's University of Toronto. During the era under consideration, McMaster became somewhat secularized, minimizing and subsequently removing the distinction between it and secular universities. This move from periphery to

---

1. This chapter is a significantly modified form of a paper first delivered at the annual meeting of the Canadian Baptist Historical Society, 13 May 2000.

2. For an overview of Chaos-Complexity Theory and its potential analytical utility in the social sciences, see Beaumont, *Nazis' March to Chaos*, ch. 1; Beaumont, *War, Chaos and History*, ch. 1; and Steinacher, "Aleatory Folk," ch. 1.

center of higher education eliminated McMaster's status as an unusual attractor within Ontario's educational basin.

Attractors are pivot points around which phenomena cluster.[3] A primary (if simple) example of a fixed-point attractor is a pendulum.[4] A pen attached to the end of a pendulum that is sent swinging will define a constantly-changing pattern that nevertheless tracks within a fixed range, demarking "swirls of trajectories that never replicate themselves, but follow roughly similar but never identical courses around [A] specific point."[5] Analytically, this combination of apparent randomness and limited order allows for the reality of ambiguity in a world that is often more analog than digital. The concept can be particularly helpful when dealing with human situations in which events are clearly intentional and thus not random, yet where clear and unambiguous vectors are absent.[6] "Dynamical systems are attracted to attractors the way fireflies are attracted to light. And just as a firefly can come from most any direction and be attracted to bright lights, so a system can start from different sets of points in phase space and still wind up as the same attractor region, called the *basin of attraction.*"[7] This evocative simile allows one to stress the gamut of McMaster student origins while retaining the ability to group students systematically and analyze the significance of the various categories of participants.

Attractors may appear in pairs, "double attractors" that represent opposing poles within a phase-state.[8] The mainline denominational colleges federating with the now-secularized University of Toronto formed the dominant pole in Ontario's intellectual basin in this era. Even the Methodists, whose rapid growth had resulted from rampant revivalism, took this academic route, leading to quicker assimilation to the mainline. Pragmatic concerns seem to have lowered resistance. Victoria College's former President Samuel Nelles (1823–1887) declared that the needs of science education were such that massive investment in equipment was necessary. As a result, "Every sect cannot have a genuine university."[9]

3. Beaumont, *War, Chaos and History*, xiii.
4. Çambel, *Applied Chaos Theory*, 59, 63. Çambel delineates four types of attractors.
5. Beaumont, *War, Chaos and History*, 11.
6. Ibid., 153.
7. Çambel, *Applied Chaos Theory*, 59–60.
8. Beaumont, *War, Chaos and History*, 11, 104.
9. Friedland, *University of Toronto*, 101.

It was against this flow toward university federation, this otherwise near-all-consuming vortex of educational centralization and secularization, that the nascent McMaster University ranged itself. In this dipolar arrangement, McMaster stood at the cultural and educational periphery, the sole independent university operating as a viable alternative to the University of Toronto and its federated colleges. While the Baptist educational philosophy underpinning McMaster will be discussed below, it should be noted here that several University of Toronto faculty members expressed contempt for the perceived confessional approach to science at their new neighbor.[10] Probably aware of such derogation, coreligionists of the late Senator William McMaster (1811–1887) nevertheless maintained their leader's goal of contributing to "the creation of a new 'strata of intellectuals'" whose work would result in a new spiritual and economic order.[11] While McMaster existed on the periphery of Ontario higher education, functioning as an alternative pole, it sought to move toward the mainline. It almost immediately commenced closing in on the center, albeit slowly, not reaching the center until it was beyond the timeframe of this chapter.

By the middle of the era under consideration, it became clear that McMaster did not simply reject an exclusivist hiring policy,[12] but set out to be more comprehensive by creating formal relationships with the Christian Connection and Disciples. By doing so, McMaster's leaders consciously curried broader connections, in effect (although they could not have described it so) expanding their role as a special node, becoming an attractor around which students predominantly from revivalist backgrounds clustered. If they came from mainline rather than revivalist denominations, students' personal inclinations towards a pietistic expression of faith may have rendered them "outsiders" in their home settings, making McMaster's vital and overt Christian atmosphere more attractive. Together, the outsiders could pursue their journey toward

10. Ibid., 105.

11. Rawlyk, "Christian Education and McMaster," 35. It is beyond the scope of this chapter to address adequately Rawlyk's contention concerning the presence of a strong, if unconscious, "consumerist" orientation among McMaster's founders, even as their own understanding of the project was the confirmation and extension of a particular form of theology and piety. See Rawlyk, "Christian Education and McMaster," 35–38, 44. This tension might also prove susceptible to more profound analysis if these impulses are viewed as a dipolar attractor structure within a single basin of attraction.

12. Moody, "Baptists and Acadia," 18.

respectability,[13] the enhanced cluster bolstering the sense of Baptist influence in public life. The limit was reached with Jewish students. Their tuition contributions were accepted, even if their welcome was ambiguous. In whatever ways Jewish students might be drawn to this alternate center, their full inclusion was denied by the straightforward fact that they were not Christians.

No fewer than thirty denominational groups were represented in the student population of McMaster University's first four decades, the "Toronto years."[14] The Baptist-sponsored university began attracting, from its earliest days, "sheep not of this fold." The allusion is to the King James Version of John 10:16, a passage in which Jesus hints of reaching beyond the Jewish nation and including Gentiles in the kingdom of God. It provides a fitting image for the non-Baptist students' welcome into the Baptist academic bailiwick.

The denominational makeup of McMaster's early student body falls into four distinct categories. Following comments about the province's cultural and educational backdrop and problems with the source material, this chapter will examine these groups under the following rubrics. First, more than two-thirds were Baptists. Second, there were denominations merely lightly represented or altogether unrepresented among students. Those lightly represented are discussed within the context of the majority Baptist population; groups absent are treated separately. Third, as one would expect, there were fairly high numbers from the large, mainline denominations. Comparison of these denominations' participation rates at Brandon College underscores the growing trend to diversity at McMaster. Last, there is a mid-range group of five denominations represented by eleven or more members yet less than 2 percent of the total. Analysis of this group constitutes roughly half of this chapter.

CULTURAL AND EDUCATIONAL CONTEXT

The "Dominion" of Canada combined, in the minds of many late nineteenth-century Protestants, both a material and a spiritual vision, evoking the image of a place of progress and even millennial hope.[15] Prominent among the reasons for such a rosy outlook was the breakdown of the

13. Rawlyk, "Christian Education and McMaster," 31.

14. Johnston, *McMaster*.

15. Stackhouse, *Canadian Evangelicalism*, 8–9; Westfall, *Two Worlds*, 3–4, 143, 145, 163–64, 187–89, 195.

antagonism between "established" churches and groups believing in voluntary maintenance of their movements. To understand this, one must realize that Anglicanism (the Church of England), Presbyterianism, and Roman Catholicism were "Constantinian" in orientation, that is, they assumed the correctness and utility of an established state-church. While no denomination enjoyed *de jure* establishment, Anglicans from Governor John Graves Simcoe (1752–1806) onward allegedly acted as if the Church of England were indeed established in Upper Canada.[16] In the early 1840s Archdeacon John Strachan (1778–1867) styled his as the "Established Church in Canada West."[17] A corollary, to their minds, was control of educational institutions by that establishment.[18] By staking this claim, Anglicans drew the battle lines in a salient struggle for control of Ontario's public life.

For Anglicans, however, this proved to be an uphill battle. Major legal changes in England, such as the 1828 repeal of the Test and Corporation Acts, the "Roman Catholic Relief Act" of 1829, and Lord Grey's "Great Reform Act" of 1832 provided a major (if incomplete) overhaul of the British electoral system and removed social and political impediments placed upon non-Anglicans in the wake of the seventeenth-century English Civil Wars.[19] The Acts also set in motion processes that eventually resulted in power shifting from landed interests to the emerging industrial areas.[20] Simultaneously, a patchwork of legislation emerged in Upper Canada that loosened the Anglican grip on public life and empowered a growing number of denominations.[21] Central, from this chapter's perspective, was removal of the requirement

16. Gibson, *Fyfe*, 84.

17. Ibid., 121.

18. Gibson discusses this struggle at length and in detail in *Fyfe*, chaps. 7, 10, 11.

19. Pugh, *Britain since 1789*, 47–50.

20. Brown, *Church and State*, 219, 226–27.

21. *Statutes of Upper Canada*, 476, 494, 504–5, 521–22, 605–7, 1086. 9 George IV (1828), Chapter II allowed religious societies associated with *specified* denominations to buy and hold land; 3 Victoria (1840), Chapter LXXIII extended this to Roman Catholics. 10 George IV (1829), Chapter I allowed Quakers, Mennonites, Tunkers, and Moravians to give evidence in court without taking an oath. 11 George IV (1830), Chapter I specified that fines payable to the Church of England under English law must in Canada be paid to the District Treasurer. Chapter XXXVI listed denominations whose ministers were permitted to register to perform marriages. 3 William IV (1833), Chapter XII removed the requirement of receiving the Lord's Supper by Church of England rites in order to hold public office.

that the "President, Members of the College Council or Professors" of King's College (precursor to the University of Toronto) be members of the Church of England.[22] By the 1850s, Anglicans were losing their *de facto* standing as an arm of the state,[23] which was in part the result of Baptist and Methodist agitation against such self-proclaimed spiritual hegemony. By century's end, Anglicans had been forced into voluntary support of their religious activities.

Furthermore, demographic changes undermined Anglican hegemony. Over the course of the nineteenth century, more Ontarians came to identify with fewer denominations, and the faction claiming no religious affiliation dropped from a quarter to less than one percent.[24] Despite the persistence of some significant differences, a broad consensus about a "Christian" society developed by the end of the nineteenth century.[25] What emerged was the legal establishment of generic Christianity as state religion, rather than one particular denomination.[26] This diluted form of Christianity focused on teaching morality and social duty,[27] tying even the most "practical and useful subjects . . . to a knowledge of religious truth."[28]

Baptists largely aligned themselves with this vision, with one major distinction. Baptists, in stark contrast to the Constantinians, were firmly "voluntarist." "Voluntarism," a term said to be distinctly Canadian in its origin,[29] was deeply rooted in Baptist congregationalist ecclesiology. Responsibility for matters ecclesiastical was believed to reside in the local fellowship. Thus, Baptists tended to be "a loose confederation of cooperating churches," unsuited to the support of major undertakings such as launching a college.[30] Cooperative work developed as increasing numbers saw the potential for task-oriented effort that was responsible to local congregations.[31] Robert Alexander Fyfe (1816–1878), thinking

---

22. *Statutes of Upper Canada*, 811. 7 William IV (1837), Chapter XVI.
23. VanDie, "Introduction," 7.
24. Westfall, *Two Worlds*, 10.
25. VanDie, "Introduction," 6–7; Westfall, *Two Worlds*, 193.
26. Gidney and Millar, "Christian Recessional," 275.
27. Ibid., 276.
28. Westfall, *Two Worlds*, 8.
29. Brackney, *Voluntarism*, 48; Gibson, *Fyfe*, 260.
30. Brackney, *Voluntarism*, 34; cf. 39, 61, 72.
31. Ibid., 159.

along English Baptist lines, averred that denominational colleges should receive only voluntary support from those of like theological mind, and if such support were not forthcoming, the institution did not deserve to survive.[32] This philosophy, on the one hand, led to several attempts to found a Baptist institution of higher learning.[33] On the other hand, it led to vigorous opposition to emerging Anglican control of the colony's tertiary education. In particular, Baptists opposed imposition of religious "tests" (that is, requiring assent to a particular doctrine or set of tenets), either for students or faculty, at state-funded institutions.[34] Furthermore, Baptists promoted the view that no denominationally-oriented school should receive either benefit or detriment from government.[35] From the mid-nineteenth to the mid-twentieth century, Baptist educational policy and practice would be shaped largely by the dipolar interaction of two attractors: their theological approach to education, and pragmatic fiscal matters. These two attractors were distinct from, but not unrelated to, the mainline/periphery pair. Financial exigencies probably account for McMaster's willingness to welcome students from other denominations, although there is little record of concerted efforts early on to recruit non-Baptists.

The question of the relationship of various denominations to McMaster University played out in the context of McMaster as an avowedly Baptist school in an era when other denominational colleges were experiencing secularization. Queen's University severed its denominational link in 1912,[36] but it would be almost half a century before McMaster would do the same. Secularization was still a remote potentiality, both chronologically and psychologically. Portraying McMaster's growth after the First World War as a shift from small Christian school to larger secular one is probably premature, evincing a sense of inevitability that may appear stronger in retrospect than the evidence justifies.[37]

32. Ibid., 48; Gibson, *Fyfe*, 143, 149.

33. These include the short-lived Canada Baptist College (1845–1849), the never-opened Maclay College, and the Canadian Literary Institute (1860–1881). After the Theological Department relocated in 1881, becoming the Toronto Baptist College, the Institute became a residential high school named Woodstock College. It closed in 1926.

34. Gibson, *Fyfe*, 140; cf. Moody, "Baptists and Acadia," 11.

35. Gibson, *Fyfe*, 137–38, 148; Ellis, "Brandon College," 70.

36. Gibson and Graham, *Queen's*, 7–8.

37. Rawlyk, "Christian Education and McMaster," 49–51. Rawlyk argues that the watershed is marked by the transition from the allegedly pious yet backward-looking

Against this backdrop, one may appreciate that the path to the creation of a "Baptist" university in Ontario was strewn with many hazards. In particular, the provincial government resisted.[38] Apparently adopting a political tactic to appear sympathetic despite actually trying to sabotage the project, educational officials allowed that if a minimum endowment of $750,000 could be raised, a university charter would be granted. This was no small sum in those days. For a body the size of the Baptist Convention of Ontario and Quebec, it was virtually impossible to collect. When Senator McMaster remade his will with the school as primary beneficiary, the government relented and passed the enabling legislation in April 1887.

Despite assent to the bill constituting the university, massive fiscal problems remained as Toronto Baptist College awaited transformation into the new university's Theological Faculty and a new Arts Faculty was created.[39] No arts degrees could be granted until the endowment was in place.[40] The school's trustees gathered for an emergency meeting on 22 September 1887 to seek solutions. Their deliberations were inconclusive. Walking down the College's front steps after the meeting, McMaster suffered what proved to be a fatal heart attack. His will provided roughly $900,000 for the nascent school, far in excess of the provincial bureaucrats' demands. McMaster University's charter could not be denied. Central Canadian Baptists had their own accredited university. Classes commenced in October 1890, with a meager sixteen scholars.

---

leadership of Chancellor Abraham Lincoln McCrimmon to the more pragmatic organizational skill possessed by Chancellor Howard Primrose Whidden. While this is true, it is arguable that a better indicator of secularization is the radical expansion of scientific education at McMaster that occurred after the Second World War. This also led to a dramatic increase in the student population, an immediate factor leading to the termination of McMaster's denominational bond.

38. "William McMaster," *Dictionary of Canadian Biography Online*.

39. Unaccredited courses, equivalent to the first two years of undergraduate work, had been undertaken at the Canadian Literary Institute, Woodstock, Ontario. The second-year-level courses were suspended in 1880, prior to the relocation of the Theological Department to Toronto as Toronto Baptist College. Undergraduate work at the renamed Woodstock College was wound down in 1890 in favor of the newly-established McMaster University. CBA: Steinacher, Unpublished Finding Aid: "Canada Baptist College to Toronto Baptist College," 4, 12.

40. Johnston, *McMaster*, 47–49.

SOURCES FOR THE STUDY

Finding source material for this study was problematic. References in official reports to the presence of non-Baptist students at McMaster are extremely rare; they were consulted where possible. While approximately forty letters to or from McMaster officials pertain directly to this chapter's subject, almost all relate to the Disciples of Christ, the Christian Connexion, and Jewish representatives. Just as the paucity of primary documentary evidence renders it hard to pin down the general theological tenor of McMaster in its Toronto days,[41] so that same *lacuna* forces scholars to a more quantitative approach in order to isolate and analyze useful information. Statistics derived from an unusual source may have to compensate for the relative dearth of qualitative primary material.

This study is possible because information about matriculating students was recorded in a single, readily-accessible source document, the Registrar's "Enrollment Book" (1890–1929).[42] This spreadsheet's contents cover the entire Toronto era. A different recording system was adopted when the university moved to Hamilton in 1930, rendering the task of compiling similar statistics too labor-intensive to justify the task. In addition to each student's full name, the "Enrollment Book" records the date of matriculation, date and place of birth, "Father's Occupation," both parents' and student's denominations, method of admission, prior school attended, "Purpose in View," parent or guardian's name, and postal address. The last registration number is 3972,[43] but the actual number of students matriculating in McMaster University in this era is less than three-quarters of that figure: 2915. Neither names nor registration numbers of individual students, nor the pages on which specific entries occur, will be footnoted in this chapter. Significant in this context are the raw numbers of students from each denomination, as well as collation and panoramic interpretation of those numbers.

Over a quarter of those listed in the book (997) were matriculants at Manitoba's Brandon College. Brandon loosely affiliated with McMaster in 1899, with its academic integration following by 1910.[44] McMaster's

41. Pinnock, "Modernist Impulse at McMaster," 199, 202–3.

42. The Enrolment Book is at CBA: Accession #96–040.

43. Enrollment Book, 230–31. There were some other minor adjustments to the total, such as removal of twenty-one redundant entries, that need not be listed in detail.

44. The first Brandon student officially matriculated within McMaster's system was #1240, in 1910. The first Okanagan student, also in 1910, was #1290.

accreditation also extended to thirty-eight Okanagan College students.[45] This chapter contains limited reference to Brandon statistics, and that only when comparison helps elucidate the situation at McMaster. Brandon's unique situation *per se* will not be included. While it is distinctly possible that the aspiration of Brandon's boosters that it become "a little McMaster on the prairies" misread local populist sentiments and damaged the Baptist cause in the West,[46] from this chapter's perspective, Brandon's significance is as a "dry run" for multi-denominationalism (as opposed to non-denominationalism) at McMaster. Brandon's increasing size also needs to be taken into account. Its student body, compared to McMaster's, ranged from a low of 22 percent in 1913 to a high of 80 percent in 1927. On average, Brandon's enrolment was 56 percent of McMaster's. As a trend, with variations smoothed by means of a five-year rolling average, Brandon grew from just over a third of McMaster's size in the early years to just under two-thirds at the end.[47] The college's Depression-initiated failure tends to overshadow this otherwise dramatic success.

McMaster's move to Hamilton accelerated the move toward entire secularization. It may be premature to peg McMaster's capitulation to secularism to the 1922 inauguration of former Brandon College Principal Howard Primrose Whidden (1871–1952) as Chancellor.[48] Apart from the continuing nominal Baptist Convention control, other factors that fuelled separation, such as medical training and advanced scientific research, were not in place until after the Second World War. Not until a quarter of a century later, in 1957, would the process of secularizing McMaster University and the creation of a separate legal

45. McMaster extended accreditation to Okanagan students from the fall of 1910 until the spring of 1915, with the last matriculants admitted in 1914. The school's enrolment had been gaining momentum, peaking at eleven in 1914, but military recruitment in the First World War drew away sufficient students to force closure of the college in 1915. Ellis also notes the failure of the speculative Diamond Coal Company as a contributing factor to Okanagan's demise. Ellis, "Brandon College," 74.

46. Ibid., 64, 66–67, 70, 82, 84–85; Rawlyk, "Introduction," x–xi.

47. The five-year rolling average for 1910–1915 was 36.3 percent; in 1925–1929 it was 63.9 percent, having edged back from its peak of 70.5 percent in 1923–1927. Sixty-one percent of McMaster's students (1,782) registered in the second half of the era under consideration, 1910–1929.

48. Rawlyk, "Christian Education and McMaster," 49–50.

entity for the Divinity College be fully implemented.[49] Given the factors in play, McMaster's secularization was both the path of least resistance and a reasonable choice. It was not, of course, "inevitable," but only the greatest of pragmatic reasons could have altered a course that was in place virtually from the university's genesis. McMaster's new charter also marked the terminus of the process by which its role as an unusual attractor was undermined as McMaster was assimilated to the mainline university attractor. Within the timeframe of this study, however, the vision of a character-building Christian university still remained in the minds of many lay-folk and faculty.

BAPTIST STUDENTS

As one would expect, the vast majority of students (2,082; 71.4 percent) were Baptists. From the school's founding until 1908, when only 68 percent reported Baptist membership, Baptists never comprised less than 80 percent of the fresh students.[50] The last year Baptists comprised more than 70 percent of incoming students was 1920 (73 percent). This dilution of Baptist representation reflects the growing impact of the total of 208 students from smaller denominations,[51] which together eventu-

49. Some still wished, however, to see that membership on the Board of Governors was restricted to Christians and that the new President would be a member of a Christian church. Explicit reference was made to the exclusion of Jews, but the impact was dismissed as inconsequential. See Thomas Bruce McDormand (1904–1988, General Secretary-Treasurer of the Baptist Federation of Canada) to P. P. W. Ziemann, 25 June 1956. CBA, files of Chancellor George Peel Gilmour (1900–1963), Box 2, File 2m.

50. The 68 percent figure is probably the result of the extraordinarily large number of students not indicating "denomination." Many of these were children of Baptists, suggesting that the person filling in the Enrolment Book assumed that it would be self-evident that students attending a Baptist university who were the children of two Baptist parents were likewise Baptist. In an era in which denominational affiliation tended to involve a higher level of commitment than a century later, this was a reasonable suggestion. If the majority of those for whom denomination is not listed were Baptists, Baptist share would exceed eighty percent. This oddity almost certainly explains the anomalous 64 percent Baptist share in 1900. For a chart including enrolment statistics by denomination, including the denomination's percentage within McMaster University's aggregate student population, see the Appendix at the end of this chapter.

51. Denominations not included in this tally were the Anglican Church, the Methodist Church, and the United Church. The 121 (4.1 percent) matriculants whose denomination was not listed were also not included. Roughly one in fourteen students belonged to these smaller denominations, which include the five that provided case studies. Another one in fourteen students was Presbyterian.

ally made up 7.1 percent of the aggregate student population of 1890 to 1929. Within those twenty-six minor denominations, twenty-one were represented by ten or fewer students (49 in all, representing 1.7 percent of the total).[52] Despite generally increasing Baptist enrolment, over time this sub-group grew at a faster rate than Baptists. On two occasions in the 1920s, Baptists almost dipped below 50 percent of the incoming student population (1923: 57 percent; 1926: 53 percent) and finally did slip to a mere 46 percent of the intake for 1929. This pattern presumably accelerated with the move to Hamilton although there is no comparable documentary source by which to track this trend easily.

As the impending move to Hamilton neared, McMaster's leadership wanted to maintain their university's Baptist character, while breaking down negative perceptions in the broader community. Internal communications acknowledge that the McMaster constituency was considered to be made up of "such narrow-minded people" that the assessment threatened to scuttle the potential relocation.[53] Their public face included the celebration of denominational diversity within both the faculty and the student body, taking particular pains to note that graduates included "a Jewish Rabbi and . . . a bishop of the Reformed Syrian Church of India."[54] Success in Hamilton would hinge largely on

52. In descending order of number of matriculants, the denominations having more than one student matriculate at McMaster were: Lutheran (10), Plymouth Brethren (9), Mennonite (5), Orthodox (3), Reformed (3), Christadelphian (2), "Evangelical" (2) and Roman Catholic (2). Denominations represented by a single student were: Apostolic, Assembly of God, Christian Catholic, Christian Science, Christian Worker, Free Church, Free Church of Finland, Free Methodist, "G. O. Catholic"[sic], Independent, Methodist Episcopal, Second Advent, and Unitarian. One of the "Reformed" may be the Jacobite Syrian student from India referred to in footnote 54. Four groups were represented only at Brandon: the "International Bible Students" (an older self-description of Jehovah's Witnesses) (2); Mission Friend (2); Muhammedan ([sic] = Muslim) (1); Non-denominational (2). No Mennonites matriculated at Brandon, which is odd, given the sizeable Mennonite population in southern Manitoba. There is no evidence from internal McMaster or Brandon sources to shed any light on this anomaly, although both a language barrier and a commitment to simplicity of life might have kept German-speaking Mennonites from enrolling.

53. "Removal of McMaster to Hamilton: Documents re: Proposal and Alternatives 1922–1926"; "McMaster University Board of Governors. Discussion of Hamilton Proposal at the Meeting of 8 November 1923," 15. The report continues: it "would be easier to get two million dollars from Hamilton for a state university than to get a million dollars for a Baptist University." All these documents are at CBA: Box 26, unnumbered file.

54. "Removal of McMaster to Hamilton: Documents re: Proposal and Alternatives 1922–1926"; undated item, "For Christmas number—Hamilton Herald and Hamilton

the transplanted university's ability to attract local students, regardless of their denomination.[55]

A similar pattern is observable in the West; the percentage of Baptists gradually drifted lower although with a regional twist. The highest Baptist share of the Brandon student population was 40 percent in 1910. This statistic varied widely over the era; its nadir was 17 percent in 1922. The drop in Presbyterian registrants allowed the Baptist share to rise to 35 percent once more by 1929 (their second highest percentage overall). Even with the recovery, Brandon's Baptists were 11 percent behind McMaster's.

As noted earlier, Brandon was well on the way to achieving parity with its parent institution by 1929, the year the "Enrollment Book" ends and the stock market crashed. Drawing upon a smaller catchment population than McMaster, in 1927 Brandon nonetheless drew four students in the West for every five garnered by McMaster in Ontario. Central to its achievement was the geographical advantage enjoyed over McMaster. Logistical problems and costs encountered in transporting students to Winnipeg for examinations of material studied at Brandon[56] would have been magnified for any considering migrating for residential study at the University of Manitoba. Both factors pushed local potential

Spectator—by Dean McLay," 1. Both in CBA: Box 26, unnumbered file. These documents state: "Though a Baptist by conviction, Senator McMaster never intended that McMaster University should be a narrowly denominational institution, and it never has been that and is not now. Its Faculty has always included members of other Christian bodies and its undergraduate body has been composed of Catholics, Jews, Anglicans, Presbyterians, Methodists, and Disciples, as well as Baptists. At present its Faculty contains an Anglican, a Disciple, a Lutheran, and several members of the United Church. One of its graduates is a Jewish Rabbi and another a bishop of the Reformed Syrian Church of India. In the light of these facts, the citizens of Hamilton may rest assured that McMaster University, though under the control of Baptists, will not be a sectarian institution, but that it will always, as in the past, offer a sound education in a Christian environment and in a spirit that will easily engage the sympathy and respect of people of varied religious faiths."

55. McMaster's self-understanding as a "regional" university apparently did not arise until later. G. P. Gilmour opposed the granting of Brock University's charter, as the new school was within what Gilmour considered to be McMaster's rightful regional catchment. See Gilmour to W. J. Dunlop (Department of Education), 4 February 1958. CBA, Box MNG, File 95.

56. Ellis, "Brandon College," 70. Again, pragmatic and philosophical issues overlap. It was not merely the inconvenience of writing Brandon exams in Winnipeg that annoyed Baptist leadership, but potential state interference with the specifically Baptist tenor of education at Brandon.

students of whatever denomination to register at Brandon. For some, having a college close enough that one could still live at home would have been the tipping point that spurred them to pursue an otherwise unattainable university education. This would not have been lost on the savvy Whidden, who continued oversight of Brandon after accepting McMaster's chancellorship. In the parlance of Chaos-Complexity Theory, Brandon served as an attractor for those not gathered into the sphere of influence of the provincial university.

Bridging the pragmatic and the philosophical was the opinion of W. Sherwood Fox (1878–1967), future President of the University of Western Ontario, that Baptists held a unique potential to break the state university's stranglehold on tertiary education in Manitoba.[57] Although it is highly unlikely his lofty goal came close to being achieved, Samuel J. McKee (1849–1937; Brandon's Principal in the 1890s) suggested that an additional reason for avoiding affiliation with the University of Manitoba was the potential for an avowedly Christian college to attain higher standards on its own.[58]

In any event, Brandon embodied a Baptist philosophy of education in which students were immersed not only in their subject matter, but in "positive Christian influences," to the end of inculcating "distinctively Christian ideals."[59] In this, Brandon paralleled the general approach to evangelical Christian higher education that had been pioneered at McMaster, where conservation of truth, rather than extension of its parameters, was the order of the day under Oates Charles Symonds Wallace (1856–1947).[60] Even under his successor, Alexander Charles McKay (1861–1946), who was more open to the active and scientific pursuit of truth, McMaster remained opposed to university federation, which it perceived as threatening its unique character.[61] The creation of unmistakable Christian character through surrender to Jesus, by means of education in an avowedly Christian school, remained a key educational motivation for McKay's successor, Abraham Lincoln McCrimmon (1865–1935).[62] Consideration must be given now to the extent to which

57. W. Sherwood Fox to O. C. S. Wallace, 27 March 1902, pp. 4–5. CBA, Box MME, File 20.

58. S. J. McKee to O. C. S. Wallace, 6 June 1898, p. 2. CBA, Box MMA, File 43.

59. Ellis, "Brandon College," 69.

60. Rawlyk, "Christian Education and McMaster," 41–42.

61. Ibid., 43.

62. Ibid., 44–45.

this educational philosophy might have acted as an attractor to students from other denominations.

DENOMINATIONS NOT REPRESENTED

At first, discussion of those groups not represented sounds like an "argument from silence." How can one meaningfully measure what is not there? One means might be to compile a list by comparing denominations recognized in the federal census with those not represented at McMaster. It is not impossible that such a list might reveal limits to McMaster's inclusiveness, but it might merely reflect those groups' small size and the relatively low level of university matriculation among the general population.

Another approach is to note those denominations represented at Brandon, but not at McMaster. There were two "International Bible Students," an older self-descriptive for Jehovah's Witnesses, among the Manitoba college's attendees; at McMaster, a Baptist student's parents were listed as adhering to "Millennial Dawnism," another label acceptable to Jehovah's Witnesses a century ago. Two students, rather than leaving the space blank, listed themselves as "Nondenominational." Another pair were "Mission Friends," members of a Swedish Pietist group with links to evangelist Dwight Lyman Moody (1837–1899).[63] Their presence is accounted for by the region's unusual demographics, featuring the presence of relatively large numbers of Scandinavians. A surprise is the presence of a "Muhammedan" [= Muslim] student, given the religion's virtual absence from Canada then.

A third angle, which allows for at least some interpretation, is to isolate denominations listed for parents, but not students. Eight students were Quaker-related,[64] not surprising in light of colonies along Yonge Street north of Toronto and eastward toward Peterborough. No student self-described as Moravian, "Pentecostal," Salvation Army, Tunker, or Universalist, although these fellowships appear under "Parents' Denomination."[65] The almost total absence of such fringe groups as the

63. Eldebo, "Moody."

64. There were two Baptists of Quaker descent, four of mixed Quaker-Baptist parentage, one Methodist of Quaker background, and one of mixed Methodist-Quaker heritage.

65. One Baptist was of Moravian heritage; one Alliance student had Pentecostal parents. The "Assembly of God" student was a member of the Pentecostal movement,

Universalists and Jehovah's Witnesses is hardly surprising, given that they would have been considered heterodox by Baptists in general and McMaster's faculty in particular. Further, none of these denominations was particularly strongly represented in the province.

While some of these groups were so small that their absence from the McMaster student body is not likely to be statistically significant, the absence of others hints at limits to the inclusiveness of a revivalist coalition against the state-church-oriented Anglicans and Presbyterians. Methodist influence among Pentecostals and the Salvation Army likely kept these often Arminian students from throwing their lot in with Calvinistic McMaster. These data also suggest that there are limits to the gravitational force exerted by an attractor. For movements with an obscurantist and anti-intellectual bent, no university would do. No human instruction could replace that of the Holy Spirit. Their non-participation underscores the Baptists' increasing tendency to drift toward the culturally-accepted view of higher education. The next group of denominations to be considered is the antithesis of the fringe. The mainline bodies were anything but obscurantist and heartily embraced all that university education had to offer.

STUDENTS FROM MAINLINE DENOMINATIONS

Precisely 7 percent of the student population was comprised of 205 students from the Presbyterian Church, the largest non-Baptist group. Presbyterian matriculants date from 1893, enrolling in fairly constant raw numbers from roughly 1900 until after the Great War. Overall, numbers declined as young men enlisted for service. As a result of their steady raw numbers, the Presbyterian percentage within the total student body began to rise around 1910, surging to roughly one in six of McMaster's students after the war. There is no straightforward explanation for this trend. The cause of the subsequent drop-off of Presbyterian registrants in 1925, however, is self-evident. Depending on whether one counts members or congregations, between two-thirds and three-quarters of Canada's Presbyterians opted to enter the newly-formed United Church of Canada. From 1925 to 1927, there were between 60 and 70 percent fewer Presbyterian matriculants. Surprisingly the numbers

but chose a different self-descriptive. Four Baptists had Salvation Army parents; two Baptists had Tunker roots; one Baptist descended from Universalists.

soon rebounded to pre-union levels in 1928, and, in 1929, the number of Presbyterian registrants exceeded the amount for the *entire* United Church. Upon reflection, the upswing is understandable. Presbyterian students became religious "refugees" at McMaster. There had always been a few Presbyterians doing Arts at McMaster in preparation for ministry, but with the loss of Queen's to the United Church and the Knox College question still unsettled, increasing numbers chose to attend McMaster. There is no indication of their theological stance, whether they were conservative or liberal. Many of the more radical Presbyterian liberals, however, had joined the United Church.

The preceding interpretation is reinforced by reference to the Brandon College statistics. More Presbyterians enrolled there (208) than at McMaster, despite the Manitoba school's affiliation for only the second half of the overall era. Presbyterian enrolment collapsed after 1925, with only seventeen students matriculating in the last four years under consideration; in 1928, only one Presbyterian entered Brandon. For two-fifths of the 1910–1929 period, Presbyterian students either equaled or outnumbered Baptists at Brandon. In 1915, each fellowship contributed one third of the students;[66] in 1923, each roughly a quarter. Presbyterians outnumbered Baptists for the first time in 1912, then again in 1918–1920, as well as 1922 and 1924. The middle years, 1918–1920 reflect the post-war surge in the enrolment of veterans. The higher rates in 1922 and 1924 probably reflect the growing acceptance of the school's reputation among the general population, with Presbyterian participation rates roughly on a par with their overall demographic share in the region.

Second among non-Baptists in the total student population at McMaster were the 141 Methodists who constituted 4.8 percent. Given the dominance of Methodists among Ontario's Protestants, this appears abnormally low, until one recalls the presence of the Methodists' own Victoria College. Victoria relocated in 1892 from Belleville to a site a mere quarter kilometer from McMaster's Bloor Street campus. This interpretation is underscored by reference to Methodist enrolment at Brandon. There, in the decade and a half between Brandon's accreditation and the creation of the United Church of Canada, 111 Methodist students were admitted. Adjusted to reflect the total enrolment of 640 between 1910 and 1924, the Brandon rate is 17.3 percent, more than thrice as high as McMaster's, yet it was still less than one might expect,

66. This was the high-water mark for the Presbyterian share of Brandon students.

given the Methodists' leading role among Canadian Protestant denominations. Again, dissonance between the Methodists' Arminian outlook
and the Baptist schools' Calvinist assumptions is a likely cause of this
underrepresentation.

Eighty members of the newly-created United Church of Canada,
or 2.7 percent of the student body, entered in the last half decade that
McMaster remained in Toronto. When one adjusts for the short sub-
period in which the United Church existed, a scant five of the forty years
under consideration (one in eight), the resulting 21.6 percent is probably not statistically significantly different from the new-born United
Church's share of the general population.[67] Almost two and a half times
as many "Union" or United Church students matriculated at Brandon
(194). The tally is higher partly because of the existence of "Union"
churches on the Prairies before 1925, but the number also remains higher in the post-union era, underscoring Brandon's multi-denominational
appeal.

The first non-Baptist student to matriculate at McMaster was an
Anglican who arrived in 1891. Given the size of the denomination in
Ontario, their aggregate count of 76 students and a participation rate
of 2.6 percent, the Anglican graduation rate at McMaster was low. The
close proximity of Trinity College is an obvious reason. On the Prairies,
where there was no Anglican college close by, 82 Anglicans[68] enrolled
at Brandon, making up 8.2 percent of the total student population. This
is still well below the rate that Anglicanism's general population share
would suggest.

The immediate significance of notable numbers of mainstream students enrolling at McMaster rested chiefly in their economic contribution. Less obvious is the evidence their presence provides of McMaster's
role as an "attractor," an alternate locus of order within the culture of
Protestant higher education in Ontario. Given the physical proximity
of McMaster's Toronto campus, it is highly unlikely that ease of access
figured among the factors leading students to enroll at McMaster. Not
unlikely for some, McMaster was a second choice when they failed to

67. I do not have the statistical background to apply the "null hypothesis" test to
this statistic.

68. A wide range of labels was self-employed by Anglicans, from "Anglican"
through "Church of England" and "English Church" to the jurisdictionally incorrect
"Established Church."

achieve admission into their denominational college. Further, a small number of registrations would almost certainly have been the result of apparently random factors.[69] While there is no hard evidence to support the following contention, it is plausible that some mainline students were attracted by the perception that McMaster's atmosphere was more revivalist than other denominational colleges. All of these factors dovetail with McMaster's function as an attractor. The forces are subtle, sometimes imperceptible, yet real. That such conjectures cannot be proved absolutely is, on another level, immaterial. The roughly one in six students who came from the mainstream represented a new revenue stream. By enrolling, they provided both literal and figurative currency to the fiscally-troubled and culturally-peripheral university.

STUDENTS FROM MID-RANGE DENOMINATIONS

This section consists of five case studies derived from the groups in the mid-range. Each contributed less than 2 percent of the total student population, yet had more than 10 individuals attend. Listed in descending order of students represented, the five are: Judaism (55; 1.9 percent),[70] Disciples/Church of Christ (37; 1.3 percent), "Christian Conference" (36; 1.2 percent),[71] Christian and Missionary Alliance (16; 0.55 percent),[72] and Congregationalists (15; 0.51 percent). Listed chronologi-

69. Canadian novelist and educator Grace Irwin (1907–2008) recounts two of her brothers' simultaneous application for work with a particular company. One received a job offer; the other did not, sending their careers on markedly different trajectories, despite their having virtually identical training. A decade later, an anomaly with their front door letter slot was discovered, leading to the recovery of five lost letters. One was addressed to the other brother, containing an identical offer of employment at the same firm (Irwin, *Three Lives in Mine*, 63–65.) This is an example of what Chaos-Complexity Theory labels "sensitivity to initial conditions."

70. Fifty-five students were Jewish, although different labels were used: Jew, Jewish, Hebrew, and Mosaic. This includes two students whose parents were listed as Jewish but who did not themselves claim a "denomination." If this identification should prove wrong, the increase caused by their inclusion does not materially affect interpretation. Additionally, two students who self-identified as "Baptist" listed their parents as "Jewish"; they were counted as Baptists. Analysis is further complicated by the failure of the Enrolment Book to indicate the branch of Judaism to which a student adhered. The Reform wing of Judaism aimed for a niche within the mainstream. See Tulchinsky, "Justice and Only Justice," 314–15.

71. Five students who self-identified as "Baptist" listed their parents as "Christian Conference."

72. One student who self-identified as "Baptist" listed his or her parents as "Christian and Missionary Alliance."

cally, by first matriculation of a member, they are Congregationalism, "Christian Conference," Disciples/Church of Christ, Judaism, and the Christian and Missionary Alliance. For the most part, the earlier a denomination's member first enrolled, the flatter the graph of their overall enrolment. This speaks to the issue of consistency. That is, the earlier a group participated, the less variation in numbers there was from decade to decade. The groups appearing later tended to experience accelerated and uneven growth. Slight modification, inserting the Christian and Missionary Alliance after Congregationalism and reversing the Christian Conference and Disciples,[73] provides an order of discussion that moves from the denomination for which the least evidence exists to explain members' motivation to matriculate at McMaster to the faction for which the most evidence exists. The reasons for such noteworthy participation rates will now be discussed based on the evidence available in the extant primary records.

For two groups, Congregationalism and the Christian and Missionary Alliance, there is little extant material to broaden interpretation beyond the mere reporting of demographics. These will be dealt with briefly before turning to the remaining three. There is significant correspondence preserved between senior administrators at McMaster University and members or leaders of the Disciples, the Christian Conference, and the Jewish community. In two cases, the Christian Conference and the Disciples, deliberate strategies or schemes existed to link denominational students and the school. The Jewish community hoped for such a link, but it was denied.

Two of the five movements in this class are "restorationist." In total, the Disciples and Christian Conference comprised 2.5 percent of the student population. Spelled with a small r, "restorationist" refers to a person or movement that seeks to "restore" what is believed to have been the essence of New Testament Christianity. In this sense, restorationism occurs throughout church history. Examples include early monasticism, the Franciscans, the Anabaptists, the Plymouth Brethren, and, possibly, the Baptists.[74] Restorationist with a capital R refers to a person or move-

---

73. The order may also be envisioned as in ascending order of matriculants, except that the Christian Conference and Disciples have been switched. The point is that there is more than one justification for the order in which the denominations are taken up.

74. Gibson, *Fyfe*, 20, 122, 346. T. T. Shields is quoted as sharing this opinion. See Rawlyk, "Christian Education at McMaster," 61.

ment derived from a loose affiliation of churches centered on the teaching of Alexander Campbell (1788–1866).[75] A point of confusion exists in the records regarding the labeling of students from three groups: Christian Conference, Disciples of Christ, and Church of Christ. "Disciples" (officially "Church of Christ/Disciples") and "Churches of Christ" appear to be used synonymously in the McMaster records. These two entities, however, had earlier parted company over issues such as the propriety of musical instruments in worship and cooperative missionary efforts, a division first officially recognized by the United States Census in 1906.[76] Treated as a unit, there were 37 of these capital R "Restorationists," 1.3 percent of the pre-1930 student body. The "Christian Conference" in Ontario has slightly older roots. Its sibling groups in Kentucky and Tennessee were virtually wiped out in the early 1830s when Campbell's "Reform Baptists" withdrew from their associations and joined with many of their neighboring "Christian" churches to form what became known as the "Disciples." Treatment of the Christian Conference's experience is longer because the body arrived at an actual agreement with McMaster, whereas the Disciples' affiliation remained informal.

The first Congregationalist student matriculated in 1896, the same year as the first Christian Conference student, making them the fourth and fifth non-Baptist denominations represented among the student population. The Congregationalists' 15 representatives (0.51 percent) are well-scattered through the four decades under consideration. Only twice, in 1897 and 1923, were there two fresh Congregationalist registrations in the same year. The Baptists' belief in congregational autonomy and insistence that education must be without religious test almost certainly proved attractive to such students. That they had no college of their own left McMaster as the most ideologically-congenial academic home. Their participation rates, however, were not out of keeping with their general population share.

The first enrolment of members of the Christian and Missionary Alliance dates from 1915, and it continued off and on until 1927. There

75. Steinacher, "Aleatory Folk," 58–63. The essential point of this extended discussion of varying Restorationist historiographies is that the interpretation of the interrelationship of Campbell's Disciples with the various "Christian" movements (led by Barton Warren Stone [1772–1844] in the West, James O'Kelly [1735–1826] in the Southeast, and the Elias Smith [1769–1846] and Abner Jones [1772–1841] in the Northeast) is driven by current denominational controversies.

76. Garrison and DeGroot, *Disciples*, 15, 19, 404, 405.

is a small cluster of new registrations around 1921–1924. There is little evidence to suggest why this pattern exists. The presence on faculty from 1919 to 1925 of Henry Simpson Curr (b. 1886), a self-admitted extremely conservative Old Testament scholar,[77] is one possible explanation for the rise. This possibility is leant credence by the only bit of firm evidence found to date about faculty attitudes toward this group. In September 1926, Dean Jones Hughes Farmer (1857–1928) lamented that the fundamentalist "Bible Union folks" were "hand and glove with the Alliance folks who are open communion and all the rest of it."[78] It is not impossible that some more conservatively-minded Baptists encouraged Christian and Missionary Alliance students to enroll, although this suggestion is pure conjecture. The reasonableness of this speculation is reinforced by the fact that no Christian and Missionary Alliance member registered in either 1928 or 1929. This coincides with the departure from the Baptist Convention of the faction fomented by the Fundamentalist leader Thomas Todhunter Shields (1873–1955). This underscores McMaster's place as a local manifestation of a continent-wide struggle between "Modernists" and "Fundamentalists."[79]

The first Disciples student (by either label) dates from 1897, just a year after the first Christian Conference enrollee. They were the seventh non-Baptist group. The foundation was laid for an expansion of this relationship through the official ties created with the Christian Conference. The commonality of adult baptism provided a superficial ecclesiological link between the Disciples and Baptists that few other denominations shared, although the precise understanding of baptism's meaning and implications kept the two fellowships separate.[80] Educators among the ecumenically-minded Disciples saw advanced educational ties with McMaster as a harbinger of greater union.[81] Active recruitment

77. H. S. Curr to J. H. Farmer, 27 May 1919. CBA, Box 251, File 2. Curr left in 1925 to become Principal of the All Nations' Bible College in London, England. See CBA, Box MMV, File 10.

78. J. H. Farmer to J. L. Sloat (of Chatham), 18 September 1926. CBA, Box 202, unnumbered file.

79. Pinnock, "Modernist Impulse at McMaster," 194, 198–200.

80. J. H. Farmer to G. S. Burt, 13 May 1919. CBA, Box HHI, unnumbered file.

81. W. C. MacDougall to McKay, 16 June 1905. CBA, Box MMF, File 70. Particular plans appear to have entailed McMaster's recognition of the Junior Matriculation examination results of the Disciples' College. See W. C. MacDougall to McKay, 30 June 1905. CBA, Box MMF, File 70. MacDougall later opined: "I sincerely hope that the day

of students to McMaster by Disciples leaders was ramped up in 1906.[82] In 1907, Fred Elmore Lumley (b. 1880), Principal of the Disciples' Sinclair College in St. Thomas, Ontario, approached the McMaster administration about the possibility of some affiliation.[83] Chancellor Alexander Charles McKay was reticent to negotiate any new terms with the Disciples, hoping that they would accept the terms already agreed to by the Christian Conference.[84]

By 1911, a Disciple had been accepted onto the faculty. Henry Franklin Dawes (1881–1953), a physicist, began a relationship with the University which would last for thirty-seven years.[85] There is no evidence, however, that this new link was promoted by the Disciples. There is meager evidence of attempts to extend the catchment area internationally, in the form of a single 1917 letter from a prospective Disciples student in West Virginia.[86] Later that same year matters got more serious, as Dawes attempted to arrange for weekly lectures in Disciples theology by an unspecified member of the movement.[87] It is not clear whether these lectures actually materialized; there is certainly no sign of increased Disciples enrolment at that time.

Negotiations to consolidate the Disciples' student body at McMaster apparently became serious again in 1925. Correspondence between the Rev. George Quiggen and Dean of Arts Walter Scott Williams McLay

---

may not be distant when we may be one people." See MacDougall to McKay, 4 August 1905, p. 2. CBA, Box MMF, File 70.

82. C. C. Lumley to McKay, 28 March 1906. CBA, Box MMG, File 8.

83. F. E. Lumley to A. C. McKay, 14 March 1907 and 13 April 1907. CBA, MMI, File 8. Lumley believed an official accord similar to that inked by the Christian Conference was necessary. See F. E. Lumley (Principal of Sinclair College, St. Thomas, Ontario) to McKay, 18 November 1907. CBA, Box MMJ, File 8.

84. McKay to F. E. Lumley, 21 November 1907. CBA, Letterbook McKay #19 (1907–1909), letter 173. McKay also suggested that McMaster should take the initiative in a formal approach to the Co-Operation of Disciples of Christ in Ontario.

85. "Former Faculty Members Biographical and Other Information" (1889–1946), CBA, Box 157.

86. J. H. Farmer to Thomas W. Bradt, 30 August 1917. CBA, Box 202, unnumbered file.

87. "Disciples of Christ—Arrangements for Students 1917–1927." CBA: Box 103, unnumbered file; cf. W. J. Hastie (Evangelist and Field Secretary for the Co-Operation of Disciples of Christ in Ontario) to A. L. McCrimmon, 20 March 1915. CBA, Box MMM, File 7; and C. L. Pyatt to McCrimmon, 9 and 15 April 1919, arguing for the presence of a Disciple as an Old Testament professor. CBA, Box MMW, File 5.

(1870–1945) reveal the Disciples' hope that their theology course might be substituted for some of the required work for an Arts degree.[88] McLay was not certain this was a good idea. In any event, enrolment moved from intermittent individuals to an average of four new students in each of the years from 1925 to 1929. The denomination bought a residence and installed a University of Chicago PhD (not Dawes) as overseer;[89] as many as ten Disciples students at a time attended lectures. T. T. Shields allegedly tried to use Disciples students' presence at McMaster to further his cause, suggesting that professors altered their teaching when Disciples were present, but he appears to have had limited success.[90]

The acquisition of property outside Toronto was to have an unforeseen impact on what had developed into a good working relationship. When McMaster moved to Hamilton, the relationship between McMaster and the Disciples ended amicably, with McLay arranging for the orderly transfer of three Disciples/Church of Church students' credits to the Methodists' Victoria College at the University of Toronto.[91] That relationship continued at least into the 1950s. Some Disciples materials are held in the Victoria University Archives.

It is not clear whether the single "Christian Church" student at Brandon was a member of the Disciples, the Church of Christ, or the Christian Conference. The latter is not impossible, as a handful of Conference members had emigrated to the West in the first decade of the twentieth century.

The "Christian Church" in Ontario was the northernmost wing of a polygenetic American restorationist movement dating from the last decade of the eighteenth century.[92] Prongs of the movement entered the northern British colonies in the first quarter of the nineteenth centu-

88. W. S. W. McLay to George Quiggen, 24 July 1925. CBA, Box HHA, File 88.

89. W. S. W. McLay to Dean Auger (of Victoria College), 18 November 1929. CBA, Box HHA, File 96.

90. J. H. Farmer to J. E. Pettit, 10 January 1927. CBA, Box 202, unnumbered file. Elsewhere Farmer intimated that some Disciples students were accusing McMaster of harboring "modernists" and that the Disciples needed to be reminded of their precise relationship to the university. See J. H. Farmer to John MacNeill, 6 December 1926. CBA, Box 202.

91. W. S. W. McLay to Dean Auger of Victoria College, 18 November 1929. CBA, Box HHA, File 96.

92. Steinacher, "Aleatory Folk," 106–22.

ry.[93] By 1900, the group maintained continuing ties with its American siblings, the closest with the New York and New England branches. These links to the United States were double-edged. On the one hand, they were problematic. Ministerial recruits went south for instruction in their peculiar tenets and never returned. Once an arrangement with McMaster was in place, not only could Conference students train in Ontario, but also American students might be lured north.

The first student from this denomination to matriculate into McMaster University did so in 1896.[94] There were also students in the early years who claimed membership in a Baptist church, but whose parents were members of the Christian Conference. One example was Ernestine Roberta Whiteside (1876–1960), daughter of a leading Conference family. "Roby" Whiteside had a prominent career in Canadian Baptist educational institutions, first as Lady Principal of the Brandon College Academy and later as Principal of Moulton College, Toronto.[95]

Christian Conference enrolment changed profoundly after John Nelson Dales (1864–late 1930s), a prominent lay-preacher and editor of *The Christian Vanguard* (the Conference newspaper), joined the McMaster faculty in 1906.[96] He had been teaching for a year at Queen's, under an arrangement that saw the church underwrite his entire salary.[97] With only about a thousand members, the denomination found the burden too great. The concept, however, appeared attractive, as already Dales had gathered around himself in Kingston a "colony" of three stu-

93. The earliest movement appears to have been into New Brunswick and Nova Scotia. Settlers from Vermont tended to spill over the border into southern Lower Canada. Preachers followed, establishing a small number of congregations (ibid., 177–79). Political entanglements during the abortive Mackenzie-Papineau Rebellions ensured the demise of the already dwindling cause. Only the denomination descended from adherents who migrated to Upper Canada exists today (ibid., 253–56).

94. One Christian Conference student, William Peer (b. *ca.* 1842), had attended the Toronto Baptist College. He converted to Trinitarianism and joined the Baptists, later leading an unusual career as a home missionary in northern Ontario. CBA: Box 767, File 32; Newmarket Christian Church: Church Minute Book, 1856–1895, 296.

95. See Whiteside to A. L. McCrimmon, 27 April 1918; and H. P. Whidden to Whiteside, 5 November 1918. CBA, Box MMN, File 15. For glowing letters of reference, consult CBA, Box MMK, File 53.

96. McMaster University, "Senate Report for 1906–1907" [typescript], 14. CBA.

97. *Minutes of the 81st Annual Conference of the Christian Church in Ontario* np: np, 1906, 20. Microform, United Church of Canada Archives.

dents: one native Ontarian, one from Vermont, and one from Rhode Island. This was no accident, but a scheme promoted by the American denomination to take advantage of lower Canadian tuition fees. Each of these students was preparing for pastoral ministry.

A new deal was reached with McMaster University by which it and the Christian Conference each paid half of Dales' salary.[98] Granted an *ad eundem* Master of Arts from McMaster, Dales became Professor of Modern Languages, mostly French. The three students from Queen's also transferred to McMaster, where they were joined by a Japanese student pastor and three more Ontarians. It is no coincidence that the Educational Secretary for the American parent denomination was a Canadian expatriate and McMaster graduate, William Garbutt Sargent (1872–ca.1953). Dean McLay considered expanding the formal relationship by appointing Sargent as an external reader of essays, but in the end opted for a more experienced academic.[99] All parties were nevertheless delighted. The goals of the new students also broadened to include teacher education and training for other professions. The thirty-six members who attended McMaster accounted for more than three percent of the Conference's entire membership, a notable rate of return.

Dales served to great acclaim by faculty and students alike until 1909.[100] After that, the story takes a bizarre twist. Dales suddenly quit, giving only two weeks' notice just before the new school year began. Evidently, Dales was dismayed when the Rev. Elmore Harris (1854–1911) attacked the teaching of University of Chicago-trained Professor Isaac George Matthews (1871–1959). Matthews, who was admitted to his Doctor of Philosophy by the University of Chicago in 1912, was Old Testament professor from 1905–1919. His developing views on Higher Criticism garnered the ire of conservatives. Harris, according to McMaster University historian Charles Johnston (b. 1926), wanted to have *all* faculty sign the statement of faith, not just theological professors.[101] Caught in the cross-fire, Dales resigned while the outcome of the entire Harris/Matthews debacle was still up in the air. Apparently

98. Ibid., 20–21.

99. W. G. Sargent to W. S. W. McLay, 22 September 1906. CBA, Box HHB, File 1: Letterbook 1906–1910.

100. McMaster University, Senate Report for 1906–1907, 14–15. CBA. Dales taught the courses for all three years of the French program and the first year German course.

101. Johnston, *McMaster*, 90–92, 98–99, 102–7, 109–12.

he feared that he might be asked to subscribe to the statement, which he could not do, given his Unitarian/Arian Christology. In that case, he would be dismissed, and his chances of ever working again at a Canadian university would be dashed.[102]

Consequently, Dales used the excuse of pursuing graduate work to cover his hasty egress. He never undertook doctoral studies, instead taking a pastorate in his hometown of Drayton, Ontario. The Conference's educational dilemma returned with Dales' exit. Without someone to inculcate their unusual tenets, students could more easily be swayed by mainstream theology.[103] Dales returned to Toronto without a university position, choosing to tutor students at an independent establishment, Kirton Hall. The Hall, purchased with a bequest by Richard Kirton (1822 or 1823–1911), opened its doors in November 1912.[104] Initially it was successful; residents provided supply preaching to small local congregations.[105] The 1914 American Christian Convention Quadrennial, meeting in Ohio, received a presentation about Kirton Hall from "Dean" Dales.[106] The outbreak of the "Great War" that same year undermined the school, as young men enlisted.

Meanwhile, McMaster officials also began to discern and question the Conference's theological oddities. A 1917 letter by Farmer specifically notes the Unitarian tendency of the Christian Conference church in Oshawa with which the local Baptist church was considering merg-

---

102. Dales's concerns would have been well-founded. Just a decade later, Ben E. Perry of Urbana, Ohio responded to an offer by McCrimmon to teach Latin: "I am much interested in the position, but unfortunately the religious requirement would appear to make my candidacy impossible. Although I was baptized by the Presbyterians, I cannot at present claim membership in any church. I attend the Unitarian." See B. E. Perry to McCrimmon, 6 January 1920. CBA, Box 251, File 1. Similarly, H. H. Bingham urged a friend not to send his child to the University of Alberta because one of the most popular professors was Unitarian: "Surely some of the State institutions are turning out rank infidels." See H. H. Bingham (pastor of First Baptist Church, Calgary) to McCrimmon, 30 May 1919. CBA, Box MMN, File 18.

103. *Herald of Gospel Liberty*, 18 July 1912, 921, col. 1; 11 February 1915, 191, col. 1; *Christian Vanguard*, 28 August 1913, 871, col. 3; 872, col. 2.

104. *Christian Vanguard*, November 1912, 10, col. 1, cf. 8, cols.1–3. Richard Kirton had been a member of the Newmarket Christian Church. The Hall was located at 513 Markham St. Cf. *Herald of Gospel Liberty*, 18 July 1912, 921, col. 1.

105. *Christian Vanguard*, 18 July 1914, 2, col. 1.

106. Ibid., 31 October 1914, 2, col. 2.

ing.[107] Dales also served as Field Secretary for the Ontario Conference, although eventually the cost of maintaining that salary proved to be too great for the small group. Moving to New York State in 1924, Dales served as the New York Central Conference's Field Secretary and church planter.[108] He never again taught at a university. As for Kirton Hall, it became little more than a dormitory for Conference undergraduates attending McMaster.[109] Without Dales' presence, numbers dropped dramatically, with only two students on site in Fall 1925.[110] The residence closed in 1928, and the property was sold in 1929, a year before McMaster's move to Hamilton.[111]

The first two Hebrews to enroll at McMaster University did so in 1908, becoming the first non-Christian group to be represented in the student body. Attendance at a Protestant university does not seem to have concerned these Jewish students. Indeed, three student rabbis undertook Arts work at McMaster.[112] This was apparently not problematic because of the role of faith-based education in Canadian Judaism. Some scholars have argued that Jewish primary and secondary education was an effect rather than a cause of group solidarity and self-image among early twentieth-century Canadian Jews.[113] According to this view, Jewish

107. J. H. Farmer to E. F. Chandler, 15 March 1917. CBA, Box 202, unnumbered file.

108. *Minutes of the 98th Annual Conference of the Christian Church in Ontario*, np: np, 1923,14; *Minutes of the 99th Annual Conference of the Christian Church in Ontario* np: np, 1924, 11,13. Microform, United Church of Canada Archives.

109. *Minutes of the 98th Annual Conference of the Christian Church in Ontario*, 1923, 22.

110. *Minutes of the 100th Annual Conference of the Christian Church in Ontario*, np: np, 1925, 30.

111. *Minutes of the 103rd Annual Conference of the Christian Church in Ontario*, np: np, 1928, 10,16–17; *Minutes of the 104th Annual Conference of the Christian Church in Ontario*, np: np, 1929, 7. The property had been sold at a loss. The new owner defaulted on the mortgage during the Depression. The Conference apparently held the mortgage, but was unable to recoup funds; the second sale netted a mere third of the original asking price. *Minutes of the 112th Annual Conference of the Christian Church in Ontario*, np: np, 1937, 9; *Minutes of the 114th Annual Conference of the Christian Church in Ontario*, np: np, 1939, 20.

112. Two were also sons of rabbis.

113. Selick, *History of B'nai B'rith*, 11, 53, 77. Also consult Weinfeld, "Educational Continuum," 202–3, 206, 209. The direction of causality is controversial. Weinfeld's discussion of the *current* setting firmly identifies Jewish education as a key factor in building Jewish identity. Even in this context he allows that what one may be measuring is actually pre-existing Jewishness. That is, those with a higher Jewish self-awareness are

students were grounded in ethnic and religious identity before undertaking sectarian education. Sectarian education did not initially exist to create such group identity.

The reception of Jewish students at McMaster was mixed. No research was conducted concerning participation at other Canadian universities. Attitudes at Queen's and McGill may best be described as frosty.[114] From the White-Anglo-Saxon-Protestant side, there were muted voices of concern. It appears that Jewish students were working hard, and that their effort was being rewarded by a larger than expected share of matriculation scholarships to McMaster.[115] This "problem," Hamilton committee members averred, would be solved by moving to their city, which "is never likely to become such a Jewish metropolis as New York, Montreal and Toronto are coming to be."[116] To be fair, some, such as McLay, were willing to court Jewish participation. In 1919, McLay nominated Henry S. Rosenberg (1900–1976) for a Rhodes Scholarship.[117] Almost a decade later, Rosenberg, by then a Toronto-based lawyer, offered to help canvas Hamilton's Jewish community for funds.[118] Of par-

---

more likely to enroll their children in Jewish education, so that the education actually reinforces identity, rather than creating it. As the clock is turned back, however, he seems more willing to allow that education is a result, not a cause, of Jewish identity.

114. Tulchinsky, *Canada's Jews*, 132–33. Tulchinsky documents both academic and personal slanders against Jewish students. A 1919 speech by Queen's Principal R. Bruce Taylor (1869–1955) (erroneously) suggested that Queen's Jewish students had evaded service during the recent World War in a cowardly manner. Tulchinsky's anecdotes dovetail with the generally anti-Semitic attitudes portrayed in Abella and Troper's *None Is Too Many*. McMaster may have been unusual in relatively welcoming Jewish students prior to World War II.

115. H. F. Dawes to McLay, 10 August 1917. CBA, McLay correspondence 1915–1917 "D"; Michell to H. P. Whidden, 2 November 1926. CBA, Box MMQ, File 22.

116. "Some Arguments Favorable to Hamilton Becoming the Home of McMaster University," p. 1. CBA, Box 302, unnumbered file. This quotation (an echo of Principal Taylor's comments about Kingston) is the fifteenth reason cited in favor of McMaster's relocation. In the event, they were wrong, as Jewish historian Gerald Tulchinsky identifies Hamilton as a "secondary" Jewish population center, whose Jewish population grew dramatically in the first two decades of the twentieth century (Tulchinsky, *Canada's Jews*, 110).

117. Letter of 24 November 1919. CBA, McLay Correspondence Box HHA, File 50. Some of Rosenberg's personal papers are on deposit in the National Archives of Canada (CAIN #261266). Accessed online URL: http://www.archivescanada.ca/english/search/ItemDisplay.asp?sessionKey=1149011692062_206_191_57_196&l=0&lvl=1&v=0&coll=1&itm=261266&rt=1&bill=1.

118. Henry S. Rosenberg (of Rosenberg and Rotenberg Barristers and Solicitors, Toronto) to McLay, 25 April 1928. CBA, Box HHA, File 113.

ticular value was Rosenberg's "experience of what McMaster really is" allowing Rosenberg to "assure the Jewish people of Hamilton that they will find nothing in the atmosphere of our University to offend their racial or religious susceptibilities and that they can support [the] campaign to their advantage."[119]

The gender balance among Jewish students is noteworthy. Education in this ethnic community had long been provided primarily to males, with girls' socialization tending to emphasize maternal and housekeeping roles.[120] Given this context, it is remarkable that ten Jewish women enrolled at McMaster between 1909 and 1926.[121] One of these women, Dora Wilensky (1901–1959), became a renowned social activist and pioneer social-worker.[122] Six of the women were born in Toronto; one in New York City; three in Russia. There is a notable reversal of the overall male trend (see below). The date of matriculation appears to have been irrelevant in terms of female registration. Since both the first three and the last three Jewish women to enroll were Toronto-born, it is unlikely that the native-born women's participation rate resulted from sociological shifts within the broader Jewish community. Furthermore, improved economic status was likely not a factor; the first Jewish woman enrolled at McMaster only one year after her first male counterpart. It appears that McMaster University's acceptance of female Jewish students helped to lower barriers to their involvement in the mainstream of Canadian society.

There was, of course, no Jewish faculty member, as all professors were required to be Christians. Instead, the rise in Jewish registration reflects a fairly straightforward demographic trend. Jews begin to enter the school in significant numbers around the time of the Great War. Between 1911 and 1931, the Jewish population rose from 0.1 percent to

119. McLay to W. J. Westaway, 7 May 1928. CBA, Box HHA, File 117.

120. Sorin, *Building*, 17–18; Tulchinsky, *Canada's Jews*, 123; Weinfeld, "Educational Continuum," 196, 198, 207.

121. Comparative gender participation rates for the rest of McMaster's student population are not available at this time, making it impossible to compare between these two different ethno-religious groups.

122. Enrollment #2189. Her stated intention upon matriculation was to become a journalist. For a short biography of the Russian-born Wilensky, consult her obituary (under "Salsberg") in the *Canadian Jewish Review*, 3 April 1959, p. 6, col.1. For a photograph and oblique references to Wilensky, consult Gerald Tulchinsky's biography of Wilensky's partner, politician and social activist Joe Salsberg, in Tulchinsky, "Quarrel."

1.5 percent of the population of Canada.[123] This coincides with a large influx of Eastern European Jews into Canada during the first two decades of the twentieth century.[124] Only fifteen Jewish students (a little more than a quarter) were Canadian-born, with all but one of those born in Toronto. Of the foreign-born, four were from New York City, four from London, England and one from Belfast. The rest were from Eastern Europe: eighteen may be identified as Russian, seven from Poland, and two from "Roumania" [sic]. Two were clearly from the area, but with overly-precise identification of their place of birth. As with the Jewish women, there appears to be no chronological pattern associated with birthplace and date of enrolment.[125] There were thirteen Jewish matriculants at Brandon or 1.3 percent of the student body, slightly lower than in Toronto, as one might expect of the more rural school. Students' birthplaces were not generally recorded, making it impossible to compare first-generation *versus* second- (or subsequent) generational behavior.

The absence of a Jewish faculty member was not for lack of effort on the Jewish community's part. J. H. Farmer, Dean of Theology, was approached in the fall of 1914 by Rabbi Julius J. Price, who had inquired about the possibility of his lecturing at McMaster.[126] Having just resigned his rabbinate at University Avenue Synagogue,[127] he appears to have hoped to secure full-time employment as a lecturer, when the tendered resignation became effective the next year. In response to Dr. Price's suggestion to add material to the curriculum, Farmer noted that it already was too full to allow expansion. Instead, he offered Price

123. Selick, *History of B'nai B'rith*, 3.

124. Between 1880 and 1920, one third of Eastern European Jews emigrated to North America, two million to the United States. See Sorin, *Building*, xv, 1. The bulk of Canadian Jewish immigrants came between 1900 and 1920, in response to changes in Canadian immigration policy in 1896 under Wilfrid Laurier (1841–1919). See Weinfeld, "Jews." Toronto's Jewish population doubled during the 1890s and Hamilton's increased by half in the same period. See Tulchinsky, *Canada's Jews*, 108–9.

125. Of the first six male Jewish students at McMaster, there were two each born in Russia and Toronto, with one each from Poland and Belfast, Ireland.

126. J. H. Farmer to Rabbi Julius J. Price, 27 November 1914. CBA, Box 202, unnumbered file. There is ambiguous and ill-defined suggestion of contact between A. C. McKay and Price in September and December 1914 (cf. McKay's Daily Journal, CBA, in an unnumbered box on shelf 4 of case 3. Its cover is marked 1913, but internal evidence suggests it had been used in 1914).

127. *Canadian Jewish Chronicle*, 20 April 1917, 8, col. 1.

a single lecture at McMaster's Theological Society. Dissatisfied with Farmer's answer, Price decided to go over the Dean's head and correspond with Chancellor A. L. McCrimmon. Price offered to lecture free of charge.[128] The manouevre failed, as McCrimmon was absent, and Farmer replied on the Chancellor's behalf.[129] In a bizarre twist, while speaking in Ottawa, Price allegedly represented himself as a member of McMaster's faculty.[130] To be fair, it may have been his local contacts who so bragged. What is relevant to this chapter is that at least some within the Jewish community hoped to replicate the kind of faculty presence achieved by two of the smaller Christian sects. The plan seems to have foundered solely because of the profound religious differences between Judaism and Christianity and not because of reluctance on McMaster's administrators' part to welcome non-Baptists.

For three of the five divisions discussed in this segment (the Disciples, the Christian Conference, and Judaism), McMaster University acted as an avenue leading to respectability. The Disciples had been organizationally suspect, the Christian Conference theologically unsound, and Judaism was, clearly, not a Christian denomination. All three groups lay at varying degrees of separation from the mainstream; all three groups experienced varying degrees of success at replicating the Baptists' elision with the Protestant mainline. In the cases of the erstwhile Protestant outliers, falling within McMaster's sphere of influence resulted in a normativizing effect. The Disciples aligned with the liberal wing of Protestantism, symbolized by their successive switch to Victoria College. The Christian Conference remained somewhat marginal, awaiting fuller integration with the emerging evangelical mainstream through interaction with another educational institution.[131] Canada's failure to accept Jewish refugees prior to the Second World War underscored their continuing outsider stance in Canadian society; McMaster's refusal to allow them into the inner circle demonstrated the limits of the power of an alternate attractor.

128. Julius J. Price to A. L. McCrimmon, 7 July 1915. CBA, Box MMM, File 11.

129. J. H. Farmer (on McCrimmon's behalf) to Julius J. Price, 14 July 1915. CBA, Box MMM, File 11.

130. Weeks to A. L. McCrimmon, undated. CBA, Box MMM, File 15.

131. This process is discussed in Steinacher, *Fighting Chance.*

CONCLUSION

Almost from its inception, the Baptist-founded and sponsored McMaster University accepted students from other denominations, "sheep not of this fold." Their presence and patterns of participation provide profound insights into an easily overlooked portion of Baptists' contribution to public life in Ontario. Analysis of these patterns may be enhanced by use of concepts from Chaos-Complexity Theory. Events may be envisioned as revolving around the poles of two distinct yet inter-related double attractor sets, one external to the university, one internal.

One set operated within the basin of Ontario's public life. Here, the Baptist university functioned on the intellectual periphery of the province's field of tertiary education, providing an pedagogical alternative to secular universities, in particular to the geographically proximate University of Toronto. This new pole emerged in the context of earlier struggles against Anglican cultural, educational, and spiritual hegemony. A generic Christianity took root in the province's public life as a variety of factors acted to dismantle Anglican dominance. The resistance by Methodists (personified by Ryerson), Baptists (embodied in Fyfe), and others rested on different grounds. The Methodists' concerns were more readily assuaged, allowing them to become assimilated to the dominant intellectual pole by the time McMaster University formed. Baptists, on the other hand, held a philosophy of education with explicit roots in the movement's genesis and voluntarist ecclesiology. Denominational colleges, they firmly believed, should exist solely by means of the support of like-minded individuals who cooperated on a free-will basis. State schools should neither support nor stifle the standards of any specific sect. As a result, McMaster initially held a distinctive position as an educational "outsider," its very formation having been resisted by bureaucrats who favored the state's system. That differentiation immediately began attracting to McMaster "outsiders" of various types, possibly focused on perceptions of energetic piety within the university's intellectual life. This applied both to students from the more than two dozen often tiny and usually theologically conservative denominations, which would never have been able to support a college on their own, as well as students from mainline bodies who embraced a more emotive spirituality than the majority within their denominations.

That said, McMaster's role as a secondary attractor, an alternate locus of order, shifted notably over this period. Almost from its inception,

McMaster was itself drawn closer to the larger and stronger mainline attractor. Even though the raw number of Baptist matriculants continued to climb, their share of the student body consistently dropped, as enrolment by non-Baptist students grew at an even stronger rate. The augmented student body imparted to McMaster both fiscal stability and a sense of cultural momentum, but at the price of diluting its particular identity. Baptists had slipped under 50 percent of the student body by 1929, a trend that clearly accelerated after the transfer to Hamilton. Yet the process of assimilation by which McMaster's alternate attractor collapsed into that of the mainline was not completed by 1930.

This era also encompasses the "Fundamentalist/Modernist Controversy." Interactions with conservative forces arrayed against McMaster's alleged tolerance of modernism form the background to the Dales incident, as well as the brief and relatively intense arrival of Christian and Missionary Alliance students. The impact of the formation of the United Church of Canada, as well as the Disciples' transference to the United Church's Victoria College relate to the liberal side of the equation. It is beyond the scope of this chapter either to validate or disprove the veracity of the perception that McMaster lurched to the theological left in the 1920s. It is possible, however, to observe that the university relentlessly moved closer to the province's theological mainstream. Of note, the flood of continuing Presbyterians after 1925 evinced their confidence in McMaster's academic and spiritual acceptability.

The continuation of this apparent outlook by the Presbyterians raises another possible motivation for non-Baptist matriculants: the potential of riding the Baptists' coattails from suspicion to respectability. This motive applied particularly to the Disciples and the Christian Conference, both of whom generated aggressive processes of directed recruitment within their memberships. Those processes included securing a denominational member on faculty and creating a student residence in the vicinity. To differing extents, the groups' goals were realized. The Disciples' adhesion was stronger, ending only because of McMaster's physical relocation to Hamilton. The Conference's link was more tenuous, as the university's leadership became increasingly aware of the group's idiosyncratic theology and as factors within the Conference reduced the number of students preparing for ministry. The self-imposed limits of the power of an alternate attractor are demonstrated, however, in McMaster's experience with students of a non-Christian background.

For Jewish students, the impermeable barrier to a faculty appointment for one of their own demonstrated that an attractor's potency is relative. Jewish students might gravitate towards McMaster's attractor, but they were not assimilated. Their path also suggests limits to the impact of the second double attractor set.

The other matched pair of attractors functioned within the basin of McMaster University's inner life, as leadership struggled with the competing poles of theological commitment and fiscal pragmatism. McMaster's collapse from periphery to mainline reflected the relatively simultaneous overwhelming of the theological attractor by the fiscal. Ironically, the theological commitment to voluntarism created the dichotomous situation by forcing the question of sound monetary management into the foreground. The first non-Baptists to be admitted were probably accepted simply because they were academically qualified and desired to participate. Expansion brought larger needs, so that deliberate schemes of advancement developed, specifically with the Christian Conference and the Disciples. Theological questions do not appear to have been raised at first; theology figured heavily, though, in Dales's precipitous departure. Pragmatic considerations appear to have become ascendant after Whidden's appointment as Chancellor. Theology, once central, was gradually (although perhaps imperceptibly to participants) being relegated to the periphery. Undue focus on Brandon's failure has obscured the reality that it stayed solvent as long as it did because of the existence of massive non-Baptist revenue streams. Drawing upon his experience at Brandon, Whidden steered a course to fiscal fitness, ultimately leading to McMaster's relocation to Hamilton and its reinvention as a regional university. The implications of adopting a new site included lessened financial impact of the internal Baptist strife in the late 1920s. This granted leaders a certain level of independence from their now-fractured original Baptist constituency. The initiative quietly but clearly slipped from theological to pragmatic considerations.

While this migration from a primarily theological orientation to a predominantly pragmatic one entailed secularization, it should be stressed that the language of an ideological attractor's competing with a fiscal one is not merely alternate verbiage for secularization. Secularization is assuredly a component of the mechanism, but not its entirety. During this period, McMaster shifted from being a monodenominational institution to a multidenominational one. Equally emphatically, it must be grasped that multidenominational is not synonymous with nondenominational. Prior to 1957, whatever Whidden or Gilmour's personal spirituality might have been, the university did not discard its overtly Christian character. Administrators' intentions were to embrace a large range of denominations, rather than focus narrowly on their original spiritual catchment basin or to cast even more broadly by abandoning a distinctively Christian outlook altogether.

The historical fact is that McMaster went on to become a nondenominational institution, in which Christian teaching became essentially irrelevant. Though exceedingly likely and predictable in the circumstances, that development was still not inevitable. While the difficulties encountered would have been monumental, the option remained to stay multidenominational. This would have radically changed the long-term development of McMaster's structure and function. If it had retained its overtly Christian atmosphere, its ability to attract students from an increasingly secular constituency would probably have been impaired, undermining its robustness. Today's educational behemoth would almost certainly not have emerged. As it is, McMaster's 1957 charter not only indicated the conflation of the alternate educational pole with the mainline one, but it marked the simultaneous final overwhelming of the theological pole by the pragmatic one, a clear-cut chronological and ideological terminal point for the ideal of a specifically "Baptist" school in which "Christian character" was deliberately fostered. This opened the ground for the emergence of a new alternate pole. Others would resurrect the vision of a religiously-based university, one infusing learning with an atmosphere of pronounced and central Christian piety. Two current examples of this blending of academics and spirituality are Redeemer University College in Ancaster, Ontario, and Tyndale University College and Seminary in Toronto. They provide other folds for the sheep.

BIBLIOGRAPHY

Abella, Irving, and Troper, Harold. *None is Too Many: Canada and the Jews of Europe, 1933–1948*. Toronto: Lester and Orpen Dennys, 1982.

Beaumont, Roger A. *The Nazis' March to Chaos: The Hitler Era through the Lenses of Chaos-Complexity Theory*. Westport, CN: Praeger, 2000.

Beaumont, Roger A. *War, Chaos and History*. Westport, CN: Praeger, 1994.

Brackney, William Henry. *Christian Voluntarism: Theology and Praxis*. Manlius, NY: REV/Rose, 1997.

Brown, Richard. *Church and State in Modern Britain 1700–1850*. London: Routledge, 1991.

Çambel, Ali Bulent. *Applied Chaos Theory: A Paradigm for Complexity*. San Diego, CA: Academic, 1993.

Eldebo, Runar. "Dwight L. Moody and the Swedish Mission Friends." *Pietisten: A Herald of Awakening and Spiritual Edification* (Dec 2008) no pages, electronic form only. http://www.pietisten.org/christmas08/moody.html. Accessed 8 August 2011.

Ellis, Walter E. "What the Times Demand: Brandon College and Higher Education in Western Canada." In *Canadian Baptists and Christian Higher Education*, edited by George A. Rawlyk, 63–87. Montreal and Kingston: McGill-Queen's University Press, 1988.

Friedland, Martin L. *The University of Toronto: A History*. Toronto: University of Toronto Press, 2002.

Garrison, Winfred Ernest, and DeGroot, Alfred T. *The Disciples of Christ: A History*. St. Louis: The Bethany Press, 1958.

Gibson, Frederick W., and Graham, Roger. *Queen's University: 1917–1961: To Serve and Yet Be Free*. Montreal and Kingston: McGill-Queen's University Press, 1983.

Gibson, Theo T. *Robert Alexander Fyfe: His Contemporaries and His Influence*. Burlington, ON: Welch, 1988.

Gidney, R. D., and Millar, W. P. J. "The Christian Recessional in Ontario's Public Schools." In *Religion and Public Life in Canada: Historical and Comparative Perspectives*, edited by Marguerite Van Die, 275–93. Toronto: University of Toronto Press, 2001.

Irwin, Grace. *Three Lives in Mine*. Toronto: Irwin, 1986.

Johnston, Charles Murray. *McMaster University: The Toronto Years*. Toronto: University of Toronto Press, 1976.

"McMaster, William." In *Dictionary of Canadian Biography Online*. Vol. 11. University of Toronto/Université Laval, 2000. No pages. Accessed February 2, 2010. Online URL: http://www.biographi.ca/009004-119.01-e.php?&id_nbr=5699&&PHPSESSI D=imv760mbq1pnd1c1m4c65bb2u3.

Moody, Barry M. "Breadth of Vision, Breadth of Mind: The Baptists and Acadia." In *Canadian Baptists and Christian Higher Education*, edited by George A. Rawlyk, 3–30. Montreal and Kingston: McGill-Queen's University Press, 1988.

Pinnock, Clark H. "The Modernist Impulse at McMaster University, 1887–1927." In *Baptists in Canada: Search for Identity amidst Diversity*, edited by Jarold K. Zeman, 193–207. Burlington, ON: Welch, 1980.

Pugh, Martin. *Britain since 1789: A Concise History*. Houndmills, Basingstoke, Hampshire: Macmillan, 1999.

Rawlyk, George A., "A. L. McCrimmon, H. P. Whidden, T. T. Shields, Christian Higher Education, and McMaster University." In *Canadian Baptists and Christian Higher*

Education, edited by George A. Rawlyk, 31–62. Montreal and Kingston: McGill-Queen's University Press, 1988.

Rawlyk, George A. "Introduction." In *Canadian Baptists and Christian Higher Education*, edited by George A. Rawlyk, x–xi. Montreal and Kingston: McGill-Queen's University Press, 1988.

Selick, Abel. *The History of B'nai B'rith in Eastern Canada*. Toronto: B'nai B'rith District No. 22 Grand Lodge, 1964.

Sorin, Gerald. *A Time for Building: The Third Migration, 1880–1920*. Vol. 3 of *The Jewish People in America*, edited by Henry L. Feingold. Baltimore and London: Johns Hopkins University Press, 1992.

Stackhouse, John Jr. *Canadian Evangelicalism in the Twentieth Century: An Introduction to Its Character*. Toronto: University of Toronto Press, 1993.

Steinacher, Christopher Mark. "An Aleatory Folk: An Historical-Theological Approach to the Transition of the Christian Church in Canada from Fringe to Mainstream 1792–1898." DTh dissertation, Wycliffe College, University of Toronto, 1999.

———. "Canada Baptist College to Toronto Baptist College." Unpublished Finding Aid, Canadian Baptist Archives.

———. *Fighting Chance: The Story of the Congregational Christian Churches in Canada*. Toronto: Bay Ridge, forthcoming.

Tulchinsky, Gerald. *Canada's Jews: A People's Journey*. Toronto: University of Toronto Press, 2008.

———. "Family Quarrel: Joe Salsberg, the 'Jewish' Question, and Canadian Communism." No Pages. Online : http://www.historycooperative.org/journals/llt/56/tulchinsky.html. Accessed 19 February 2010.

———. "'Justice and Only Justice Thou Shalt Pursue': Considerations on the Social Voice of Canada's Reform Rabbis." In *Religion and Public Life in Canada: Historical and Comparative Perspectives*, edited by Marguerite VanDie, 313–28. Toronto: University of Toronto Press, 2001.

VanDie, Marguerite. "Introduction." In *Religion and Public Life in Canada: Historical and Comparative Perspectives*, edited by Marguerite Van Die, 3–12. Toronto: University of Toronto Press, 2001.

Weinfeld, Morton. "The Educational Continuum: A Community Priority." In *From Immigration to Integration, The Canadian Jewish Experience: A Millennium Edition*, edited by Ruth Klein and Frank Dimant, Chapter 13. Toronto: B'nai B'rith Institute for International Affairs, 2001.

———. "Jews." In *Encyclopedia of Canada's Peoples*, edited by Paul R. Magocsi, 864–65. Toronto, University of Toronto Press, 1999.

Westfall, William. *Two Worlds: The Protestant Culture of Nineteenth Century Ontario*. Montreal: McGill-Queen's University Press, 1989.

APPENDIX

Denomination\College	Okanagan	Brandon	McMaster	TOTAL	%McMaster	%Brandon
Anglican	1	82	78	161	2.7	8.2
Apostolic			1	1	0.03	0
Assembly of God			1	1	0.03	0
Baptist	25	259	2082	2366	71.4	26
Christadelphian			2	2	0.07	0
Christian and Missionary Alliance			16	16	0.55	0
Christian Catholic			1	1	0.03	0
Christian Conference			36	36	1.2	0
Christian Science		5	1	6	0.03	0.4
Christian Worker			1	1	0.03	0
Church of Christ/Disciples		1	37	38	1.3	0.1
Congregationalist		6	15	21	0.5	0.7
Evangelical			2	2	0.7	0
Free Methodist			1	1	0.03	0
Free Church			1	1	0.03	0

APPENDIX (cont.)

Denomination\College	Okanagan	Brandon	McMaster	TOTAL	%McMaster	%Brandon
Free Church of Finland			1	1	0.03	0
G. O. Catholic [sic]			1	1	0.03	0
IBSA "International Bible Students"		4		4	0	0.2
Independent			1	1	0.03	0
Jewish		13	55	68	1.9	1.3
Lutheran		8	10	18	0.3	0.7
Methodist	7	111	141	259	4.8	11.1
Methodist Episcopal			1	1	0.03	0
Mennonite			5	5	0.2	0
Mission Friend		2		2	0	0.2
Mohammedan [sic]		1		1	0	0.1
Non-denominational		2		2	0	0.2
Not given	5	90	121	216	4.1	9.4
"Orthodox Christian"/Orthodox			3	3	0.1	0

APPENDIX (*cont.*)

Denomination\College	Okanagan	Brandon	McMaster	TOTAL	%McMaster	%Brandon
Plymouth Brethren		1	9	10	0.3	0.1
Presbyterian		208	205	413	7	21.2
Reformed			3	3	0.1	0
Roman Catholic		10	2	12	0.7	0.8
Second Advent			1	1	0.03	0
Unitarian			1	1	0.03	0
United/ "Union"	38	194	80	247	2.7	17.9
REAL TOTAL		997	2915	3950		
Duplicates	0	1	21	22		
TOTAL RECORDED		998	2936	3972		

9

A Missed Opportunity

Central Canadian Baptists
and the Forward Movement, 1919–1920

DONALD A. GOERTZ

THE 1919 FORWARD MOVEMENT was at a time of great optimism. From the perspective of the day, the War to end all wars had been won by great sacrifice; civilization had triumphed over barbarism; the League of Nations had been born, and reconstruction was in full gear. Canadian churches believed that they had the opportunity to ride this wave of sacrifice and optimism to engage the nation and the world in a new mission.

For Baptist self-understanding, this was also a pivotal moment. Baptists saw in the Forward Movement the possibility of becoming a significant force among Canadian churches. It was time to move from the margins into the center and become a significant force in the nation-building agenda. Yet, as quickly as this grand vision had emerged, it unraveled. By 1927, the Baptist Convention of Ontario and Quebec and its sister group, the Baptist Union of Western Canada, fractured and then split into warring camps. The 1919 Baptist Forward Movement frequently used the metaphor of "Kadesh Barnea" to call forth willingness to risk. Like the original story, it would turn out to be a lost opportunity.[1]

While the Forward Movement was launched with great fanfare and carried with it the language of grand dreams of the kingdom of God as

1. Deuteronomy 1:19–46.

it related to Canada, it quickly disappeared from sight in the denomination's narratives. This would suggest that for the leadership of the various denominations it was regarded as a failure, one they hoped would simply vanish and be forgotten. Scholarly literature on the period has facilitated this appearance of failure. Despite the immense effort expended in the Forward Movement there is little research on the topic.[2]

This chapter will explore the 1919–1920 Forward Movement as it was developed in the Baptist Convention of Ontario and Quebec. It will look at the various forces and factors that came together to launch the movement, analyze the goals it set for itself, and then outline how it was executed. It will also analyze what happened and how all of the possibilities could so quickly evaporate.

The Forward Movement of 1919–1920 provided Baptists in Ontario and Quebec with an opportunity to deepen their unity as a community of churches and to do this around an understanding of a mission involving the larger Canadian church and focused on reforming public life in Canada. While there was an initial move in these directions, concerns over losing traditional Baptist beliefs led to a pulling back from the larger goals of the movement and a refocusing on more explicitly spiritual values. As a result, the churches were not able to find a new unifying center rooted in a sense of mission and engagement in the life of their local communities. It is important to examine this major effort by the Canadian Baptists as it represents a missed opportunity to move forward as a community. It brought together all of the key leadership in central Canada and provided them with an opportunity to work together and to hear each other's visions. Had it been successful, it would have opened up the opportunity to move forward in a concerted, unified manner and to become involved in the larger life of the nation. As it was, the Forward Movement was unable to slow the fragmentation already at work. By the time it wound down, the denomination was moving into a full-blown battle over theological nuances.

CONTEXT: GROWTH AND CHALLENGE

Forward Movements emerged in the late nineteenth century and continued with a variety of functions until after the Second World War. They

---

2. The most significant discussions are found in Allen, *The Social Passion*, and Baswick, "Social Evangelism."

were not a continuous movement, but rather a series of focused campaigns to address particular needs. Arthur T. Pierson, writing in 1898, noted that "previous forward movements called for a revival of evangelical piety and a renewal of its connection to service."[3] This linking of piety and service is what differentiated them from the better known evangelistic crusades.

Prior to the First World War they were primarily lay-led movements with limited powers, committed to fostering denominational unity and downplaying denominational distinctives.[4] This ecumenical impulse was strengthened by pulling together leadership from across the spectrum of Protestant denominations; often the YMCA was a key catalyst. The movements provided business people an opportunity to use their professional training in the service to the church. Committed to efficiency, effectiveness, and economy, they brought a desire and an ability to develop integrated promotional materials and methodologies and to get information into the churches. David Dawson points out the significance of this development: "Following the lead of business and industry, churches developed models of efficiency, consolidation, and specialization that had the effect of producing the 'corporate denomination.'"[5] With these competencies, a key component of the forward movements became the raising of money.

There were two major forward movements that shaped the Forward Movement of 1919–1920. The first emerged in 1898 when the American Board of Commissioners for Foreign Missions decided to launch a Forward Movement to connect missionaries with individual churches, families, and people.[6] In the aftermath of the formation of the Student Volunteer Movement there were large groups of college students volunteering to go overseas as missionaries. Business people saw their place in this as finding ways to raise the money to facilitate these students' dreams. They did this by developing in this Forward Movement a model of direct and personal giving. The larger Forward Movement served as a centralized hub that was able to encourage other forward movements within the various denominations. Over time this Forward Movement for missions was co-opted into the denominational structures, and,

3. Dawson, "Funding Mission," 155.

4. Brown, *Church in America*, 252.

5. Dawson, "Funding Mission," 155.

6. Ibid.

led by John R. Mott, it became the Laymen's Missionary Movement in 1907.[7] The success of this movement was a key motivating factor for the 1919–1920 Forward Movement.

The other highly influential Forward Movement was the Men and Religion Forward Movement of 1911–1912.[8] It was born out of a growing unease around the seemingly low rate of male involvement in the churches, something seemingly confirmed by the 1905 U.S. census with its data pointing out that mainline Protestant denominations were two-thirds female.[9] This movement set out to provide what were seen as appropriate activities to engage males and to involve them in the life of the church. To accomplish this goal, the initiative brought together the various men's organizations from all of the major Protestant denominations, as well as parachurch groups, especially the YMCA. Like the Forward Movement in missions, this effort also brought business principles and models of organization into the church. By taking on more the look of a rationalized corporation, it was believed that the church would be seen as more masculine and therefore become more attractive to men.[10] There was an element in this movement that had the feel of a gigantic advertising campaign. The scale of its endeavor was huge. There were hundreds of thousands of dollars spent, and "seventy-six major cities and 1,083 small towns participated."[11] But it was much more. There was a conscious attempt to harness what was seen as men's aggressive, business orientation and to fix it on a new goal, the Christianizing of the social order. This was to be accomplished by a balanced focus on individual salvation and a deep social concern.

Bederman argues that the social gospel movement appropriated this Forward Movement as a means of popularizing its message.[12] Sidney Mead concurs when he writes that this was the popular peak of social Christianity in America. He goes on to quote C. Howard Hopkins, who, according to Mead, "describes it as 'the most comprehensive evangelistic

7. Ibid., 157. Wilson has a brief discussion of this movement in "Baptists and Business," 225–26.

8. For a fuller exploration of this Movement, see Putney, *Muscular Christianity*, and Allen, *Rise Up, O Men of God*.

9. Bederman, "Women Have Had Charge," 438.

10. Ibid., 441.

11. Ibid., 432.

12. Ibid., 448.

effort ever undertaken in the U.S.,'" and he adds, "it was 'virtually converted . . . into a social campaign.'" Rauschenbusch had concluded in 1912 that "the movement has probably done more than any other single agency to lodge the social gospel in the common mind of the Church."[13]

Bederman also argues that in the long run the social gospel was co-opted as "advocates of masculinization appropriated the Social Gospel to the services of defeminizing the church."[14] Once men found their place in the church through the projects of the social gospel they turned out to be more concerned with "masculinization, than about social justice."[15] Yet, these movements did mark a shift of focus from the individual to the collective, from an understanding of Christianity as primarily a quest for personal salvation to an additional concern, that of caring for the poor and broken in an industrial society.[16]

Forward movements continued into the mid-twentieth century and occurred in many of the emerging churches. For example, in 1932, there was an "All-India Forward Movement in Evangelism" sponsored by India's National Council of Churches. In Canada the last significant Forward Movement was launched in 1945, the "Crusade for Christ and His Kingdom" in which the Baptist Convention of Ontario and Quebec also participated.[17]

The years prior to the First World War had been years of great optimism and challenge for Canadian Baptists. There had been a number of decades of growing centripetal impulses pulling together the various dissonant factions. Over the last dozen years of the nineteenth century, the Baptist Convention of Ontario and Quebec had been formed, along with McMaster University. As well, the Toronto Bible Training Institute (later Toronto Bible College) was begun in Walmer Road Baptist Church to train laity. In 1900, the first All Canada Baptist Congress was held in Winnipeg, carrying with it dreams of a national organization. At this Congress the cornerstone was laid for Brandon College. In 1907, the Baptist Convention of Western Canada was formed, followed by the Canadian Baptist Foreign Mission Board in 1911. Those years had also

13. Mead, *Lively Experiment*, 182.

14. Bederman, "Women Have Had Charge," 448.

15. Ibid., 445.

16. Salzman, *Reform and Revolution*, 108.

17. For a discussion of this 1945 Forward Movement and its impact on Canadian Baptist life and faith, see Gillespie, "Recovery."

witnessed significant numbers of baptisms, for Baptists the greatest sign of God's work. Finally, a theological storm around a professor at McMaster University had passed, and many seemed satisfied with the final resolution.

These powerful centripetal forces were all at play within the context of the great challenges facing the nation. Cities were growing, urbanization and industrialization were transforming Canada, and rapid immigration was reshaping the country as the north European Protestants of English Canada found themselves sharing their cities with growing numbers of new arrivals from the non-Protestant parts of Europe. The outbreak of the War brought a halt to much of this growth. But the great sense of optimism, along with an awareness of growing problems within the nation, was not forgotten as the nation ground through those trying years. S. J. Moore, who chaired the Toronto Baptist Forward Movement, wrote, "Many during the tragic years of the war looked forward eagerly and prayerfully to a time of spiritual revival which they hoped would come to the church . . . after the war madness had passed."[18] War was a time of testing and preparation.

As the First World War dragged on, it led to the reshaping of religious categories and language. This was as true for Baptists as for everyone else. As Duff Crerar writes, "the war offered both the chaplains and the men a chance to experience self-sacrifice."[19] The language expressing this became a vehicle for shaping expectations of sacrifice for those at home as well. A new vocabulary emerged, born in the trenches, and it made the church, including Baptists, used to the calls to sacrifice wealth and sons on the altar of nationhood in order to preserve a godly society.

As the war ended and the men returned home from the front, there was tremendous optimism. Stories of large scale conversions among the troops had been reported by both the field chaplains and the YMCA. Crerar reminds us of the power of the experience of the front on those who were there: "Padres had, after all, encountered admirable soldiers whose qualities of self-sacrifice and dedication to the cause were an inspiration to them."[20] The padres then took these stories and retold them at home with powerful effect. The assumption was that these men, newly recommitted to their faith, had learned how to sacrifice for God,

---

18. Moore, "What Is the Forward Movement?"
19. Crerar, *Padres in No Man's Land*, 230.
20. Ibid., 231.

King, and country, and that this willingness to put everything on the line would carry over into religious life back home. This led to a widespread belief that with this attitude of sacrifice, all of the problems that had been growing before the war could be encountered and overcome. The Forward Movement was born of that assumption and was its resulting vision.

Drawing on these themes of sacrifice, the unifying effect of the war,[21] and the momentum of the Men and Religion Forward Movement, the Inter-Church World Movement in the United States was launched in December of 1918. Richard Allen draws attention to the optimism that was a part of the church across the continent:

> In 1919 there emerged on the North American scene a church movement with broad vistas and high ambitions for the fulfilling of the social and world responsibilities of the church. To this end it planned to link the energies and programs of some thirty churches. The first project of this Inter-Church World Movement in the United States was to raise $1,300,000,000 over five years."[22]

There was a deep concern for Christian unity and reform that needed expression. The first step to realizing its goals was to raise $300 million. Charles Harvey develops the roots of this movement in his article on its primary benefactor, John D. Rockefeller, Jr.:

> The Movement itself had been conceived by officers of the foreign mission boards of the major Protestant denominations as a cooperative fund-raising campaign to meet the providential opportunities of the postwar era. It reflected the complex impulses of the Progressive period and the synthesis of evangelical and social gospel enthusiasm that was such a vital element of Progressivism. It climaxed in a series of forward movements to expand church involvement in the emergent industrial-urban society.[23]

This movement, chaired by John R. Mott, worked similarly to the Men and Religion Forward Movement, using a central organization to coordinate the movement and develop shared materials and promotion for each of the participating denominations. It tried to use the spirit of sacrifice and the call of duty that had been developed and worked so

21. Marsden, *Understanding Fundamentalism*, 53.

22. Allen, *The Social Passion*, 137.

23. Harvey, "Rockefeller," 199.

effectively during the war as a motivating force for reform. In the end, it failed to raise this money. Harvey points to disillusionment with "crusading social reformism" combined with the growing theological controversies as the cause.[24] George Marsden agrees with the latter point, seeing a resurgent conservatism as the key factor: "By the summer of 1920 the Interchurch World Movement was in shambles. Conservative opposition brought about a fate much like that of the League of Nations . . ."[25]

In Canada a similar movement began to simultaneously take shape. Richard Allen writes:

> The Inter-church Forward Movement, as it was called in Canada, was born in the winter of 1917–18 and formally established on 6 March 1918 under the guidance of a Central Committee of Forty, representing the Methodists, Presbyterian, Anglican, Baptist, and Congregational churches, and the Missionary Education movement.[26]

While the American movement would have influenced the Canadians, this was a completely separate movement. As Allen points out, in scale it was unprecedented: "The campaign was the greatest single example of church co-operation to date, and in its scale could be matched by few, if any, other combinations of Canadian voluntary organizations."[27] The earlier Laymen's Missionary Movement had involved leaders from a similar range of denominations, but now the denominations themselves were participating.

In these decisive early stages Canadian Baptists were very engaged. The goal of working together as the Protestant church in Canada was one that they affirmed. T. T. Shields, in his Forward Movement sermon, commented on this longing among Baptists: "Much has been said in recent years about 'union' and 'cooperation' and Baptists are not indifferent to these discussions."[28] The concern for "social evangelism" was also embraced. Social evangelism was not, however, some clearly defined program. Rather, it worked at bringing together the twin themes

---

24. Ibid.
25. Marsden, *Understanding Fundamentalism*, 54.
26. Allen, *The Social Passion*, 138.
27. Ibid.
28. Shields, *Plot That Failed*, 183.

of social service and traditional evangelism.[29] There was a shared belief that by bringing these two themes together the church would be able to relevantly engage its world and draw back many who had become disillusioned by what they deemed to be irrelevant theological debates.[30]

THE HOPES OF 1919

Baptist discussion of the proposed Forward Movement and its implications had to be delayed. The influenza outbreak in the fall of 1918 pushed the regularly scheduled October Convention Assembly to January of 1919 and with it any decision regarding Baptist participation.

The new post-war era broke in for Baptist with 1918 and the election of Joseph N. Shenstone as President of the Baptist Convention for that year.[31] He had a broad vision that led to Baptists considering participation in a variety of ventures, most notable the Forward Movement. For Baptists, this idea of larger involvement was tentative at best, and only the credibility of Shenstone and a small group of established older leaders allowed it even to be discussed.[32]

Shenstone's personal integrity and spirituality shaped his tenure. He not only fulfilled his term, but also left his mark on the Convention. Most importantly, his call for what were well-attended days of prayer and fasting leading up to the Assembly created an impression among the constituency that the Convention was in the hands of godly people. As a result, there was a markedly spiritual tone at that Assembly and a number of significant things were proposed and passed. Key leaders believed

29. Baswick, "Social Evangelism," 305.

30. Christie and Gauvreau, *Full-Orbed Christianity*, 4–11.

31. Joseph Shenstone was one of the most powerful men in the Baptist Convention. The brother-in-law of Elmore Harris, he sat on the Boards of the Toronto Bible College, the YMCA, the Laymen's Missionary Movement, and a variety of faith missions, as well as serving as President of the denomination. He was also President of Massey Harris and on the boards of a wide range of business and service organizations. His business acumen combined with his deep spirituality made him a man of great influence.

32. Shenstone had also been involved in the ecumenical Laymen's Missionary Movement. At its 1909 Congress he gave an address entitled, "The Stewardship of Business Talents and Possessions." Other Central Canadian Baptists involved in this Congress were S. J. Moore, who served as Chairman of the Congress Executive; James Ryrie; Thomas Urquhart, a former mayor of Toronto who spoke on "The Best Methods of Missionary Finance"; and John MacNeill, who gave the closing address.

that they were in a moment of crisis. The Convention sat poised. Would it be able to realize its potential?

Shenstone's presidential address was entitled "Christian Nationality." In it he called for Baptist involvement in the Forward Movement and for an engagement of its larger vision of the role of the church in the national arena. But the title also was a play on words. This was significant, for while he was calling on the church to begin to shape national agendas, one begins to see here the unique themes that were essential to the Baptist vision. He argued, "If the political world is to be ruled by democracy then it is evident that the ecclesiastical world must sooner or later adopt the same principle of government. There may be a bitter and prolonged struggle before this comes to pass . . . Yes, the church must be made safe for democracy."[33] For Baptists there was a conviction that democracy was a part of God's ultimate order for all of society and in this the state had much to teach the church. Not only was the state to be reshaped, but also mainstream Protestantism. So, while his vision was more ecumenical, it also highlighted the uniqueness of Baptist beliefs.

Shenstone did not stop there. In pleading for Baptist participation in the Forward Movement he also drew on war metaphors. Darryl Baswick points to the patriotic and nationalistic language of the movement, and argues that it used the war metaphor to prepare the church for the challenges ahead.[34] Shenstone models this as he challenged Baptists to see the Forward Movement as a spiritual extension of the war, now being fought on the home front. Clear attempts were made to build on a spirit of self-sacrifice engendered by the war effort. There was a need for a deep-seated change in the nation, which could only be achieved by voluntary enlistment and sacrifice. In particular, the strongest, noblest, and best educated were needed to enlist in order to instruct everyone in their duty. The goal was to develop a sense of mission in which the distinctions between home and foreign missions were broken down. This would require stewardship of time, talent, and personality. There was already the ability to do this, Shenstone argued, because the Laymen's Missionary Movement had put a model in place.

The power of this metaphor was seen a year later when S. J. Moore, in the first issue of the Baptist *Forward Movement News*, wrote, "Many

33. Shenstone, "Presidential Address: Christian Nationality," *Canadian Baptist*, 16 January 1919, 2.

34. Baswick, "Social Evangelism," 306.

of those who were profoundly stirred by the sacrifice made by the nation's best manhood, believed that this example must of necessity find its
counterpart in a period in which heroic spiritual service would be rendered by those who were followers of the Prince of Peace."[35] The proper
response to honor those who died would be to give a thank offering for
peace. The Forward Movement could be that. O. C. S. Wallace pointed
out that the war necessitated a special effort because the war had created
new conditions. Forces of sin and worldliness, of unbelief and wicked-
ness, had been released in the trenches.[36]

The most significant decision of the January 1919 Assembly was
to take the step and launch a Forward Movement. A Committee was
struck to plan the events. The motion's preamble captures the concerns
and dreams:

> Believing that the present world situation, presenting as it does,
> not only serious problems, but also unparalleled opportunities,
> constitutes an urgent call to all Christian people for a higher stan-
> dard of Christian lives than is generally practiced, and greatly en-
> larged Christian effort and sacrifice for the saving of men and the
> extension of the Kingdom of God. Therefore, be it resolved . . .[37]

While this pre-amble was very general and made liberal use of traditional Baptist language with no attempt made to enlarge definitions,
particularly around understandings of the Kingdom, this was not unusual. As Baswick points out, social evangelism was not a "concrete plan
of action or strictly defined practical means of achieving this . . . Rather,
it was an idealized vision of what the churches should be stressing in all
aspects of their work . . ."[38] As a result, each denominational community
was able to tailor-make it to their context.

The Committee was given two basic objectives that the Assembly
wanted to achieve; to make the fundamental truths of the gospel applicable to every aspect of life, and to impress on people the implications
for stewardship. To realize these there were eight specific goals spelled
out.[39] These eight were:

35. Moore, "What Is the Forward Movement?"

36. O. C. S. Wallace, "The Forward Movement's Something New, Additional,
Special, Over and Above," *Movement News* 1, 14 January 1920.

37. *Canadian Baptist*, 30 January 1919, 3.

38. Baswick, "Social Evangelism," 305.

39. These are listed and explained in the *Baptist Yearbook for Ontario and Quebec*

1. To institute family worship in every Baptist home

2. To stimulate the people to daily Bible study

3. To win converts through personal testimony

4. To improve the work of the Sunday Schools to make sure young people caught the Christian vision

5. To identify in the churches thirty gifted young people for pastoral and mission work and two hundred recruits for the schools

6. To encourage the reading of Christian literature, especially the *Canadian Baptist* and other denominational magazines

7. To battle sin and vice in the community and see the law of Christ worked out corporately

8. To place support of missions on a war basis and raise the funds needed to meet the unprecedented challenges of society

These goals represented an acceptance of the larger challenge of the Forward Movement. While the first six were cast in the framework of a traditional Baptist definition of renewal, the seventh and eighth goals included the larger agendas of social evangelism and a commitment to engaging public life. The language here is very similar to that of the larger movement. The question was, could the Baptist constituency accept this?

Richard Allen argues that the social gospel was central to the Baptist goals:

> Baptists were urged by Dr. F. W. Patterson of Winnipeg to recognize their complicity in social guilt, and were driven, according to W. J. MacKay, editor of the *Canadian Baptist*, to better appreciate the possibilities of life, to include in their sphere of interest all the world of God's concern, and to see the vision of the Kingdom of God come on earth.[40]

He goes on to say that readers must overlook the language of concern over personal sin and see a primary preoccupation with the "issues of industry, class, nationalism, race."[41] While recognizing that there were

---

and Western Canada, 1918, 32–33. See also *Canadian Baptist*, 23 January 1919, 3.

40. Allen, *The Social Passion*, 138.

41. Ibid., 139.

dissonant voices, Allen places the weight of the opposition around immi-gration and concerns over race when he writes, "Jingoistic Baptist pub-licity spoke alarmingly of 'enemies of righteousness' and the withering of 'fair flowers of virtue.'"[42] This picture reflects the views of many Western and Eastern Baptists. The Convention Baptists, however, were less at ease with this larger agenda than their sister denominations. George Rawlyk has argued persuasively that Convention Baptists reached their high point in a social gospel vision with the 1913 twenty-one point plat-form of the Social Service Committee.[43] This platform was much more radical than the constituency, and after the War the social radicals were clearly on the defensive.[44] The Forward Movement reflected this reality.

A vigorous debate followed in which an amendment was added confessing the coldness and indifference of the Baptist churches. Shenstone spoke to a deep concern that the movement must be first and foremost about the spiritual life, not money. Finally, a committee of five was struck to arrange the work, consisting of three from Walmer Road Church (Pastor John MacNeill, Jones H. Farmer, who was a deacon and Dean of Theology at McMaster, and Joseph Shenstone) and two from Jarvis Street Church (businessmen James Ryrie and S. J. Moore). The *Canadian Baptist* on 6 February 1919 carried a call to action in a front page article signed by all five. It closed with the words; "Brethren of the Churches! This is the 'tide in the affairs' of our Baptist denomination. Let us prepare to take it 'at the flood.' 'Speak unto the children of Israel that they may go forward.'"[45] There was every indication that a groundswell was beginning.

While the Assembly had decided to join in the launching of a Forward Movement, there were still unresolved concerns in the con-stituency. To allay these concerns, a group led by Shenstone success-fully argued that a prior time of prayer and consecration was necessary. Preparations for the Forward Movement began with a Convention-wide Prayer Conference, which was to be held from February 24 to 26 at the Jarvis Street church. This was to be followed, from March 2 to 9, by a time in every local church dedicated to "special humiliation and prayer, thanksgiving and consecration, with a view to a more perfect fulfilment

42. Ibid.
43. Rawlyk, "Champions of the Oppressed," 109.
44. Ibid., 111.
45. Quoted in Shields, *Plot That Failed*, 94.

. . . of that vow of death to self and life to God to which they pledged themselves in their conversion and baptismal confession."[46]

It was this call to pray that led various Baptist leaders to consider lending their support to a Forward Movement. In the two decades prior to the war there had been a variety of forward movements, and now the proposal to renew this strategy was viewed with scepticism by many. The views of O. C. S. Wallace were an example of such reticence:

> The phrase "Forward Movement" had come to sound unpleasant in my ears. Various "forward movements" have been undertaken in recent days which, from the standpoint of spiritual devotion to Christ, were mere oscillations, some little agitation occurred, but when things grew normal again it was found that we thought was "movement" was only "motion." Other "forward movements" have been concerned with raising unusual sums of money, or "challenging the attention of the world" with something spectacular in method or extraordinary in numbers. I know that I have not been alone in my recoil . . .[47]

There was a feeling that prayer might safeguard the movement from the urge to be spectacular or novel.

T. T. Shields opened up the Jarvis Street church for this conference. Leslie Tarr writes of the meeting:

> A Convention-wide prayer conference was convened for February 24 to February 26. The response was electrifying. Nearly seven hundred delegates registered and hundreds of others joined them to tax the seating capacity of the Jarvis Street Church. Morning, afternoon and evening witnessed a great volume of prayers, and there was every indication of a "grass roots" longing among Baptists for a revival.[48]

The leaders were elated by this evidence and went into the local church meetings with tremendous optimism. John MacNeill of Walmer Road Church gave the closing address at the Jarvis Street conference:

> [He] expressed the conviction that the Lord is ready to use any denomination that . . . will put itself in His hands to do with a whole heart the real will of God. We are reminded of the fact that in Moody's earlier life someone had said in his hearing that

46. *Baptist Yearbook for Ontario and Quebec and Western Canada, 1918*, 32.

47. *Canadian Baptist*, 13 February 1919, 4.

48. Tarr, *Shields*, 65.

> it remained to be seen what the Lord could do with one man who was wholly surrendered to His will. Moody registered a vow that, with God's help, he would be that man, and the results we all know.[49]

This challenge bore the desired fruit. Revival services following the Prayer Conference were judged a success, and everyone seemed optimistic heading into the Ottawa Convention that October. The Walmer Road Church minutes reflected the Convention's optimism as they looked back on this sequence of events. These minutes emphasized that the Assembly

> was remarkable for the deep spiritual tone culminating in the last day so markedly that it was decided to call a special Spiritual Conference for the last week in February. Much of the special power of that Convention was due to our own Deacon J. N. Shenstone, who was its President. The Special Conference was almost unique in the history of denominations in Canada, and its influence was poured into the Associations in June and carried over into the Ottawa Convention last October . . .[50]

Everywhere they looked, the signs of a great work of God among Baptists and in Canada seemed to be in evidence.

Yet the issues were not resolved. Baptists had initially been interested in the larger Forward Movement and, while entering late, had begun the process of putting things in place. When it seemed that the timelines were not going to work for them due to internal issues, the Baptist Advisory Committee asked the National Interchurch Executive to postpone the United National Campaign. This was rejected and the Baptists then withdrew from the planning in April 1919. What the internal issues were was never stated. But, it is likely that there were Baptists who saw Forward Movements as being first and foremost about money and activity, not spirituality.

The ecumenical element of the movement was also generating misgivings. This is clearly seen in that T. T. Shields, in his official Forward Movement sermon, addressed an ongoing question around the Baptist participation: "The question arises, therefore, whether we, as Baptists, have any special aptitude for the spiritual interpretation of life. While other Christian bodies discuss the possibilities of various forms or or-

---

49. *Canadian Baptist,* 20 February 1919, 2.

50. WRM, 14 January 1920.

ganic union, have we still any logical reason for standing apart from such discussions?"[51] This sermon is significant in that it both developed this theme and was preached at every large Convention Baptist Forward Movement gathering. The deep-seated belief that Baptists had a unique gift to offer the church was seen as threatened. Consequently, Shields, on behalf of the Baptist Movement, preached on Baptist core beliefs in rallies that were part of a movement characterized by a larger concern for Christian unity.

There are also other signs of a stepping back from a larger social evangelism agenda. This was evident in how Baptists responded to the Winnipeg General Strike, May-June 1919. There is very little evidence of any support for the strikers within the Baptist Convention. While there were sympathy strikes in Brandon, Vancouver, Calgary, Edmonton, Regina, Saskatoon, and Prince Albert, and related strikes in Toronto, Sydney, and Amherst, the Baptist response was best captured by the *Canadian Baptist*. It never once even mentioned the strike. If anything, this would suggest a move toward more traditional understandings of how the world was to be engaged.

Baptists did later chose to re-enter the movement in the fall of 1919 with a separate but almost simultaneous campaign. The reason was not that they were happy with the way things were working out, but rather that their Foreign Missions Board was in desperate need of money,[52] and they believed that if they did not enter the campaign at this time they would miss a vital fund-raising window. The fund-raising effectiveness of the Forward Movement for missions was well known. A shift in emphasis was occurring; it would be funding the missions agenda that would now drive the Baptist Forward Movement.

The centrality of the missions agenda can be seen in the financial goals and allocations. They set out to raise $300,000, an average of $5 each from the 60,000 members. Of this, the Foreign Missions Board was to receive $110,000, the Home Missions $60,000, Western Missions $10,000, the Grande Ligne Mission $40,000, the Christian Education Board $60,000, the Sunday School Board $10,000, and the Pastor's Superannuation Fund $10,000. This breakdown of the funding reflects the agendas at play: the priorities were missions and education.

51. Shields, *Plot That Failed*, 170.

52. "Report of Ottawa Convention," *Canadian Baptist,* 6 November 1919, 8.

The conversations leading up to the 1919 Convention in Ottawa were colored, not by a discussion of the possibilities that lay ahead, but by T. T. Shields's letter attacking a *Canadian Baptist* editorial of 2 October 1919, which he believed questioned inerrancy. Shields continued his attack and call for an official response and censure of the magazine by the Assembly. Shields's letter of 16 October 1919 linked orthodoxy with the discussion of the Forward Movement.

> We are talking of a "Forward Movement." Forward whither? And to what? Is it to be in the direction to which your editorial points? . . . If the only principle for which Baptists now stand is the much-vaunted "liberty" to doubt everything and to be sure of nothing—except that those who believe the Bible to be the inspired and authoritative Word of God are "partially educated" and not to be classed with other "intelligent Christian people," it is a principle which few will sacrifice to "forward."[53]

While the issue around the editorial was resolved, it left questions of confidence in leadership for some. It also meant that the actual launch of the Forward Movement was undertaken in the context of an affirmation of traditional doctrine, not new visions of church and Kingdom.

Despite these clouds, as the Convention met for its annual Assembly in Ottawa, 22–28 October 1919, there were signs of optimism everywhere. Ironically, while people in attendance at the Assembly saw it as an affirmation and celebration of unity, it would be remembered in history as the beginning of the fracturing of the Convention. It was at this Assembly that Shields's motion regarding the article in the *Canadian Baptist* was debated.

The highlight for those attending was the election of John MacNeill as President of the BCOQ and the unanimous approval of the report on the Forward Movement. When the Forward Movement was launched at the Ottawa Assembly, the Convention immediately set up a two-tiered structure of leadership. The Executive Committee was composed of Albert Matthews as Chair, John MacNeill as Chair of Spiritual Aims, O. C. S. Wallace as Chair of the Editorial Committee, Fred Ratcliff as Treasurer, J. R. Webb, Charles H. Schutt, and Joseph Wright. They then approached MacNeill to serve as overall President of the Forward Movement.

53. *Canadian Baptist*, 16 October 1919, 4.

MacNeill immediately requested that T. T. Shields join him.[54] These two would essentially be the Spiritual Aims Committee and the public face of the movement. Both were released by their churches for this and spent considerable time together. This was costly for their congregations, and the Walmer Road deacons later recorded the price the church paid:

> That hope of the Church was not disappointed, though it means to us immediate and serious loss in congregations, collections and otherwise. The Pastor has been leading the Movement with great energy and success, and we are confident in some way God will make up to us the loss we have incurred for His kingdom's sake.[55]

Jarvis Street made an even greater sacrifice, also releasing its second pastor, B. W. Merrill, to serve as the Secretary of the Executive. For MacNeill, the contributions Shields made were crucial. He wrote that it "was far reaching in practical guidance and inspiration."[56]

The coming together of the two most significant pastors in the Convention for a lengthy period of time was important. MacNeill and Shields were provided with this opportunity to get to know each other well. Prior to this they had been part of the same Association of churches, had worked together on a wide range of projects, and had been the public voice and face of Ontario Baptists. But they had always done it from their own narrow locations with their own local agendas. Now, out of a shared location, they had an opportunity to hear and understand each other's vision and passion for the gospel and for the church. There was an opportunity to work together and develop both a shared vision and a personal friendship.

THE FORWARD MOVEMENT

The BCOQ launched the Forward Movement in November 1919 as a part of a coordinated move by Canadian Protestants to refocus their mission, renew their churches and win the nation. By many standards the Forward Movement was a success as it worked itself out in the life

54. While the Forward Movement was a high point of Convention life, Tarr makes only a passing mention of it and of Shields's crucial role. See Tarr, *Shields*. Shields quickly downplayed the movement, so it was remarkably magnanimous of him to serve as an assistant to MacNeill in this way.

55. WRM, 14 January 1920.

56. *Baptist Yearbook for Ontario and Quebec and Western Canada, 1920*, 64.

of the churches. Yet, as Baswick points out, it was seen as only partially meeting its goals. The question around its success or failure lies in understanding the goals of the churches as they went into it. It is against these that it must be measured.

The Forward Movement held a two-fold emphasis for Convention Baptists: stimulating a deeper spiritual life, and raising a lot of money. This created tremendous internal tension, however, for what was really the most important? Published material left no doubt. The banner for the Forward Movement issue of the *Canadians Baptist* on 13 November 1919 read "Collecting a Great Sum of Money Is Not the First or Chief Aim of the Baptist Forward Movement." Rather, it was to be evangelism and a deeper sacrifice for service. John MacNeill opened the campaign with its kick-off sermon in Montreal.

> First, the movement forward has begun . . . there is a spirit of "readiness" abroad. Second, only great spiritual achievements will satisfy our people; a spirit of soul-dissatisfaction and heart yearning is manifest. Third, the financial objectives can be reached, and surpassed if . . . a spirit of "sacrifice" is evident.[57]

But, if these were the goals, how would they be measured? Here there was less clarity, although attempts to define success were made.

The Forward Movement had revised the original eight goals down to six prior to the actual launch. The six were,

> to yield ourselves in personal consecration to God to be holy men and women for His indwelling; to give ourselves with new faith to prevailing prayer as individuals, as families, and as churches; to devote ourselves to personal service, definitely linking our lives with some distinct task in the Kingdom; to acquaint ourselves more fully with the Word of God, the work of the denomination and the great movements of God in the world; to intensify our evangelism, seeking from God a commission to become His messenger in salvation to some soul; to maintain the standards of sacrificial giving which were set in the Forward Movement.[58]

How these six goals were understood can be seen best in the measurements of success they assigned to each. MacNeill spelled out the specifics.[59] The first of these had no measurable criteria developed. It was

57. *Canadian Baptist*, 27 November 1919, 3.

58 *Baptist Yearbook for Ontario and Quebec and Western Canada, 1920*, 66.

59. MacNeill spelled these out in an article entitled, "Progress of Our Spiritual Aims."

understood to be deeply personal, between God and the individual. The second, prevailing prayer, set up three measurements: 650 intercessors on a list, the distribution of 10,000 daily prayer cards, and 20,000 homes asking for and using Bible study and family worship materials. Their third goal, Christian instruction, sought for a 33.3 percent increase in Sunday School attendance and 1,200 new subscriptions to the *Canadian Baptist*. Goal four was personal service, measured by a 50 percent growth in the Baptist Young People's Union and a collection of names from pastors for potential ministerial candidates. Here one can see a dramatic step back from the larger social evangelism agenda of goals seven and eight in the earlier list. This new way to measure personal service now excluded almost all adults. Fifth, evangelism was left up to each family, which was asked to "seek a commission from God to become His messenger of salvation to some one soul." The final goal, sacrificial giving, was set out in very specific terms: $300,000, or $5 per member. They also recommended that each Association set up a group to stimulate the spiritual side of the movement. In these six goals there was a shift in emphasis from the earlier eight. All social evangelism themes were removed. The result was a very personal and less tangible movement. Any impact it would have would be felt primarily within the Baptist congregations.

The movement kicked off with meetings in Montreal on 16 and 17 November 1919. Shields described the strategy as a series of meetings or conferences held in a variety of centers. These were the central churches for each of the Associations within the BCOQ. In this manner they were able to address the membership of the Convention within the course of a month, with the exception of Northern Ontario, which he and MacNeill visited in January 1920.[60] The format was simple:

> It was agreed that the afternoon session of each conference with the churches be given to organization, and the evening session be given to two inspirational addresses, Dr. MacNeill concluding the session as President, with an address on "The Baptist Mission," and I preceded him with an address on "The Baptist Message."[61]

There is no text of the sermon preached by MacNeill, but Shields's "The Baptist Message" is preserved in *The Plot That Failed*. It was a

60. Shields, *Plot That Failed*, 162.
61. Ibid.

classic Baptist sermon focusing on the core historic Baptist emphases of Christology and Scripture.[62] While these themes were historically shared by all Christians, Shields argued that they played a particularly important role in defining Baptist faith. What is of particular importance regarding these sermons is that both focused on Baptist distinctives. A key goal of the Forward Movement had been to foster a deeper sense of Christian unity among the churches. These two sermons functioned almost as an apologetic for not being a formal part of the larger Forward Movement and for rejecting any part in the church union talks. Rather, support of the Baptist Forward Movement would make sure that these unique emphases that had been entrusted to the Baptist community would not be lost.

The Forward Movement had put together templates for the denominations to use in order to ensure a common and a comprehensive promotion. Baptists used this very selectively. In contrast to material developed by the Presbyterians and Methodists in particular, there was no national vision or meaningful call for social engagement.[63] There was also a common template developed for daily prayer. A comparison of the prayer material produced by the Baptists[64] and the Methodists[65] highlights the extent to which the Baptists had stepped back from the initial goals of the movement. For the Sunday prayer, Baptists asked people to pray for the Forward Movement in Canada and the United States while Methodists were asked to give thanks for the victory in the war, for the great heroism and self-sacrifice of the soldiers, and for a larger fellowship among Anglo-Saxon races and the success of the League of Nations. On Monday, Baptists and Methodists both offered prayers of consecration. Tuesday Baptists prayed for a sense of stewardship. Methodists did as well, but with an added call to sacrifice that the world would be conquered for Christ. On Wednesday, Baptists turned to prayers for a

62. Ibid., 169–84.

63. The *Forward Movement of the Presbyterian Church in Canada*, June 1919, No. 5, would be an example of the larger vision. It carried articles on social service work, on the growth of the nation and the challenges presented by this, on the challenges of non-Christian populations arriving in British Columbia, the church and social work, and overseas mission. Baptist material was all framed in traditional language of spiritual renewal, mission, and evangelism.

64. *Let us Pray.* Toronto: Baptist Forward Movement, Form No. 5.

65 *A Cycle of Prayer*, Methodist National Campaign/United National Campaign, Pamphlet No. 1.

revival of personal devotion and prayer life as well as for volunteers for missions and ministry. Methodists prayed a wide range of home missions prayers, including prayers for a blending of the diverse races and a united Dominion, for a reaching of the masses and caring for the poor and needy, rescuing the fallen, "that the united energy and influence of the church may be exerted to suppress all social evils, promote Christian brotherhood and establish ideals of the Kingdom" and "that aboriginal races be not allowed to fade away without the touch and sympathy of the Gospel of love." The very basic and personal prayers of the Baptist material carry on for the week. There was in this material a deliberate decision made not to use the resources of the larger movement, other than for an outline of themes. What had started in late 1918 and early 1919 as a broader call for a wide-ranging social and national engagement had become a narrow agenda about the personal concerns and boundaries of the Baptist community.

The culmination of this first stage of the movement was held at Massey Hall, Toronto, on 5 February 1920. After that the movement conducted a series of carefully staged actions. They began with a thorough canvas of the BCOQ's members and adherents. From February 15 to March 6 there was a twofold visitation; both a financial canvas and a survey of every church family to identify any unconverted. For the week of March 7–14 there was a time of consecration with special meetings for the Christians in every congregation. From the 14th to the 21st of March they committed to engage in two-by-two visitation of every unconverted person identified earlier and to call on all of the professing Christians not yet members. Finally, these were to be followed by classes for new converts and evangelistic meetings in the days from March 21 to Easter Sunday April 4, when it was anticipated that there would be concluding large scale baptisms.

Despite all of its momentum, reports of the movement slowly began to disappear from the pages of the *Canadian Baptist*. This fading out of sight began to occur just as the key elements of the movement were scheduled to take center stage. The last front page headline story regarding the Forward Movement was 1 March 1920. On March 18 the *Canadian Baptist* had dropped the reporting to a single item on page 5, "Over the Million." This was a reference to the total money raised in the Baptist communities across Canada. The next issue again had one entry, also on page 5, and then on April 1 it was totally absent.

While it was always stated that money was not the movement's real goal, every mention since February had been about money raised. The evangelistic push was to be in March, climaxing with the great baptismal service the first Sunday of April. Yet, there were no articles of encouragement and no material on how the evangelistic push might be maximized. At the end of March, B. W. Merrill wrote,

> The month of March is almost gone. April 4th will soon be here. What have our churches been doing with this program? What has been the success of their evangelistic campaigns? How many rejoicing believers will be baptized in Easter Sunday? Let us hear from you soon.[66]

There were, however, no letters forthcoming telling the larger community of conversions and outpourings of the Spirit in local churches. The *Canadian Baptist* carried no stories about Easter baptismal services. This, more than anything else, suggests that the movement did not realize what it set out as its key goal.

Financially the campaign was a great success. The Convention set $300,000 as its goal. That was quickly raised to $400,000. When the totals were in, the final tally reached $640,000.[67] As well, every Board in the Convention saw its regular receipts for the year rise.

They did not, however, submit any statistics in the Report for the spiritual results. Two reasons were listed.[68] First, "because it is impossible to make an accounting of souls as one makes an accounting of money," and second, "because spiritual efforts have no time limits, and the Divine accounting of the Forward Movement is not yet finished." What they did provide were general statements and anecdotal evidence. There was no doubt that a number of people had been converted, churches renewed, evangelism rediscovered in many churches, youth engaged, prayer increased, prospective missionaries and pastors recruited, and 1,500 subscribers added to the *Canadian Baptist*. The tone of the presentation, however, gives a clear impression that their goals were not reached. As a

---

66. *Canadian Baptist*, 25 March 1920, 5.

67. Baswick points out that the movement reached 125 percent of its financial goals. Baptists exceeded theirs by over 213 percent. See Baswick, "Social Evangelism," 308.

68. *Baptist Yearbook for Ontario and Quebec and Western Canada, 1920*, 65. Baswick states that the denominations reached "well less that 50% of their membership goals. They also failed in urging their members to play larger roles in the church" (Baswick, "Social Evangelism," 309).

result, people were called to celebrate the money raised and to ask God to continue the hidden work that had been begun.

Why did the results turn out this way? Baswick argues that finances were easier to promote, and the spiritual aspects failed "because social evangelism failed."[69] He explains that the theological issues were too obscure; the clergy had not taken ownership of the social evangelism and came to believe that social evangelism was emphasized at the expense of traditional evangelism.

There seems to be little doubt that the money was easier to promote. As well, most church members were already in the money-giving mode. They had made financial contributions to the war effort. This was a comfortable way to feel involved. The point about the failure of social evangelism does not, however, explain the Baptist situation. Rather, between January and November 1919 there had been a stepping back from the social evangelism agenda and a reinstatement of a highly personal and Baptist theology. The MacNeill/Shields message focused very much on traditional spiritual themes. While others may have pushed for a larger place for the social agenda, it was not coming from the leadership of the Forward Movement. The six goals they promoted were very traditional, as was the language used to describe them. It would seem that some other factors were also involved.

Walmer Road Baptist Church embraced and applied the Forward Movement very personally and traditionally. If their pastor was out calling on the churches "to rally to Christ's call in full surrender to His holy purpose," it was imperative that his vibrant, growing home congregation set the example. They saw a clear problem and expressed it in traditional terms, "we must at the same time make humble confession that we are unprofitable servants. There is much room for improvement. There has been all too much worldliness in our thinking; too much of confidence in the flesh; too little faith and love and far too little prayer and concern for souls."[70] They also saw very tangible temptations in the affluence of the world around them:

> Selfishness is abroad, filling the world with strife and suffering. Profiteering has been rife. There is a general tendency now that the war is over to revert to the old, easy-going, self-indulgent life of pleasure and ambition. That is the way to destruction. Only

69. Baswick, "Social Evangelism," 311.

70. WRM, 14 January 1920.

Christ can meet the world's need; only He can save. His work alone is sufficiently radical.[71]

These were not only personal temptations, but larger social evils to battle. Yet the deacons' call to the church was this:

> Our Baptist Forward Movement is on. Our Pastor is busy call-ing the churches of the Convention to rally to Christ's call to full surrender to His holy purposes. Shall we fail him here at home? For his sake let us rally as one man and resolve to rise to a higher plane of Christian life and service and stay there. Nay, for the sake of Christ, the Chief Shepherd, who laid down His life for us, shall we not renew our baptismal vow of death to the old order and life to God in the new, and so consecrate ourselves—body, soul and spirit—to carrying out His Great Commission?[72]

The Walmer Road response is significant, because it was the church with the largest and most fully-orbed social engagement. Its Memorial Institute was the largest single mission ever undertaken by a Canadian Baptist church and the themes of the social gospel were very much a part of that community.[73] Yet, when it spoke about its vision and interpreted the goals of the Forward Movement, it did so in deeply traditional terms.

While all of the goals had not been realized, the project itself was still seen as a great success with unfinished business. The success narra-tive quickly emerged as the results of the financial canvas became known. They saw these as confirming that the movement had been blessed by God, so it made sense to them to complete the unfinished aspects of the movement. As a result, a Forward Movement Continuation Committee was established.

This Forward Movement Continuation Committee was in reality to carry on the agenda of the Spiritual Aims Committee. We see this clearly spelled out in a strategy meeting of the Committee. Dean Farmer of McMaster and Shields formed a resolution expressing the conviction that

> the church is, above all else, a Society for the Evangelization of the world; that we commit ourselves to a special evangelistic campaign, with the objective not only of winning souls, but of greatly promoting the practice of constant evangelism; the de-

71. Ibid.

72. Ibid.

73. Goertz, *Century for the City*, 41, 42–46.

tails of such a campaign be left in the hands of the continuation committee.[74]

The Committee would have as its primary task to move the spiritual life emphasis to the Associational level, making sure that it was taken up by the pastors and individual churches.

After the 1920 Assembly, the Continuation Committee began to work in a more focused way. It set as its first priority a call to start the New Year with two weeks of prayer in conjunction with the larger Forward Movement. The prayer topics reflected general goals and were very broad,[75] and the response to this call to prayer was very positive. Continued prayer was the key because, as J. G. Brown summed things up, "The general revival that was anticipated would follow those meetings did not come, though here and there blessing was received. It is evident that even yet the denomination, as a whole, was not ready."[76] Yet, even as the Continuation Committee began its work there were signs beginning to emerge that the centripetal forces were losing their energy and powerful centrifugal forces were brewing.

RESULTS

As the BCOQ's year drew to a close with its 1920 Assembly, it was up to John MacNeill, the Convention and Forward Movement President, to provide an assessment of the year's efforts. His evaluation evoked images of Bunyan's great Baptist classic of the Christian life in his Presidential Address entitled, "The Pilgrim Spirit." Clearly, this was a journey requiring both thanksgiving and persistence.

> A year ago this Convention solemnly dedicated itself to this task. For the great blessing that has visited our churches we humbly and devoutly thank our God . . . Much of it lies beyond human reckoning, but this we can record—many precious souls were won to Christ, churches were quickened, hundreds of young people dedicated themselves to Christian service, the spirit of intercession was extended and intensified, Sunday School attendance greatly increased, Bible study was undertaken, home altars were set up, many prospective ministers and missionaries were recruited, 1,500 new subscriptions secured for "The Canadian

74. As quoted in Tarr, *Shields*, 74.

75. *Canadian Baptist*, 16 December 1920, 1.

76. *Canadian Baptist*, 23 December 1920, 4.

Baptist," and such a sacrificial response—gifts that the original financial objective was more than doubled. It was truly a great visitation from God and to him we render grateful thanks.

Much, however, as we rejoice in the efforts and results of the Forward Movement, we may very well pause to ask if in this Kingdom enterprise we have earned the proud distinction of pilgrims.[77]

While these were certainly the central goals in terms of the promotion of the movement, MacNeill did want to keep a larger vision and the unfinished business before the delegates. MacNeill at this point shifts the focus of the unease. Up to this point, the concern was over the lack of baptisms. MacNeill, while not a social gospel advocate, was the pastor of a city church in downtown Toronto, and prior to that, one in downtown Winnipeg. He saw the problems first hand and realized that solutions required a more comprehensive response. So he spelled out the larger vision he felt was necessary to merit the title "pilgrim."

> The Kingdom enterprise calls for a fuller acceptance of the responsibilities of Christian citizenship. A new world order is upon us. Human interests are more clearly seen to be social as well as individual. Whether we like it or not, Jesus had a gospel for society as well as the soul. We cannot escape our duties there. Community evils must be crushed, social wrongs righted, the public conscience quickened, national obligations expounded, and enforced in the light of the Kingdom of God. There is danger that an over emphasis of the sacred and central doctrine of individualism may blind us to the equally sacred duties in the life of society—duties that range from the welfare of the child in your street . . . to the League of Nations in the world.[78]

The tone of the speech was clearly that this particular goal had not been achieved. He had hoped to see a larger mobilization, but that had failed. Then the Forward Movement had narrowed down its goals, withdrawing from a larger public engagement and explicitly excluding goals of this nature. MacNeill had not publically opposed that decision, but when the Forward Movement was officially over, he brought out these larger themes of social evangelism and of a national and global vision and put these issues back on the agenda. MacNeill called Baptists in

---

77. *Canadian Baptist,* 28 October 1920, 2.
78. Ibid.

Canada to an awareness that they had influence, and yet they remained on the margins, convinced that they should be shut out of power. He wanted that to change, and he argued that Baptists needed to take their place on the larger national stage and become participants in the task of nation and city building. However, MacNeill was a lone voice, for his call was not officially heeded. The Continuation Committee that was subsequently formed reflected nothing of his vision.

Allen argues that the Forward Movement's understanding of society and the Kingdom were part of a growing movement. He concludes:

> Here was a revelation of the anxiety of the church leadership about growing wealth of the laity, an anxiety which had caused apprehension about the fruition of the social gospel. Now it seemed possible as a result of the Inter-Church campaign success to see in a new relationship between a socially conscious clergy and the well-to-do laity, a force, Chown claimed, "surpassing in influence for human results in business life anything that could be achieved by formal conferences between capital and labor." Whatever the minor accomplishments of the national Industrial Conference, the Inter-Church campaign had been a resounding success, not simply in raising money, but also, it seemed, in promoting a new social conscience among the business community and a new alliance for social progress in the church.[79]

Baswick challenges Allen's interpretation, arguing that social evangelism lacked any widespread appeal. As a result, while the Forward Movement drew in business leaders and was a success in raising money, "the failure of the spiritual aspect . . . showed that when they abandoned this type of (evangelical) message they risked losing their hold on the same people who made the financial campaign such a success."[80] MacNeill's reflection on the experience of Convention Baptists would also challenge the conclusion of Allen. There did not seem to be any new links emerging in the Baptist community between business and the social evangelism advocates. Shields, later reflecting back, saw the Forward Movement as a wasted moment. He drew on the Kadesh Barnea image, the spying out of the Promised Land, but emphasized that fear had overcome the community and it had not been able to complete its call to a spiritual renewal.[81]

---

79. Allen, *The Social Passion*, 140.

80. Baswick, "Social Evangelism," 315.

81. Shields linked the Ottawa Assembly and his challenge of the *Canadian Baptist*

The movement raised a considerable amount of money, and in that had been a significant success. As Allen points out, the Forward Movement as a whole in Canada raised 125 percent of its goal, $15,000,000.[82] The BCOQ had set out to raise $300,000 and was able to raise $640,000. This more than doubling of its goal allowed the missions it funded to continue. That would be particularly significant in establishing the work in Western Canada.

S. J. Moore, President of the Convention for the next year, stated that 1920 was to raise money. But now, in 1921, it was time to get serious about the most important things. "Many have felt that the spiritual ingathering has fallen far short of our expectations and even our faith, but the conviction is deepening that the promised blessings are only postponed in order that they may be more abundant."[83] Moore was speaking of this feeling that many had. But, measured against the goals set, how did they actually fare?

The Forward Movement had six goals. The first, personal consecration, they made no attempt either to define or to quantify as it was too personal. The second was to raise up intercessors, measured by a list of 650, the distribution of 10,000 daily prayer cards and 20,000 homes using resources for family worship. There is no record of this, although there must have been some numbers kept of material mailed. Rather, the record consists of only general statements as in MacNeill's "Pilgrim Spirit" speech, which refer to family altars being establish and many more praying. The third, fourth, and sixth goals do provide quantifiable criteria. Christian instruction would be a success if the Sunday Schools increased by a third and there were 1,200 new *Canadian Baptist* paid subscriptions. As the chart below indicates, the subscription numbers grew significantly and held their growth until 1927, when the Shields controversy led to significant cancellations. The Sunday School did not grow by a third, but it did begin a steady period of growth that continued right through to the split. Personal service was defined by a 50 percent growth in the Baptist Young People's Union (BYPU) and a collection of names of potential ministerial candidates.

---

editorial with the Forward Movement. Together they formed a perfect opportunity for the Convention to take a stand and reform itself. See Shields, *Plot That Failed*, 149–63.

82. Allen, *The Social Passion*, 140.

83. *Canadian Baptist*, 13 January 1921, 1.

Statistical Chart of Categories Defined as Markers of Success[84]

Year	1918	1919	1920	1921	1922	1923	1924	1925	1926	1927
Canadian Baptist Subscribers (paid)	6,271	6,727	8,343	8,090	7,893	7,581	8,120	8,500	8,350	No stats: controversy
Sunday School Scholars (enrolled)	49,577	47,032	45,909	48,756	49,494	51,147	50,956	53,895	55,317	56,004
B Y P U (total)	4,505	5,311	6,921	8,110	8,874	8,572	10,207	11,386	12,375	12,698
Baptisms	2,646	1,934	2,267	2,578	3,149	2,634	2,843	3,333	3,658	2,871
Churches	513	515	507	492	489	489	495	502	506	504

84. Statistics based on Board Reports, *Baptist Year Book for Ontario and Quebec and Western Canada.*

This is significant precisely because it speaks only of the youth. The BYPU grew dramatically, more than doubling by 1924. The list of potential ministerial candidates was gathered, but never made public, so there is no way to see how many actually followed through and entered ministry. Money, the sixth goal, was their big success. $300,000 turned into $640,000. While there are no specific goals given for evangelism, the way Baptists have historically measured this is by baptisms. Here we notice that there was a significant upturn. It was slow and steady, but by 1924 was up just over 36% and it continued to grow right to 1927 when it was up over 89% above the 1919 total. The emphasis of the Forward Movement's social service element was the recruiting of youth, and in this it was quite successful. The dramatic growth of the Young People's Union accounted for the growth in baptisms, for typically most baptisms in a Baptist church at this time were coming from the BYPU.

Central Canadian Baptists ultimately entered the Forward Movement when they did because they saw a desperate need to raise money for foreign missions. In that they succeeded. But there was also a larger context of foreign missions that was not seen on the home front. In 1920 the foreign mission boards of the Baptists, Congregationalists, Methodists, and Presbyterians, along with the Canadian Council of the Missionary Education Movement, joined forces to produce *Canada's Share in World Tasks*. It was edited by a Baptist, H. C. Priest. A number of those involved also had ties into the new faith missions. In the book's forward Priest wrote:

> The Forward Movement marked a new era in Canadian Church life . . . The magnificent response revealed the readiness of the people to do large things for the Kingdom of God . . . "Canada's Share in World Tasks" is sent forth not simply as a summary of the share that our country has taken in the foreign mission enterprise, but as challenge, in view of the appalling need, the compelling opportunities and the large resources with which God has entrusted to us, that Canada may do her full share in establishing His dominion in the earth.[85]

A study of the Canadian Baptist Foreign Mission Board reveals strong growth over subsequent years. New schools were opened in India, and by 1930 the India mission had ninety Canadian missionaries along with 1,200 paid Indian leaders. The Bolivia work was smaller, but

85. Priest, *Canada's Share*, ix, xi.

also was able to open new schools and build a number of new church buildings.[86]

When measured against the goals set prior to the Forward Movement's launch, one can see that a significant number of them were met. However, those without quantifiable criteria were difficult to evaluate and that difficulty led to a sense of disquiet. Nevertheless, while there was an impression that things were not as they should be, the statistics indicate that the movement actually did fare very well over time. Had it not been for the growing theological controversy, it may well have been remembered as a wide-ranging success.

CONCLUSION

The Forward Movement of 1919–20 was possible because of its timing. The existing leadership was well established, trusted, active, and engaged. They were able to draw the Convention into this larger movement because of the trust they had earned. Walmer Road, the Convention's undisputed cathedral church, was the location of many of the key older leaders in the Convention. They were, however, aging. Health would force McCrimmon out of the McMaster Chancellor's chair in 1922, Joseph Gilmour would die very unexpectedly in 1924, as would Farmer in 1928. Professor Campbell retired amid a storm of protests from Shields in 1926. He was seventy-eight.[87] By the later part of the 1920s, MacNeill's healthy was also fragile. While he, along with Shields, was to be a part of the next generation who would take over the Convention, he would die prematurely.

A young, new generation of leaders arrived in this period and stepped into the vacuum. H. P. Whidden, the new Chancellor, arrived in 1923. In 1925 both L. H. Marshall and Nathaniel Parker arrived to teach in the Faculty of Theology. These three men became a part of Walmer Road's mother church, Bloor St. Church, which moved up to St. Clair and Yonge in 1927, becoming Yorkminster Baptist. This church, led by William Cameron, was to be the new home of the Toronto Baptist elite. It made no attempt to hide its desire to be the Baptist cathedral, taking

86. Daniel, *Moving with the Times*. Chapter 8, "Further Developments," covers this period.

87. *Gospel Witness*, 4 November 1926, 39. This is the "Ichabod" issue. A key argument of Shields was that the 76-year-old Campbell and the 77-year-old Keirstead were forcibly retired.

for its design the plan of Yorkminster Cathedral in England. Its location, between the exclusive Forest Hill and Rosedale communities, positioned it to fill that role. While this new group of leaders clearly identified themselves with the Baptist financial elites, they had not yet earned the trust of the community.[88] The events of the 1920s would be dramatically influenced by this evolution within Baptist leadership.

The Forward Movement was the last significant event organized and led by the older leaders. It brought together MacNeill and Shields and opened the possibility of a friendship and new alliance of the bridge generation, but that was not to be. For thirty years Central Canadian Baptists had been in a slow process of building structures and institutions that united them, but a new series of centripetal forces was about to be unleashed that would ultimately split the Convention.

In 1921, Jarvis Street Baptist Church underwent a serious internal battle and ultimately a split. The issue was around Christians and amusements. There was a call by Shields for Jarvis Street members to refrain from any activities that compromised holiness, in particular worldly amusements. Things such as theatre attendance were cited. This set off a storm of controversy within the church, which also turned Shields into a larger media sensation. Tarr, writing on this, says that Shields was simply acting on a Forward Movement resolution.

> When the Executive Committee of the Forward Movement had previously met in Toronto, there had been the same expressed concern. The meeting passed a resolution stating that one of the greatest hindrances to the spiritual progress of the churches was the participation of church members in worldly amusements. The resolution proceeded to call upon the Committee to draw the problem to the attention of the churches.[89]

According to Tarr, Shields maintained that he was simply the only one with the courage to act on this resolution and its call to be living out the first of the Forward Movement's goals.

A theological storm was clearly shaping up at the 1922 Convention held at Walmer Road. Jarvis Street had been the scene of a power struggle in 1921 in which Shields only barely managed to hold onto power.[90]

88. For a discussion of this leadership shift, see Rawlyk, "McCrimmon, Whidden, Shields."

89. Tarr, *Shields*, 77.

90 The battle ended in the fall of 1921, when 350 of the more affluent Jarvis Street members left to form what would become Park Road Baptist Church. The story of this

Charles Johnston observed, "It was to Walmer Road and its pastor, John MacNeill, that some evicted members of the Jarvis Street church who could not tolerate Shields's personality or his theology had transferred their loyalty."[91] Others founded the new Park Road Church, which was immediately recognized by the Convention. These moves illustrated the two emerging camps within the Baptist Convention. Any possibilities of moving forward together were now gone.

Looking at the Forward Movement of 1919–1920 one can only reflect on what might have been. It is relatively easy to look at the goals that were set and to reflect on the degree to which they were realized. This is not an insignificant question. Certainly the speed at which the leadership distanced themselves from the movement is a clear indication that they were ambivalent regarding its record. The Forward Movement was concerned with developing deeper unity across denominational lines and uniting the Protestant denominations in a mission that would renew the church and transform the nation. For Central Canadian Baptists, the call to join this movement was one that tempted them sorely. They had been in a long process of coming together and growing in influence on the national scene. The social evangelism promoted by sister denominations and strongly present among Baptists in the United States and in both eastern and western Canada had a strong appeal. However, while they came to the point of initial commitment, they could not follow through. There was still a belief that Baptists had a unique role to play. Their mission was to see both the nation and the other Protestant denominations changed. Ultimately the uniqueness of their message was not one they could compromise.

While the Baptists were very concerned to see a revival in their churches, they were not able to imagine it in a way that was not in the traditional crisis-conversion model. It was only by the transformation of individuals that larger change could occur. As a result, their prayers focused on personal consecration and the raising up of pastors and missionaries.

---

struggle from Shields's perspective was recounted in the book *The Plot That Failed*, written in 1937.

91. Johnston, *McMaster University*, 172. While Northway transferred to Walmer Road, most of the Jarvis Street opponents of Shields opted to start their own church. It became Park Road church, which later, after a fire destroyed their building, merged with Yorkminster Church to become the current Yorkminster Park Baptist Church.

As the Forward Movement came to a close, there was a feeling of unparalleled success and abject failure. The blessing seen in the raising of the money encouraged them to see God at work and to hope for something more in the future. And it was precisely in these areas of mission and evangelism that they would see great future results. They entered the movement to provide funds for the overseas work and that work grew dramatically over the decade of the 1920s. They prayed for evangelistic success and while the great Easter celebration they had hoped for did not materialize they did see significant increases in numbers of baptisms over the next six years.

Within this larger context was this smaller but very significant side story, the lost opportunity for a relationship between John MacNeill and T. T. Shields. The Forward Movement was one of those rare moments when a community finds its older leaders, well respected and trusted, coming together in a project with the next generation who are in the process of taking over the reins of power. John MacNeill and T. T. Shields were the most important of this next generation. The failure of these two men to use this opportunity to forge an understanding that involved mutual respect and trust would cost Canadian Baptists dearly. Instead of working together to build on the foundations laid in the three decades prior to the war, they set in motion a centrifugal force that would spiral out of control. It untimely stole all of their creative energy and strength. What might have been used to energize the Convention was rather turned to managing a split and its aftermath. There is a profound sense of irony in the Forward Movement. What was to have been the impetus for a great move forward in mission and Christian unity turned out to be the beginning of a breakup within the denomination.

BIBLIOGRAPHY

Allen, L. Dean. *Rise Up, O Men of God: The "Men and Religion Forward Movement" and the "Promise Keepers."* Macon, GA: Mercer University Press, 2002.

Allen, Richard. *The Social Passion: Religion and Social Reform in Canada 1914–28.* Toronto: University of Toronto Press, 1973.

Baptist Yearbook [1918, 1921] for Ontario and Quebec and Western Canada. Toronto: Standard Publishing Co.

Baswick, Darryl. "Social Evangelism, the Canadian Churches, and the Forward Movement, 1919–1920." *Ontario History* 89 (1969) 301–19.

Bederman, Gail. "'The Women Have Had Charge of the Church Work Long Enough': The Men and Religion Forward Movement of 1911–1912 and the Masculinization of Middle-Class Protestantism." *American Quarterly* 41, no. 3 (1989) 432–65.

Brown, William Adams. *The Church in America: A Study of the Present Condition and Future Prospect of American Protestantism.* Whitefish, MT: Kessinger, 2007.

The Canadian Baptist, 1919.

Christie, Nancy, and Gauvreau, Michael. *A Full-Orbed Christianity.* Montreal and Kingston: McGill-Queen's University Press, 1996.

Crerar, Duff. *Padres in No Man's Land. Canadian Chaplains and the Great War.* Montreal and Kingston: McGill-Queen's University Press, 1995.

A Cycle of Prayer. Methodist National Campaign/United National Campaign, Pamphlet No. 1. CBA. Forward Movement Folder 1.

Daniel, Orville E. *Moving with the Times.* Toronto: Canadian Baptist Overseas Mission Board, 1973.

Dawson, David G. "Funding Mission in the Early Twentieth Century." *International Bulletin of Missionary Research* 24, no. 4 (2000) 155–58.

Forward Movement of the Presbyterian Church in Canada, June 1919, No. 5. CBA. Forward Movement Folder 1.

Gillespie, William. "The Recovery of Ontario's Baptist Tradition." In *Memory and Hope: Strands of Canadian Baptist History,* edited by David T. Priestley, 25–37. Waterloo: Wilfrid Laurier University Press, 1996.

Goertz, Donald. *A Century for the City: Walmer Road Baptist Church, 1889–1989.* Toronto: Walmer Road Baptist Church, 1989.

Harvey, Charles E. "John D. Rockefeller, Jr., and the Interchurch World Movement of 1919–1920: A Different Angle on the Ecumenical Movement." *Church History* 51, no. 2 (1982) 199–209.

Johnston, Charles Murray. *McMaster University.* Vol. 1, *The Toronto Years.* Toronto: University of Toronto Press, 1976.

Let Us Pray. Toronto: Baptist Forward Movement, Form No. 5. CBA. Forward Movement Folder 1.

Marsden, George M. *Understanding Fundamentalism and Evangelicalism.* Grand Rapids: Eerdmans, 1991.

Mead, Sidney E. *The Lively Experiment: The Shaping of Christianity in America.* New York: Harper & Row, 1963.

Moore, S. J. "What Is the Forward Movement?" *Forward Movement News* 1, 14 January 1920, 1.

Priest, H. C., ed. *Canada's Share in World Tasks.* Toronto: Canadian Council of the Missionary Education Movement, 1920.

Putney, Clifford. *Muscular Christianity: Manhood and Sports in Protestant America, 1880-1920*. Cambridge, MA: Harvard University Press, 2001.

Rawlyk, George A. "A. L. McCrimmon, H. P. Whidden, T. T. Shields, Christian Higher Education, and McMaster University." In *Canadian Baptists and Christian Higher Education*, edited by G. A. Rawlyk, 31–62. Montreal and Kingston: McGill-Queen's University Press, 1988.

———. "The Champions of the Oppressed? Canadian Baptist and Social, Political and Economic Realities." In *Church and Canadian Culture*, edited by Robert E. VanderVennen, 105–23.New York: University Press of America, 1991.

Salzman, Neil V. *Reform and Revolution: The Life and Times of Raymond Robins*. Kent, OH: Kent State University Press, 1991.

Shenstone, Joseph N. "The Stewardship of Business Talents and Possessions." In *Canada's Missionary Congress*, 139–43. Toronto: Canadian Council, Laymen's Missionary Movement, 1909.

Shields, T. T. *The Plot That Failed*. Toronto: Gospel Witness, 1937.

Tarr, Leslie. *Shields of Canada*. Grand Rapids: Baker, 1967.

Urquhart, Thomas. "The Best Methods of Missionary Finance." *Canada's Missionary Congress*, 201–6. Toronto: Canadian Council, Laymen's Missionary Movement, 1909.

Wallace, O. C. S. "The Forward Movement's Something New, Additional, Special, Over and Above." *Movement News* 1, 14 January 1920.

WRM = Walmer Road Baptist Church Minutes, 14 January 1920. CBA.

Wilson, Paul R. "Baptists and Business: Central Canadian Baptists and the Secularization of the Businessmen at Toronto's Jarvis Street Baptist Church, 1848–1921." PhD dissertation, University of Western Ontario, 1996.

Watson Kirkconnell
An early Baptist prophet of multiculturalism.
Used by permission of the Acadia University Archives.

10

For Whose Kingdom?

Central Canadian Baptists, Watson Kirkconnell, and the Evangelization of Immigrants, 1880–1939

Robert R. Smale

L ESS THAN A CENTURY ago, Canadians confronted what some charged was an influx of a "hungry, poverty-stricken, skin-clad population of wild-eyed Asiastics and Eastern Europeans" who posed a serious threat to the nation. In 1929 one commentator remarked,

> The admission of any race that cannot blend satisfactorily is a menace, and may become an increasing menace both socially and politically in the future. Race problems in Canada are sufficiently serious at the present without increasing them unnecessarily.[1]

Another commentator decreed "Few national issues have given rise to so many different shades of opinion as has immigration."[2] Many Canadians of the day saw the continued influx of "foreign hordes" as a serious threat to their political, social, and economic institutions and way of life. They charged that the foreign peril—the colored races—would "submerge the white races just as the dusky sons of the Arabian deserts and the savage hordes of Tartary submerged the Roman Empire."[3] The effect of the growing preponderance of foreign groups within society was feared,

---

1. Carrothers, "Immigration Problem in Canada," 521.
2. Hurd, "Quota," 147.
3. Sir Donald Mann, as cited in ibid.

343

therefore, not only because it would lead to a mixing of the races, which for some was "biological suicide," but also because these foreign groups failed in other respects to measure up to the basic stock of the country. In advocating a case for a restrictive immigration policy, W. Burton Hurd, in a 1929 article published in *Queen's Quarterly*, remarked, "Clearly, then, the Southeastern and Central Europeans as a class are our least desirable immigrants, not only from the stand point of intermarriage and educational status, but from that of obedience to the laws of our land."[4] Thus, many Canadians of the period had strong opinions on who should be admitted to Canada. How much were these opinions shared and shaped by the nation's churches?

The Protestant churches of the nation also entered this debate on immigration policy. The presence of large numbers of "undesirable immigrants," the vast majority non-Protestant, in the nation's urban centers left many progressive clergy uneasy. At first the churches sought to head off this influx by opposing immigration and upholding the virtue of rural life. When this response failed, the churches set out energetically to establish their presence within the mushrooming immigrant communities by sending missionaries to convert the newcomers. Beyond evangelism, every attempt was made to convince new immigrants to adopt the virtues of "solid Canadian ways."[5] Like the majority of "native" Canadians, church clergy believed that if immigrants were going to be admitted to Canada, the country's welfare depended upon the rapid assimilation of immigrants, especially those non-Protestant "foreigners" from southern and eastern Europe.

Often such attitudes and concerns surrounding this nationalist vision are linked with conservative religious forces. Certainly T. T. Shields, the fundamentalist Baptist leader, "subscribed to the powerful idea of 'His Dominion'"[6] as did other conservative Protestant (and Baptist) leaders. Yet, progressives were also among the chief proponents of assimilation. Caught up in the enthusiasm of the social gospel, these progressive Protestant churchmen and women also combined xenophobic social fears and anti-Catholic bigotry in their efforts to proselytize in the cities. Since the majority of immigrants found their way to the cities, evangelizing them often became linked to the "new evangelism"

4. Hurd, "Quota," 156. See also Angus, "Underprivileged Canadians," 455–56.

5. Slater, *Religion and Culture in Canada*, 17.

6. Wright, "Canadian Protestant Tradition," 151.

of the social gospellers and their efforts to serve society.[7] Conservative evangelicals may have stressed personal salvation, while liberal evangelicals emphasized the redemption of society at large, but both parties agreed that Canada ought to be fashioned into "God's Dominion"— a Protestant Christian and preferably British nation from sea to sea.[8] As N. K. Clifford notes,

> The inner dynamic of Protestantism in Canada during the first two thirds of the century following Confederation was provided by a vision of the nation as "His Dominion." This Canadian version of the Kingdom of God had significant nationalistic and millennial overtones, and sufficient symbolic power to provide the basis for the formation of a broad Protestant consensus and coalition . . . The vision of Canada as "His Dominion" implied a homogeneous population which shared a heritage of political democracy and evangelical Protestant Christianity.[9]

In their determination to ensure that Canada became "His Dominion" from "sea to sea," many Protestant church leaders, guided by a sense of national righteousness, set out to engage this social phenomena, which they saw as a threat not only to the denominational and national strength of the nation, but also to the deep-seated rural values they held so dear.[10] As John Stark, President of the Baptist Convention of Ontario and Quebec, warned delegates in 1900, "All that is choicest and best in our national life is trembling in the balance."[11]

However, while the initial reaction of the churches to what they regarded as a threat to the religious and civil order was one of concern and alarm, it also became apparent that such changes afforded new opportunities for service in establishing the Kingdom of God from sea to sea. In this regard, the vision of His Dominion provided Protestant church leadership with both an ideological and theological framework from which to launch a campaign of moral and spiritual activism against

7. Airhart, "Ordering a Nation," 130.

8. Wright, "Canadian Protestant Tradition," 151.

9. Clifford, "Vision," 24.

10. They also saw the need to address two other social phenomena of this period: urbanism and industrialism.

11. *Baptist Yearbook*, *1900*, 47. Stark served as President from 1899 to 1900. He was also a member of McMaster University's Board of Governors until 1904, the Church Edifice Office until 1908, and served as President and Treasurer of the Home Mission Society.

these threats that seemed poised to undermine the best of Canadian identity. As N. K. Clifford maintains, "The Protestant reaction to these newcomers reveals how the vision of Canada as 'His Dominion' helped not only to define the threat of immigration, but also to direct their response into a crusade to Canadianize immigrants by Christianizing them into conformity with the ideal and standards of Canadian white Anglo-Saxon Protestants."[12]

All of the major Protestant denominations in this period exhibited similar nativist reactions to those immigrant groups whom they judged to be a threat to their vision of Canada as His Dominion. While some extremists advocated exclusion of these groups, and a radical fringe pressed for massive deportation, especially after the First World War, the majority of Protestants were confident of their ability to make these new-comers embrace the values and standards of Anglo-Saxon Protestantism. For many of these Protestants, being Canadian and Protestant were one and the same. To them it seemed impossible that one could be a "real" Canadian and not be Protestant (French Canada aside). This inevitably led to a home mission crusade designed to Canadianize the immigrants by Christianizing them. The churches, therefore, felt that it was their God-given duty to implant Canadian ideals of citizenship. One Baptist spokesperson believed that the "'Open Bible' approach would prepare people for citizenship by weaning them away from the superstition and extravagant rites that characterized many Old World religions."[13] In this regard, "Canadianism" became a favorite term in Protestant circles, "imply[ing] both a loyalty to British institutions and conformity to Victorian moral standards."[14] Thus, in their efforts to both evangelize and Canadianize, which were really one and the same objective, Protestant church leaders believed they were acting in the best interests of the na-tion and the immigrant population.

To date, the most noteworthy critical studies of Baptist work amongst immigrants are essentially introductory in nature. They consist of Jarold K. Zeman's introductory essay "They Speak in Other Tongues: Witness amongst Immigrants," David T. Priestley's essay "The Effect of Baptist 'Home Mission' among Alberta German Immigrants," and a chapter in J. B. Scott's dissertation on "Responding to the Social

---

12. Clifford, "Vision," 24.

13. See Petroff, "Macedonians," 30.

14. Grant, *Church*, 96.

Crisis: The Baptist Union of Western Canada and Social Christianity 1908–1922."[15] Thus, a critical analysis of Canadian Baptist responses to immigration policy in the years from the1880 to 1939 is most definitely warranted. It is a theme too long neglected in the annuals of the history of Christianity in Canada and one that must be undertaken in order to comprehend fully how Protestant churches in this period, and Baptists in particular, responded to major social changes, in part brought on by mass immigration.

Invariably, the response and action of the church leaders during this period were linked to a broader issue of national identity "an issue with which Canadian religious communities have had to wrestle ever since the colonies of British North America showed promise of developing into a nation or nations."[16] John W. Grant noted, however, that when Stewart Wallace wrote his pioneer work, *The Growth of Canadian National Feeling*, he did not find it necessary to outline the contribution of churches to the nation-building debate. Nor, for that matter, did others who followed his work.[17] Consequently, the contribution of the churches to the development of a distinctively Canadian awareness and the cultivation of a specifically Canadian consciousness has generally been viewed as "somewhat peripheral to the interests of the churches."[18] However, "[i]f the churches have occupied themselves only fitfully with the quest for a Canadian *identity*, they have been deeply engaged from the beginning in an attempt to create a Canadian *character*. Their interest has been less in the existence of Canada than in its essence, their concern not so much *that* Canada should be as *what* it should be."[19] As one Baptist publication of the era noted:

> [O]n our Baptist churches in Canada rests a challenging responsibility for the building of the Canadian character. Baptist churches are Christian democracies, and, in the opinion of many, the nearest approach to Christian democracies which are possible. Christian democracies alone can lead the world to its highest and best efforts. Our responsibility, then, as Canadian Baptist

15. My own doctoral thesis sought to fill in the gaps to this historical record, cf. Smale, "For Whose Kingdom? Canadian Baptists and the Evangelization of Immigrants."

16. Grant, "Religion," 8.

17. Ibid.

18. Ibid.

19. Ibid., 8–9.

churches, for our own Canada, for Canada as part of the Empire,
and for Canada as part of the world, is as clear as daylight. If we
are as true to our responsibility as our predecessors have been,
we shall not fail.[20]

As such, the missionary impulse of Protestant church leaders at home
(as real as abroad)[21] was influential in the shaping of a Canadian character. The turn-of-the-century infatuation of Protestant church leaders
with the manifest destiny of the Anglo-Saxon people led inevitably to a
crusade for the Christianization of national life in which all barriers to
the establishment of Christ's Kingdom in Canada had to be addressed.
As Jennie M. Pearce, a Canadian Baptist missionary remarked: "'*And
He shall have Dominion also from sea to sea and from the River unto
the ends of the earth.*' And then Canada shall have fulfilled her 'manifest
destiny.'"[22] Baptist churches, then, adopted a theology of tribalism that
equated their own conception of piety with patriotism.

Like other Protestant denominations, central Canadian Baptists
belonging to the Baptist Convention of Ontario and Quebec (BCOQ)
believed they had a unique calling, a role to play in shaping the nation
in these formative years into His Dominion. This vision expressed itself
in a determination to establish the Kingdom of God in the new country.
But the Baptist response was to some degree atypical of those of other
Protestants. The Baptist vision of Canada as His Dominion found practical expression in a unique set of Baptist missionary activities, reform
movements, voluntary societies, educational programs, and institutions.
In this manner, Canadian Baptists sought to socialize immigrants into
the mainstream of Canadian life to the extent they deemed possible. Only
by Christianizing the "foreign element" could they be Canadianized,
and thereby, the essence of an Anglo-Saxon Protestant Dominion would
not only be preserved but also expanded. As a result, throughout this
period Baptists expressed strong anti-Catholic sentiments bordering on
bigotry, since they believed the influx of large numbers of Catholic im-

20. Hardy, "Canada's Historical Background," 6.

21. For an analysis of Protestant foreign missions during this period that deals with
attitudes to immigrants, see Gagan, *Sensitive Independence*, 177–203. Presbyterians
began their mission work first overseas and only later turned their attention to home
mission, unlike the Methodists and the Anglicans. See Brouwer, *New Women*, 22–24;
Austin, *Saving China*.

22. Pearce, "Ontario West," 262.

migrants posed the greatest single threat to the preservation of Canada as an Anglo-Saxon Protestant Dominion. Thus, for most Baptists of the period, religion was deemed more important in assessing an immigrant's ability to be assimilated than the relation of that immigrant's ethnic origin to Anglo-Saxon culture.

This chapter will use five principle Baptist publications as the basis for its analysis: the *Baptist Yearbook*, the *Canadian Baptist*, the *Baptist Link and Visitor*, the *Gospel Witness*, and the *Western Baptist*.[23] These publications represent the collective published voice of central-Canadian Baptists, and they will be used to ascertain how Canadian Baptists responded to the vision of "His Dominion." The published works of Baptist Watson Kirkconnell (1895–1977) will also be examined. Primarily this chapter will focus attention on Baptist identity, history, theology, and mission, and it will be argued that these factors shaped Baptist responses to immigrants from 1880 to 1939. At a time when many contemporary Baptists are sympathetic, if not inclined to support, the agenda of the right on matters related to immigration policy, a critical analysis of the past may also provide insight into some of the hidden motives for contemporary responses and their underlying appeal.

Traditionally, Baptists had resisted Protestant monolithic uniformity as much as they resisted Catholic monolithic uniformity. However, in the years 1880 to 1939, that vision was blurred as Baptists, like other Protestants in Canada, sought to transform the nation into His Dominion. Their distinctive ecclesiology should have impinged directly upon the notion of fostering a uniform Canadian national identity. However, when combined with their identity as evangelicals, their anti-Catholic sentiments, their predominant post-millennial eschatology, "practical Christianity," and a loss of their own historical experience, Baptists strove instead with fervent zeal to create a monolithic culture—an Anglo-Saxon Protestant Canada.

Inspired by a sense of religious duty, millennialism, fear of Roman Catholicism, and a growing sense of national and civic duty, Baptists

---

23. The *Western Baptist* is used to a less significant degree in this study due to the chapter's focus on Baptists in Ontario and Quebec. It has nevertheless been consulted and cited at times because of the mission work carried out and sponsored by Baptists from Ontario and Quebec in the Northwest during this period. The publications of the United Baptist Convention of the Atlantic Provinces have generally not been consulted due to the relatively small numbers of immigrants who settled in this region during the period under review.

met the challenge of immigration with a range of attitudes and programs that sought to assimilate the "foreign element" in Canada or prevent its admission into the country altogether. Baptists were as much drawn into schemes of Christianization and Canadianization as their Protestant counterparts, seeking to mold the nation into His Dominion. This vision of Canada was shared by both liberal and fundamentalist Baptists and was only seriously questioned in the 1930s, when a Baptist intellectual, named Watson Kirkconnell, began to question the morality of assimilationist and protectionist policies, and in their stead extolled the virtues of ethnic pluralism. He was a father of multiculturalism in Canada.

THE FORMULATION OF "HIS" DOMINION: BAPTISTS AND THE EVANGELIZATION OF IMMIGRANTS, 1880–1914

The thirty-four years from 1880 to 1914 were a period of significant transformation for Canada. During these decades the nation underwent tremendous social, cultural, economic, and political change. To a large extent three phenomena were responsible for bringing about this transformation of Canadian society: immigration, industrialization, and urbanization. Their combined effect fostered the growth of a nation that was new in both quality and spirit. The new Canada that emerged from this period, while a product of its past, was in other ways fundamentally different. Consequently, these "years should be seen as a history of a people attempting to bring its institutions into conformity with the demands of a new, unfamiliar kind of society."[24]

Two government officials were largely responsible for shaping Canada's immigration policy during these critical years of national development. Clifford Sifton and Frank Oliver served as Sir Wilfrid Laurier's Ministers of the Interior from 1896 to 1911.[25] Between 1896 and 1914, some two and a half million immigrants came to Canada, largely from Britain, the United States, and continental Europe. Contrary to popular perception, not all of these immigrants settled in western Canada. In fact, many were attracted to the growing cities and towns of the east. Nevertheless, more than a million settled in the west during the peak

24. Brown and Cook, *Canada*, 2.

25. Sifton served as Minister of the Interior from 1896 until his resignation in 1905 following a bitter dispute over separate schools in the newly created provinces of Alberta and Saskatchewan. Oliver served as Minister of the Interior and Superintendent of Indian Affairs from 1905 until 1911.

years 1901–1911.[26] The chief planner and promoter of this policy was
Sifton. Sifton brought much-needed reform to the Immigration Branch
of the Ministry of the Interior, made efforts to free railroad lands and
Dominion lands for immediate settlement, and brought about improvements in transportation. His program also planned to settle the west
with farmers and farm laborers no matter what their ethnic or national
origin. In an article he wrote for *Maclean's* magazine in 1922, Sifton remarked, "I think a stalwart peasant in a sheepskin coat, born on the soil,
whose forefathers have been farmers for ten generations, with a stout
wife and half-dozen children, is good quality."[27] Thus, agriculturalists
from Britain along with those from Sifton's two new areas of recruitment, the USA and Central and Eastern Europe, were given priority over
all other types of immigrants.[28]

While Canada did receive a large number of good agricultural
settlers from Europe during this period, nearly "70 percent of the
newcomers obtained work in industry and transportation."[29] These predominately urban dwellers were the types of immigrants that Sifton's
policy was designed to discourage, fearing similar socio-economic problems in Canadian cities that such an immigration policy had brought to
American cities. Furthermore, Sifton had encountered much opposition
to his western settlement plan and made many enemies. Critics argued
that his immigration policy was non-selective and indiscriminate. He
was admitting "illiterate Slavs in overwhelming numbers," whom the
Anglophone conservative press deemed the scum of Europe—"physical
and moral degenerates not fit to be classed as white men."[30] His successor as Minister of the Interior, Frank Oliver, a westerner, attacked
Sifton's policy in this way: "there is nothing [the westerners] more earnestly resent than the idea of settling up the country with people who

26. Knowles, *Strangers at Our Gates*, 88–89.

27. Sifton, "The Immigrants Canada Wants," *Macleans*, 1 April 1922, 16, as cited in
Palmer, *Immigration*, 35. Sifton's main effort to attract and recruit farmers for Canada
was made south of the border in the USA. See Troper, *Only Farmers Need Apply*, 7–31.
Black settlers were, however, excluded from Sifton's American campaign. See ibid.,
121–45.

28. Avery, *Reluctant Hosts*, 23–42.

29. Knowles, *Strangers at Our Gates*, 103.

30. Lehr, "Peopling the Prairies with Ukrainians," 184; See also "Tower of Babel,"
Calgary Herald, "The Character of Our Immigration," 18 January 1899, as cited in
Palmer, *Immigration*, 44–45.

will drag on our civilisation and progress. We did not go out to that country simply to produce wheat. We went to build up a nation, a civilisation, a social system that we could enjoy, be proud of and transmit to our children; and we resent having the millstone of this Slav population hung around our necks in our efforts to build up, beautify and improve the country, and so improve the whole of Canada."[31] Clearly, in the eyes of western Canadians, though these immigrants might be excellent farmers, this did not qualify them as suitable. Only those settlers who could assimilate easily into the predominately Anglo-Saxon culture, and who posed no real threat to its values and institutions, were deemed acceptable to Canada.[32] Thus, Oliver embarked on forging a new immigration policy, producing two new acts in 1906 and 1910 designed to deny entry to Canada to those immigrants deemed "undesirable."[33] Clearly, for Oliver, the ethnic and cultural origins of prospective immigrants took precedence over their occupation. Assimilation into mainstream Anglo-Saxon society became the benchmark for "Oliver's hierarchy of settlers for the West."[34] Like Oliver, many of Canada's clergy also began to express concerns over the racial composition of the nation.[35] Canada's churches thus entered the debate on immigration policy.

The changes brought on by urbanization, industrialization, and immigration became a growing preoccupation for the country's churches. Sometimes, only vaguely aware of the nature of the transformation that was occurring around them, Canadian churches largely attempted to either minimize what they understood as the negative impact of these changes or retard their effects altogether.

The late nineteenth century found Protestantism in general, and Canadian Baptists in particular,[36] largely on the defensive. In the intel-

---

31. *House of Commons Debates* 54, 12 April 1901, 2939, as cited in Troper, *Only Farmers Need Apply*, 22.

32. See Lehr, "Peopling the Prairies with Ukrainians," for a discussion of opposition to Ukrainian settlers in western Canada. Doukhobors were the other major group in the West who were the subject of much hatred during these years. In British Columbia it was Asian immigrants who were largely subject to such hatred and discrimination. See Anderson, "Idea of Chinatown"; Gouter, *Guarding the Gates*, 35–86.

33. Knowles, *Strangers at Our Gates*, 105–26; Kelley and Trebilcock, *Making of the Mosaic*, 134–38; Gouter, *Guarding the Gates*, 11–87, 115–44.

34. Knowles, *Strangers at Our Gates*, 107.

35. For example, see Woodsworth, *Strangers within Our Gates*.

36. In 1881, there were 296,525 Baptists in Canada (6.9 percent of the population).

lectual arena, Darwinism had shaken the theological foundations of the faith by drawing into question the inerrancy of Scripture. The Roman Catholic Church seemed poised to expand its influence as its membership continued to increase. "In 1901, 2.2 million of Canada's population of just over 5.3 million were Catholic; a decade later, Catholics numbered 2.8 million, and in 1921, there were 3.4 million in a population of 8.8 million . . . it seemed only a matter of time before Canada would have a 'Papist' majority."[37] Furthermore, urbanization was becoming a more significant factor in Canadian life, but the urban proletariat seemed less amenable to church attendance or accepting of the Protestant message.[38]

These challenges were made more acute by the large numbers of immigrants who entered the country during this period. Increasingly, these immigrants came from vastly different religious traditions than evangelical Protestantism.[39] Consequently, if they were not openly hostile, these immigrants were, at the very least, largely distrustful of the hopes and dreams that groups such as Baptists had for immigrants. Clearly, visions of a homogeneous (Protestant) Christian civilization were seriously challenged. However, despite these challenges, optimism remained relatively high. Pastor A. A. Cameron's sermon to the annual Manitoba Missionary Convention in 1884 is reflective of this optimism:

In 1911, there were 382,666 Baptists in Canada (5.3 percent). See Airhart, "Ordering a Nation," 104. The experience of Maritime Baptists was quite different from that of central and western Baptists, for Nova Scotia and New Brunswick Baptists comprised one of the largest Protestant groups in the Maritimes.

37. See Bothwell and Granatstein, *Our Century*, 39–40.

38. The secularization thesis has recently been questioned by Michael Gauvreau, who argues that this approach strips the early twentieth century of "its historical distinctiveness." Gauvreau, *Evangelical Century*, 218–54; See also Christie and Gauvreau, *Full-Orbed Christianity.*

39. Canadians had listed their origin in the 1901 census as follows: British, 3 million; French, 1.6 million; other Europeans, 500,000; Asians 23,000; and Aboriginals, approximately 125,000. Ten years later the 1911 census noted: British, 4 million, French, 2 million, other Europeans, 1 million, Asians 43,000; and Aboriginals, 105,000. Many of these "other Europeans" tended to stay in Canada, while many American migrants returned home, and some British immigrants either left for the United States or returned to the United Kingdom. Furthermore, "[t]o the horror of many British-Canadian Protestants, large numbers of the newcomers were Roman Catholic, Ukrainian Orthodox, or Greek Orthodox. In 1901, 2.2 million of Canada's population of just over 5.3 million were Catholic; a decade later, Catholics numbered 2.8 million, and in 1921, there were 3.4 million in a population of 8.8 million . . . it seemed only a matter of time before Canada would have a 'Papist' majority." See Bothwell and Granatstein, *Our Century*, 39–40.

> Now, the question comes to us, is the church as much in earnest in making this country Christian, as the government in making it populous? We may rest assured there can be no true advancement of this country unless there be first aggressive evangelization . . . The text speaks of making disciples of all nations; but we need not go very far for them, as nearly all nations come to us. The Mennonites and Lutherans of Germany; the Jews of Russia, are here. They are here from China and Iceland; from Great Britain and the United States; as well as from all the Eastern Provinces of the Dominion. In our home work we shall soon have to provide for the foreign element. German Baptist Missionaries are needed even now. Oh! What a magnificent field is ours . . . We are called upon to make and baptize disciples while the foundations of the Empire are being laid.[40]

Thus, Canadian Baptists initially viewed the influx of immigrants as a magnificent opportunity to help shape the destiny and foundation of the nation. They viewed their arrival as a providential moving of God to hasten the goal of world evangelism and hence, the ushering in of the Millennium. Their attitudes and responses to the increasing "foreign element" during these years also reveal much about the way a culture acts to protect and preserve its values when it is (or is perceived to be) threatened. In many respects, the reactions of Canadian Baptists paralleled the fears of many others throughout the nation. In this context, their views perhaps reflect one way in which a native subculture seeks to meet the challenge of what it considers "foreign."

As part of the evangelical Protestant tradition, Canadian Baptists were committed to the propagation of the gospel of Jesus Christ. Their goal, therefore, was the reproduction of Christians—individuals in union with God by means of spiritual regeneration. Pursuant to this goal was the desire to establish Baptist churches, which were viewed as the closest bodies to the New Testament *ekklesiai*. Consequently, Baptists steadfastly remained committed to regenerate church membership and believer's baptism. However, such beliefs and convictions only partially explain the motives that undergirded Baptist efforts to proselytize immigrants.

Baptists also saw themselves as playing a decisive role in shaping the transformation of Canadian society that was occurring in these years. First of all, as heirs of the Protestant Reformation, Baptists were committed to the principle of *sola scriptura*. The Bible was to be the sole authority

---

40. *Baptist Yearbook, 1884*, 52–53.

in matters of faith and practice. But more than that, the Scriptures were to serve as an everyday guide book for life. Morals, values, and standards for living were to be based upon the teaching of Scripture. Second, Baptists adhered to the doctrine of the priesthood of all believers. This belief meant that they rejected the sacramental and mediatory role of the Catholic priesthood. Third, and perhaps most importantly, Baptists stressed the belief in religious liberty. Consequently, Baptists propagated the separation of church and state. This conviction was the key source of traditional antipathy to the Roman Catholic Church, as well as to the established churches of England and Scotland.[41] Baptist aversion to ritual also made them largely anti-Catholic by definition. Finally, Baptists were strongly committed to the principle of local church autonomy and democratic cooperation between churches. Consequently, one should not speak of a Baptist Church in Canada, but of a loose federation of Baptist churches. Their religious associations and conventions were formulated solely on a voluntary basis. Consequently, Baptist ecclesiology was democratic in nature, predicated on the principle of congregational rule. Baptists rejected more hierarchical forms of ecclesiology, regarding these as not only anti-democratic but also unscriptural. Notions of a Pope were anathema, since such an office presented a direct challenge not only to religious liberty in the church but also to the state. What Canadian Baptists sought, along with their evangelical counterparts, was the creation of a "sanctified nation"—one that was "moral, enlightened and dedicated to the principles of the Protestant Reformation."[42]

In their efforts to achieve these goals, Canadian Baptists did not exist or function in a kind of supra-cultural biblical vacuum. They were not isolated from an increasingly secular society. They were, in fact, a very real part of it. As such, they were forced to assume a dual identity, namely that of Canadians, and of evangelical Christians. At times the distinction between the two identities was blurred, given the fact that the majority of Baptists were native-born whites of British heritage. Canadian Baptists, therefore, were engulfed within a largely Anglo-Saxon Protestant community, which regarded itself as co-existent with, and having a proprietary right to, the nation's character and institutions.

---

41. See Torbet, *History of the Baptists*, 46–57.
42. Grant, *Church*, 76.

In terms of actual numbers, however, Baptists were the smallest of the four dominant Protestant denominations in Canada.[43]

As John Webster Grant pointed out, Canadian Protestant churches in those years embarked on large-scale missionary endeavors among immigrants with a clear view of what they wanted to achieve but no clear view of what it was possible to achieve. Grant notes that at least three motives were significant in this regard. The first, and perhaps the most powerful motive, was the simple recognition of the needs of these "strangers in a strange land." The second was the evangelical impulse to propagate the gospel amongst these "heathens." And the third impetus, which became significantly more important as the franchise was granted to increasing numbers of these immigrants, was a desire to implant Canadian ideals of citizenship.[44]

Such views of Canadian nationalism were not, however, exclusive to the Protestant community in Canada. Mark McGowan argues that English-speaking Catholics also "cultivated their own unique vision of Canada" that shared an affinity with that of their Protestant adversaries. English-speaking Catholics believed Canada was "destined to be English in speech but Catholic in faith." Armed with their own brand of "Canadianism," English-speaking Catholics proved just as zealous as Protestants in their efforts to evangelize and assimilate immigrants into Canadian society. As McGowan notes, these foreigners "were offered the Catholic faith and the English language as the prerequisites to solid citizenship." This attempt to assimilate immigrants in the final analysis, however, only succeeded in making English-speaking Catholics more "aware of their own identification with Canada, its institutions, opportunities and freedoms."[45]

While Protestant leaders regarded these aims as essentially complimentary, they found it increasingly difficult to keep them in balance. What is clearly evident here is that racial thought was part of the Canadian Protestant imagination. Groups that came to Canada who were deemed unfit, whether socially, racially, morally, politically, or

43. The four largest Protestant denominations were Methodist, Presbyterian, Anglican, and Baptist.

44. Grant, *Church*, 96.

45. McGowan, "Toronto's English-speaking Catholics." This work by English-speaking Catholics among immigrants further reinforced Baptists fears about the dangers of Catholicism for Canadian society and the urgency of their own missions with the immigrants entering Canada in those years.

religiously, could become "legitimate members" of the society only by assimilating "Canadian" ideals and values, which were indistinguishable from Protestant ideals and values. And all of this was tempered by racial fear of the non-Anglo-Saxon. In their immigrant assimilationist crusade Baptists,

> essentialized social and cultural differences and condemned certain groups as alien, foreign and unwanted. In this way, racial categories legitimized the social and cultural forms of native-born Protestants and defined other groups as illegitimate. Race was also an ideological medium through which power and dominance were played out. Racialism explained and justified social inequality and determined which immigrant groups' morals, social values, faiths and political traditions fit [Canadian] needs.[46]

These racial assumptions would dominate Baptist and Protestant ideology up until the Second World War, and would only begin to be seriously questioned with the emergence of Fascism in the 1930s.

Anglo-Saxonism, with its overt biological intimations, privileged direct descent from British lineage and was expressive of an indigenous nationalism. Furthermore, Anglo-Saxonism and loyalty to the British Empire were regarded as extensions of Canadian patriotism. As Carl Berger notes in *The Sense of Power: Studies in the Ideas of Canadian Imperialism*, "Canadian imperialism was one variety of Canadian nationalism—a type of awareness of nationality which rested upon a certain understanding of history, the national character, and the national mission." The sense of mission, Berger contends,

> grew out of [a] conception of the immanence of God in the world: history has not accidentally placed millions of the "weaker races" under the protection of the Empire, nor was the evolution toward a stronger union a fortuitous and fitful process. The main justification for imperial power was work directed toward the Christianization and civilization of these races. Such work would not only fulfil God's purposes, but would also burn away the selfishness and pride bred by power.[47]

---

46. Katerberg, "Protecting Christian Liberty," 9.

47. Berger, *Sense of Power*, 226–27, see also 9, 49, 230–32. For a discussion of how the imperialists saw "the strangers" impacting upon the national character of Canada, see ibid., 147–52.

The Empire was seen, therefore, as a "divine agency of progress and civilization" and the "attainment of a nation . . . contingent upon the acceptance of the white man's burden." Consequently, Canadians were largely proud of their country "precisely because of its British roots."[48]

In contrast, Canadianization implied a loyalty to British institutions that covered a much broader range of social, ideological, political, and religious concerns. This concept also included an enunciation of the pragmatic implications of racialism and nativism. The concept of nativism had developed in the United States, where it perhaps "took more virulent and violent forms than it did in Canada." The term describes the "amalgam of ethnic prejudice and nationalism." John Higham, in his study of nativism in the United States, defined it as "intense opposition to an internal minority on the ground of its foreign . . . connection." Higham noted that there were three strands of American nativism: Anglo-Saxon, anti-Catholic, and anti-radical.[49] Some Canadian historians feel that the term "nativism" is inapplicable to Canada given the very different historical development of Canada than the United States.[50] Howard Palmer, however, asserts that the term is "indeed a useful tool for Canadian historians . . . [and] while a comparison between Canadian and American nativism reveals some differences, it does show that the three strains of nativism (Anglo-Saxon, anti-Catholic, and anti-radical) identified by Higham had considerable influence in . . . Canada prior to World War II."[51] The Methodist W. H. Pike outlined the goals of Canadianization in 1919:

> The general notion "Canadianization" appears to denote the adoption of English speech, of Canadian clothes and manners, of the Canadian attitude of politics. It connotes the fusion of the

48. Katerberg, "Protecting Christian Liberty," 10. See also Heath, *War with a Silver Lining*, 3–20, 88–117, which outlines Canadian Protestants' enthusiastic support for Britain in the South African War of 1899–1902 and how it produced stronger ties to the Empire.

49. Higham, *Strangers*, 4.

50. For arguments against the use of the term nativism in a Canadian context, see Jaenen, "Unique Qualities." Katerberg has also strongly criticized the use of Higham's model by Canadian historians. See Katerberg, "Irony."

51. Palmer, *Patterns*, 8–9; Palmer, "Mosaic," 167–68. For discussion of the use of the concept of nativism in a Canadian context, see Ward, *White Canada*, ix–x, and Barber, "Nationalism." For a general discussion of Anglo-Saxonism and Christian theology, see Davies, *Infected Christianity*, chap. 4.

various bloods, and a transmutation by the miracle of assimilation of Poles, Russians, Ukrainians, Jews, Germans, and others
into beings similar in background, tradition, outlook, and spirit
to the Anglo-Saxon backbone of the country.[52]

Canadianization was a program whereby the immigrants were to be
transformed into not only reflecting, but also accentuating the values of
Anglo-Saxon culture.

The goals of Canadianization thus focused on acculturation and
assimilation. Canadianization programs, therefore, involved inculcating Canadian ideals—civic, social, political, and religious—as well as
preventing pockets of immigrants from forming. But Canadianization
was more than simply naturalization. Naturalization was a change in
legal status. Immigrants to Canada could become "naturalized" by applying for "naturalization" after a specific period in Canada free of legal
problems. Assimilation, in contrast, was a change in worldview. It involved adopting the culture and values of the host nation. Naturalization
was, therefore, not the same experience as assimilation. As Rev. John
A. Cormie, Superintendant of the Home Missions Board of the United
Church of Canada, remarked in 1931: "Every social problem in the
country is markedly influenced by immigration . . . naturalization does
not mean Canadianization. It merely signifies the intention of the immigrant to make a more or less permanent home in Canada and the
desire to share in the country's political destiny."[53] So long as southern,
eastern, and central European immigrants avoided assimilation, Cormie
and other like-minded Protestant clergy asserted that "a problem of serious magnitude will certainly emerge."[54] Canadianization schemes were,
therefore, driven by an urgency that aimed to create a culturally homog-
enous society as soon as possible.

Immigration also provided the churches with an opportunity to
exercise their overlapping duties to God and country. R. G. Welsh, writing in 1924 for the *Presbyterian Witness*, argued that "Christianity helps
to fit citizens for enfranchisement and the use of liberty. Further, the
type and method of community life in the Christian fellowship will help

52. W. H. Pike, "Slavic Stock," *Christian Guardian*, 3 December 1919, 11, as cited in
Katerberg, "Protecting Christian Liberty," 11.

53. Cormie, *Canada*, 14.

54. Ibid., 15.

guide the reconstruction of the civic and political order."[55] As William H. Katerberg remarks, "the work of the churches and the needs of the nation were twofold: democracy was the product of Christian nations and, to be a positive force, liberty required adherence to Christian morality."[56] Consequently, Protestant churches were emphatic on the need of immigrants to adapt to Canadian life, and Canadian life without Protestantism was hollow. Sometimes this attitude displayed itself in overtly racist attitudes towards particular immigrant groups, like Blacks, while on other occasions it "assumed the superiority of the Anglo-Saxon race, but allowed for acculturation."[57] In either case, it was obvious that Anglo-Canadians associated their British heritage with Protestant Christianity and democracy and that Canadianization schemes were at best permeated with "naive paternalism," or at worst "unvarnished bigotry," in which stereotypes and prejudices abounded.

During the early part of the nineteenth century, many of Canada's aboriginal peoples were subjected to a similar application of these ideals. Certainly this program of acculturation of Canada's Native Peoples, "pressed by the state not as mere expedience but as part of the moral responsibility of the British people,"[58] sounds strikingly similar in a variety of ways to the goals of "Canadianization" with respect to immigrants that W. H. Pike espoused approximately a century later. In both instances, the eradication of the cultural norms, values, and customs of undesired minorities was the stated objective. Given the racial overtones inherent in Protestant missions to both Canada's Native Peoples and immigrants, was the framework of Canadian Baptist responses to immigration in this period motivated by purely evangelistic goals? Was it diluted or even dominated by an impassioned Canadian nativism dedi-

55. Welsh, "Why I Believe in Missions," *Presbyterian Witness*, 24 February 1924, 7–8, as cited in Katerberg, "Protecting Christian Liberty," 13.

56. Katerberg, "Protecting Christian Liberty," 13.

57. Ibid., 12.

58. See Grant, *Moon*, 75–95. While "Europeanization" may have been the catch-phrase earlier in the century, the goals of this assimilation scheme were in many ways parallel to the "Canadianization" schemes towards immigrants in the latter half of the century. As John W. Grant notes, the Aboriginal peoples of Canada were forced, as a matter of survival, to become like Europeans. This meant learning to adapt to European customs, technology, economic patterns, manners, and dress. Missionaries and administrators, Grant maintains, provided the Aboriginal peoples with "all possible help" that was necessary "to cultivate the European values of sobriety, frugality, industry and enterprise" (p. 75).

cated to the preservation of Anglo-Saxon ideals and institutions? In order to answer these questions it is necessary to examine the evangelical aspect of Baptist identity and determine the role this played in shaping the attitudes and responses of Baptists to immigration.

As evangelicals, Canadian Baptists took seriously the command of Christ to make disciples (Matt 28:19). Their "loyalty to the truth" obligated Baptists to fulfill this mission, and they felt uniquely qualified to carry out this task. The following remarks, taken from the 1901 *Baptist Yearbook*, reflect the principles and policy that the denomination established in order to regulate its Home Mission work in this capacity:

> There are first of all the general and well recognized principles that constitute the bases of all Christian Mission work, whether home or foreign, viz.: The evil and lost condition of the human family; the possibility of the human family being saved from this evil and lost condition, and the belief that the gospel of the Lord Jesus Christ is the only agency for the accomplishment of this great salvation. (b) And secondly, [t]he special principles that must form the basis of Home Missions work.
>
> The first of these is the one the late Alexander Grant used to emphasize with great force, viz.: "Responsibility in life and work always increases with proximity." Hence our duty as Christians is to see to it that no part of our land shall remain either unsupplied or insufficiently supplied with the gospel in its purity and entirety. And the second is like unto the first, viz.: "Home Mission work is basi[c] work" . . . The simple fact that a very considerable proportion of the best workers in our self-supporting churches, and about two-thirds of all the pastors, are drawn from our Home Mission Churches, is sufficient proof of the basi[c] character of this work. Another basi[c] principle of Home Missions is that we believe our distinctive principles as a denomination to be of sufficient importance to justify us a separate existence and work in every community in which such work is a reasonable possibility. When this principle shall cease to be recognized and acted upon by any religious denomination, it is high time that such a denomination should withdraw from the field and cease by its existence to perpetuate schism in the body of Christ. Another principle is that we believe our denominational progress will depend largely upon our so planning and organizing and conducting our work, that every Baptist in our own country may have Baptist preaching and pastoral watchcare. We are strongly convinced that this last is a principle to which we, as a denomination, have not given sufficient attention, and because of our failure to act upon this

principle hundreds of Baptist families, and thousands of Baptists, have drifted beyond our reach, and the life and power which we so much need has been absorbed by wiser and more aggressive bodies of Christians.[59]

Officially, at least, the Home Missions policy of the BCOQ reflected a commitment to an evangelistic mandate coupled with the promotion of denominational distinctives like religious liberty. What ultimately needs to be ascertained is whether there was any substantial variance or departure from this policy in addressing the immigrant phenomenon during this period.

In one respect, 1901 must be regarded as a significant turning-point in Baptist responses to immigration. In the years from 1880 to 1901, the focus of Baptist Home Missions in Canada was primarily concerned with those of German and Scandinavian extraction, largely in Ontario and the Northwest, and French Catholics at the Grande Ligne Mission in Quebec. However, the years from 1901 to 1914 witnessed a gradual shift in emphasis away from what has sometimes been deemed "old immigration" to "new immigration"—namely, people of eastern and southern European descent, especially Slavs.[60]

J. K. Zeman attributes this change to the volume of nearly three million immigrants who entered Canada between 1901 and 1914.[61] Certainly the large number of immigrants presented the churches of the Convention with a monumental challenge, yet with challenge came opportunity. No simple numeric explanation is, of itself, adequate in trying to explain this sudden conceptual shift in focus. While three million immigrants entered Canada during these years, the greatest period of mass immigration in Canada's history, the majority still were people from traditional sources, like the British Isles, the United States, and northwestern Europe. Consequently, other factors must also have fostered this shift.

Rather than quantity, the origin of an increasing number of these immigrants was a critical factor. "Old immigrants," as has been noted,

59. *Baptist Yearbook, 1901*, 41–42. Much the same thought was echoed by the Canadian Baptist Women's Home Mission magazine in September of 1894. See *Baptist Visitor*, September 1894, 6.

60. Zeman, "They Speak in Other Tongues," 69, points out this shift in Baptist concern; cf. Petroff, *Sojourners*, 60.

61. Zeman, "They Speak in Other Tongues," 69.

consisted of people from British, American and northwestern European heritage, namely Germans and Scandinavians. As such, they shared many of the same beliefs, values, institutions, and practices that Baptists in Canada would endorse. Most were also Protestant of one type or another. Martin E. Marty has noted that part of the contrived racial theory of the day was the belief that Anglo-Saxon democracy was born in the forests of ancient Germany.[62] Germans were viewed as a cultured people who could easily fit into the mainstream of Canadian life. Alexander Grant, Baptist superintendent of Canadian Home Missions from 1884 until his tragic death in 1897, asserted that in Germans "we have no better class of colonists than they."[63] Grant further commented, "It may also be affirmed with confidence that Germans are as intelligent thorough-going Baptists, when they are Baptists, as can be found."[64] German willingness to become a part, not only of the civil, but also the (Baptist) religious life of the country, heightened their desirability as immigrants in the view of many Baptists.[65]

Baptists did not confine their "praise" solely to German immigrants during these years. Scandinavians, namely Swedes, Norwegians, Finns, and Danes, those "hardy Norseman," were also looked upon in highly favorable terms. In fact, they were regarded as "among the most valuable of immigrants when they turn toward our shores."[66] The positive endorsement of this group of people, whom many in Baptist circles regarded as the "best class of settlers," was predicated on the fact that they were regarded as being "peaceful," "law abiding," "frugal," and "industrious." Even their compatibility with regions of northern climate was viewed in a positive way by Baptists.[67]

Thus, rather than posing any direct threat or challenge to existing norms in Canadian society, these people were seen by Baptists as those

62. Marty, *Protestantism*, 129–30.

63. Goertz, "Alexander Grant."

64. *Baptist Yearbook, 1893*, 158; see also 154–58.

65. *Baptist Visitor*, May 1911, 6.

66. *Baptist Visitor*, September 1901, 4. For further discussion of this "ethnic pecking order," see Palmer, *Patterns*, 22–37.

67. *Baptist Visitor*, January 1912, 6. Yet at the same time these qualities were perceived to be simply the raw material for making these immigrants into good Canadian citizens, rather than worthy attributes in their own right. The perception of the foreigner as "primitive" and "benighted" still dominated Protestant thinking of the period. Enrico C. Cumbo notes that "the supremacy of the Anglo-Saxon and the spiritual superiority of Protestantism led many to patronize the foreigner." See Cumbo, "'Impediments,'" 162.

who could make a positive contribution to the development of the nation. The fact that most of them were Protestant, and many were even Baptist, only served to buttress these feelings and was probably the most significant factor in the formation of such attitudes among Baptists. Consequently, the general consensus within the BCOQ was "that of all immigrants coming to our country, there are none who give promise of making better citizens than do the Scandinavians. And to become a nation, such as God would have us to be, we must wreathe into our citizenship the laurels of christian grace."[68]

So long as immigrants were perceived to re-enforce existing social and religious norms, Baptists were largely content to confine their missionary activities to the propagation of the gospel in order "to exert an influence in advancing the Redeemer's Kingdom."[69] But not all Protestant groups shared the same degree of enthusiasm towards northern or western Europeans. Some asserted that even those immigrants from the "Nordic" race of Northern Europe needed to be Canadianized because, although very receptive to Anglo-Protestant ideals, on arrival in Canada they did not necessarily share the ideals and morals on which a democracy like Canada depended. As a result, all immigrants needed to be ranked according to how much they differed from the Anglo-Saxon ideal. Though American and northern European immigrants did not invariably present major problems when it came to Canadianization, those from other parts of Europe, and especially Asia, whose languages, cultures, and ideals were considered more radically distinct, required far more scrutiny.[70]

Increasingly after 1901, even Baptist attitudes and responses to ethnic diversity began to change. As one commentator remarked, "Christian civilization is at stake by the godless influences of these European and Asiatic peoples."[71] After 1901, Baptists who had regarded the possibilities for evangelism afforded by immigration as a wonderful opportunity now perceived immigration to be the greatest peril facing the nation.

68. *Baptist Visitor*, September 1901, 6.

69. *Baptist Yearbook, 1894*, 158.

70. Katerberg, "Protecting Christian Liberty," 11. Howard Palmer noted, "Public debate over Slavs focused on whether they should be allowed to enter Canada. But debate over blacks, Chinese, and Japanese focused on whether they should be allowed to come to Canada at all." See Palmer, *Patterns*, 32–37. For a discussion of Protestant clergy's response to Oriental immigrants, see Ward, "Oriental Immigrant."

71. *Baptist Visitor*, May 1904, 9.

In 1909, the *Baptist Yearbook* expressed the fears of many Canadian Baptists:

> It is equally certain that this fact is creating one of the gravest problems that the Canadian government and the Canadian people have ever faced . . . Some of these people are easily assimilated and incorporated into our life and brought into a fair conformity to our national ideals. They are anxious to learn and to become Canadians in the truest sense of the word. But this is not true of the largest proportions of them. They are here for one and only one purpose—that of securing an easier and better living than they could get in their own land. They think nothing about our national ideals and care nothing about the making of the nation. Notwithstanding this, we are convinced that they are capable of being transformed into *good citizens. But we must remember that they are coming to us as raw material. They are bringing with them all their religious and racial prejudices, all their socialistic and anarchistic* tendencies, all their disregard for the Christian Sabbath and all their callous indifference to the value of human life. We believe that nothing but the Gospel of Jesus Christ will effect the needed transformation, and we would [argue] that this problem is everyday becoming vaster in its proportions and more urgent in its character.[72]

Clearly, interests of national security rather than eternal security were increasingly becoming the preoccupation of evangelistic endeavors, since many of these immigrants were deemed a menace to Canadian civilization.

Howard Palmer has rightly noted that the response of Protestant churches to the new immigrants must be viewed "within the context of the relationship between Protestant religious values and nationalism."[73] One of the main goals of the Protestant churches, including Baptists, was the creation of a Christian nation. N. K. Clifford argues that this religious vision and its relationship with immigration not only

> provide[d] the basis for the formation of a broad Protestant consensus and coalition . . . but also a host of Protestant-oriented organizations such as temperance societies, missionary societies, Bible societies, the Lord's Day Alliance, the YMCA's and YWCA's utilized this vision as a framework for defining their task within

72. *Baptist Yearbook, 1909,* 65. Italics original.

73. Palmer, *Patterns,* 41.

the nation, for shaping their conceptions of the ideal society, and for determining those elements which posed a threat to the realization of their purposes . . . Amongst the threats to this vision was the massive immigration to Canada, between 1880 and World War II, of people who did not share it.[74]

The reform movements that emerged in Canada prior to the First World War were dedicated to the task of "righting the social ills" that plagued the nation and "building a truly Christian Canada." Three of the major social reform movements, the social gospel, prohibition, and women's suffrage, all expressed concern over the "'threat' the new immigrants posed to the type of 'progressive' society they envisioned." While some reformers believed the social problems of the immigrant neighborhoods could be remedied through education and assimilation programs, a tiny minority believed they were "biologically determined and sought a solution to the problem in exclusionary immigration laws."[75]

The social gospel, the underlying ideology of many of these reform movements, sought the creation of a Protestant Christian Canada not only through the salvation of individual souls, but also through the salvation of society itself.[76] In their efforts to build this truly Christian society, social gospel clergy and lay people saw "the immigrant" as one of their major stumbling blocks.

> The root cause of the ever expanding "hydra-headed social monster," at least in the minds of the theologically enlightened and socially motivated Protestant churchmen of the period, was the combination of a large influx of European immigrants and the industrialization of North America.[77]

74. Clifford, "Vision," 24. The Laymen's Missionary Movement should also be included with this group.

75. Palmer, *Patterns*, 38. Palmer notes that despite the widespread concern among reformers over the impact of the new immigrants, as long as Clifford Sifton remained Minister of the Interior the Liberal government of Wilfrid Laurier basically ignored demands for tighter controls on immigration, since they believed immigration was necessary to sustain economic growth, as well as to provide cheap labor for railroad construction. However, when Frank Oliver became Minister of the Interior in 1905 following Sifton's resignation, "some concessions were made to nativists in the form of tightened immigration regulations governing central and eastern Europeans." See Palmer, *Patterns*, 45–47.

76. See Scott, "Western Outlook," 6; cf. Allen, "Social Gospel," 381–82.; Allen, *Social Passion*.

77. Scott, "Responding to the Social Crisis," 272.

Southern and eastern Europeans and Asians were singled out for missionary activity not only because they were viewed as "inferior to other immigrants," but also because they "were not Protestant and 'lacked the desirable Anglo-Saxon qualities.'"[78] As this missionary work proceeded, Howard Palmer notes that "proselytizing to Protestantism came increasingly to be seen as secondary to the task of assimilating the immigrants to the standards of Canada's English-speaking majority." The Protestant clergy believed that "assimilation would both alleviate the social problems facing immigrants and prevent the deterioration of 'Canadian' or 'British' institutions, which were regarded as synonymous." Consequently, assimilation, which was "first seen as a means of facilitating conversion . . . eventually came to be an end in itself."[79]

While the responses of Protestant churches to the social crisis of the late nineteenth and early twentieth centuries were markedly similar, J. Brian Scott notes that the crisis did not consume Baptists in the same fashion "that it consumed Methodists and Presbyterians." Scott asserts that "a Calvinistic reverence for pursuit of rugged individualism in the form of free enterprise . . . seems to set Western Baptist social gospel apart from its prairie counterparts."[80] Nevertheless, "[t]here is little doubt that the Baptist Union embarked upon its missionary endeavor with a strong evangelical intent of both Christianizing and Canadianizing the rising tide of new immigrants."[81]

Somewhat surprisingly, little overtly racist material against immigrants appears in the Baptist literature of the period other than a few scattered remarks depicting Hindus, Chinese, and Japanese as "heathens," Italians as possessive of "impulsive temperament[s]," and Galicians as "stolid," "indifferent," "ignorant," and "illiterate."[82] Nothing in the way of anti-Semitic comments could be found other than a reference to "the shrewdness of Hebrews" and the statement "And oh, the Jews, the Jews,"[83] which in the context of the address seemed to carry a degree of negativity, during these years of Baptists mission. The 1930s,

78. Palmer, *Patterns*, 40.

79. Ibid., 41.

80. Scott, "Responding to the Social Crisis," 276; Scott, "Western Outlook," 18.

81. Scott, "Responding to the Social Crisis," 270.

82. *Baptist Yearbook, 1912*, 86; "Who Are Canadians?" *Baptist Visitor*, January 1912, 6–8; *Baptist Yearbook* (1901), 7.

83. *Baptist Yearbook, 1912*, 86; *Baptist Visitor*, January 1912, 8.

however, would clearly show that anti-Semitism was very much a part of Baptist attitudes during this period.[84]

The most overtly negative comments about immigrants were found in a single article entitled "Who Are Canadians?" which appeared in the January 1912 edition of the *Baptist Visitor*, the Women's Home Missions publication. The article attacked immigrants for becoming too "dependent upon our public charities." It also asserted that "thirty percent of those cared for in our asylums are foreign born [and] among the criminal class, thirty-eight percent are foreign."[85] The article also sought to draw a distinction between the characteristics and ideals of different foreigners, arguing that Scandinavians and Germans were by far the best classes. As for others,

> Ignorance of our language, disregard for our institutions of law and order, indecency, immorality, drunkenness and crime, make of their city hives, but city dives. High rents, high prices of food, aggravate the troubles, and disease, dirt and degradation pollutes these foreign quarters. We must steadily, patiently, constantly keep at this work of Christianizing the foreigners. We must do it because we cannot afford to neglect it. Our national life demands it. He who puts to this work his best effort and energy is as true a patriot as was ever he who shouldered a musket in the defense of his country.[86]

The article concludes with an assertion that Christian love and the glorification of Christ ultimately must serve as the impetus to eliminate the monumental problems of these immigrants. Was the salvation of "our national life" the more pressing motive? If so, what facilitated this shift in

---

84. See Smale, "Canadian Baptists." Historian David Rome notes in *Clouds in the Thirties*, 11:510, that "The reluctance of the Canadian government to admit Jewish refugees in any great numbers was a fair reflection of public opinion [. . .] which was a strong Anglo-Saxon nativism permeated with Anti-semitism."

85. In 1911 the population of Canada that was Canadian born was 5,620,000 and the population that was foreign born was 1,587,000. The foreign-born population of Canada thus amounted in 1911 to 28.2 percent of the total population. Source for statistics: Canada Employment and Immigration Commission, Immigration Statistics, 1984.

86. *Baptist Visitor*, January 1912, 8; See also the highly negative tone of Cameron, *Foreigners*. This highly racist publication would be reissued in the 1920s under the title, *The Call of Our Own Land*, and used to instruct Baptist youth of the period. See Cameron and Schutt, *Call*. Each of these publications demonstrates that stereotypical negative attitudes towards most foreigners were widely held by many Baptists of the period.

motive? Why were certain classes of immigrants deemed more desirable than others?

The answer to each of these questions seems to be more ideological than ethnically rooted. Germans, Scandinavians, British, and Americans were all "highly prized" immigrants for Baptists of this period, because they were, by and large, Protestant. Their basic values and beliefs tended to essentially endorse rather than undermine fundamental Canadian values and institutions of the period. Such groups were generally not seen to present any serious threat to Baptist aspirations of wanting to ensure that Canada remained a Christian nation. However, increasingly after 1901, the religious affiliation of more and more of the immigrants who came to Canada was Catholic. For Baptists this reality posed a serious threat to their notions of a Christian Canada.[87]

Throughout the course of Canadian history, clashes between Protestants and Roman Catholics were common. During the later part of the nineteenth century, open hostility to Roman Catholicism was a popularly expressed phenomenon. This anti-Catholicism was not simply politically motivated; it also had a theological and social inclination as well. As J. R. Miller points out, "a proper appreciation of the emotive force of anti-Catholic feeling requires an exploration and understanding of its several surfaces [nevertheless] [t]here could be no mistaking the liveliness of Catholicism as a public issue during the Victorian period."[88] Roman Catholicism was attacked as morally and politically degenerate, responsible for criminal, poor, and unattractive societies, a brutalizer and degrader of women, a corrupter of the minds of youth, and biblically and spiritually bankrupt. In making their case against Roman Catholicism, nineteenth-century Protestants asserted, "that Rome was heretic, schismatic, and riven with dissension."[89]

But of even greater concern to Protestants of the nineteenth century was Rome's claims to and lust for power. As one significant Protestant publication of the period commented, "Popery 'never can be satisfied

---

87. Scientific racial theories of the period tended not to regard Slavs and other Eastern Europeans as white. Yet the *Baptist Visitor*, in October 1900, referred to these people as "a white race, healthy and good looking." This suggests that ethnicity was not the sole or even the critical factor in fostering changes in Baptist attitudes. See *The Baptist Visitor*, October 1900, 4. For Protestant reaction to the changing religious composition of Canada, see Bothwell and Granatstein, *Our Century*, 39–40.

88. Miller, "Anti-Catholic Thought," 474.

89. Ibid., 487.

with less than complete domination, and that, too, in matters political as well as spiritual'; in fact, with the logical Romanist the one is the natural consequence of the other."[90] T. C. Haliburton, in 1851, further remarked that Catholics "always aim . . . at supremacy; and when supreme, they are ever intolerant. They can never be affectionate subjects to a Protestant monarch."[91] The natural outcome of all this, many Baptists charged, was centuries of persecution and tyranny on the part of Rome. Consequently, by the turn of the century many Canadian Protestants, including Baptists, viewed Roman Catholicism as a threat, not only to basic fundamental civil liberties, but also to ties with the Empire and later on to the Commonwealth. Brent Reilly has pointed out that "[t]he maintenance of democratic freedoms and of the links with Great Britain were twin impulses which drove some Protestants to organized defence against what they perceived as Catholic aggression."[92]

Recent scholarship in the area of Protestant-Catholic relations in Canada suggests that the confrontationalist approach "typified by the 'Belfast of Canada' motif seems overly simplistic given the variegated nature of relations between the city's [Toronto's] Catholics and Protestants." John Moir argues that the Protestant press "seldom mentioned Roman Catholicism" and very infrequently made reference to "their Catholic neighbours." Moir further contends that Protestants were less "anti-Catholic" than they were "anti-papal," since they feared the interference of the Vatican, a foreign power, in their domestic affairs. This, however, is a rather fine theological distinction. How much did the average lay person draw such a distinction and how capable were people of doing so? Were anti-papal and anti-Catholic really two sides of the same coin? Was it possible to attack the embodiment of Catholicism without attacking its institutions and its members? Even T. T. Shields tried to claim his attacks were not against individual Catholics, but against the Catholic system. "I would contend for the religious liberty of my Roman Catholic

---

90. See *Protestant Landmarks*, 35, 24 as cited in Miller, "Anti-Catholic Thought," 491.

91. T. C. Haliburton, *Rule and Misrule of the English in America*. New York, 1851, 353–54, as cited in Miller, "Anti-Catholic Thought," 491; Mark McGowan's recent analysis of English-speaking Catholics seems to draw this into question. English-speaking Catholics, he maintains, espoused their own form of Canadianization, advocating a vision of Canada that was "English in language," and "respectful of British laws and governance" although "Catholic in faith." See McGowan, *Waning of the Green*, 218–49.

92. Reilly, "Baptists," 181.

fellow citizens as earnestly as I would my own. . . . People who are wrong religiously . . . have the right to be wrong if they want to . . . But it is to Roman Catholicism as a political system we are especially opposed, a political system that claims religious sanction and special privileges because it is religious."[93] In the final analysis does Shields's argument justify his actions or make him any less of a bigot? Despite Shields's assurances, it is difficult to make such a fine distinction between people and policy.[94] Moir contends that "[a]lmost invariably, political perceptions not religion stirred Protestant fears."[95] While the nineteenth century was certainly marked by episodes of sectarian violence between Protestants and Catholics, "[f]or Toronto, 1858 seemed to mark a turning point in the tide of religious violence." [96] Moir notes that "[p]hysical violence was largely replaced by verbal attacks, in which Catholic editors referred to their neighbours as 'grunting Methodists' and 'canting Presbyterians.'"[97]

The Jubilee Riots of 1875 represented the "last gasp of physical confrontation between Protestants and Roman Catholics in Toronto."[98] In the decades that followed the Jubilee Riots, relations between Protestants and Catholics gradually improved, but fluctuated with political perceptions and economic realities of the day. Consequently, Moir contends that the period following Confederation "inaugurated an age of increasing toleration, or even reconciliation" between Protestants and Catholics, which climaxed in the reforming spirit of the Second Vatican Council.[99]

McGowan also views the analysis of Miller and Reilly as too one-dimensional. McGowan argues that Protestant-Catholic relations in Canada functioned at least at three different levels—institutional, public, and private. The analysis of Miller (and a few other scholars), McGowan contends, focuses only on the institutional level and provides insights into the reasons for Catholic-Protestant hostilities at a theoreti-

---

93. "It is against principles and not against personalities we protest," Shields contended in "The Pope's Fifth Column—Everywhere," *Gospel Witness*, 8 August 1940, 3; See also *Gospel Witness*, 16 November 1922, 3; *Gospel Witness*, 17 December 1925, 4.

94. See Smale, "Voice."

95. Moir, "Toronto Protestants," 314.

96. See Grant, *Profusion of Spires*, 204–20.

97. Moir, "Toronto Protestants," 317.

98. Ibid., 317–18; Wicks, "No Drawing Back," 33–39.

99. Moir, "Toronto Protestants," 320, 324.

cal level. McGowan asserts that interdenominational relations "among the ordinary rank and file" were often "frequently in conflict with popular perceptions of institutional and public peace or violence." Generally the "bishops spoke of peace between Protestants and Catholics" and Protestant families were "on good terms with their Catholic neighbours," although there were regional variations. The Episcopal Reports of 1900–1901, McGowan notes, make it clear that Catholic bishops did not regard direct proselytism as a major concern, but the everyday contact between Catholics and Protestants. Such social interaction, it was feared, "could subtly disarm Catholics, create moral and devotional laxity, and finally imperil their faith itself." What especially concerned the bishops was the number of mixed marriages, still eminently regarded as a "danger to religion." What this suggests to McGowan is that relations from "the perspective of the pew" were vastly different from those from the institutional perspective. From the day-to-day perspective of living, working, and interacting with one another, traditional hostility between some Protestants and Catholics was beginning to subside, and this was reflected in the growing number of mixed marriages.[100]

But this change in attitude also reflected something more. Religion was gradually being relegated more and more to the private rather than the public sphere. This was true for growing numbers of Christians, as well as the society at large. With increasing secularization, religious concerns became less important in the public realm. Religious affiliation for some no longer represented the totality of who they were, but only one aspect of their personal identity. As religious distinctiveness and issues of the past became increasingly less important, greater cooperation and interaction with traditional foes at various levels was to be expected. Not all, however, embraced this new era of reconciliation and toleration with the same spirit of enthusiasm or cooperation.

Given the distinctives of Baptist theology, it is not surprising that Baptists would not generally share these reconciliatory sentiments. Baptists held a rather low opinion of the Catholic Church, regarding it as essentially ignorant, semi-pagan, hostile to free institutions, and committed to a deliberate plan of world domination. As such, Catholicism posed a direct challenge to Baptist dreams of a Christian Canada. The *Baptist Visitor* prefaced an 1895 article with a caption that stated this

---

100. McGowan, "Rethinking"; See also McGowan, *Waning of the Green*, 89–117.

"would read as appropriately for us if Canadian was inserted in the place of American." The *Home Mission Monthly* charged:

> Rome is not content with a religious sphere of action, but aspires to political supremacy, and craves uncontrolled sway in national affairs. Even this, reprehensible as it is, would not be so alarming were it not for the fact that the Church of Rome is intrinsically anti-American [anti-Canadian], and to that extent is a continued menace to our free institutions. The dogmas of the Vatican and their supremacy in the Church, including the infallibility of the Pope and his supreme temporal and civil reign, projected into American life [Canadian life], threaten to subvert and under-mine our national freedom and its particular institutions.[101]

Baptists feared that the burgeoning Roman horde would ultimately foster the demise of Canadian civilization. They saw their duty as not only resisting the further encroachment of Roman Catholic power, but also rescuing those who were already under the curse of its bondage.

But it was not just the Roman ideology that many Baptists feared. Socialism, communism, secularism, and even general religious indifference were also perceived as a threat.[102] Consequently, Baptists were gravely concerned over the way the ballot box was being "recklessly" handed over to these new immigrants, fearing that it was being transformed "into a bludgeon for our heads."[103] The critical issue for many Baptists became "[h]ow [to] mold the heterogeneous mass of immigration, formed of one hundred foreign elements, into one people making

---

101. *Baptist Visitor*, January 1895, 7; See also the *Canadian Baptist*, 30 August, 1900, 8–9, where J. H. Farmer notes, "Most of the readers of the *Baptist* . . . have been trained into an attitude of hostility to, and almost contempt for, the Roman Catholic Church . . . Rome has been weighed in the balances and found wanting." See also "Protestant Torchbearers," *Canadian Baptist*, 16 August, 1900, 9; "Shall the Truth be Told concerning Romanism?" *Canadian Baptist*, 22 February 1900, 8; "Catholicism: Roman and Anglican," *Canadian Baptist*, 8 February, 1900, 10, asserted "the foundations of Catholicism are false." Justin D. Fulton in "A Manly Christianity," attacked those Protestant churches calling for a "diluted gospel that shall not touch Romanism" and condemned a leading publisher associated with temperance reform for giving away the plates of a book that attacked the "aggressions of Romanism" thereby surrendering "the truth" in order "to get some priests to join in the temperance work" (*Canadian Baptist*, 15 February 1900, 2); *Canadian Baptist*, 26 July 1900, 1, notes that the "Pope does not wish it understood that the policy of the Vatican is against England."

102. *Baptist Yearbook, 1908*, 64–65; *Baptist Yearbook, 1897*, 73.

103. *Baptist Visitor*, January 1912, 6.

them moral and intelligent citizens, loyal to our free institutions and capable of self-government."[104]

Their solution to this problem was as much political as it was religious. As C. J. Cameron, Assistant Superintendent of Home Missions, explained, not only was it necessary to assimilate the foreign element, it was equally important to prevent those who were deemed inassimilable, particularly blacks and the "yellow races," from entering the country, since their presence would only serve to undermine the ideals and values of a free and nominally Christian society. Cameron maintained that,

> we must endeavor to assimilate the foreigners. If the mixing process fails, we must strictly prohibit from entering our country all elements that are non-assimilable. It is contrary to the Creator's law for white, black, or yellow races to mix together. If the Canadian civilization fails to assimilate the great masses of foreigners admitted to our country, the results will be destruction to the ideals of a free and nominally Christian nation which will be supplanted by a lower realm of habits, outcomes and institutions.[105]

For Cameron, the basic threat of the immigrant was political. "The millions of aliens admitted to Canada," he asserted, "have transported to our soil political notions which we cannot tolerate. 'The continental ideas of the Sabbath, the nihilist's ideas of government, the communist's ideas of property, and the pagan's ideas of religion.'"[106] Consequently, assimilation of this "foreign horde" became a matter of paramount importance in the minds of church leaders. While acknowledging that the public school, press, and political institutions were doing much to instill in these foreigners "a sense of citizenship," these agencies were limited in their effectiveness to inspire true values of Canadian citizenship, because they failed to touch upon "the inmost springs of life, and unfold the noblest qualities of the soul." The only means whereby this goal could be achieved was to "Canadianize the foreigner by Christianizing him." Cameron maintained that immigration represented "our greatest opportunity and our gravest responsibility," since failure to Christianize would inevitably result in the foreignization of Canada.[107] Such work,

104. Cameron, *Foreigners*, 14.

105. Ibid., 14; See also Cameron and Schutt, *Call*, 143.

106. Cameron, *Foreigners*, 15; See also Cameron and Schutt, *Call*, 144.

107. *Baptist Visitor*, May 1909, 8.

Baptists believed, was the means to building a nation and one for which they were uniquely qualified. Given their own democratic ecclesiology, Baptists felt that no other denomination was better suited to meet these people and lead them along in the right direction on the ideals of nationhood and citizenship. Baptist churches were not merely centers for "teaching men the way to God and holiness and Heaven, but also for the dissemination of the great principles of liberty, justice, equality and fraternity which have been the foundation principles of all organized Baptist life."[108]

Hence, the years from 1880 to 1914 saw a form of Baptist dualism develop with respect to immigration. On the one hand, certain groups were perceived rather favorably with the recognition that they had the potential to become good citizens and contribute to the enrichment of Canadian life. In this capacity, Baptists believed that a Protestant environment, and more specifically their churches, had sufficient vitality to improve the foreign elements they encountered. On the other hand, as the sources of immigration began to shift increasingly after 1901, those new groups whose beliefs and customs were deemed alien and threatening to the foundations of the society were regarded as undesirable. The dread of radicalism, a belief in the superiority of Anglo-Saxon values and institutions, combined, in these later years, with an inherent anti-Catholic theology to produce a growing concern, amongst Baptists in Ontario and Quebec, about immigration. Hence, Canadian nativism became a major motivating factor behind Baptist missionary activities. This was the result of the view that the religion of the immigrant was more significant than the relationship of his ethnic origin to Anglo-Saxon culture.

Two factors did, however, work together to mitigate this growing nativistic tendency somewhat. The first was the belief that the immigrant was part of God's providential plan for helping to build a Christian nation (even though some felt more and more that it was the Pope's plan). The second was a more practical restraint. Certainly, if the immigrants were to be reached for Christ, care had to be exercised so as not to offend them overtly. Despite these mitigating factors, Baptists in the BCOQ increasingly saw the "incoming horde" as a debasing influence intent on the destruction of the nation—that is, an Anglo-Saxon Protestant Canada.

108. *Baptist Yearbook, 1908*, 65.

These formative years in Canada witnessed significant economic, social, political, and cultural changes that had a profound impact on the churches of the land. The Baptist churches of Ontario and Quebec sought to address this change. With respect to immigration, a change in motive and attitude occurred after 1901. The Baptist reaction to a new wave of immigrants is not primarily explained by the large numbers of immigrants, nor is the answer found in the state of the nation's economy. The Baptist response was molded in large part by the religious nature of such immigration, which they believed raised serious questions about the type of society that would emerge in English-speaking Canada. Certainly, among Baptists few ever thought "that [Anglo-Saxon] values might not be the apex of civilization which all men should strive for."[109] As a result, Baptists readily accepted and propagated an assimilation-ist agenda in which immigrants were expected to renounce their home culture, values, traditions, and particularly, religions, in favor of those of Anglo-Canadians and Protestantism.

Ultimately, these Baptist churches would fail in their efforts to win significant numbers of immigrants. Even work among the Germans and Scandinavians, which had proved fruitful in the early years, would end in bitter disappointment as many of these churches splintered away, forming their own associations.[110] But the success or failure of Baptist efforts should not be judged solely in terms of conversions. As John Webster Grant has pointed out, Protestant missionary endeavors in this period helped to ease the way for many immigrants into Canadian society.[111] Baptist fears about the destruction of Canadian society as a result of Catholic infiltration were also subsequently proved wrong, though many today question the legitimacy of public funding of separate schools in the Province of Ontario.

In another respect, Baptists were proven right. The Catholic Church is the largest religious group in Canada today.[112] Nevertheless, in their

109. Palmer, "Reluctant Hosts," 193.

110. Ellis, "Baptist Visions," 75–76. In 1881 there were 296,525 Baptists in Canada (6.9 percent of the population). In 1911 there were 382,666 Baptists in Canada (5.3 percent). These figures were garnered from Airhart, "Ordering a Nation," 104.

111. Grant, Church, 97.

112. The largest denomination in Canada has always been and continues to remain the Roman Catholic Church. Roman Catholics continued to grow in Canada in terms of numbers from 10,320,024 in 1981 to 12,624,403 in 2001. Immigration is a major factor in this. According to Statistics Canada, one third of immigrants to Canada in

efforts to address the immigrant question in these formative years of nationhood, BCOQ Baptists attempted to serve two kingdoms—that of Jehovah and that of Victoria, Edward, and George, a distinction in these years that became blurred. In the end it would seem that God's Kingdom increasingly took second place.

The coming of the Great War temporarily put to rest Baptist fears surrounding the enormous influx of immigration, since the war effectively closed Canada's borders during the years 1914 to 1918. Following the war, however, Canada once more saw a mass migration of Europe's "great unwashed" to Canadian soil. This reality reignited Baptist fears. Baptists would once again be "armed and ready" with their program of Canadianization and Christianization. And like other Protestant churches, Baptists were among the leading advocates calling for a change in government policy regarding immigration. Their first priority became a restrictive immigration policy.[113]

By the late 1920s, however, some Baptists were expressing their misgivings about the prevailing Baptist view. One of the more moderate and eloquent of these dissenting voices was that of Watson Kirkconnell. His challenge of the assimilationist perspective and his advocacy for pluralism are the next focus of this chapter.

"THE PROPHET OF CANADIAN MULTICULTURALISM": WATSON KIRKCONNELL AND THE STRUGGLE AGAINST CANADIANIZATION

Throughout the 1920s and 1930s, Baptists continued almost unabated in their efforts to "Anglicize" and "Canadianize" immigrants. Anglo-conformity was believed essential to the successful development of Canadian society and the preservation of those Anglo-Saxon traditions that Baptists both nurtured and prized. The First World War, it seemed, had done little to dampen their vision of turning Canada into His Dominion.[114]

---

the 1980s and one quarter in the 1990s were Catholic. As University of Lethbridge sociologist Reginald Bibby points out, "The Roman Catholic Church continues to be a prominent player on the national religious scene—indeed, the most prominent player." See Coggins, "State of the Canadian Church II and IV."

113. See Smale, "Broad Is the Road."

114. For a further discussion of Baptist attitudes in the period, see ibid.

By the late 1920s, however, some Baptists began to adopt a some-what moderate view of assimilation, at least partially out of the recognition that immigrants could make valuable cultural contributions to Canada. These assimilationists envisioned a kind of merging of Anglo-Canadianism with the immigrants, "and a blending of their cultures into a new Canadian type."[115] The essence of assimilation was not fundamentally questioned. Like Anglo-conformity, this Canadian version of the melting pot was also deemed necessary in order to ensure immigrants fit into Canadian society.[116]

With the onset of the Great Depression, "nativist" fears were once again aroused.[117] The decade marked the "high point of discrimination against non-Anglo-Saxons," as xenophobia gripped the nation.[118] Yet, despite the "continuing dominance of the old stereotypes concerning non-Anglo-Saxons and continuing dominance of assimilationist assumptions, the 1930s also saw the emergence of the first full-blown pluralist ideas [albeit in a] somewhat ambiguous form."[119] One of the advocates of this pluralist ideology was a Baptist, Watson Kirkconnell. In contrast to most who discussed immigration in Canadian society, Kirkconnell sought to promote tolerance towards ethnic minorities through a sympathetic portrayal of their cultural backgrounds and countries of origin and by demonstrating the cultural creativity of these minorities through translating and publishing their writings.[120]

Kirkconnell attacked the fundamental assumptions of both Anglo-conformity and the melting pot. In their place he advocated a "multicultural" vision of society that would allow immigrants to maintain pride in their heritage. As Kirkconnell himself asserted in his memoirs, *A Slice of Canada*, the Preface to his 1935 work *Canadian Overtones*

115. Palmer, "Reluctant Hosts," 202.

116. In other words, the melting pot was still an "Anglo-Saxon pot." See Palmer, "Reluctant Hosts," 202.

117. For an analysis of nativist politics in Canada, see Robin, *Shades of Right*, 1–124; Lloyd, "Immigration and Nation Building," 55.

118. See Palmer's summary of these fears in "Reluctant Hosts," 203–5.

119. Ibid., 205.

120. The other major advocate of pluralist ideas in this period was John Murray Gibbons (*The Canadian Mosaic*). See Palmer, "Reluctant Hosts," 205. For further discussion of changing Protestant attitudes towards missions and a moving away from paternalism and ethnocentrism to a more heterogeneous conception of Protestant Christendom, see Wright, *World Mission*, 142–77.

set out his "philosophy of the multicultural state in categorical terms."[121] Kirkconnell was not advocating a form of separatism for ethnic minorities in order to preserve their culture. He firmly believed that integration needed to occur in the realm of political and economic values as well as in institutions. At the same time he believed "that some of the conservative values and folk-culture of immigrants could be preserved."[122]

Thus, Kirkconnell did not believe that ethnic diversity was incompatible with national unity. In his judgment, unity did not mean uniformity: "Unity does not, however necessarily mean uniformity. A country in which all people spoke the same language, attended the same church, and had the same opinions on all important subjects would be in sorry danger of developing sleeping sickness."[123] He believed that the existence of many different European traditions in Canada only served to heighten both the "hazards and possible rewards of a multi-national state." Nevertheless, such a state was the "surest guarantee of progressive and intelligent national policies." Allowing for divergence of opinion and opposing points of view, Kirkconnell believed, added value to the cultures of others and provided the "opportunity for developing the highest qualities of citizenship through facing the problems of national harmony."[124] Kirkconnell reflected not only a commitment to ethnic minorities, but also a dedication to liberal ideals. As he once expressed it, "[b]asic to the liberal ideal is faith in the dignity and the worth of the individual. The freedom of the Canadian democracy is intimately bound up with the freedom of the single citizen and his right to individual differences of thought and action."[125]

It was during his eighteen-year stay in Winnipeg that Kirkconnell championed the cause of immigrants and ethnic minorities in Canada. He maintained that the nation had remained "effectively bifocal for me . . . until 1922, when I went west to live in Winnipeg. There I found a population as different from that of the East as the Prairies are from the St. Lawrence basin . . . This was still Canada, but a Canada profoundly different from the little towns of my boyhood."[126] The city reminded him

121. Kirkconnell, *Slice*, 280.

122. Palmer, "Reluctant Hosts," 206.

123. Kirkconnell, *Canadians All*, 11.

124. Ibid., 12.

125. Kirkconnell, *Liberal Education*, 15.

126. Kirkconnell, "European Elements," 4. For further discussion of his years in Winnipeg, see Perkin and Snelson, *Morning*, 15–24. Perkin writes: "He was one of the

of his travels and his experiences in Europe, "and these [the linguistic and cultural traditions] as the living ingredients in an evolving commonwealth." Kirkconnell was one of the first to recognize that the aspirations of the immigrant communities were not any different from those of any other communities in Canada. Both established and immigrant communities were striving to create the best possible life for themselves and their descendants. The fusion of this mosaic of peoples, languages, and cultures "into a Canadian people of diversified richness caught my imagination" and became not only Kirkconnell's "vision," but also his lifelong goal for Canada.

Beginning in 1928, he commenced work on translating a series of twenty-four volumes of European literature, by which he hoped to enlighten "our Canadian culture ... of all the noble traditions that were blending in our common life."[127] After completing work on only three volumes, his publisher went bankrupt in 1930, and the project lapsed. Nevertheless, Kirkconnell soon discovered that many of these new Canadians were producing "a good deal of significant literature in their own mother tongues," and so in 1935 he produced a volume of Icelandic, Swedish, Norwegian, Ukrainian, Modern Greek, Italian, and Hungarian poetry that revealed the experiences of these peoples in adjusting to pioneer life on the Canadian frontier. The book was entitled simply *Canadian Overtones*. Much of the poetry Kirkconnell translated was dedicated to showing the heartfelt thanks many of these immigrants felt to Canada, as well as their dedication and loyalty to the nation.

Kirkconnell not only dedicated himself to promoting the values and virtues of immigrant cultures, but also to extirpating the ignorance, stereotypes, and racist attitudes that so many "old Canadians" held. The root of much of this, he believed, was ignorance. Far too few "old Canadians" or "their newspapers," he once remarked "have even an elementary knowledge of the history of Central and Eastern Europe."[128] In responding to "a hysterical newspaper letter from a Saskatchewan bishop," that urged "true British Canadians to unite against the admission into Western Canada of 'non-British stocks,'" Kirkconnell maintained that diversity was not a determent to the growth and development of a

first to recognize and draw upon the polyglot literature of the new Canadians who flooded to the Prairies after the First World War" (p. 21).

127. Kirkconnell, "Tale of Seven Cities," 10.

128. Ibid., 24–25.

civilization, but rather "a positive enrichment of national life." So long as ignorance and intolerance were allowed to flourish, a nation would be prevented from achieving its true greatness. Cultural diversity in Canada was thereby the means through which the nation could ultimately develop to its full potential.[129]

With the publication of *Canadian Overtones*, Kirkconnell had tactfully chastised his fellow countrymen for considering new Canadians to be "minimal races" who were "incapable of intellectual development and fit only to serve their masters."[130] This task, however, was not popular, and Kirkconnell was vilified on the left for advocating the use of cheap labor and on the right for his compromise of Anglo-Saxon values.[131] Nevertheless, the work was a significant milestone in not only pointing out the erroneous beliefs and prejudices of so many "old Canadians," but also in laying the foundation for the progress of future generations of those ethnic nationalities for whom he expressed concern, by providing for them an important link to their ancestral heritage. In this sense, Kirkconnell hoped that, however Anglicized and Canadianized these immigrants and their future generations might become, their assimilation would not be complete.

His goal was not to deny the value of a national culture or traditions, but to enrich it: "I do not wish to belittle or deny the value of a national culture and a national tradition in giving a warm core of spiritual significance to our Canadian community. I hope for the fullest possible development of such a national culture, blending and cherishing here all the rich legacies of European gifts that are found in our land."[132] In other words, any national Canadian culture had to encompass the cultural legacies of its diverse ethnic components if it was to become a truly national culture. Canada's rich ethnic diversity, Kirkconnell believed, had something to offer to the definition of nationhood.

With the onset of the Great Depression, Kirkconnell's task became even more daunting. In a period of growing hostility and resentment toward ethnic minorities[133] he was increasingly challenged both to inter-

---

129. Kirkconnell, "Western Immigration," 706–7.

130. Andrusyshen, "Canadian Ethnic Literacy," 33.

131. Kirkconnell, "Tale of Seven Cities," 7.

132. Kirkconnell, "European Elements," 17.

133. See Robin, *Shades of Right*, 125–55, which examines the growing intolerance towards Jews and the emergence of "embryo Nazism" in Canada. See also Kelley and

pret these new Canadians to the rest of the country, and to defend their loyalty as well. Many Canadians, including Kirkconnell's own Baptist brethren, saw these immigrant communities as breeding-grounds for all kinds of seditious and pagan ideologies bent on the destruction of Canadian democracy and ending their vision of Canada as an Anglo-Christian nation.[134]

While acknowledging the fact that these immigrant communities were "susceptible to the gospel of revolutionary Communism," since as a result of the onset of the Depression they were most often the first to be laid off by industry, Kirkconnell nevertheless charged that "[t]he smallest success of the conspirators, whether Nazi or Communist, has been amongst the European Canadians. These people know far better than the average English or French Canadian the reality of the horrors that rule in Europe today."[135]

While *Canada, Europe and Hitler* was Kirkconnell's "categorical statement" of his anti-Nazi position, it was equally his conscious attempt to discount the fears of many "old Canadians" that immigrant communities were likely to become partisans of Communist agitation and that those of German heritage in Canada posed a serious threat.[136] Following an exhaustive, more than seventy-page survey of the European press in Canada, Kirkconnell came to the conclusion that it "shapes itself nev-

---

Trebilcock, *Making of the Mosaic*, 216–49; Avery, *Reluctant Hosts*, 108–25; Roberts, "Shoveling out the 'Mutinous.'"

134. *Baptist Yearbook, 1932*, 227; Note similar charges in "'Canadianize!' Evangelize," *Canadian Baptist*, 24 February 1938, 3; "Bible as the Basis of the British Empire," *Canadian Baptist*, 24 February 1938, 11; "The Task at Home," *Canadian Baptist*, 2 August 1934, 7; "More Settlers," *Canadian Baptist*, 11 April 1935, 2; "Necessity for Work among Our New Canadian Citizens," *Canadian Baptist*, 15 May 1944, 4. We must recognize that enemy activity is "one of the most serious threats which endangers our life as a unified democratic nation." These threats are present within a "large body of people who have not been assimilated into our national life and are separated from us and each other by many bars," particularly "language and race." Some Baptists even went so far as to call for the deportation of such radicals. See "Home Mission Work," *Canadian Baptist*, 21 November 1935, 5. The Convention, however, to its credit, did object to the government's utilization of Sections 40/41 of the Immigration Act that provided for the deportation of non-Canadian citizens on relief (*Baptist Yearbook, 1933*, 203).

135. Kirkconnell, *Canadians All*, 17.

136. Kirkconnell, *Canada, Europe and Hitler*, 117. Critics of the work said it was "too emotional" and was "lacking in objectivity." See also Perkin and Snelson, *Morning*, 22.

ertheless into a pattern of quite astonishing unanimity on the issue of supporting Canada and its armed opposition to Hitlerian aggression."[137]

In short, Kirkconnell argued that there was no reason to question the loyalty of these new Canadians: "Canadians of all origins are today thinking as Canadians and responding as Canadians to the greatest responsibility our country has ever had to face."[138] In defending the loyalty of these multi-ethnics, Kirkconnell argued that it did not nor did it necessarily have to include filial affections for all things British. Their allegiance was to Canada. That allegiance precluded any corresponding affection for Britain, which would not only be historically impossible for them, but also equally hypocritical to assume.[139] Perhaps Kirkconnell was somewhat of an idealist, given the immensely partial attitudes of his day. But he possessed a keen understanding of the human psyche. By creating an environment of respect and toleration, Kirkconnell believed he could help immigrants feel more confident and willing to make a contribution to the general welfare of the nation. In this respect, the more immigrant communities felt that they were a part of Canada, and that their traditions were respected, the more willing they would be to accept Canada's broader cultural values and social norms.

Kirkconnell passionately believed that Canada as a liberal democracy had the responsibility to meet the demands of social justice, and at the same time, the country must protect the values of the individual. As such, he challenged "old Canadians" to show "tolerance and justice" toward the loyal majorities in all new immigrant communities, and he called on these Canadians to "help them rather than malign them in their almost universal struggles against the [seditious] minorities in their midst."[140]

137. Kirkconnell, *Canada, Europe and Hitler*, 188.

138. Kirkconnell, *Canadians All*, 19. Kirkconnell also pointed to the fact that most of these folk of the second generation insisted that they were Canadian, and how could their loyalty be "contradicted" when "they signed up for their citizenship with their blood."

139. Kirkconnell, *Canada, Europe and Hitler*, 197–202.

140. Kirkconnell, *Christian Social Order*, 8. See also his impassioned plea in "Twilight of Canadian Protestantism," *Canadian Baptist*, 1 December 1942, 2, where he argued that "vociferous loyalty to the British crown is not enough. It needs to be followed by a conscientious application of the principles for which Britain has stood in her best and highest moments—principles of liberty, justice and goodwill. If we can [constitute] a political and social [order] in which there is no hint of discrimination against any group, we shall have done much to ensure the future welfare of the Canadian people."

When Kirkconnell left Winnipeg in 1940 to become Head of the English Department at McMaster University in Hamilton, Ontario, the *Winnipeg Tribune* paid him the following tribute: "No man has done more to help the peoples of Winnipeg to live as neighbours . . . He will be able to interpret the life and thought of the new peoples who today are making some parts of Ontario as cosmopolitan as Winnipeg. To this extent the exchange may be to national advantage."[141] In 1940, Louis Rosenberg, Executive Director of the Canadian Jewish Congress Western Division, claimed that Watson Kirkconnell was "unique in Canadian life." He added, that Kirkconnell "has gone out to meet us more than half way, and when he ceases to be an isolated phenomenon and becomes one of many there will be greater hope for mutual understanding in Canada."[142]

The pioneering efforts of Kirkconnell in an era of indescribable nativism and support for immigration restrictions were praised by a few but dismissed by many. But this does not mean that his ideas had no impact, especially in the long run. His thinking, so revolutionary in its day, helped pave the road to the Canada of today. As J. R. C. Perkin asserts:

> Kirkconnell is one of that small band of individuals who, to a significant degree, helped create modern Canada. He would not have liked every part of today's Canada any more than he approved of every aspect of it in his own day, but if the worst excesses of racial prejudice have been avoided, and if the experiment to create a cultural mosaic has been partly successful, some of the credit is surely due to him.[143]

He was among the foremost Canadians of his age and, perhaps surprisingly, given the usually conservative tone of Baptist thinking, he helped to effect an eventual concord between his own national heritage and those who had most recently arrived seeking new lives and a new land.

141. "Editorial," *Winnipeg Tribune*, 15 June 1940 (Watson Kirkconnell Clippings, Canadian Baptist Archives). Kirkconnell himself remarked that "Winnipeg taught me the vital importance in our national life of the two million Canadians whose ancestry is neither English nor French" (Kirkconnell, "Tale of Seven Cities," 12). For further discussion of his years in Hamilton, see Perkin and Snelson, *Morning*, 25–31.

142. Louis Rosenberg, *The Israelite Press*, as cited in Kirkconnell, *Slice*, 274.

143. Perkin and Snelson, *Morning*, 63. For more on Perkin's assessment of Kirkconnell, see Perkin, "Giants."

Kirkconnell rightly deserves, in the words of the late George F. G. Stanley, to be recognized as the "prophet of Canadian multiculturalism."[144] Unfortunately, few Canadians and few Baptists during the first half of the twentieth century were willing to adopt his vision of Canada.[145] Despite this opposition, Kirkconnell steadfastly and passionately believed that the recognition of the cultural contributions of ethnic minorities would not only heighten their sense of belonging to Canada, but also strengthen national unity. In the end, Kirkconnell was a Baptist voice "crying in the wilderness"—a wilderness unfortunately still dominated by discrimination and racism, and a wilderness inhabited by many, but by no means all, of Kirkconnell's fellow Baptists.

CONCLUSION

Armed with the belief that their vision of Canada was under attack by foreigners holding alien worldviews, evangelical Baptists formulated a mission that was designed to defend their Anglo-Saxon Protestant culture and values. Baptist leaders during this period believed that the church had a significant role to play in the assimilation process of immigrants. While Baptists' faith in their ability to convert and assimilate the immigrant generally remained strong, gradually it came to include advocacy of more restrictive immigration measures, particularly in the aftermath of the First World War and in the growing economic distress of the 1930s. Thus, what had begun as a campaign designed to "win"

144. This epithet was used by Stanley in his address delivered at the dedication of the Watson Kirkconnell Room in the library of Acadia University on 12 October 1979. See Zeman, "They Speak with Other Tongues," 81, 85.

145. It would appear that Kirkconnell was having at least some influence on his Baptist brethren by the late 1930s. Lewis F. Kipp, editor of the *Canadian Baptist*, in an article entitled "Strangers within Our Gates," 1 December 1941, 3, for the first time clearly enunciated and admitted the racist attitudes of the church towards immigrants. Kipp wrote: "that some non-English families are not desirable neighbours is admitted, but it is equally true that not all English-speaking are of angelic type. There are fine and undesirable people in every race, colour and creed. No district has a right to withhold its hand of fellowship to a newcomer simply because he is not of its race or language . . . race feeling exists in the Dominion [and] the racial colour splinter that we find in some other eye should not blind us that there are splinters in our own . . . In this ostracism of other races and colours the church has not always been without fault . . . He (the foreigner) will not think well—can you blame him—of a religion that teaches brotherliness in its place of worship on Sunday, but which is anything but brotherly on Monday. This country of ours would be a great deal lovelier if the Spirit of friendly brotherhood was extended to take in the brother of other tongues, colours and different habits."

the immigrant for the Kingdom eventually came to be demands that the immigrant be kept out of the Dominion. Many of the immigrants who experienced the home mission endeavors of Canadian Baptists saw nothing but racism in their attacks on Roman Catholic religious traditions and non-Anglo-Saxon cultural values.

The public talk about welcoming new Catholic immigrants that often dominated Baptist discussions of immigration in the wider Canadian context was in part an attempt to paper over Baptist anti-Catholic sentiment. In determining the long-term desirability of an immigrant, purging him or her of Catholicism was a critical component in the Baptist assimilationist plan. During the 1930s, ethnicity, race, and religion became increasingly significant measures of an immigrant's desirability, and some Baptists were swept up by "scientific" race theories. Such views fostered a nativism that was replete with religious bigotry and prejudice. This anti-Catholicism, which amplified Baptists' fears of foreign "isms" and a belief in Anglo-Saxon superiority, translated into a general suspicion of the "strangers within our gates." Therefore, in the face of ever-increasing numbers of immigrants from Catholic non-English-speaking countries, Baptists generally sided with those who advocated for the cultural dominance of an English-speaking Protestant tradition in Canada.

When translated into action, the Baptist vision of "His Dominion" required the acceptance and implementation of an assimilationist agenda. One desired result of this "providential gathering" was that Canada would become the Kingdom of God on earth. This millennialist view of Canada's future as a Christian nation prepared the way for the propagation of the social gospel. Baptists, therefore, "succeeded in welding together their millennial hopes for the establishment of Christ's kingdom in Canada with their deep desire to serve the nation and to save it from racial and ideological contamination."[146] In the end, the Baptist vision of a "terrestrial Jerusalem characterized by Puritan morals, social justice and English supremacy did not materialize."[147] As historian Ramsay Cook notes, "it remained easier for a camel to pass through the eye of a needle than for Canadian society to become the kingdom of God on earth." In fact, the "union of the sacred and the secular," Cook argues, produced not the intended kingdom of God, but "the birth of a secular

146. Clifford, "Vision," 32.
147. Ellis, "Baptist Visions," 68.

view of society."[148] In the process, Baptists had become missionaries not just for God's Kingdom, but for mainstream Anglo-Saxon values—the advocates of a monolithic culture.

"It is never too late to give up our prejudices," wrote one commentator in the *Canadian Baptist*.[149] It was not until the 1930s, however, that negative attitudes towards immigrants began to change, and the whole program of Canadianization began to be questioned. In Baptist circles, Watson Kirkconnell played a leading role in making both the church and mainstream Canadians aware of the cultural contributions that immigrants had made and would continue to make for Canada.

148. Cook, *Regenerators*, 227, 231.
149. *Canadian Baptist*, 1 March 1923, 5.

BIBLIOGRAPHY

Airhart, Phyllis D. "Ordering a Nation and Reordering Protestantism, 1867–1914." In *The Canadian Protestant Experience, 1760–1990*, edited by George Rawlyk, 98–138. Burlington, ON: Welch, 1990.

Allen, Richard. "The Social Gospel and the Reform Tradition in Canada, 1890–1928." *The Canadian Historical Review* (December, 1968) 381–99.

———. *The Social Passion: Religion and Social Reform in Canada.* Toronto: University of Toronto Press, 1971.

Anderson, Kay J. "The Idea of Chinatown." In *Immigration in Canada: Historical Perspectives*, edited by Gerald Tulchinsky, 223–48. Toronto: Copp Clark, 1994.

Andrusyshen, C. H. "Canadian Ethnic Literacy and Culture Perspectives." In *The Undoing of Babel—Watson Kirkconnell—The Man and His Work*, 31–49. Toronto: McClelland & Stewart, 1975.

Angus, H. F. "Underprivileged Canadians." *Queen's Quarterly* 38 (1931) 445–60.

Austin, Alvyn J. *Saving China: Canadian Missionaries in the Middle Kingdom 1888–1959.* Toronto: University of Toronto Press, 1986.

Avery, *Reluctant Hosts: Canada's Response to Immigrant Workers, 1896–1994.* Toronto: McClelland & Stewart, 1995.

Baptist Yearbook [1884, 1093, 1894, 1897, 1900, 1901, 1908, 1909, 1912, 1932, 1933] for Ontario and Quebec [and Manitoba and and Western Canada/the Northwest and British Columbia]. Published by the Baptist Convention of Ontario and Quebec.

Barber, Marilyn. "Nationalism, Nativism and the Social Gospel: The Protestant Church Response to Foreign Immigrants in Western Canada, 1897–1914." In *The Social Gospel in Canada*, edited by R. Allen. Ottawa: National Museums of Canada, 1975.

Berger, Carl. *The Sense of Power: Studies in the Ideas of Imperialism 1867–1914.* Toronto: University of Toronto Press, 1970.

Bothwell, Robert, and Granatstein, J. L. *Our Century: The Canadian Journey in the Twentieth Century.* Toronto: McArthur, 2000.

Brouwer, Ruth Compton. *New Women for God: Canadian Presbyterian Women and Indian Missions, 1876–1914.* Toronto: University of Toronto Press, 1990.

Brown, R. C., and Cook, Ramsay. *Canada 1896–1921: A Nation Transformed.* Toronto: McClelland & Stewart, 1974.

Cameron, C. J. *Foreigners or Canadians?* Toronto: Standard Publishing Company, 1913.

Cameron, C. J., and Schutt, C. H. *The Call of Our Own Land.* Toronto: American Baptist Publishing Society, 1923.

Carrothers, W. A. "The Immigration Problem in Canada." *Queen's Quarterly* 36 (1929) 517–31.

Christie, Nancy, and Gauvreau, Michael. *A Full-Orbed Christianity: The Protestant Churches and Social Welfare in Canada, 1900–1940.* Kingston and Montreal: McGill-Queen's University Press, 1996.

Clifford, N. K. "A Vision in Crisis." In *Religion and Culture in Canada*, edited by Peter Slater, 23–43. Waterloo: Wilfrid Laurier University Press, 1977.

Coggins, Jim. "The State of the Canadian Church in 2008." Part II, "Shifting Traditions." Part IV, "The Impact of Immigration on the Church." *http://www.canadianchristianity.com/nationalupdates/071213state.html.*

Cook, Ramsay. *The Regenerators: Social Criticism in Late Victorian English Canada.* Toronto: University of Toronto Press, 1985.

Cormie, J. A. *Canada and the New Canadians.* Toronto: The Social Service Council of Canada, 1931.

Cumbo, Enrico C. "'Impediments to Harvest': The Limitations of Methodist Proselytization of Toronto's Italian Immigrants, 1905–1925." In *Catholics at the "Gathering Place,"* edited by Mark G. McGowan and Briane P. Clarke, 155–74. Toronto: Canadian Catholic Historical Association, 1993.

Davies, Alan. *Infected Christianity: A Study of Modern Racism.* Montreal and Kingston: McGill-Queen's University Press, 1988.

Ellis, Walter E. "Baptist Visions of the New Jerusalem." In *Celebrating Canadian Baptist Heritage.* Hamilton: The McMaster Conference, n.d., 68.

Ellis, Walter E. "Baptist Missions' Adaptation to the Western Frontier." *Canadian Baptist History and Polity.* Hamilton: McMaster Divinity College, 1982.

Gagan, Rosemary R. *A Sensitive Independence—Canadian Methodist Women Missionaries in Canada and the Orient 1881–1925.* Montreal and Kingston: McGill-Queen's University Press, 1992.

Gauvreau, Michael. *The Evangelical Century: College and Creed in English Canada from the Great Revival to the Great Depression.* Montreal and Kingston: McGill-Queen's University Press, 1991.

Gibbons, John Murray. *The Canadian Mosaic.* Toronto: McClelland & Steward, 1938.

Goertz, Donald. "Alexander Grant: Pastor, Evangelist, Visionary." In *Costly Vision: the Baptist Pilgrimage in Canada,* edited by Jarold K. Zeman, 1–22. Burlington, ON: Welch, 1988.

Gouter, David. *Guarding the Gates: The Canadian Labour Movement and Immigration, 1872–1934.* Vancouver: University of British Columbia Press, 2007.

Grant, J. W. "Religion and the Quest for a National Identity: The Background in Canadian History." In *Religion and Culture in Canada,* edited by Peter Slater, 525–49. Waterloo: Wilfrid Laurier University Press, 1977.

Grant, John Webester. *The Church in the Canadian Era.* Burlington, ON: Welch, 1988.

Grant, John W. *Moon of Wintertime: Missionaries and the Indians of Canada in Encounters since 1534.* Toronto: University of Toronto Press, 1984.

Grant, John Webster. *A Profusion of Spires: Religion in Nineteenth Century Ontario.* Toronto: University of Toronto Press, 1988.

Hardy, E. A. "Canada's Historical Background." In *From Sea to Sea: A Study Book of Home Missions,* 1–6. Toronto: Publications Committee of the Women's Baptist Missionary Society of Ontario West, 1940.

Heath, Gordon L. *A War with a Silver Lining: Protestant Churches and the South African War, 1899–1902.* Montreal and Kingston: McGill-Queen's University Press, 2009.

Higham, John. *Strangers in the Land: Patterns of American Nativism 1860–1925.* New York: Athenaeum, 1967.

Hurd, W. B. "The Case for a Quota." *Queen's Quarterly* 36 (1929) 131–59.

Jaenen, Cornelius. "The Unique Qualities of Canadian Ethnic Studies." University of Toronto Ethnic and Immigration Studies Programme Lecture Series, 5 October, 1978.

Katerberg, William H. "The Irony of Identity: An Essay on Nativism, Liberal Democracy and Parochial Identities in Canada and the United States." *American Quarterly* (1995) 493–524.

————. "Protecting Christian Liberty: Mainline Protestantism, Racial Thought and Political Culture in Canada, 1918–39." *Canadian Society of Church History Papers* (1995) 5–33.

Kelley, Ninette, and Trebilcock, Michael. *The Making of the Mosaic: A History of Canadian Immigration Policy*. Toronto: University of Toronto Press, 1998.

Kirkconnell, Watson. *Canada, Europe and Hitler*. London: Oxford University Press, 1940.

————. *Canadians All—A Primer of Canadian National Unity*. Ottawa: The Director of Public Information, 1941.

————. *Canadian Overtones*. Winnipeg: Columbia, 1935.

————. "European Elements in Canadian Life." An address to the Canadian Club, 4 November 1940.

————. *Liberal Education in the Canadian Democracy*. Hamilton: McMaster University Press, 1948.

————. *A Slice of Canada*. Toronto: University of Toronto Press, 1967.

————. "A Tale of Seven Cities." An address given at a public dinner in his honor by the Women's Civic Club, 9 April 1948.

————. *Towards a Christian Social Order*. Toronto: Baptist Board of Social Service and Evangelism, 1945.

————. "Western Immigration." *The Canadian Forum* 8, no. 94 (July 1928) 706–7.

Knowles, Valerie. *Strangers at Our Gates: Canadian Immigration and Immigration Policy, 1540–2006*. Toronto: Dundurn Press, 2007.

Lehr, John C. "Peopling the Prairies with Ukrainians." In *Immigration in Canada: Historical Perspectives*, edited by Gerald Tulchinsky, 177–202. Toronto: Copp Clark, 1994.

Lloyd, George Exton. "Immigration and Nation Building." In *Immigration and the Rise of Multiculturalism*, edited by Howard Palmer, 55–56. Issues in Canadian History. Toronto: Copp Clark, 1975.

Marty, M. E. *Protestantism in the United States: Righteous Empire*. New York: Scribers, 1986.

McGowan, Mark. "Rethinking Catholic-Protestant Relations in Canada: The Episcopal Reports of 1900–1901." *CCHA Historical Studies* 59 (1992) 11–32.

————. "Toronto's English-speaking Catholics, Immigration, and the Making of a Canadian Catholic Identity, 1900–1930." In *The Place of English-speaking Catholics in Canadian Society, 1750–1930*, edited by T. Murphy and G. Stortz, 204–40. Montreal and Kingston: McGill-Queen's University Press, 1993.

————. *The Waning of the Green: Catholics, the Irish and Identity in Toronto, 1887–1922*. Montreal and Kingston: McGill-Queen's University Press, 1999.

Miller, J. R. "Anti-Catholic Thought in Victorian Canada." *Canadian Historical Review* 66, no. 4 (December 1985) 474–94.

Moir, John S. "Toronto Protestants and Their Perceptions of Their Roman Catholic Neighbours." In *Catholics at the "Gathering Place": Historical Essays on the Archdiocese of Toronto, 1841–1991*, edited by Mark McGowan and Brian P. Clarke, 313–50. Toronto: Canadian Catholic Historical Association, 1993.

Palmer, Howard. *Immigration and the Rise of Multiculturalism*. Issues in Canadian History. Toronto: Copp Clark, 1975.

————. "Mosaic versus Melting Pot?: Immigration and Ethnicity in Canada and the United States." In *A Passion for Identity*, edited by David Taras et al., 82–96. Toronto: Nelson, 1993.

————. *Patterns of Prejudice: A History of Nativism in Alberta.* Toronto: McClelland & Stewart, 1982.

————. "Reluctant Hosts: Anglo-Canadian Views of Multiculturalism in the 20th Century." In *Readings in Canadian History*, edited by R. Douglas Francis and Donald B. Smith, 192–210. Toronto: Holt, Rinehart, & Winston, 1990.

Pearce, J. M. "From Ontario West." In *From Sea to Sea: A Study Book of Home Missions*, 259–62. Toronto: Publications Committee of the Women's Baptist Missionary Society of Ontario West, 1940.

Perkin, J. R. C. "There Were Giants in the Earth in Those Days: An Assessment of Watson Kirkconnell." In *Canadian Baptists and Higher Christian Education*, 89–110. Montreal and Kingston: McGill-Queen's University Press, 1988.

Perkin, J. R. C., and Snelson, J. B. *Morning in His Heart: The Life and Writings of Watson Kirkconnell.* Wolfville, NS: Lancelot, 1986.

Petroff, Lillian. "Macedonians: From Village to City," *Canadian Ethnic Studies* 9 (1977) 29–41.

————. *Sojourners and Settlers: The Macedonian Community in Toronto to 1940.* Toronto: Multicultural Historical Society of Ontario, 1995.

Priestley, David T. "The Effect of Baptist 'Home Mission' among Alberta's German Immigrants." In *Memory and Hope: Strands of Canadian Baptist History*, 55–68. Waterloo: Wilfrid Laurier Press 1996.

Reilly, Brent. "Baptists and Organized Opposition to Roman Catholicism 1941–1962." In *Costly Vision*, edited by Jarold K. Zeman, 181–98. Burlington, ON: Welch, 1988.

Roberts, Barbara. "Shoveling out the 'Mutinous': Political Deportation in Canada before 1936." In *Immigration in Canada: Historical Perspectives*, edited by Gerald Tulchinsky, 265–96. Toronto: Copp Clark, 1994.

Robin, Martin. *Shades of Right: Nativist and Fascist Politics in Canada, 1920–1940.* Toronto: University of Toronto Press, 1992.

Rome, David. *Clouds in the Thirties: On Anti-Semitism in Canada 1929–1930.* 12 vols. Montreal: Jewish Historical Society of Canada, 1981.

Scott, J. Brian. "Responding to the Social Crisis: The Baptist Union of Western Canada and Social Christianity, 1908–22." PhD diss., University of Ottawa, 1989.

————. "The Western Outlook and Western Baptist and Baptist Social Christianity, 1908–22." *Canadian Society of Church History Papers* (1983) 1–21.

Shields, T. T. "The Pope's Fifth Column—Everywhere." *Gospel Witness*, 8 August 1940, 3.

Slater, Peter, ed. *Religion and Culture in Canada.* Waterloo: Wilfrid Laurier University Press, 1977.

Smale, Robert R. "'Broad Is the Road and Narrow Is the Gate Leading to the Land of Promise': Canadian Baptists and Their Voice in Restricting Immigration Policy, 1914–1929." *Canadian Society of Church History Papers* (2006) 103–25.

————. "Canadian Baptists and the Jewish Refugee Question of the 1930s." *Canadian Society of Church History Papers* (1999) 5–28.

————. "For Whose Kingdom? Canadian Baptists and the Evangelization of Immigrants and Refugees 1880 to 1945." EdD diss., OISE/University of Toronto, 2001.

———. "'The Voice of One Crying in the Wilderness' or Verbal Bigotry—T. T. Shields, *The Gospel Witness*, and Roman Catholicism, 1922–42." *Canadian Society of Church History Papers* (1997) 5–27.

Torbet, Robert G. *A History of the Baptists*. Valley Forge: Judson, 1950.

Troper, Harold M. *Only Farmers Need Apply: Official Canadian Government Encouragement of Immigration from the United States 1896–1911*. Toronto: Griffin, 1972.

Wallace, W. Stewart. *The Growth of Canadian National Feeling*. Toronto: Macmillan, 1927.

Ward, W. Peter. "The Oriental Immigrant and Canada's Protestant Clergy, 1858–1925." *BC Studies* 22 (Summer 1974) 40–55.

———. *White Canada Forever: Popular Attitudes and Public Policy towards Orientals in British Columbia*. Montreal: McGill-Queen's University Press, 1978.

Wicks, Linda Frances. "'There Must Be No Drawing Back': The Catholic Church's Efforts on behalf of Non-English Speaking Immigrants in Toronto, 1889–1939." MA thesis, OISE, 1999.

Woodworth, J. S. *Strangers within Our Gates*. Toronto: F. C. Stephenson, 1909.

Wright, Robert A. "The Canadian Protestant Tradition 1914–1945." In *The Canadian Protestant Experience 1760–1990*, edited by George A. Rawlyk, 139–97. Burlington, ON: Welch, 1990.

Wright, Robert. *A World Mission: Canadian Protestantism and a Quest for a New International Order, 1918–1939*. Montreal and Kingston: McGill-Queen's University Press, 1991.

Zeman, J. K. "They Speak in Other Tongues: Witness among the Immigrants." In *Baptists in Canada: Search for Identity amidst Diversity*, 67–86. Burlington, ON: Welch, 1988.

Name Index

Subject Index

Abolition, 2

Alberta, 80, 88, 289n102, 346, 350n25, 391

America, 1n1, 2, 14–15, 19, 50, 90, 104, 118, 124n90, 125, 129n109, 134, 137–39, 163, 169, 176, 178–94, 209, 222, 240, 244, 256, 258, 286–89, 300, 306–7, 311, 339–40, 351, 353n39, 358, 363–64, 369, 370n91, 373, 389. *See also* United States

American Bible Union, 237

Anglican Church, 147, 160, 170, 174, 237, 242–43, 267–69, 311, 348, 356, 373; and education, 10, 14–16; clergy reserves, 27; and General McNaughton, 99; Fenian Invasion, 174, 178–82; enrollment at McMaster, 267–68, 278, 280, 295; statistics, 301

Anglo-Saxon, 250, 253, 291, 324; values related to, 2, 381; imperialism, 206–7; culture, 346–52, 355–68, 375–78, 385–87

Baptism, 309, 317, 328, 330; adult/ believer's baptism, 14–15, 354; services, 284, 325–26, 334, 338; statistics, 333

Baptist Convention of Ontario and Quebec (BCOQ), 54–55, 103, 217, 246, 270, 304–5, 308, 345, 348

Baptist Yearbook, The, 314n39, 317n46, 321n56, 322n58, 326n68, 339, 345n11, 349, 354n40, 361, 362n59, 363n64, 364n69, 365, 367n82 & 83, 373n102, 375n108, 382n134, 388

Bible, as instructional tool, 10, 14, 17, 35–36, 54–55, 59, 115, 123, 153, 234, 237, 239, 244, 277, 315, 320, 323, 329, 346, 354; Unions of, 237, 284; societies, 230, 233–34, 238, 242, 274n52, 365

Brandon College, 8, 145, 151–53, 163, 266, 289n35, 271–72, 275n56, 276n59, 279, 287, 299, 308

British Columbia, 8, 88, 217, 324n63, 352n32, 388–89, 392

Boer War, 182n62, 217. *See also* South African War

Bond Street Baptist Church, 226n25, 229–30, 237–38

Calvary Baptist Church (Weyburn), 145, 153, 157

Canada, Dominion of, 80, 88–90, 133, 204, 212, 266, 325, 354, 386; as a biblical concept, 88, 127, 174n26, 199, 334, 344–51, 377, 386